The Voyage of the *Peacock*

Dr. Benajah Ticknor

The Voyage of the *Peacock*

A Journal by Benajah Ticknor, Naval Surgeon

Edited by Nan Powell Hodges

Ann Arbor

THE UNIVERSITY OF MICHIGAN PRESS

1994   1993   1992   1991   4   3   2   1

Library of Congress Cataloging-in-Publication Data

Ticknor, Benajah, 1788–1858.
  The voyage of the Peacock : a journal / by Benajah Ticknor :
edited by Nan Powell Hodges.
      p.   cm.
  Includes bibliographical references and index.
  ISBN 0-472-10201-X (cloth : alk.)
  1. Asia, Southeastern—Foreign relations—United States.
2. United States—Foreign relations—Asia, Southeastern.   3. United
States—Foreign relations—1827–1837.   Asia—Description and
travel.   5. Peacock (Ship)   I. Hodges, Nan Powell.   II. Title.
DS525.9.U6T56   1991
327.73059—dc20   90-23797
                                                           CIP

Maps drawn by Corinna Campbell

Cassis tutissima virtus

The safest protection is virtue

motto on the seal of Dr. Benajah Ticknor

Acknowledgments

In the course of editing this journal, I have been helped by many people whom I would like to acknowledge. In 1980, Dr. Robert M. Warner, then director of the Bentley Historical Library of the University of Michigan, gave me the courage to begin transcribing Benajah Ticknor's journals from the copy owned by the library. Almost more important for an independent researcher unaffiliated with any university, he gave me private space in which to work. To him, his successors, and all the staff of the Bentley Library, I owe a profound debt of gratitude.

I would like to thank Professor W. Andrew Achenbaum of the University of Michigan for his constant encouragement and his invaluable critique; Professor Jacques M. Downs, University of New England, who helped me sort out American merchants and sea captains in pretreaty China; Professor Paul Pascal, University of Washington, for translating Ticknor's Latin motto; and my husband, Robert M. Hodges, a physician, who helped me understand medical and pharmaceutical terms in the text.

Bits of knowledge on the Ticknor family came to me by way of George and Mary Campbell, Wystan Stevens, Glenn Hendrix, the late Herbert Bartlett, the late Donald and Frances Ticknor (descendants of Heman Ticknor), Raymond Ticknor, and other members of the Ticknor family in Ann Arbor. I am grateful to them all.

I am very indebted to Donald Ticknor Warner of Sharon, Connecticut, the great-great-grandson of Dr. Benajah Ticknor, for being allowed to see and photograph personal possessions of Dr. Ticknor. It is with his kind permission that I publish Dr. Ticknor's portrait.

My research took me almost around the world from Ann Arbor, Michigan, to Bangkok. In every place I received generous help on all my inquiries. I would like to convey my thanks to the following: Judith Ann Schiff, chief research archivist, Manuscripts and Archives, Yale University Library, and Marjorie G. Wynne of the Beinecke Library of Yale; M. Frances Hainer of the Naval History Section, Armed Forces History Division, National Museum of American History, Smithsonian Institution; the Western Reserve Historical Society; the Manuscripts Division, Library of

Congress; the Rare Books Library, University of Michigan; Houghton Library, Harvard University; the University of Delaware Library; the New Hampshire Historical Society; the Maryland Historical Society; the library of Peabody Museum of Salem; and the library of the School of Oriental and African Studies, London University.

The manuscript of Journal II of the Benajah Ticknor Papers and a facsimile of pages 410 and 464, Journal II are published with the permission of Manuscripts and Archives, Yale University Library. Benajah Ticknor's letter to Elisha Whittlesey, July 3, 1833, is published with the permission of the Western Reserve Historical Society.

Contents

Introduction

When the USS *Peacock,* a sloop of war, "stood out to sea" at 11 A.M. on March 8, 1832, the United States embarked on its first diplomatic mission to three mysterious and fabled countries: Cochin China (Vietnam), Siam (Thailand), and Muscat (Oman). This mission was so secret that except for Commander David Geisinger, none of the officers or crew was told the destination. On board, listed as captain's clerk, was a civilian named Edmund Roberts from Portsmouth, New Hampshire. Tending the sick was another New Englander, Dr. Benajah Ticknor, surgeon in the U.S. Navy, the author of this journal. The chance meeting of these two men on board the *Peacock* is the reason for this story.

Dr. Benajah Ticknor and Edmund Roberts had been brought together by a change in American foreign policy. During the 1820s, the United States had been preoccupied with continental expansion and content to proclaim the Monroe Doctrine in the Western Hemisphere under the somewhat benign approval of Great Britain. The proud, young U.S. Navy, at full strength at the end of the War of 1812, had confined itself to showing the flag in ports of South American countries that were then undergoing revolutions or to battling pirates preying on American shipping in the Caribbean.

By the 1830s, the United States government was forced to consider a more venturesome foreign policy as American merchant ships took over the pepper trade in the East Indies and came into direct competition with the East India Company, a British trade monopoly, in the lucrative opium and tea trade with China. Demands were being made in Washington for legal protection of trade through treaties as well as nine-pounder protection against the fierce Sumatran pirates.

These complaints were finally taken seriously in 1831, toward the end of President Andrew Jackson's first administration, when Sumatran pirates at Kuala Batu attacked the *Friendship* of Salem, Massachusetts, capturing the ship and killing several crew members. Jackson immediately ordered the USS *Potomac*, Commander John Downes, to go to Sumatra to find and punish the murderers. The *Peacock* was ordered to follow and act as a backup warship to the *Potomac*.

Prior to this crisis, Jackson had been persuaded by his advisers—particularly his secretary of the navy, Levi Woodbury of New Hampshire—that to protect American trade from the west coast of Africa to Japan, the United States must negotiate reciprocal trade treaties, even if it meant competing directly with Great Britain, the dominant power in the East. Many of Levi Woodbury's ideas had come from an aggressive American trader—Edmund Roberts.

In 1828, Roberts had run into frustration when attempting to trade without a commercial treaty in Zanzibar, an island off the west coast of Africa that was owned by Seyyid Said bin Sultan of Muscat. Roberts found that U.S. traders, in contrast to British traders, who were covered by a treaty, were subject to impossibly high export taxes and moorage fees; and he had the audacity to complain to the sultan in a public audience about this discrimination. He found a very sympathetic ear and returned to America with the sultan's suggestion that a diplomatic mission be sent to Muscat to negotiate a trade treaty. He talked at length about his experience to his old friend and kinsman, Levi Woodbury, who later entered Jackson's cabinet. He continued to lobby to be appointed head of this mission, and with Woodbury's influence he was appointed special agent to carry out trade negotiations with Muscat, Cochin China, Siam, and Japan.

The British had successfully negotiated a commercial treaty with Siam in 1826, but had been unsuccessful in Cochin China. No Westerners, with the exception of a few Dutch traders at Nagasaki, had penetrated Japan since 1641. An attempt to open Japan (where Britain had failed) to provide a supply base for American whaling ships would be the height of Yankee conceit. Adding these countries to the mission to Muscat meant challenging the British lion on its own turf. To avoid alarming the British or give any advance warning to the closed kingdom of Japan, Edmund Roberts was sworn to secrecy and put on the payroll of the *Peacock* as captain's clerk. At the same time, the voyage served as a vehicle to advance Roberts's fortune.

In contrast, Dr. Benajah Ticknor came to his assignment on the *Peacock* with great reluctance. He was forty-three years old, tired of the navy, and convinced that he would never become fleet surgeon, the top rank in the navy's medical corps. Even his last assignment at the naval hospital in

Baltimore had become a disappointment, when in March, 1831, he was detached from his comfortable position and told to hold himself in readiness to go to sea. He had been replaced by a younger surgeon who had spent little time at sea, but had strong allies in the chief clerk in the Navy Department and a senator from Maryland.

Ticknor found it useless to appeal directly to the secretary of the navy and retired to his brother's home in Salisbury, Connecticut, to wait assignment. He soon learned that his next sea duty was as surgeon on board the *Peacock*, the flagship of a two-vessel fleet, rumored to be going to the East Indies. His bitterness at being denied the rank and pay of a fleet surgeon was too much to bear. For the first time since his naval career began in 1818, Ticknor asked a friend—Congressman Elisha Whittlesey of Canfield, Ohio— to intercede with the Navy Department on his behalf.[1]

His old friend was happy to do so. In a confidential letter to Whittlesey, Levi Woodbury, secretary of the navy, hinted that later in the year the *Peacock* would cruise the Indian Seas—a voyage whose length normally required a fleet surgeon. Nevertheless, he would have to deny Ticknor the post of fleet surgeon as long as the ship remained a part of the Brazilian Squadron off South America because an older surgeon in the squadron held this rank. Dr. Ticknor accepted the news rather than complain and make known Whittlesey's breach of confidential information. He was reconciled to another hazardous sea voyage by the anticipation of visiting new places that he had always wanted to see.[2]

Thus the eager ambassador and the reluctant doctor first met as the *Peacock* slipped out of Boston harbor. They were almost the same age, Roberts having been born in 1784. Each had traveled extensively and spent long periods of time in South America—Roberts as a merchant in Buenos Aires and Ticknor as a doctor on several naval cruises off the coasts of South America. Edmund Roberts, a widower, was well-educated and formerly a wealthy businessman. Now heavily in debt, he had sought the prestige and pay of a diplomat in order to support eight daughters.

Dr. Benajah Ticknor had essentially made his way on his own. The oldest of nine children of Benajah and Bethiah Bingham Ticknor, he was born May 22, 1788, on a frontier farm in Jericho, Vermont. His childhood was spent mainly in Salisbury, Connecticut; then in 1805, his family followed the frontier west to Windham, New York. There, on a farm that was no more than a dense forest with five acres partially cleared, young Ticknor shared a rude log house, approximately eighteen by twenty feet, with his parents, six brothers, and one sister. Friends later testified that Benajah, who had virtually no formal education, had snatched every moment he could spare from the chores of survival to satisfy a passion for learning.

One day in January, 1806, Ticknor left the house with his father to cut wood. Less than an hour later, the neighbors bore home the body of his father, killed in a tree-felling accident. At seventeen, Benajah was suddenly the head of a family. He tried his hand at teaching school, but, discouraged perhaps by his own inferior education, he continued only long enough until the next oldest son, Luther, could take over the family responsibilities. In 1808, Benajah left home "with but one dollar in his pocket and poorly clad, to seek his fortune elsewhere."[3]

He was fortunate to be taken in by Dr. J. B. Dodge, a practicing physician in Sharon, Connecticut. Ticknor pursued medical studies with this rural doctor and was qualified several years later. It was here that he probably acquired Latin, the language of all medical texts, and began the serious pursuit of classical studies, mathematics, and science, interests that preoccupied him for the rest of his life. Sometime later he taught himself Greek and Hebrew in order to read the Bible in its original languages. Through study and travel while in the navy, he gained a reading knowledge of French, Italian, German, and Spanish.

During the War of 1812, Ticknor applied for a post as surgeon's mate in the U.S. Navy, hoping to increase his knowledge of surgery, but the war ended without his having received any reply to his application. He then joined the westward migration of Connecticut families into Ohio. In 1814, at the invitation of Judson Canfield, founder of Canfield, Ohio, he settled there as the town's first physician.

Late in 1815, Dr. Ticknor learned by accident that he had been appointed surgeon's mate in the navy. He accepted his commission on December 15, 1815, but did not receive his first assignment until 1818, when he was ordered to Boston to serve as surgeon's mate on the USS *Macedonian*. In the interval he had met and married Canfield's first woman schoolteacher, Getia (Gesie) Bostwick, the daughter of the late Reverend Gideon Bostwick, an Episcopal minister in Great Barrington, Massachusetts.

When late in August, 1818, Ticknor received his orders in Canfield, Ohio, to report to Boston, he obeyed with a speed that astonished friends. Within three days, he had wound up his affairs, left his wife with her sister's family in Canfield, and set off on horseback for Boston. He arrived three days later at 2 A.M., having ridden the last hundred miles without food or rest. A few hours later he presented himself with "trembling steps, and palpitating heart" at the office of Commodore Isaac Hull to report for duty. Fortunately for Ticknor, the great man was out, and Ticknor had a few more hours to collect himself. When they finally met, Hull wanted to know why he was late arriving but was magnanimous when Ticknor pointed out that he had been in Ohio when his orders were received. Ticknor went immediately to the frigate where forty sick sailors demanded his attention.[4]

Thus began Benajah Ticknor's career as naval surgeon. An insecure country doctor, obsessed with the importance of duty, he embarked on a three-year voyage around the coasts of South America. He and his family received no word of each other during the entire voyage. Ticknor had promised his friends an account of his travels, and during those three years of isolation and loneliness on the USS *Macedonian,* he wrote the first in a series of journals that cover most of his life from 1818 to 1852. Seven of these journals survive and are on deposit in the manuscripts and archives division of Yale University Library in New Haven, Connecticut.

Ticknor established his writing pattern in this first journal. He included events on shipboard or in port and his impression of life in each new country visited. Perhaps more important for his sanity, he wrote about the often difficult personal struggle of a pious and sensitive village doctor to adapt to the harsh life of a frigate with its drunken officers and whiplashed crew. Finding living conditions appalling and intellectual companions nonexistent, he resolved to keep himself aloof from men whose dissolute life he detested and "to devote all the time not employed in the duties of my station, to such studies as would most effectually divert my mind from my ignominious condition."[5] Although his living conditions and status improved on future voyages, he always remained a bit apart from his shipmates.

After the initial voyage, Ticknor's naval career advanced slowly. During 1822–23, he served as surgeon's mate aboard the USS *Congress,* on pirate patrol in the West Indies. Promoted to surgeon in 1824, he survived a near fatal assignment at Key West, Florida, by being invalided home with malaria. After a tour of duty (1826–28) as surgeon on the *Macedonian* off the coasts of Brazil and Argentina, he was at last, in 1829, given shore duty in Baltimore, where he was commander of the naval hospital until he was detached abruptly in 1831.

The cruise of the *Peacock* began auspiciously and Benajah Ticknor, an experienced and more confident naval surgeon, settled down to the rhythm of a well-run ship to fill several notebooks with his impressions of foreign travel. Conscious that he was going to visit countries and seas unknown to

Americans, he kept a very careful account of sailing directions and geographical descriptions. His chapter subtitles and the subjects covered seem to imply that he intended to write a travel book—the best-seller of the 1830s.

Edmund Roberts, as captain's clerk, kept the ship's log and also a personal journal as part of his responsibility as special agent. Both Ticknor and Roberts were each aware that the other was collecting material and writing personal observations about the voyage. There seemed to arise between the two men a genuine friendship built on shared opinions, books, and excursions on shore. That Ticknor not only witnessed but also participated in the diplomatic negotiations in Cochin China and Siam indicates the closeness of their relationship.

When the *Peacock* stopped in Rio de Janeiro on the homeward voyage in January, 1834, she was detained until she could be released from the Brazilian Squadron. Edmund Roberts hurried ahead to New York to deliver the treaties made with Siam and Muscat and to report to the State Department. He carried with him an introduction written by Dr. Ticknor to Congressman Elisha Whittlesey. Later, when the State Department could come up with no money to repay Roberts for $7,297 in personal funds he had been forced to spend on unexpected gifts and expenses, Roberts decided to petition Congress for payment and asked Ticknor to write to Whittlesey for aid in steering the petition through Congress. His friend did so willingly with the result that Whittlesey took up Roberts's cause in Congress in late 1834.[6]

Ticknor's immediate response to Roberts's financial need was a further example of his selflessness. The first example had arisen as a result of a hasty and excited letter that Ticknor wrote to Roberts on May 31, 1834, a week after the *Peacock* finally arrived in New York. Ticknor had been persuaded by friends and his younger brother, Dr. Caleb Ticknor, that a book could be made out of his journal. He informed Roberts that he had "endeavoured to plead off by saying that perhaps Mr. Roberts will publish a journal, & if so, it will not be best for me to publish." But his friends had not been deterred, and to please them, he had talked with Harper and Brothers about a book. They had agreed to publish it, suggesting only that he supplement the text with some drawings. Lt. Hugh Y. Purviance, who during the voyage had made drawings that were now in Roberts's possession, had consented for Ticknor to use them. Ticknor concluded his letter with the request that Roberts forward the drawings to him "if you are not going to turn author."[7]

But Roberts, heavily in debt and in desperate need of cash, *was* going to publish his journal, as soon as the State Department would give him permission to use parts of the official report. He informed Ticknor of his intention, and Ticknor, true to his word, "instantly dismissed all thought of publishing."[8] Edmund Roberts was the agent of the U.S. government and a gentleman; in Ticknor's world of virtue and duty, these were sufficient reasons to step aside.

Roberts worked furiously to prepare his manuscript for publication by Harper and Brothers before he left in March, 1835, on his second voyage on the USS *Peacock*—this time to return the ratified treaties to Muscat and Siam. He left a mass of papers, uncorrected portions of his journal, illustrations, and a jumble of last minute instructions on the book with his son-in-law, Amasa J. Parker.

Roberts wrote one last time to Ticknor and mentioned that the State Department did not wish him to include anything in the book on the failed negotiations in Cochin China. Late in 1835, when asked by Elisha Whittlesey why he had never published his journal, Ticknor pointed out that it was as well that he had deferred to Roberts's intention to publish. He felt that he had written so freely on forbidden subjects that he might have been forced out of the navy.[9]

The two friends never met again or exchanged correspondence. After safely delivering the treaties to Muscat and Siam, Roberts contracted dysentery in Siam; he died in Macao on June 12, 1836. He was buried there in the English Protestant cemetery not far from the grave of the Reverend Robert Morrison, first Protestant missionary to China. Years later on another voyage to Canton (1846), Ticknor visited the cemetery in Macao to view the graves of Edmund Roberts, Robert Morrison, and Morrison's son John Robert Morrison.

Edmund Roberts's journal, *Embassy to the Eastern Courts of Cochin-China, Siam, and Muscat During the years 1832-3-4*, was published posthumously, without illustrations, in 1837 by arrangement with Harper and Brothers. His mass of papers and notes was put in order and prepared for stereotyping by Jeremiah N. Reynolds, a well-known author who had been hired by Amasa J. Parker. Reynolds undertook the work for $300 and the assurance that Parker would use his influence to have Reynolds's biography of George Washington, *Vita Washingtonii,* adopted as a textbook by the New York schools.[10]

Dr. Ticknor's life and naval career began to improve with his appointment as commander of the Charlestown naval hospital in Boston in 1834. He had time to write medical articles on tropical disease, and, in 1836, he received an honorary M.D. degree from Yale University Medical School. As an investment and a future retirement home, he purchased a farm, to be managed by his brother Heman, in Ann Arbor, Michigan. In 1837, he was finally appointed fleet surgeon for a survey mission to the Antarctic Ocean, commanded by Commodore Thomas Ap Catesby Jones. When confusion and poor planning resulted in Jones being relieved of command, Ticknor resigned rather than serve under the new commander, a junior officer whom he judged inexperienced—Lt. Charles Wilkes. Thus he missed serving as fleet surgeon to the celebrated Wilkes Expedition to the South Seas.

His next assignment, in 1838, was the most choice in the U.S. Navy for a medical officer—fleet surgeon on the USS *Ohio,* Commodore Isaac Hull, for a Mediterranean cruise. Unfortunately, Ticknor and a group of five young officers ran afoul of the aged Hull's paranoia before the ship left port, by complaining openly about their quarters being taken for Mrs. Hull, her niece, and a maid. The incident seemed to be forgotten during eighteen months of peaceful travel, which included visits to the antiquities of Athens and Rome and an audience with Pope Gregory XVI, but then Ticknor and the young officers were suddenly accused by the vindictive Hull of insubordination and sent home in disgrace. Fortunately, an investigation by the secretary of the navy cleared Ticknor from the charge, and he was next assigned to command the Brooklyn Navy Yard hospital.

The shocking experience of being unjustly discharged from a ship was soon followed by the death in 1840 of his youngest and dearest brother, Dr. Caleb Ticknor. As a result, Benajah Ticknor underwent a period of deep melancholy, which was reflected in his diary and correspondence. His need for a permanent residence for his wife and two adopted daughters became more pressing. By 1844, Ticknor had built a fine classic revival cobblestone house on his farm in Michigan. He lived there between naval assignments in the role of gentleman farmer and, in his friendship with leading professors of the University of Michigan, he found at last the intellectual companionship that he craved.

Ticknor was forced to interrupt his pleasant life in Ann Arbor to go to sea one last time. In 1845, at the age of fifty-seven, he was named fleet surgeon on the USS *Columbus,* Commodore James Biddle, for another diplomatic mission to the Far East. This voyage took him back to China for the exchange of the ratified 1844 Treaty of Wanghia, to Japan for an abortive attempt to open that country to trade, to Hawaii, to California—then in the throes of the Mexican War—and home again in 1848 via Cape Horn for a complete circumnavigation of the globe. His diary of this voyage, Journal

V, contains one of the few eyewitness accounts of Commodore Biddle's humiliation in being struck by a Japanese soldier and the resulting break-off in negotiations to open Japan.

Ticknor served two more brief tours of duty in Boston before he asked to be relieved from duty in 1854 because of poor health. He died at his home in Ann Arbor, Michigan, on September 20, 1858. His extensive library of medical, historical, and classical books was donated by his widow to the University of Michigan. In 1974, Dr. Benajah Ticknor's house on Packard Road, owned by the city of Ann Arbor and on the National Register of Historic Places, became a museum called Cobblestone Farm, open to the public.

The story might have ended here—one diary on the shelf and one published to the posthumous acclaim of its author. In the course of some general research on the life of Benajah Ticknor, I read for the first time Edmund Roberts's *Embassy to the Eastern Courts* in order to compare the two accounts of the voyage of the *Peacock*. I had expected their versions to be parallel, but I was unprepared to find several passages in Roberts's book to be almost word-for-word duplicates of passages in Ticknor's journal. Immediately the question arose: Did Roberts copy Ticknor's journal? The search for the answer was one of the motivating factors that started me on the interesting process of editing Benajah Ticknor's journal.

In an analysis of the manuscript of *Embassy to the Eastern Courts,* which is found among Edmund Roberts's papers in the Library of Congress, I discovered that most of Roberts's book is a collection of articles and chapters from seminal sources about life and culture in East Asia, interspersed with his own personal journal. Sections of chapters were lifted without acknowledgment from *The Chinese Repository* (vols. 1 and 2), a monthly newspaper published in Canton by Elijah Bridgman; from Robert Morrison's *Chinese Miscellany* (1825); from John Crawfurd's *Journal of an Embassy to the Courts of Siam & Cochin China* (1830); and from many other titles identified in Roberts's hand by page number and point of insertion in the manuscript. Having been a virtual bystander in Cochin China, he printed intact the manuscript "Journal and Conversations with the Officers of Government During the Stay of the Mission at Vunglam in Cochinchina," written entirely by his eighteen-year-old secretary, John Robert Morrison. It is a fascinating task to separate the real Edmund Roberts from his ghosts. Roberts's book embodies a quotation found in his papers, "I am a collector of other men's scraps."[11]

Roberts's most direct quote from Dr. Ticknor's journal is the account of the first death from cholera of a seaman aboard the *Peacock* while at Manila (*Embassy,* 63–64). Since Roberts was living ashore at the time, he could not have given such a detailed account without reference to Ticknor's journal or medical report. Roberts and Ticknor seemed to have thought alike, later in Mocha, on the creepiness of climbing a dark staircase whose very walls might have been stained with the blood of victims (*Embassy,* 345). There are other, less direct, instances where a similar incident or thought appears in both texts. For Edmund Roberts, Benajah Ticknor's journal was just another useful source.

In a time when there was no copyright protection and travel writers were not criticized for a bit of plagiarism, Roberts's use of some of Ticknor's material would not have been noticed. Whether Ticknor ever saw or read *Embassy to the Eastern Courts* is not known. After copying over his own journal in 1836, suppressing whole passages of his more personal remarks about Commander David Geisinger, captain of the *Peacock,* Ticknor laid it aside. He accepted the fact that his second journal would not be read beyond a circle of family and friends.

Today, Dr. Benajah Ticknor's journal of the voyage of the *Peacock* offers much of interest both to the general reader and the historian. Ticknor wrote in a clear, straightforward way about what happened on board the *Peacock* in the almost unbearably tight-knit company of men at sea. The hardships, the danger, the drunkenness and abusiveness of the captain, the petty jealousies, and the boredom of life on a slow-moving sloop are set down alongside descriptions of his duty as surgeon. However, on shore Ticknor assumed the role of enlightened traveler rather than naval officer or physician.

Above all he was curious. He was a pragmatic observer, not content to prejudge new people or cultures before viewing them himself. His observations of urban and rural life, mores and manners, and physical characteristics and differences among Asian peoples suggest the systematic collection of data of a social historian or anthropologist. Despite his loathing of filth or his shock when an impoverished Vietnamese woman offered to give her baby to him, he refused to condemn a people because of their poverty and lack of education.

Ticknor's description of Canton before the Opium War affords another glimpse of the fascinating minute world of cohong and traders. Taking tiffin with Dr. Robert Morrison, the remarkable English missionary and Chinese scholar, and sightseeing with the Reverend Elijah Bridgman, the first American missionary in China, gave Ticknor a chance to know two of the most famous Westerners in pretreaty China. Living among merchants whose trade was opium, Ticknor neither approved nor disapproved of an illegal drug generally considered a simple commodity. Despite the strange customs of the Chinese, Ticknor was not contemptuous of these people, and he generally admired their artistry and skill in manufacturing. His views were in marked contrast to those of other contemporary travel writers, including Edmund Roberts.

His criticism of navy discipline, and particularly drunkenness among midshipmen and young officers, did not stem entirely from his strict New England background. Ticknor saw firsthand the effect of the abuse of alcohol on his patients. His voice was part of the reform movement in the navy in the 1830s and 1840s to establish a more professional officer corps, to forbid dueling, and eventually to abolish the twin evils of grog rations for seamen and flogging.

Ticknor's Christian conscience was not selective while traveling. He wrote with passion on the evils of slavery in Brazil and refused to accept current arguments that slavery there was less onerous than in the United States. Judged today, Ticknor might be thought a racist, but in 1832, his views would have been considered dangerously liberal. He was sympathetic to the antislavery position of the abolitionists and even attended some of their meetings, but his innate caution and his respect for established authority prevented him from totally espousing their cause.

From the point of view of medical history, the reader will be surprised to find how infrequently Ticknor writes about the medical problems he dealt with day to day. The common bilious remittent or intermittent fevers were well known in America, hence unworthy of note. But the dread spasmodic Asiatic cholera was only reaching America's shore in 1832. Ticknor described his treatment and its success or failure, compared it with that of local physicians, and questioned venesection as a method of curing the disease. Despite his strict adherence to the prevailing miasmatic theory of disease, which located the source of all disease in the noxious atmosphere of swamps and decaying organic matter, he was careful to record his experience with cholera to add to the general body of medical knowledge. When he could not cure the patient, he tried to ease him into death with the application of prayer and his unfailing belief in life after death for anyone who accepted Christ.

With Ticknor's focus on the diplomatic side of the mission, we have another perceptive witness to the very beginning of American diplomacy in

Southeast Asia. Misunderstanding and lack of preparedness in Cochin China are evident despite his defense of Roberts's attempt to gain a treaty. In Siam, Ticknor is uneasy in the face of Roberts's impatience and quick anger at imagined affronts to his dignity. He describes the crucial role of Carlos da Silveira, the Portuguese consul, in advising Roberts during the treaty negotiation. He fills in the background that Roberts carefully omits when recounting the articles of the treaty.

Ticknor's conscience is unable to ignore two examples of naval gunboat diplomacy: the seizure of the Falkland Islands by the USS *Lexington* in 1831 and the revenge enacted against Kuala Batu by the USS *Potomac* in 1832. He makes very negative comments based on private inquiries about both incidents. However, his underlying hostility to naval authority at that moment in his career cannot be ruled out.

Unfortunately Ticknor's journal of the whole voyage is not complete. The original journal written on shipboard covers the voyage from Boston to the ship's arrival off Siam (Journal II, 1–539); there is only a fragment remaining of this journal to describe the voyage home from Anjer to Mozambique (Journal II, 888–1130). A revised version of the journal, made by Ticknor in 1836, is almost an exact copy of the original (with many deletions) and extends the story of the voyage through the first half of the visit in Siam (Revised Journal II, 1–248). All the rest of the revised journal is lost. There is enough, nevertheless, to depict an intelligent, thoughtful observer, a kind compassionate doctor, and an enthusiastic recorder of people and events, who was not averse to a bit of humor and gossip. With the publication of his journal, Dr. Benajah Ticknor will at last join his more well-known cousins, George Ticknor, leader of the Boston brahmins, and William Davis Ticknor, publisher, in the world of New England letters.

My editorial task has been to interfere as little as possible. Ticknor wrote his original Journal II in 8″ by 9¾″ notebooks bound in three-quarter leather. He wrote in a clear hand with few blots or errors despite the rolling of the ship. There are almost no unintelligible words. Ticknor's punctuation style would be judged unusual today because of his excessive use of commas and the use of semicolons for commas. His spelling was good but not consistent throughout; I have not corrected spelling errors in the original manuscript unless absolutely necessary for meaning. Editorial insertions of full names or simple definitions are enclosed in square brackets. More extensive explanations and editorial comments are confined to notes at the end of the book.

When Ticknor recopied and revised his original journal in 1836, he corrected his spelling, broke the body of the text into shorter paragraphs, and excised from the text lengthy sailing directions and most of his personal opinions. The result is an interesting account of his voyage bereft of immediacy and passion. I have chosen to reproduce his original journal wherever possible rather than the more polite version of the story in his revised Journal II.

Chapters I through VIII of this book comprise the bulk of the original journal. They were written in two notebooks, the first of which is entitled, "Journal, 1831–1832, of a trip from Boston to Manila aboard the Sloop-of-War, Peacock." When Ticknor revised his journal, he combined two chapters (because of deletions) and simplified the subtitles of his chapters. In order to link chapters I through VIII of the original journal with chapter IX, which is entirely from his revised 1836 journal, I have used the paragraphing, chapter subtitles, and chapter divisions of the revised journal. I have inserted a simple geographic title for each chapter and italicized all names of ships. Instead of deleting the somewhat embarrassing opinions that Ticknor excised, I have enclosed them in braces. With this method, we can read the original text and see Benajah Ticknor editing his own work.

In chapter IX—the chapter on Siam from the 1836 revised journal used to replace the missing chapter in the original—the reader will see the result of Ticknor's editing. His descriptive writing is tighter and personal opinions are fewer and more guarded. We can only regret the revised journal ends halfway through the visit to Bangkok, and we do not have Ticknor's reaction to the exotic courts of Rama III or the colorful funeral procession of the second king.

I have attempted to bridge the gap between chapter IX and the partial chapter XI by inserting a letter written by Ticknor in Batavia to his friend Elisha Whittlesey. In his long correspondence (1818–52) with Whittlesey, he often duplicated passages from his journal in his letters.

With chapter XI we return once more to the original journal. This section continues into chapter XIII where it breaks off with the departure from Mozambique. There are no chapter subtitles and the text is less polished, perhaps reflecting Ticknor's fatigue and the illness he suffered in Muscat.

Geographical descriptions and latitude and longitude have been checked wherever possible. The latter are not accurate because of inexact chronometers. Place names have not been modernized or changed. I have found them consistent with the names used in the twenty-eight charts of

Horsburgh's East India Pilot (London: Kingsbury, Parbury, and Allen, 1824). Both Ticknor and Edmund Roberts cite James Horsburgh as the navigational authority used on the *Peacock*. I have attempted to identify every person mentioned in the journal, but for a few this was not possible.

In going through Edmund Roberts's papers at the Library of Congress, I was able to see and identify for the first time the original drawings of Lt. Hugh Y. Purviance, which Ticknor had requested from Roberts. In the haste to publish the book, perhaps, or because of lack of funds, they were not used in *Embassy to the Eastern Courts*. Several of these views are now included in this publication of Benajah Ticknor's journal.

The editing of this journal was challenging because of the historical, geographical, and medical knowledge needed to fill in the background of Benajah Ticknor's world. For me, it was an interesting private education and an immense amount of fun. I am grateful that it lay "on the shelf" until I could find it.

CHAPTER I

Boston to Port Praya

Departure from Boston; The ship, officers, crew, &
passengers—Accident to Mr. Baylies; Arrival at Port Praya,
on the island of St. Jago; Party on board; Visit on shore;
Description of St. Jago & Port Praya; Mr. Martinez;
Productions of St. Jago; Description of other islands;
Departure from P. Praya.

On the 17th. of December, 1831, I received an order from the Navy Department, to proceed to Boston and join the Sloop of war, *Peacock,*[1] fitting
out at that port for a cruise; and on the 29th. of the same month, I arrived
in Boston and reported myself for duty. From what I had casually learned
before I left home, I supposed the destination of the ship, was either the
coast of Brazil, or the Indian Ocean; and I expected on arriving at Boston,
to obtain satisfactory information of the subject. In this however, I was
mistaken. All I could learn respecting the destination of the ship was, that
she was fitting out for a long cruise, and would proceed to the south,
probably across the torid zone & into a cold climate to the southward of it.

Several of the officers destined for the *Peacock,* had arrived at Boston
before me, but had not yet entered upon their duties. The ship was said to
be nearly ready for sea, and I was required to provide the necessary supplies
for the medical department without delay. The commander destined for the
ship was looked for every day, though no one knew who he was to be. In
this state of suspence we remained for about a month, when Capt. Geisinger
[Master Commander David Geisinger][2] arrived as her destined commander.

Preparation for sailing was now hastened as fast as circumstances would
permit; and about the 10th. of February the crew was selected and the officers

began to mess on board. They occupied the ward-room,[3] and being provided with a stove, they lived quite comfortably, notwithstanding the weather was extremely cold, the mercury being sometimes below zero, and frequently not more than ten degrees above it. Towards the last of February, it was ascertained, as had been conjectured, that Mr. Baylies [Francis Baylies],[4] recently appointed Chargé des affaires at Buenos Ayres, and his family, were to go out in the *Peacock,* and preparation was accordingly made for them.

About the first of March the ship hauled out into the stream and as we had a long cruise before us and were therefore anxious to enter upon it as soon as possible, that we might the soonner come to the termination of it, every thing was done to hasten our departure.

Every preparation being finally completed, and Mr. Baylies and his family having come on board, on the 8th. of March, at 11 O'clock a.m. we weighed anchor, and with a fair wind stood out to sea. While I am writing, at half past 9 O'clock, the wind continues fair and the weather pleasant, and we are urging our way through the "dark blue waters" to distant regions, at the rate of 8 to 9 miles an hour. At present, our prospects seem flattering, and we all seem disposed to look forward to our cruise with the expectation of being in some measure repaid by what we shall meet with, for the privations to which we must be subjected. But while it is right for us in our present situation, separated from our friends and country and consequently from the principal blessings of life, for two or three years, to take as favourable a view as possible of our prospects; still it is best to bear in mind at the same time, that as all our calculations concerning future events, are founded upon an extremely uncertain basis, we may not realize one of our agreeable anticipations. For my own part, I wish to divest myself of all solicitude respecting the events we are to meet with, and to commit myself unreservedly to the disposal of divine Providence, knowing that whether my anticipations are realized or not, the course of events will be so ordered as shall, in the final result, prove to be best. To describe the feelings that are called forth for taking leave of one's family and friends for the long period of two or three years, and perhaps forever, and with the prospect too of receiving no intelligence from them during the long separation, would be impossible. It is not in the power of language to convey an adequate idea of the emotions that agitate the heart in such circumstances as these. The person who has experienced them knows what they are, and it is only by experience that they can be known. Happily for us, however, these feelings do not long remain this vivid; if they did, no one, I am sure, would ever voluntarily place himself in a situation to experience them a second time. But I shall pursue this subject no farther.

Much of the comfort of life depends on the harmony which exists between ourselves and those with whom we are most intimately associated; and this is especially the case with those who are brought together on ship-board, and compelled to live for years in almost constant contact with each other. How it will be with us in this respect, it is too soon to judge with any certainty; but so far as I have become acquainted with officers of the ship, I have reason to believe that we shall harmonize well, and consequently so far as this can contribute to it, we may promise ourselves a pleasant cruise. On the part of our Commander, a disposition is manifested to promote the comfort of the officers to the utmost of his power; and if this disposition is reciprocated on the part of the officers, as I hope and trust it will be, one of the most fruitful sources of discontent on board ship, and of the unpleasantness of a cruise, will be removed.

The number of officers and men belonging to the ship, is about a hundred and seventy [166]. There are in the ward-room eight officers, namely, Lieutenants White [Lt. John White], Cunningham [1st Lt. Robert B. Cunningham], Purveyance [Lt. Hugh Y. Purviance], Mr. Brent Sailing Master [Acting Lt. Thomas W. Brent], Lieut. Fowler, Marine Officer [2nd Lt. Henry W. Fowler], myself & assistant, Dr. Gilchrist [Asst. Surgeon, Dr. Edward Gilchrist], and Lieut. Rodgers, passenger [Lt. John G. Rodgers]. The number of midshipmen in the steerage is [9]. The ship being provided with an upper deck like a frigate, possesses nearly the same accommodations, and must be much more comfortable than an ordinary sloop of war. As to her lading etc, I can speak better hereafter.

In consequence of having the minster on board, we are somewhat restricted as to room; but I expect we shall be amply compensated for this inconvenience by the agreeable society of Mr. Baylies and his family, which includes three females, namely, Mrs. Baylies [the former Mrs. Elizabeth Moulton Deming] and a daughter about nine years old [Harriet Baylies], and a Miss Sampson, who, it is said, goes out as governess.

March 12. We have now been out four days, and have been more favoured with respect to wind and weather than we had reason to expect. The wind has continued fair most of the time, and the weather, with the exception of a few hours day before yesterday, while in the Gulf-stream, has been pleas-ant. It is usual to experience squally unpleasant weather in the Gulf-stream, and the sea there is generally rough, especially when the wind and current are opposed to each other; but fortunately for us, at least for our passengers, the wind was nearly in the direction of the stream, and our ship laboured much less than she otherwise would, and there was consequently much less suffering from sea-sickness. Notwithstanding these favourable circumstances, however, there were a good many sea-sick. Mrs. Baylies suffered a good deal for one day, and her daughter and Miss Sampson have kept their beds most of the time till today. The weather has now become so mild that it is quite comfortable on deck, and the ladies have spent several hours there today, enjoying the pure air, and the view of the surrounding ocean gently agitated with the rising breeze.

Night before last there was considerable rolling of the ship, and during a heavy roll, Mr. Baylies was thrown down, and received a contusion of his side, which has caused him considerable uneasiness, and rendered it necessary for him to keep as quiet as possible. There is reason to believe, however, that there is no fracture of the ribs, and that he will consequently soon recover from the injury.[5] He presented me today, with his History of Plymouth, consisting of two volumes, which I expect to find quite an interesting work.[6]

{As we have no Chaplain on board, the Capt. proposed to me today, that I should read prayers next Sunday, if the weather should permit; which I very readily consented to do, believing most firmly, that the performance of this religious service will, if regularly observed, produce very salutary effects on the crew. Nothing, indeed, I am persuaded, can tend more strongly to preserve order and harmony among the crew and to render punishment unnecessary, than the regular performance of religious duties; and I view the Captain's attention to this subject as an evidence of a most excellent trait in his character.}

March 19. Yesterday being Sunday and the weather pleasant, religious service was performed as the Captain proposed some days ago, and in such a manner as to show, that if we continue as we have begun, the best effect may be expected to result from our religious exercises. All the passengers, officers and crew being assembled on the quarter-deck, the articles of war were first read by the Lieut. of the watch, and then such parts of the morning service as were deemed appropriate, together with the psalter, and a part of the service for vessels at sea, were read, and the responses made by Mr. & Mrs. Baylies, and by the Capt. and some of the officers, in as regular a manner, as I have ever known them made at church. {Those officers who did not join in the service, as well as the crew manifested an interest in it, and conducted [themselves] with the greatest order and decorum. After the service was ended, the crew were mustered, and a crew of more healthy and fine looking men, I have never seen. Besides exhibiting a better appearance than any ship's crew I have ever seen before, our men are more quiet and orderly in their conduct, especially on Sunday, than any crew I have yet sailed with. Sunday is usually considered on board a vessel of war, not as a holy day that ought to be spent in religious reading & meditation; but as a day of recreation, on which every one is at perfect liberty to amuse himself in any manner he chooses. And, as might be supposed among such men as usually compose the crew of a vessel of war, the day is almost always spent either in the most noisy and boisterous kinds of mirth, or as is very often the case, in angry dissentions and fighting. I was very much pleased to observe, however, that our men spent the day in a very different manner. They seemed to be aware that they owed at least a decent respect to the day, which they endeavoured to manifest in their quiet and correct deportment. Thus passed the second Sunday that we have spent at sea, and if every succeeding Sunday shall be spent in the same manner, as I sincerely hope it may, I can not but anticipate the most pleasant cruise that I have ever made. I feel myself very illy qualified to perform the duties of a Chaplain in a proper manner, and had much rather that some one else should undertake this office; but if it shall be required of me to take the lead in the performance of religious service, I shall do it with pleasure, and an earnest prayer to Heaven, that it may be done in such a manner as shall meet with the divine acceptance.

Until last night the wind continued fair, and our progress was as rapid as could be reasonably desired, even by those who are anxious for a short passage to Rio Janeiro; but the wind last evening became adverse, and still continues so. The weather, however is fine, and the ship comfortable, so that we ought to be contented, although the wind may not blow from the right quarter again for several days.}

{March 23. Our prospect of a short passage to Rio, becomes less and less every day. For the last four days the wind has continued constantly ahead, accompanied with a heavy swell, in consequence of which we have advanced but a very little way on our destined course. During these four days showers of rain have been frequent, and the ship has consequently been wet and uncomfortable. The temperature, however, has been mild, so that, although our comfort has been a good deal abridged by the continued wet weather, and our spirits have suffered a corresponding depression; yet our condition has been much less unpleasant than it usually is in such a state of the weather, for the heat is generally so great in these latitudes where we are most apt to meet with rainy weather, as effectually to destroy every thing like comfort. With respect to myself, however, so long as I can have daylight enough to enable me to read and write, I am comparatively but little incommoded by unpleasant weather. And as to the direction of the wind, and the progress we are making, I feel quite indifferent; for since our cruise is to be of two or three years duration, it is of no consequence to me whether our progress is rapid or slow. At present, however, it is desirable to reach our destined port as soon as possible, that we may disencumber ourselves of a large quantity of baggage belonging to the Minister, and thereby render the ship both more comfortable, and less likely to become unhealthy in the hot climates to which it is supposed we are going. It is particularly important in tropical climates, that the lower decks and hold [of] a vessel of war should be kept clear and well ventilated and so long as this is duly attended to, there is but little danger to be apprehended from sickness, however great the heat of the climate may be. As I shall probably have occasion to bring this subject again under consideration, I shall make no farther remarks upon it at present.

A sail was seen yesterday in the forenoon from aloft, but we were unable to make out what she was, or in what direction she was standing. Our passengers had the satisfaction yesterday, for the first time, of seeing a whale, but so far off that they had not a distinct view of it. They will probably have opportunities of fully gratifying their curiosity with a sight of this monster of the deep, before we reach Rio Janeiro. This is the first object of curiosity with most persons on first embarking upon the ocean, and particularly with those who have read and believe, what is related in the Bible of the Prophet Jonah. To see, not only the monarch of the deep, but as we have reason to believe, the longest of animated beings that inhabit our globe, is highly satisfactory to any body capable of experiencing any delight in viewing the stupendous works of the creator; but it is peculiarly satisfactory to him who believes the Bible, to behold one of that species of animal that was employed as an agent for manifesting the miraculous interposition of divine power, in preserving the life of a disobedient prophet, while endeavouring to evade the commands of his God.

Towards night yesterday, something was seen floating at the distance of about half a mile from the ship, which it was supposed, might be deserving of particular notice; and the sea being smooth, and the ship not making any headway, the first Lieut. with two other officers, took the whale-boat and went in pursuit of it. In about an hour they returned, towing a piece of the railing of a large ship, which had probably been carried away in a severe gale of wind; but whether the ship to which it belonged was lost or not, it is impossible to say. It is a source of melancholy reflections, however, to meet with fragments of vessels at sea, since they are an evidence that the vessel to which they belonged must have been in danger if not perhaps lost; and that those on board of her, must consequently have endured a degree of suffering, probably as great as we should experience in the same circumstances.

Our latitude today is 36°.12′, and our longitude is probably about 38°. The thermometer for the last eight or ten days, has been 67, at mid-day in the cabin; today it is 65. The barometer for the last five or six days, has been fluctuating between 30.15 & 30.30 inches, thus giving a very correct indication of the state of the weather.}

April 9. For several days after my last date our progress was very slow, the wind being generally ahead, and very light. We expected to have taken the trade-wind as far north as 30°; but we did not meet with it till we had advanced to about 24, and then it was unusually light, and blew from the east, or east-south-east; so that if we had not run about as far to the eastward as we wished to, we should have been unable to pursue our destined course.

Until we had been out about twenty days, and on account of head-winds had given up the expectation of a short passage to Rio Janeiro, which the Capt. was desirous to make, it was not the intention to stop at the Cape de Verd Islands; but after it became evident that our passage at the best, could not be a short one, and that it might be so long as to endanger our suffering for want of water, the Capt. determined to stop at Port Praya in the Island of St. Jago, and take in a supply of water. It is usual for ships of war on long voyages, to be on an allowance of water, commonly two quarts to each person; but it is always desirable, when circumstances will admit of it, to allow the men as much water as they want, only taking care that it is not used in a wasteful manner. With only this restriction it has been used on board this ship, and that we might continue to use it thus freely, an additional supply would become necessary. Accordingly we have been shap-ing our course for the last ten or twelve days, for Port Praya, the only watering place in the Cape de Verds; and yesterday, at day-light we made the Island of Sal, the northernmost of the group. When first seen, it was about twenty miles to the westward of us.

{This is a barren uninhabited Island, and is only valuable on account of the salt that is obtained here. The salt is formed, as I am told by our first Lieut. who had frequently visited these Islands in the merchant service, in the small lagoons which are filled with sea water at high tide, and the heat of the sun being intense they are soon covered with a layer of salt in consequence of the rapid evaporation. This island is four or five miles in length, as I should judge, and exhibits in some places a level surface apparently of sand and in others hills of various height, but all apparently made up of rocks and sand, and without any signs of vegetation. In the afternoon we passed another Island called Bonna Vista, about 20 miles to the south-west of that which I have described, and presenting nearly the same appearances, though of a rather more uneven surface, and rising into hills of a greater elevation.

In the evening we had an indistinct view of the Island of Mayo to the south-east which we passed in the night, and were so far from it this morning, that we could see nothing more of it than its brown naked hills.

The weather being fine yesterday, we had Divine service on the quarter-deck, as indeed we have done every Sunday except one, since we sailed. Yesterday, however, for the first time, we went through with the whole service in a regular manner, with the exception of the litany; and the responses were made in a very proper and devout manner by the Capt. & first Lieut. as well as by Mr. & Mrs. B-s [Baylies], Miss - S. [Sampson] & Mr. R-s [Edmund Roberts]. I felt so much interested in this performance of our duty myself, that I did not suppose any one could possibly find fault with the exercises on account of the time spent in them; but I was mistaken. For although the time spent in them did not exceed twenty-minutes, still one of the officers expressed himself much dissatisfied, and thought it would be better to dispense with religious service altogether, than to spend so much time in it. It is not likely, however that his wish will prevail, since the Capt. seems to be much pleased with the service; and being satisfied of its beneficial influence on the crew, expresses his determination to have it continued.[7]

At day-light this morning, we found ourselves on the southside of St. Jago, and at the distance of eight or ten miles from it. As we advanced we approached so near to it as to have a distinct view of its most striking features, which are indicative of arid sterility in the highest degree. It being much larger than the Islands which have been mentioned, its mountains rise much higher, but seem equally destitute of verdure. Towards the southern extremity of the Island, a few scatered dwellings were seen at a little

distance from the shore in the ravine, where there is probably some vege-
tation, though none can be seen. Having coasted along the east side of the
Island, we doubled around its southern extremity, and anchored in Port
Praya at 10 oclock A.M. after a very pleasant passage of thirty-two days from
Boston.}

Port Praya

Immediately after coming to anchor, a boat was sent ashore with the junior
Lieut., Mr. Brent, and the Marine officer, Mr. Fowler, to the American
Consul, and Governor of the Island. About 12 o.c. the boat returned with
the Consul — Mr. Merril [William G. Merrill], and soon after, the customary
salute was exchanged with the battery on shore. Mr. Merril was originally
from Boston, and has been here most of the time for nine years, and
consequently may be supposed qualified to give correct information respecting the Island and its inhabitants.

The following particulars comprize the amount of the information
which he communicated. The whole population of the Island is supposed
to amount to about thirty-five thousand, of whom only about four hundred
are whites. The blacks are nearly all slaves. Some of them, however, are free,
and own slaves themselves, whom they treat with kindness, contrary to the
usual practice of negro slave holders. Most of the inhabitants of the Island
are collected into villages which are chiefly situated in the valleys, the only
habitable parts of the Island. The population of the town is from fifteen
hundred to two thousand, and the better part of this population, according
to the Consul's account, are those who have been banished from Portugal
by the cruel and blood thirsty [Don] Miguel.[8] This detestable tyrant has but
very few friends on the Island, and these are so only on account of the offices
with which he has invested them; and their fidelity will therefore continue
no longer, than he retains his power. There is at present a prospect that his
bloody reign is nearly at an end, and that Pedro will soon take possession
of the crown of Portugal.

The consul related the following ingenious proceeding on the part of
Pedro, of which information has just been received here, and from the result
of which, it appears that the Portuguese are only waiting for an opportunity
to throw off the yoke of their inhuman Master. In order to strengthen the
hopes of his friends in Portugal, and to make them acquainted with his
plans, that they might act in concert with him, and for the purpose also of

ascertaining the strength of his party, Pedro issued proclamations designed to accomplish these important objects, of which he caused a great number to be put up in barrels, and sent a small vessel with them as near to the harbour of Lisbon as the vessel could approach with safety; and at a favourable time of the tide, the barrels were thrown into the sea and drifted directly ashore. Being immediately discovered, and opened, their precious contents were quickly circulated throughout the kingdom and produced a very great effect, with which means were found to make Pedro immediately acquainted.

There has been no rain here for about twenty months, and there is consequently but little vegetation, and provisions of all kinds are dear. The inhabitants of the neighbouring Islands, particularly of Fogo, (a volcanic Island to the westward, the summit of which is visible from the ship) have suffered much from famine, and several thousands have fled to this Island to save themselves from utter starvation.

{This being the only watering place among these Islands, American vessels frequently stop here on their way home; and it is only three days ago, that a vessel sailed from this port for Boston, by which we might have sent letters to our friends, if we had arrived a little soonner.}

April 13. In order to return the kindness and hospitality of a countryman of ours who resides here, and also to strengthen the favourable opinion which the Islanders are disposed to entertain of the people of the U. States, the Capt. had a party on board night before last, consisting of some of the most respectable people of the place besides the gentleman to whom I have alluded, and the American Consul, who are the only Americans in the place.

The name of the gentleman to whom we are indebted for most of the satisfaction that we have realized here, is Mr. Gardner [Ferdinand Gardner]. He was formerly from Hudson in the state of N. York, and has been a resident of these Islands most of the time since 1819. Until 1827, he resided on the Island of Mayo; but since that time, he has resided at this place. His wife is a Portuguese woman, and the daughter of a Mr. Martinez of whom I shall have occasion to speak more particularly.

For the accommodation of the party, the quarter deck was very tastefully fitted up, on one side of which a supper-table was set, and furnished with such articles both for eating & drinking, as it may be persumed our guests are [surely] accustomed to partake of. The other side of the deck was to have been occupied as a ballroom; and the music was to have been supplied by Mrs. Bayleys' piano, which was accordingly placed on the after part of the quarter-deck.

A little before 5 o.c. the company from shore arrived, consisting of six or eight ladies, & ten or twelve gentlemen. The ladies were received on the quarter-deck by Mrs. B. & Miss S. As our ladies were ignorant of the Portuguese language, as their visitors were of English, they were of course unable to entertain each other with conversation; but this soon ceased to be a subject of regret, for they had not been half an hour on board, before two or three of them became extremely sea-sick, which rendered their stay short, & considerably lessened the entertainment of the evening. Some of the ladies were able to partake of the supper, which took place about 6 o.c.; and shortly afterwards, they all took leave, and went ashore. Before supper, however, we had a specimen of their waltzing, and in as graceful and modest a style as I have ever witnessed it; but still I cannot help feeling a strong dislike to it, for reasons, which, it appears to me, must be obvious to every one that has seen it.[9]

The ladies being accompanied ashore by some of our officers, the gentlemen who came with them, staid some time longer, and so far as a profuse supply of wine and especially of champaigne, can contribute to enjoyment; they must have realized it in a high degree. Among these gentlemen, were Mr. Martinez, & a Physician who was banished from Portugal some two or three years ago, by Don Miguel, and a Priest, who was also banished at the same time. The latter played on the piano, and performed exceedingly well. About 10 o.c. the party broke up, and our guests left the ship highly delighted, I have no doubt, with their visit. {But whatever reason they may have had to be pleased with the transactions of the evening, I could not regard them all with feelings of approbation. When I hear young Midshipmen urged to drink, and told repeatedly not to spare the Champaigne; and when I see them in consequence of this, empty one full glass after another, till they become too much excited to sit longer at the table, and then go reeling about the deck; I see no cause of satisfaction, and cannot participate in the least degree, in the pleasure which others seem to enjoy on such occasions. On the contrary, I see such consequences likely to result from Midshipmen, being not only permitted, but urged to drink to excess, that I am constrained to consider such conduct as exceedingly reprehensible. But what shall be said, when example is added to persuasion, to induce the young inexperienced officers to drink to excess? It is so obvious that the most serious evils must result from it, that I need not point them out. The subject is a most unpleasant one, and I regret extremely that I have occasion to mention it.}

Yesterday [April 12] I went ashore at the town for the first time, in company with the Capt., Mr. Roberts, Mid^nCarroll [George R. Carroll]. We called on our hospitable countryman, Mr. Gardner, and after spending about an hour there, during which time I prescribed for Mrs. G. & her niece, both of whom have been suffering for a long time under purulent ophtalmia, we took a walk about the town. The former has entirely lost the sight of one eye, and the sight of the other is considerably impaired. The eyes of the niece were still a good deal inflamed, notwithstanding two years have elapsed, since the disease commenced. Her sight is considerably impaired, but with proper management the disease may be prevented from proceeding farther.[10] After spending about an hour at Mr. Gardner's we took a survey of the town, which ocuppied us but about an hour; when we returned, and after making a short call on the Consul, went again to Mr. G.s where we dined. It being late in the afternoon when dinner was over, it was concluded to stay and spend the evening.

A small party was made up of ladies and gentlemen and the evening was passed very pleasantly, at least to those who could participate in the amusement, of music and dancing. The exiled priest was again the performer on the piano, and he seemed as well acquainted with ball-room music, as if he had made it a chief subject of study and practice. The company here consisted principally of those who were on board the evening before. The ladies appeared very well, though their complexion and features, exhibit evident marks of a mixture of African blood. These were a few exceptions, however, and it was remarked as something anomalous, that the lady whose complexion was fairest, and who seemed to be most free from the African [cast], was a native of Africa. {This young lady, indeed, had as fair a skin as any of my fair country-women, and seemed to be no more nearly allied to the negro race than they are. With regard to dress, I shall only observe, that however inferior these residents of a barren Island may be in those qualities which constitute the most essential part of female beauty; they certainly exhibit a much greater share of modesty & decorum in their dress, qualities which used to be considered of some importance among the fair daughters of America, but which, I am sorry to say, are now regarded as marks of prudery, and a want of that gentility which ladies would above all things, be thought to possess.}

At 9 o.c. we took supper, which consisted of fish, fowls, omelets, cakes, sweetmeats, coffee, tea, etc. After supper the dancing was resumed, and continued till after 10 o.c. when we took our leave & returned aboard the ship.

Having now obtained all the information respecting these Islands, that can be obtained by the most diligent inquiry that I have been able to make; I shall here insert such particulars as seem to be worth remembering.

The Island of St. Jago is about thirty-two miles in length, and of an average breadth of five or six miles. Its surface is extremely uneven, and exhibits as great a degree of barrenness as can possibly be conceived of. Mountains and hills seem to occupy almost the whole of its surface; and these appear to consist entirely of rocks and a reddish sand. Some of the highest peaks of the mountains are probably three thousand feet above the level of the sea. There are many appearances which indicate the volcanic origin of the Island, and these are particularly conspicuous in the neighbourhood of the harbour. A perpendicular bank bounds the harbour to the distance of half a mile east of the town, which presents a horizontal stratum of sand, generally two or three feet thick, and at the height of twenty or thirty feet from the surface of the water. In this stratum of sand, as well as in the superincumbent stratum in contact with it, are marine shells & petrifactions in abundance; from which it is evident that it has been raised to its present situation by volcanic fire. The superincumbent stratum is in some places fifty or sixty feet thick, appears to consist principally of the scoriae and other products of a volcanic eruption; as also does the subjacent stratum.

The population of this Island is said by those who have better means of knowing the truth than the Consul has, to be only twenty-seven thousand, of which not forty families are whites.

The town of Port Praya is situated on a hill about a hundred feet above the sea, and contains a population of about two thousand. The principal part of the town surrounds an open space on the top of the hill, which is level to the extent of about [three] hundred rods. There is but one principal street, which runs along the west side of the public square, and is nearly half a mile in length. This, as well as one or two other short streets, have paved side walks. The buildings are mostly made of stone, and the best of them are plastered & white washed, both within and without, which gives them, at a distance, quite a pleasant appearance. There are no public buildings that deserve to be mentioned. The residence of the Governor, is a most miserable looking hovel externally; and in such a ruinous state that it has to be propped up, to prevent its falling. The best private dwelling in the place belongs to a Mr. Melloe, and is really a very neat and comfortable residence. It stands on the western brow of the hill which forms the site of the town, and overlooks a large and pleasant garden in the valley a hundred feet below. This garden is the property of the above gentleman, and he is bestowing much labour and expense upon it; for which he will no doubt be amply repaid by its productions.

The hill on which the town stands is surrounded by a deep valley, the bottom of which is level and from twenty to sixty rods wide. This valley is now perfectly dry, but in the rainy season it is covered with water, and becomes the source of bilious fevers, which sometimes assume the character, if I am correctly informed, of the most malignant yellow-fever.[11] It was only in this valley that any signs of vegetation were to be seen, and even here but little else than the date and palm trees. The date tree is a species of the palm, and grows here to the height of fifty or sixty feet. They only bear during a rainy season, which sometimes occurs only once in several years. The fruit in its fresh state, is considered by the people here very unwholesome.

The principal productions of the Island are orchilla, a vegetable used in dyeing, coffee, skins & hides. The former is a royal monopoly, and of course nobody can profit by it except the king & his agents. Mr. Martinez, the gentleman whom I have already mentioned, [father-in-law of the American merchant Ferdinand Gardner] is the agent for this monopoly, from which he derives a considerable profit. As this gentleman is the first among all the residents of these Islands, both for intelligence and influence, some account of him will not be considered improper. He is a native Portuguese, but has been long a resident of the Islands, and in 1822, was a member of the Cortez for framing a constitution for Portugal. His possessions are very extensive, and his wealth immense. He owns the whole Island of Sal—has a large estate at Bonna Vista—owns a coffee plantation in this Island—another in Brazil, opposite Rio Janeiro; and besides all this, he has possessions in Portugal. He upholds the present government of Portugal, but only on condition that no persecuting measures are had recourse to in the Islands. It is owing chiefly to his influence, as his son-in-law, Mr. Gardner told me, that the people do not declare themselves in favour of Pedro. He is very intelligent, and speaks English very well. He speaks freely of the degeneracy of his countrymen from their ancient character, and says that the Portuguese nation, whatever it may once have been, is nothing now. Their spirit and enterprize are gone, and it matters but little, he says, whether Miguel or Pedro is their master: the players may be different, but the flag will be the same.

But to return to the productions of the Island. The orchilla which constitutes the chief article of export, is a kind of lichen or moss, which grows on the rocks, and is gathered every year. It is put up in large packages, and shipped to Lisbon. The king pays five dollars a hundred for it, and sells it for about seventy-five. There is a commission, however, and some other expenses to be added to the original cost of the article. It is used chiefly as a set to several kinds of dye, but particularly as I am told, to that of scarlet. I did not learn the amount of the yearly export of this article.

Coffee has been cultivated here but a few years, and last year, about thirty tons were exported. It is very fine, and said to be even superior to the mocha coffee. The trees begin to bear at the age of three years, & continue bearing seven; when the old tree is cut down, and new shoots come up, which bear & die in the same manner as the parent tree. Each tree produces about three pounds annually.

Sugar is made in sufficient quantity for the consumption of the inhabitants, but none for exportation.

The government of the Island is of course despotic; but owing to the restraining influence of Mr. Martinez, and of the Chief Justice, there is probably less oppression here than anywhere else in Miguel's dominions. The Chief Justice is a negro, a real African, but a very intelligent, good looking man. He is very highly respected, and is said to exert a very extensive and salutary influence over his countrymen.

A small garrison is kept up here, but the troops are badly paid, and consequently serve with great reluctance. The officers are sometimes more than a year without pay, and when received it is so small as scarcely to afford a subsistence. On the verge of the hill towards the harbour is a battery mounting upwards of thirty guns, some of which are twenty-four pounders. The harbour is good for vessels of any size. We anchored within about half a mile of the town, and in eight fathoms water.

Bonna Vista. The principal production of this Island is salt, which is made in the manner I have already mentioned, except that instead of forming a crust on the surface of the water in the lagoons, the salt falls to the bottom in the form of chrystals, till at the end of the season for making it, which is the beginning of September, it is from one inch to six inches thick for nearly a mile in length and half that distance in width. It is sold at the rate of ten or twelve dollars for sixty bushels. The population of this Island is four or five thousand, and nearly all blacks. Mr. Martinez has introduced the coffee there, which will probably become a valuable article of export from that Island, as well as from St. Jago.

Mayo. The populations of this Island is only fourteen or fifteen hundred, and its only production is salt.

Sal. The whole of this Island, as I have already stated, belongs to Mr. Martinez, where his preparations for making salt, or rather for transporting it from its natural manufactory to the sea, has cost him a hundred thousand dollars. Twenty-seven thousand dollars were expended in making a tunnel through a hill to serve as a passage for transporting the salt.

Fogo. This Island is inhabited by about sixteen thousand blacks, who are at present, and have been for some time past, in a state of great suffering for want of provisions. Heretofore this Island has produced not only sufficient corn for the consumption of its inhabitants, but considerable for exportation. They are now, however, in consequence of the long continued drought, reduced to the most extreme distress, and great numbers, it is said, have perished. Some thousands have come to Praya, where they receive all the assistance which the inhabitants, who are poor themselves, can afford. A vessel with a hundred and fifty of these miserable sufferers has just arrived, and I saw some of them yesterday on shore; and more wretched looking objects I have rarely seen. Our Capt. has sent them such a supply of provisions, as will satisfy the immediate wants of many, and perhaps save them from utter starvation.[12] I regret much that the condition of these poor creatures could not be immediately known in the U.S. for I have no doubt that a ship load of provisions would soon be sent to them.

Having taken in a sufficient supply of water, and provided ourselves with such vegetables and fruits as the place afforded, we sailed from Port Praya at 12 o'clock today [April 13], with a fine breeze & very pleasant weather.

CHAPTER II

Rio Janeiro

Departure from P. Praya; Passage to Rio Janeiro; Arrival; Walk
on shore, visit from Mr. Wright; Visit to the Botanic Garden;
Dinner at Mr. Wright's; New Empress; Education; Climate
of Rio Jan.; Commerce etc.; Police of Rio Jan.; Slavery;
J. Burkhead & Co.; Visit to Mr. Gardner's; Scenery about Rio;
Harbour of Rio; Praya Grande; Death of Mr. R.

{April 18. Since leaving Port Praya until today the wind and weather have
continued very propitious; indeed we have advanced several degrees nearer
to the equator with the north-east trade-wind than is usual. This wind
seldom prevails farther south, than seven or eight degrees of north latitude;
but we are now in four and the breeze still continues, though it has become
very light, and will probably cease in the course of the day. We may now
expect to meet with calms and light baffling winds for several days, before
we reach the south-east trade. Until today, there has scarcely been a cloud
in the sky since we left St. Jago, and although the days have been hot, yet
the nights have been remarkably pleasant, so as to make up for the discomfort occasioned by the heat of the day. The ladies especially have enjoyed
these pleasant evenings, and have generally remained on deck from teatime,
till nearly 10 o'clock.

The scene is now, however, about to change for instead of the clear &
azure sky, we are today surrounded by bodies of dark heavy clouds, which
threaten us with abundance of rain in the course of the day. The thermometer is now 81° & it was the same yesterday.}

{April 23. While writing the last page, a heavy squall came on, which

31

continued two or three hours, and put an end to the trade-wind. During this squall considerable rain fell, though it did not descend in such torrents as it usually does between the two trades. This was the heaviest rain we had while passing through these rainy latitudes, and it is remarkable that we had no thunder, and but very little lightning.

After about three days of light baffling winds, and unsettled weather, we met the south-east trade, which is now wafting us along at the rate of seven or eight miles an hour, and with a clear sky and a dry pure atmosphere. We had advanced within about a degree of the equator, when we took the south-east trade, which is very unusual, as this wind is almost always met with several degrees north of the line.

Night before last about 9 o'clock, we crossed the line and entered the southern hemisphere. It had been expected that his submarine Majesty, Neptune, would pay us a visit on this occasion, there being so many on board who had never crossed the line before, and some preparation was made for the purpose; but the claims of Neptune were satisfied with a liberal [treat] of sour punch served out to the crew, and thus his visit was dispensed with.[1] This childish and ridiculous ceremony is now but seldom observed, and it is to be hoped that it will soon go entirely into disuse, especially in our ships of war, as it tends to introduce disorder and insubordination.

Yesterday being Sunday, we had divine service as usual, with which the men seem to be much pleased. The Sunday before, we had a sermon, one of Buckminister's,[2] which was a very good one and was listened to very attentively. I suspect that this is the only public ship now in service, not provided with a Chaplain. It is to be hoped, however, that this will not long be the case, for it cannot fail to produce a salutary effect, at least so far as good order and correct deportment among the men are concerned; and it may be the means of leading some to turn their attention to the subject of religion in such a manner, as shall result in the salvation of their souls.

As we have now passed through the region of calms, and are fairly within the limits of the south-east trade-wind, which will probably carry us to Rio Janeiro, we can estimate with considerable certainty, the time that will be spent in the remaining part of our voyage. In twelve days, at farthest, if no accident befals us, we may expect to be at anchor in the harbour of Rio.}

May 5. With the exception of one day, the trade-wind continued to blow as steadily, and as fresh as we could desire, till the 3d. inst. when we made Cape Frio, about sixty miles to the eastward of the harbour of Rio Janeiro.

The night before we made the Cape, the breeze was unusually fresh, and for the first time since we left the U. States, we run at the rate of ten miles an hour, for two or three hours. We found ourselves within about twenty miles of land at day-light, which proved to be the Cape, though we were not able to make it out to our satisfaction, until we had passed it some distance, and had a view of the highlands about the harbour of Rio. At about 3 o'clock in the afternoon, we had a distinct view of the Sugar Loaf at the entrance of the harbour, and of that remarkable ridge of mountain to the southward of the harbour, called Lord Hood's Nose. We were now five & twenty miles from the harbour, and had the fresh breeze continued, we might have run in before dark; but about this time the wind died away, and we lay becalmed till seven or eight o'clock in the evening. A land breeze then sprung up, with which we run in within four or five miles of the entrance of the harbour, and then stood off till day-light; at which time we were about ten miles from it. Soon after sun-rise, the breeze died away, and we remained becalmed through the day. Although the thermometer was not so high now, as it was several days in the neighbourhood of the line, yet we felt the heat more sensibly than we have done before during the voyage. There being no prospect of our having a breeze that would enable us to enter the harbour, the Capt. sent in a boat with the Second Lieutenant about 4 o'clock in the afternoon, to apprize the Commodore [Commodore George W. Rodgers] of our arrival, and deliver the despatches & letters for himself and the officers of the squadron. Before the boat had arrived at the entrance of the harbour, a black cloud was observed in the south-west which emitted an occasional flash of lightning, a sure presage of unpleasant weather and frequently of a severe gale of wind.

About this time a favourable breeze sprung up, and the Capt. having determined to run in and anchor, if possible, all sails were set, and we approached the harbour at quite a rapid rate. In the mean time the lightning in the southwest became more vivid, the black clouds began to rise and every thing portended an uncomfortable night. The Sugar Loaf now became so obscured that it could not be seen, though not more than two or three miles distant, and the wind having freshened, and inclined more ahead, it was apprehended that we should be compelled to stand out to sea again. The bearing of the entrance of the harbour having been taken, however, before dark and there being no shoal or other obstacle in the way, we continued to stand on before a fresh breeze, in darkness, and rain for about half an hour; when the clouds broke away, and the moon came out, so that we had a distinct view of the Sugar Loaf, which bounds the entrance of the harbour on the left hand, and of the Fort of Santa Cruz on the other. Until now, considerable anxiety had been felt, respecting the event of the attempt we were making to run into the harbour in a dark stormy night; but, when the clouds dispersed, and we had a view of the objects which bounded our course, all apprehension was dismissed, and we proceeded on towards our anchorage without any farther concern. As we passed the fort, two guns were fired & blue lights burnt, which is the usual signal when vessels enter the harbour at night. Before this signal was made, however, we were hailed from the fort, but in an unintelligible manner, and an answer was returned, which must have been equally unintelligible. A little farther up the harbour, we passed another fort, where we were again hailed as before, and another gun was fired & a blue light burnt.

It had been the Captain's intention to anchor near the Sugar Loaf, but this wind being favourable and the navigation safe, he determined to keep on till he reached the usual anchorage ground. Not being able, however, to designate the place where vessels of war usually anchor, and being desirous to advance sufficiently far into the bay, we found, after we came to anchor, that we were considerably above all the other vessels of war in the harbour; and day-light disclosed to us this morning, a reef of rocks at a very small distance from us, on which we should have struck in two minutes more if the wind had not at that moment, suddenly died away.

Immediately after we were safe at anchor a boat was dispatched with a midshipman to a French frigate, lying next below us, to obtain information respecting the Commodore. The boat returned in a short time, with information that he had sailed fifteen days before for the River Plate [Rio de la Plata], on account of some disturbances respecting the Falkland Islands.[3]

Soon after daylight, the boat that had been sent in with the second Lieut. returned, without having accomplished any thing, there being no American man of war in the harbour. Before the boat reached the harbour the shower came on, which compelled her to stop at the first vessel she came to, which proved to be a Portuguese man of war, where the officers & crew passed the night; and were very hospitably entertained by the Capt. who was an Englishman. Several others, among whom were two or three ladies, had been compelled by stress of weather, to take refuge for the night on board the same ship.

In the course of the forenoon, the Consul, Mr. Baker [John Martin Baker], came on board, and the Captain received the instructions which had been left for him by Commodore Rodgers;[4] and which directed him to proceed as soon as possible to Buenos Ayres. No satisfactory information could be obtained from the Consul respecting the transactions which had occasioned the Commodore's visit to the River; but in the course of the day we learned the following particulars from a Mr. Gardner, another American resident here.

{In consequence of some proceedings at the Falkland Islands, on the part of Governor Vernet [Governor Louis Vernet], which were considered Piratical, our Consul at Buenos Ayres, Mr. Slacum [George Washington Slacum], wrote to the head of the Government, to know whether they acknowledged Vernet as acting under their authority; but no satisfactory answer was returned. This led Capt. Duncan [Commander Silas Duncan] of the *Lexington* to declare to the Government, that on such a day, if no satisfactory answer to the Consul's inquiry were previously given, he should sail to the Islands, and take up the establishment there; and at the time appointed he did sail, and succeeded in carrying his threat into full execution. A man by the name of Brisbane [Matthew Brisbane] had been left in command there by Vernet, who, with about thirty others, became a prisoner of Capt. Duncan. All but six of the principal agents in the alleged piratical acts, were liberated; and these were still on board the *Lexington*. This news renders Mr. Baylies very anxious to be at Buenos Ayres, as soon as possible; and it is probable we shall sail in the course of next week. It is further stated in relation to the troubles at Buenos Ayres, that the Government has suspended the function, of our Consul, in consequence of the proceedings of Capt. Duncan, of which they complain in the bitterest terms.}

May 7. Yesterday being Sunday, we had divine service on board as usual; and several of our countrymen from shore, who had come on board to pay their respects to the Capt. and Minister, attended. After dinner, the ladies were desirous to go ashore at Praya Grande, for the purpose of exercise; and Lieutenants Purviance & Brent, and myself accompanied them. We landed on the beach at the lower part of the town, and walked back about three quarters of a mile among groves of orange trees loaded with fruit, and gardens of coffee, bannanas, etc. and richly adorned with a variety of flowers. In the course of our walk, we passed several dwellings which had a very neat and comfortable appearance, and exhibited as much evidence of the ease and contentment of their possessors, as I have any where met with. We also saw a good many people, both white and black, collected together in groups, or scattered about on the hills which bounded our path on both sides; and they all appeared to be happy & contented. {And, indeed, no reason can be seen why they should not be so, unless it may be those unfortunate slaves who have tyranical and cruel masters; for the ground is so fertile, that with very little labour, enough is produced to satisfy all the reasonable wants of life. In this delightful walk we spent about an hour, and then returned to the ship, where we arrived just as it began to grow dark.}

Today I had the pleasure of seeing Mr. Wright [William H. D. C. Wright], our former Consul here, whom I knew while on this station before, and of whom I then entertained, and do still entertain a very high opinion. The cause of his being superseded he tells me, was his detecting some fraudulent proceeding in the custom-house in relation to an American vessel, and representing it to the Government here in strong, but respectful language. This so offended them that they complained to the Government of the U.S. and requested that he should be removed. With this request, unjust as it was, our Government readily complied; but at the same time addressed a letter to Mr. Wright, expressing the most entire approbation of his conduct.[5] I am happy to learn that his business does not sustain any injury, in consequence of being thus unceremoniously dismissed from an office, the duties of which he had faithfully performed.

It was not till today, that arrangements could be made respecting a salute; and this afternoon seventeen guns were fired, and the same number returned by the fort. This was rather an unfortunate salute for the Captain, for the first gun broke two fine looking-glasses in the cabin, which had been placed against the bulk-head, in such a manner as to receive the full force of the concussion.

May 12. Yesterday I made a visit to the Botanic Garden, in company with Mr. Roberts & Lieut. Fowler. We left the ship at about half past 9 o'clock, and landed at Bota Fogo, about four miles south of the city, and three from the Garden. Bota Fogo is one of the most pleasant and romantic places that I have ever seen. It is a small village situated at the bottom of a small bay that sets back about half a mile on the west side of the harbour just above the Sugar Loaf; and is bounded by hills varying much in form and elevation, but most of them richly clothed with verdure.[6] Between the base of these hills and the bay, is a plain of small extent on which the town stands; and which produces in the greatest profusion all kinds of tropical fruits and flowers. We passed several gardens here, which exhibited an astonishing degree of the luxuriance of nature, in every thing that can please the eye, or gratify the taste. There is generally a sea breeze blowing here, which renders this the most pleasant place of residence, that is any where to be found in the neighbourhood of the city, and far more pleasant than the city itself.

We left Bota Fogo for the garden at 11 o'clock, and passing along the base of Corco Vado, a point of rock, nearly a thousand feet high, and along the shore of a small beautiful lake, we arrived at the Garden a little past twelve. The Garden gates we found closed, and were informed that they were not to be opened till 2 o'clock. Being unwilling to return without accomplishing the object of our visit, and learning that it was not far to the sea in a southerly direction we determined to prolong our journey [farther] where we were told we should be able to make a good collection of shells. After walking about half a mile along the shore of the lake [Lake Rodrigo de Freitas], we came to a venda [an inn], and beginning to feel the need of refreshment, we stopped and called for dinner; which was ready in a few minutes, and consisted of a dozzen and a half of eggs, bread & butter & coffee. After dinner, we resumed our walk and having laboured more than a mile through the deep sand, we came to the sea. Our labour was but poorly rewarded, as we found no shells worth picking up. On the way we passed through a little village of negro huts, surrounded by orange trees bending under a load of fruit. There was the appearance here of as much comfort and independance, as the African race seem capable of enjoying any where.

We returned to the Garden about half past three, and found the gate open. There has been considerable improvement in the Garden since I was there last in 1827. We found there most of the eastern exotics, with which we are acquainted, in great perfection; as the clove, cinnamon, camphor & nutmeg trees; the tea, cardam[on], pepper etc. The Garden comprized, as I should judge, at least twenty acres, and is in a state of high cultivation. It is laid out with taste, and adorned with a great variety of flowering plants and shrubs, most of which are to be found only within the tropics.[7]

Having spent about half an hour in the Garden, we left it at 4 o'clock, and with no little sense of fatigue, we set out on our walk of seven miles to the city, where we had requested a boat to meet us at sunset. It was too late, however, for us to reach the city by sunset, so that we proceeded at such a rate as suited best our fatigued condition. We reached Bota Fogo, about 5 o'clock, and after spending half an hour there in searching on the beach for shells, we pursued our weary way to the city, where we arrived at half past six. The boat was at the landing-place waiting for us, which took us immediately on board the ship; where we arrived at 7 o'clock, after a walk of about fifteen miles, and as might be supposed, a good deal fatigued, though well pleased with our excursion.

May 14. Day before yesterday [May 12] I dined with Mr. Wright, our former Consul here, in company with Mr. Baylies, Capt. Geisinger, Mr. Roberts, Lieut. Brent, & Lieut. Fowler. Besides the party from the ship, there were several other gentlemen, namely Mr. Brown, our Chargé [Ethan A. Brown], Mr. Maxwell, the partner of Mr. Wright, Mr. Giraud [Daniel Giraud], & Mr. Foster, American merchants here. The party was favoured with the company of three ladies, namely Mrs. Wright, Mrs. Maxwell, & Miss Wright. Mrs. Baylies & Miss Sampson had been invited, but the landing was so bad on account of the surf, that they were deterred from going. We left the ship at 2 o'clock, and landing at the lower part of the city in a high surf, we walked about two miles to Mr. Wright's residence at Praya Flamengo. The guests had assembled when we arrived, except Mr. Brown, who did not make his appearance till we had taken our seats at the table. During the hour that elapsed before dinner was announced, I had considerable conversation with Mr. Maxwell, who is a very intelligent man, and from his long residence here, of twenty-seven years, is well qualified to give correct information of the place & people. From him I learned, that in some respects, at least, the condition of this country has been considerably improved within a few years, and particularly with regard to the Monastic orders, of which there were several here whose members were numerous, and a heavy burden upon the industrious part of the community. None of these orders now exist, and Mr. Maxwell says there are not a hundred & fifty monks in Brazil. Several of these religious orders possessed large funds, all of which have been expended, ostensibly for the benefit of the public, but in reality I suppose, for the benefit of the Emperor. Of the secular clergy, I know nothing worth recording, except that the Bishop, who resides here, is a most worthy and learned man, & a member of the Senate. His income is from twenty-five to thirty thousand dollars a year, of which he expends nearly the whole in acts of charity.[8]

With respect to the abdication of the Emperor, [Don Pedro I], it was voluntary, and proceeded, as is supposed, from a design to unite the kingdom of Portugal with the empire of Brazil, and to subject both to the sway of his arbitrary will.[9] But if such was his design, he will most assuredly fail of accomplishing his purpose; for, if he should gain possession of Portugal, which, however, is very doubtful, it will never be in his power to unite the two kingdoms, the hostility of the Brazilians to such a measure being too determined & deep-rooted for him ever to overcome it. He might have continued to reign here, though probably not in the arbitrary manner, to which his inclination would lead him; yet with the good will, & the benefit of his subjects. It is said that the new Empress [Don Pedro's second wife, Empress Amelia, a Bavarian princess from Leuchtemberg] introduced considerable changes into the Palace, which must have been productive of effects highly gratifying to the people. She had prevailed on the Emperor to pay some attention to study, and to allot a certain portion of his time every day to the improvement of his mind. Another portion of the day was appropriated by her arrangement, to business; and the remainder to meals, the instruction of their children, & amusements. It had been the custom of Pedro, after the example of his father, to dine by himself; but the new Empress abolished this custom, and induced him to dine with the family. Her influence was farther exerted in the abolition of another ridiculous custom, which was requiring those who waited upon him, when they handed him any thing, to do it on their bended knees. This practice, a relic of feudal servitude, she induced him to abolish; and wherever her influence extended, it was exerted for the welfare of the people. Hence she soon became exceedingly popular, and if she had remained here, there is no doubt, that she would have contributed greatly to the improvement of the Brazilians, and effected an important change in the state of society.

There is more attention paid to the important subject of education than there formerly was, several colleges having been established within a few years, where the usual course of collegiate instruction is pursued, and the several degrees conferred. There is no college in the city of Rio Janeiro, where it might be supposed a litterary institution would be more likely to flourish, than any where else in the empire; but the reasons assigned for there being no college in the capital of the empire, are undoubtedly well founded, and the same which render the colleges in our large cities, less flourishing than those that are situated in places where the population is comparatively small. These reasons are, the greater number and variety of alluring temptations in a large city, which exert a most baneful influence on the minds and morals of young men; and the greater expense for board, clothing etc. The colleges are said to be in a flourishing state. The term of study prescribed for graduation is seven years, but if a student does not wish to graduate, he is at liberty to leave the college at the end of three years. No one is admitted for a less term than three years.

The medical profession is also in an improving condition. Formerly almost all the medical men of the country were obliged to go either to

Portugal or Paris for their professional education; but now there is a medical school [Hospital da Misericordia] here where the medical student enjoys nearly the same advantages that he would in Europe, and where degrees are conferred. From what I can learn, however, the native practitioners do not rank very high for professional science & skill. The English & American residents, employ a Scotch physician by the name of Coates, who is well informed in his profession, and highly deserving of all the confidence that is reposed in him.[10]

It rarely happens that the physicians here are called upon to treat any form of acute disease, the complaints requiring medical treatment being almost wholly of a chronic character. These complaints are generally seated in the liver and other organs concerned in the process of digestion; and are owing to the debilitating influence of the climate, and the mode of living.

The heat is not very great here except about four months of the year, when the thermometer on shore ranges between 90 & 100: during the rest of the year, the range of temperature is generally between 70 & 80. The former is the rainy season, and comprizes the months of December, January, February & March. During this period, more or less rain falls almost every day, and frequently it pours down in torrents for hours together. There is much less rain during the other season, but then it frequently happens that there is a shower every day for several days in succession, and sometimes it rains almost incessantly for two or three days together. Hence there is always a good deal of humidity in the atmosphere, which, even with the temperature that prevails here during the cool season, exerts a debilitating influence on the human body.

The principal diet of the people here, which is assigned as another cause of the gastric and hepatic disorders that prevail among them consists of beans stewed in pork fat. This is a kind of food, which must be difficult of digestion, and its flatulent properties, no doubt, occasion that general appearance of corpulence, which attracts the notice of a stranger.[11]

No malignant epidemic has ever been known in Rio Janeiro, for which it is difficult to assign a satisfactory reason; as all the causes, so far as we can judge, exist here that produce epidemic diseases of a malignant character in other places within the tropics. The streets of the city are generally narrow & extremely dirty, there being apparently as little attention paid to cleanliness here, as I have observed any where. There is consequently a great mass of animal and vegetable matter constantly exposed to the action of the two principal agents in the process of decomposition, heat and moisture; and as these agents act as powerfully here as they do in other places where the most fatal epidemics prevail, we should conclude with good reason, that they would rage here with as great violence as they do any where, and especially in our cities, where the utmost pains are taken to remove all the causes from which they originate, so far as these causes are within the reach of human agency. The fact, however, as we have seen, is far otherwise. A city, which we should suppose, by reasoning on the subject, would be liable to the most terrible ravages of the yellow-fever, and other destructive diseases of tropical climates, enjoys a perfect immunity from them; while the cities of the U. States; which the same train of reasoning would lead us to consider as secure against these calamities, have experienced their repeated and severe visitations. It is evident, therefore, that we are yet ignorant of much that is most essential to be known, respecting the origin of epidemic diseases, and the laws which govern them; and until we acquire this knowledge, all our reasoning on the subject is but little avail.

{May 18. Today we expected to have taken our departure for the River Plate, but the heavy rain yesterday, prevented the transaction of some business, which must be settled before we sail. It is probable, however, that I have made my last visit on shore here till we return from the east; and I shall therefore conclude the remarks I have to make respecting the place & people.}

With respect to the city itself, there seems to have been but little change since I left here in 1828. But very few buildings have been erected since that time, and these are in the outter limits of the city, where the poorer classes of the population generally reside. The reasons of this trifling increase of the city are obvious to any one who witnessed the active and lucrative commerce four or five years ago, and observes its languishing condition at the present time. Arrivals were then very frequent, especially from England and the U. States, and every arrival was a source of profit to the merchant, and an advantage to the whole city in keeping alive its industry and enterprize; but now, the arrivals are comparatively few, and even these occasion a loss to all who are concerned in them. Mr. Burkhead, the principal American merchant here [James Birckhead & Co.], told me the other day, that they were sorry to see an American vessel come into port, as they sustained a loss on every vessel consigned to them, and had done so for some time past. This is attributed in a considerable degree to the abdication of the Emperor, and the consequent unsettled state of the country, which renders every branch of business unsafe, no one knowing how soon another change in the government might take place, and his property be taken from him.[12]

Such continues to be the unsettled state of the country with regard to politics. There are two great parties here, and also throughout the empire, between which nearly all the people of any character are divided, and almost equally. One party goes with the Regency, and the present ministry; the other, which is said to be headed by the Andrada family, one of the most intelligent and influential families in Brazil, is opposed, not to the present form of government, but to the persons who constitute the executive branch of it; and their principal design is, to effect the removal of these individuals, and to take the offices which they hold into their own hands.[13] This party is now a large minority in the House of Delegates, but in the Senate their force is quite small. {They are making every effort, however, to gain the ascendency, and the event is said to be very doubtful. If they should succeed, it is expected that great commotions will take place, and that lives and property will be exposed to the greatest hazzards.} There have been recent attempts at a revolution, and it is believed that, if the English and French Admirals had not rendered assistance, the malcontents would have triumphed, and that the destruction of the city would have followed.[14] The American merchants here feel themselves quite insecure, and they are endeavouring to circumscribe their business, and prepare themselves for any event that may occur.

Notwithstanding this agitated state of the public mind, however, it is said that the police of the city is much better than it was while the Emperor was here; and from what I have seen, I have no doubt of the fact. Formerly assassinations were extremely frequent in the city, and so little thought of, that an English resident here told me, he could procure the murder of any man for a quarter of dollar, without subjecting himself to the least hazzard of punishment. At the present time, however, assassinations are rare, and depredations on property, are also seldom committed. This is certainly an important step towards an efficient, and well regulated police, such as would render the life and property of the citizen secure; and it is probably as great an advance towards that state, as can be made, while the slaves, who have no interest in the preservation of peace & good order constitute so large a proportion of the people.

The slave trade is abolished, [1831] through the intervention of the English government; but slavery still exists here in all its horrors. It is said that the slaves here are treated with great lenity, and are as happy as they would have been at home. This may be true in part, but whoever walks the streets of Rio Janeiro, and sees the labours which this unfortunate race of beings are compelled to perform, cannot avoid concluding, that slavery subjects its miserable victims to the same evils here that it does elsewhere, and that the kind treatment which they receive here, is only a less degree of cruelty. Can that be called mild treatment which compels the slave to perform all the labours of beasts of burden through the day, and leaves them to seek for their shelter at night wherever they can find it? In fact, I do not hesitate to declare from my own observation, that brute animals receive much more humane treatment here from their owners, than man receives from his fellow-man. For the former are worked moderately, when worked at all, which is but seldom, compared with the unremitting toils of the latter, and when their labours are ended, they are provided with a comfortable shelter, and with a sufficient supply of proper food; but the latter are worked without mercy through the day, and at night are turned adrift to seek food and shelter wherever they may happen to find them. A hundred times, perhaps, have I seen the miserable slave performing the labour of a dray-horse, either in dragging heavy loads through the streets, or in carrying burdens on his head, which would make a sufficient load for a horse. The transportation of all heavy articles is performed by slaves. Hogsheads of molasses, sugar etc, and large boxes, are placed on low trucks with four wheels, and drawn by six or eight slaves. Bags of coffee, and any thing contained in sacks not weighing more than two hundred pounds, the slaves carry on their heads. It is astonishing to see what immense burdens these poor creatures are made to carry on their heads; and it is painful to witness the effort which they are obliged to make to sustain these enormous loads. When employed in this kind of labour, there is generally a company of ten or twelve together, and as they move along at a kind of half-running gate, they all join in a kind of song, which seems not only to regulate their movement but also to lighten their burden. But violent and exhausting as these efforts must be, the exertions of those employed in dragging the loaded trucks through the streets, appear to me to be still more so. Indeed, I have often thought, when I have seen these miserable wretches tugging at a load which would have required all the strength of the stoutest horse, and have witness[ed] the writhing of their muscles, and the perspiration running in streams down their naked bodies; that the human frame was incapable of making more violent efforts.

Such are the employments in which a large proportion of the black population of the city are constantly engaged; and it is therefore absurd to say, that the slaves here are generally well treated, and are contented with their condition. There are slaves here, I have no doubt, who are treated with kindness and humanity, and whose condition is consequently as well adapted, perhaps, to their capacity for enjoyment, as any they could be placed in. But these constitute, as I have reason to believe, only a small part of the slave population. The rest are reduced to a state of suffering and servitude, as completely destitute of every thing that can constitute human enjoyment as we can easily conceive. They manifest a degree of contentment, it is true, but if they do, it is that kind of apathy and insensibility, which is the result of their abject and degraded state. This, however, is not a higher degree of contentment than is realized by the brute. The slave does not complain, nor manifest a desire to change his situation, because he dreads the additional pain that will be inflicted on him, if he dares to complain; and as to any change in his condition, he is made to look upon every change for the better as utterly hopeless.

{Now, such being the condition of a large proportion of the black population of Rio Janeiro, we must draw an unfavourable conclusion, I think, with regard to the condition of the whites: for it appears to me that the moral and intellectual condition of any people must be very low, who treat their fellow creatures, however abject and degraded they may be, in the manner that slaves of Rio are treated. Man without sympathy can scarcely be supposed to possess any moral sense, or understanding the force of those obligations which unite men together in society and can that man possess the sympathies of human nature, who inflicts such suffering on an unfortunate class of his fellow-beings, as those slave-owners do, to whom I allude? I would not hastily, nor without sufficient reason, form an unfavourable judgement of the citizens of Rio Janeiro, but when I see the power which circumstances have given them over the poor african, exercised in a more merciless manner than it is over the brutes, I am unavoidably led to conclude that their moral character must be extremely defective.

I am aware, that this conclusion, as well as the fact from which it is drawn would be denied with indignation by the people of Rio; but until they can show, that the manner in which the slaves are employed there, is not an evidence of bad treatment, but is voluntary on the part of the slave, that conclusion that I have drawn must stand uncontroverted. It may be farther said, indeed it is often said, in extenuation of the crime of slavery here, that the slaves in Brazil, are treated with greater humanity, and enjoy greater privileges than they do in any other country where slavery is tolerated; but before we give implicit credit to such assertions, we must consider by whom they are made, and we shall find that it is by the very persons themselves, to whom we are to give the praise of superior kindness and humanity.}

It may indeed be true, that there are many slave-holders in Brazil, who treat their slaves better than many even in the U. States; but I find no reason to conclude that the general condition of slaves here is better than it is in other slave-holding countries, and not so good as it is in the U. States. In judging of the condition of slaves in Brazil, as compared with that of the slaves in the U. States, in relation to the treatment which they receive; we should take into consideration the difference of climate, which affects very materially the condition of the slave. The climate of Brazil is such that the slave requires very little attention from his master in providing him with shelter and clothing, and is always earning something to his master except when disabled by disease, instead of being a source of expense to him, wheras in the U. States, the climate is such during some months of the year that the slave is unable to perform any profitable labour for his master, and must be furnished with the means of protecting himself against the cold at his master's expense. If there were, therefore, any superiority in the condition of the Brazilian slave over that of his unfortunate brother in N. America, it should be attributed rather to the greater mildness of the climate in which his destiny has placed [him], and to the greater facility of procuring the necessaries of life, than to the greater humanity of his master. But even admitting that the slaves of Brazil were treated as well as it is pretended they are; still slavery is a most fearful evil to the country, and one from which the most dreadful consequences must be apprehended at some future day. There is nothing wanting, indeed, at this moment, to render the blacks the masters of the whole country, owing to the great majority of their numbers over that of the whites, but a general concert among them, and men of sufficient intelligence to direct their efforts in a proper manner. It is sincerely to be hoped, however, that the slave-holders of Brazil, will become sensible of the danger to which they are exposing themselves by retaining so many of their fellow creatures in a state of the most abject and degrading bondage, before it shall be too late to avert the evil.

The day before yesterday [May 16], I spent on shore and dined at Mr. Burkhead's in company with several of the officers, where we were entertained in a very friendly & hospitable manner. This gentleman is one of the oldest American merchants here, and has succeeded so well in business, that he has acquired quite a large fortune. On his first engaging in business here, he was associated with two other Americans, whose names were Bedwell & Boyd. In 1827, while I was at Rio, both of these gentlemen were in bad health, in consequence of their close attention to business, and of the influence of a debilitating climate. The latter, Boyd, embarked on board the Brig *Cervantes* for the U. States, for the recovery of his health, and was never heard of afterwards; the other was taken worse about the same time, and died after a very short confinement to his room. Until about the period that I have mentioned, the house of Burkhead & Co. transacted nearly all the American business in the place; but other American houses began about that time, to take a share of the business, and have also succeeded very well.

The principal, and indeed almost the only article of export from Rio Janeiro, is coffee, of which, from seventy to eighty millions of pounds were exported last year. The principal season for gathering coffee is the month of August; but more or less of it is brought into market during the whole year. This is owing to the difference of the seasons in the lowlands and on the mountains. The coffee on the former ripens much soonner than it does on the latter; and on both, it is considerably earlier in the neighbourhood of the city than it is in the interior. The price of coffee at Rio is 8 or 9 cents a pound.

After dining with Mr. Burkhead, Mr. Roberts, Lieut. Purviance & myself took a walk out to Mr. Gardner's about two miles out of the city. On passing along one of the principal streets of the city, our attention was arrested by the voice of a large number of blacks collected together in the street that we were crossing; and on inquiring of a boy the cause of the disturbance, he replied, "muerto," that is, someone is dead. We approached the scene of contention, for it was manifest from their words and gestures, that they were contending about something; and we found that they were quarrelling over the dead body of a black female, which was lying in a sack in the street, and which they were about to transport to the place of burial; and the quarrel seemed to have arisen about the privilege of assisting to bear the body to its final resting place. Such a scene will serve to convey some idea of the state of society in this large city, where we should expect more refinement than any where else in Brazil.

It was four o'clock when we set out for Mr. Gardner's, and we arrived there about sunset, where we found several American gentlemen, who had also been invited to spend the evening there. Mr. G. has his family with him, which consists of his wife, sister, brother, and a little son. This is a very agreeable family, and the evening was spent very pleasantly. Mr. G. occupies a situation on one of the hills which surround the city, where they enjoy an extensive and delightful view, and a comparatively pure and refreshing air. Their house is surrounded by orange trees bending under the weight of their golden fruit; and just below them on the plain, was a large and beautiful garden, where could be seen at their proper seasons, almost all the fruits and flowers of the torid zone.

Having directed a boat to be at the landing for us at 9 o'clock, we left this agreeable family about 8 and commenced our walk back to the city. Just as we entered the road that was to conduct us to the city, we observed two men carrying what we supposed to be a dead body in a sack suspended from a long pole, which they bore on their shoulders. The foremost bearer carried a torch; and as they were going in the same direction with ourselves, we had the curiosity to observe their movements. They had not proceeded more than a quarter of a mile, however, before they stopped at a house, and rapping at the door, a feeble voice proceeded from the supposed dead body in the sack; from which we concluded that some sick person had thus been conveyed home, or perhaps to the Doctor, because too poor to pay the fee for a visit. This incident is too trifling to deserve notice, if it did not serve to show a trait of semi-barbarism in the Brazilian character.

{While we feel ourselves compelled to speak in less favourable terms than we could wish, of the character and intelligence of the citizens of Rio Janeiro;} it is difficult to find language to convey an adequate idea of the magnificent scenery by which they are surround[ed], and of the immense source of wealth which they enjoy in the astonishing richness of their soil. On all sides, except that bounded by the bay, the city is surrounded by hills and mountains of every possible variety of form, and every degree of elevation up to three or four thousand feet. The most striking objects, however, in this grand panorama of nature, as beheld from the harbour, are the Sugar-Loaf, the Corco Vado, and the Organ Mountains. The former bounds the southern entrance of the harbour, and rises from the water's edge at an ascent of about 45°, to the height of more than seven hundred feet. On the western side it is nearly perpendicular. It appears to be a solid rock of granite, and a more stupendous one, has rarely if ever been seen.

The second is situated about two miles to the westward of the harbour, and its height is estimated at fifteen or sixteen hundred feet. On the north west side the ascent is so gradual that people ride to the top on horse-back; but on the other side, it presents a perpendicular face of solid rock, eight or nine hundred feet high. Near the top is a chasm in the rock, over which there is a bridge; and quite at the summit is a telegraph,[15] which was occasionally used during the late war with Buenos Ayres, but is now wholly neglected. At the base of this peak on the north side, the aquaduct which conveys the water into the city, has its source. A small body of water is formed there by the rain, and the condensed vapours with which the thick foliage of trees on the sides and at the base of the mountain are almost always loaded; and from this reservoir, which rarely ever fails, a stream of water five or six inches deep, and eight or nine inches wide, runs in a channel made in a bed of stone, a distance of at least four miles on an inclined plane into the city, which it supplies abundantly with most excellent water.

The Organ-Mountains are situated to the northward of the bay twenty or thirty miles from the city, and consist of three sharp peaks which shoot up to a considerable height, and bear some resemblance to the pipes of the instrument from which they are named; though by no means so striking, that every beholder would perceive it.

Most of the hills and mountains which constitute the ground-work of the grand scenery about Rio, are clothed to their summits with perennial verdure; which is partly the spontaneous product of nature, which is nowhere more prolific than here, and partly the product of human industry.

{Besides the objects which have been mentioned, there is another peculiar feature in this grand exhibition of nature's work, which deserves particular notice; and that is what is called by Englishmen and Americans, Lord Hood's Nose.[16] This is formed by what is called the table mountain from the level appearance of its top, as seen on its eastern side from the harbour. It is situated about four miles to the southward of the harbour, near the sea, and is probably about two thousand feet high. As viewed from the sea, the top of this mountain presents a very strong resemblance to a Roman nose; and taken in connection with the adjacent hills, which bear a considerable resemblance to the other parts of the human countenance, it constitutes a remarkable land-mark, which can never be forgotten by those who have once seen it.}

Such are some of the principal features of the scenery about Rio, which present themselves to the view on entering the harbour; but the less prominent points of this magnificent landscape, from their great variety and beauty, are equally deserving of our admiration. There is no pleasure, however, without alloy; and while beholding with admiration the rich and luxuriant scenery, which everywhere meets the eye from the harbour of Rio; we find the pleasure which this view is calculated to produce, considerably diminished, on reflecting that this rich verdure conceals a great variety of the venomous reptiles and insects, with which tropical regions are infested, and among them some kinds of snakes of enormous size. Mr. Maxwell, the partner of Mr. Wright, our former Consul, who owns a plantation a few miles out of the city, told me when at his house four years ago, that snakes ten or twelve feet long, were seen almost every day on his grounds, and that his slaves were sometimes bitten by them. The bite was highly dangerous, but he had discovered a remedy, he said, in the Balsam Copaiba,[17] taken internally in as large quantity as the stomach would bear, and also applied externally to the wound. These monsters, however, of the serpent race, as we are disposed to consider them, are mere pigmies compared with those which exist in the interior, and of which Mr. Gardner gave me an account the other evening when at his house. There they are so large, that their skins are tanned, and used for boots and shoes, and saddles. It is common, Mr. G. says, to see them 40 or 50 feet long; he had often seen them of this size. Not long ago, a gentleman in England sent to his friend in Rio to procure him the preserved skin of a snake 70 feet long, if he could possibly obtain one of that astonishing length. After some inquiry, his friend informed him, that he could not procure him one preserved of the length that he specified; but he could send him one that was tanned, 90 feet long. This relation may seem incredible, but I have no doubt of its truth.

Having said so much about the scenery which delights the eye of the beholder in the harbour of Rio, it will be proper to say a few words respecting the harbour itself. And as the works of nature which surround this harbour, are probably not surpassed by any in the world for variety and beauty; so there is probably no harbour in the world, that rivals this in its extent, security, and ease of access. From its entrance to its upper anchorage, where merchant vessels usually lie, the distance is about five miles, and the general width of the bay is about three miles. The anchorage is good, and the depth of water is ten or eleven fathoms. The distance at which vessels of war usually anchor from the town, is about a mile.

The entrance of the harbour is narrow, being only about a quarter of a mile wide. On the south side it is bounded, as I have already observed, by the Sugar Loaf, and on the other side by an immense mass of rock, which rises by a gradual ascent from the water to the height of fifteen or twenty [feet]. The summit of this mass of rock is occupied by Fort Santa Cruz, which is of considerable extent, and might be made capable of affording very effectual protection to the harbour. It is now, however, apparently in a decaying condition; and I should judge that two English or American ships of the line, with a fair wind, would easily overcome all the opposition which this fort would make to their entering the harbour. A little distance above Santa Cruz, is another fort on what is called Round Island, situated a little to the left hand of the passage up the bay; but this fort is small compared with that which I have just mentioned. Still farther up the bay, and nearly in a line with Round Island, is another island of a larger size, which is also surmounted with a fort. Both these last mentioned forts, however, seem to be in quite as ruinous a state as that of Santa Cruz, and capable of making but a very feeble opposition to any hostile force that might be disposed to enter the harbour.

At a little distance above the anchorage, and so near the city as to leave only a narrow passage between them, is the Island of Cobras, on which there are foundries, work-shops for a variety of mechanical arts, store-houses etc; which render this island a very important appendage to the city. The base of this island on the north consists of solid rock, and it was here where I saw four years ago [1828] the iron rings which Capt. Cook [Captain James Cook] had fastened in the rock, for the purpose of careening and repairing his ships.[18] A dry dock has since been commenced there.

Between the anchorage and the town is a small island consisting almost entirely of rock, called Rat-Island, which is used for drying hides, and sometimes as a place of deposit for stores. Observations are conveniently made here for ascertaining the rate of chronometers, and other purposes. This island has also been the theatre of duels, and when I was on this station in —27, an Assistant Surgeon belonging to one of our ships of war, was killed there in a duel.

Farther up the bay, which extends fifteen or twenty miles to the north, there are many islands visible from the anchorage, some of which are of considerable size and inhabited, while others are small and destitute of other occupants than birds and reptiles. They are all covered with verdure, and with the white buildings which are seen in contrast with the surrounding green on the largest of them, they altogether present a variegated view of the most pleasing character. {Such are the principal objects in the harbour of Rio that are deserving of notice.}

On the opposite side of the bay from the city is Praya Grande, a small village consisting of white-washed buildings, which at a distance, make a very neat and pleasant appearance. The village extends along the shore of the bay about the distance of [a] mile, and is divided by a small stream of water, into two unequal parts; the lower of which, or that towards the sea is called St. Domingo, and the other is properly the Praya Grande. Hills of various elevation and of great diversity of form, and all verdant to their summits with a rich and luxuriant vegetation, constitute the landscape in the rear of this pleasant village. Judging from the view which this village presents, we should consider it a delightful place of residence in the hot season, where one could enjoy the pleasure of breathing a pure air, and of being refreshed by the cool shade which is always to be found in the numerous gardens & orange groves, which surround the village.

It was here where I attended one of my countrymen [Mr. R.] in 1828, during the closing scene of his life; and witnessed a state of mental agony which I shall never forget, and which I hope never to witness again. This man had been a resident of Monte Video, where I first saw him in 1826, with every appearance of the most perfect and robust health. He led a dissolute life, however, and no soundness of constitution, or vigor of health, can long withstand the deadly influence of dissolute habits. In the latter part of the year 1827, I was again at Monte Video, and saw this man, but so altered that I scarcely knew him. He was pale, emaciated, and so feeble as scarcely to be able to endure the most gentle exercise. Early in 1828, we returned to Rio Janeiro, and had not been long there, when to my great surprise, this man came on board the ship to consult me respecting his health. He was now evidently in the last stage of consumption; and knowing the course of his past life, and that he had consequently much to do, in order to be prepared for the awful event which seemed to be rapidly approaching, I lost no time in expressing to him my opinion of the extreme danger of his situation. This made but little impression upon him and he returned to Praya Grande, whither he had come for the purpose of regaining his health, with the expectation that he should soon recover, at least so far as to be able to return to the U. States. From this time I made him a visit at his lodgings as often as he required; and finding him worse at every succeeding visit, I endeavoured by all proper means to make him sensible of his situation, but all to no effect. At last, I received a message from him very early one morning, saying that he was worse and wished to see me immediately. I went as soon as possible, and found the symptoms of death upon him. His reason was perfect as it usually is in consumption till the last moment of life. He had evidently but a few hours to live, and no time was to be lost in trifling with hopes which could certainly never be realized. I told him plainly that he must instantly abandon all hope of life, and think only of making preparation for death, which was now very near. He gazed at me at first with incredulous surprize, and said he felt able to get up and walk about the room, and asked with extreme anxiety, if he could not so far recover as to be able to return to his family at Monte Video. I told him he certainly could not, and he must not deceive himself with such a delusive hope. His feelings soon convinced him of the dreadful truth, that death was already closing up the avenues of life, and that in a very short time he would cease to be numbered with the living. A most dreadful agony now seized him, manifested not by words, for he spoke no more, but by a heartrending groan which accompanied every breath; and by the large drops of perspiration which covered his pale and ghastly face. In this state he continued about three hours, when the mortal struggle ceased, and his spirit took its flight to that world, where its destiny is fixed forever. Such was the miserable termination of a life, which had been spent wholly in worldly pursuits, and in vicious indulgencies, and probably without a single thought having been bestowed upon the subject of death and a future state.

{Before closing my account of Rio Janeiro, it is proper that I should say a few words respecting the light-house, and certain islands, which serve as guides to the entrance of the harbour. The light-house is situated on what is called Rosa Island [Raza Island], to the southward of the entrance of the harbour, and about ten miles from the town. The island on which the light-house stands is probably thirty feet above the sea, and the light-house is of such a height, that the light can be distinctly seen fifteen or twenty miles. The light revolves, and at every third revolution appears of a bright red, by which it may be distinguished from any other light that might be seen in its neighbourhood. At a little distance from Rosa Island, is another island called Redondo [Round Island], which presents a round summit, that rises to the height of sixty or seventy feet. On approaching the harbour, two islands are passed at the right hand, the first of which is about two miles from Santa Cruz, and the other about one. These are of nearly a circular form, of about the same size, and forty or fifty feet in height. Besides these islands, there are several others in the neighbourhood of the harbor but they are not deserving of particular notice.

Vessels bound to Rio Janeiro, usually make Cape Frio, about sixty miles to the eastwards and then steering nearly west, the Sugar Loaf soon becomes visible, and designates the course to the entrance of the harbour. In approaching the harbour at night, the safest way is to keep four or five miles to the northward of the light, and within a little distance of the two islands which I have last described. By observing these directions, it is perfectly safe to run into this harbour in the darkest night without a pilot; and when once inside of Fort Santa Cruz, vessels may anchor with perfect security. There is usually a land breeze, however, blowing out of the harbour at night, which renders it impossible for vessels to run in during this time. The land breeze commonly dies away at nine or ten o'clock in the morning, and is succeeded by the sea breeze, which continues till about seven o'clock in the evening. It is only during the time of the sea-breeze, or while a south-westerly wind is blowing, which is almost always accompanied with bad weather, that vessels can enter this harbour; and it is only while the land breeze prevails, which blows generally from north to northwest, that they can go out. Hence they usually get under way very early in the morning, the time when the land breeze is generally most fresh, and by the time it is met by the sea-breeze, they are as far out of the harbour as to have sufficient sea room from whatever direction the wind may blow.}

CHAPTER III
Buenos Ayres

Departure from Rio Janeiro; Passage to Buenos Ayres; First
visit on Shore; Landing of Mr. Baylies; Dinner at Mr.
Zimmerman's; Description of B. A.; Departure from the River
Plate; Description of Monte Video; Throwing the lazo; Pass
Tristan de Acunha; The barometer; Make the island of
Amsterdam; Severe gale; Pass Christmas Island;
Arrival at Bencoolen.

On our arrival at Rio Janeiro, and finding that we were to join the Commodore as soon as possible, at Buenos Ayres; we expected to have resumed
our voyage in a week at farthest, and made our arrangements accordingly.
The weather, however, being rainy, and more time being consequently taken
up in painting the ship, and making the other preparations, than was
calculated for; our stay was prolonged from seven to seventeen days, and it
was not till the 20th. of May, that we took our departure from Rio, and
shaped our course for the River Plate.

On Sunday the 20th. at 8 o'clock in the morning we weighed anchor,
and stood out of the harbour, well pleased that we were about to leave a
place where the almost incessant rains had in a great measure deprived us
of the satisfaction which we might otherwise have enjoyed.

The wind being very light, our boats were sent ahead to tow the ship
down the harbour, but being too few and too small to make much progress,
the other ships of war in the harbour, namely the English, French, and
Brazilian, sent their boats to our assistance. The English Admiral's ship,
the *Warspite* 74, commanded by Sir George Baker, was lying about a mile
below us; and as we passed her within a little distance, her band commenced

playing, and continued it till we were nearly out of hearing.[1] This is a complement that is frequently paid by vessels of war of different nations to each other, and especially by those of England and America; but circumstances which it is not necessary to mention, lead me to suppose, that on the present occasion, the compliment was rather intended for the ladies on board our ship, than for any body else. However, this may be, the compliment was duly appreciated, and in return for it our flag was lowered as we passed the Admiral's ship.

Besides the *Warspite*, there were two or three other small English vessels of war lying in the harbour, one of which, the *Beadle* [HMS *Beagle*], was destined for a surveying expedition, but where I did not learn.[2] The French force consisted of a forty-four gun frigate, and a brig, the latter of which is the vessel, it is said, which carried Napoleon from the island of Elba to France.[3]

We succeeded very well, notwithstanding the light wind, in making our exit from the harbour; and we had no sooner got fairly out, than a favourable breeze sprung up, which bore us along at the rate of seven or eight miles an hour, till we had run a distance of about two hundred miles. The wind then became adverse, light and baffling, and continued so about twenty-four hours, when it returned again to its former point, and continued there with but little variation about three days; during which we made very good progress, and flattered ourselves with the prospect of a short passage to the River. In this, however, we were disappointed, for when we were within about a day's sail of Cape St. Mary, which bounds the entrance of the River on the north side, the wind again became unfavourable, and continued for three days to blow quite fresh from the southward, and raised so heavy a sea, that we were unable to make any progress on our destined course. The weather during this time was cloudy, and there were occasional heavy showers of rain. At last, the clouds dispersed, the wind became fair, and we made all sail towards the cape, for which we were now about 150 miles distant. This was on the 29th of May, and early the next morning, we made the highlands to the northward of the Cape, and about 10 o'clock in the forenoon, we had the Cape itself in sight. The Cape is a low sandy point which runs out to the southeast, and cannot be seen from deck more than fifteen miles. The highlands seen to the northward of the Cape, appear to consist of a ridge five or six miles in extent, and have an elevation, as I should judge, of from five to seven hundred feet. Soundings extend a hundred miles or more from the coast, and at the distance of seventy miles, there is only about fifty fathoms water.

About the time we made the land on the 30th, the wind became so light that our progress was only at the rate of one or two miles an hour; so that it was night before we passed the cape. About this time the breeze freshened, and during the greater part of the night we pursued our course as rapidly as we wished. Our course for the cape was about south-west, the direction of the Island of Lobos, a small oblong island siting fifteen or twenty feet above the water, and situated near the mainland about forty miles above the cape. {The usual track of navigation is very near the south side of this Island; but in order to avoid the danger of running upon it, we steered so far to the south, that when day light appeared and we had a view of the Island, we found ourselves at least fifteen mills to the southward of it.} The fair wind had now died away to a calm, and a thick fog came on which continued through the day. It occasionally broke away, however, and gave us an opportunity of extending our field of vision to the distance of some miles. During one of these intervals a brig was discovered at the distance of a mile or two above us coming down the River, and our boat was sent to make inquiry respecting our squadron. She returned in a short time with the melancholly news that Commodore Rodgers was dead. No event could have been more unexpected than this, as no man, judging from the opinion of those who were acquainted with him, had a fairer prospect of a prolonged life than he had. All calculations, however, with regard to the duration of life are founded on too uncertain a basis to be entitled to the least confidence. {The Commodore has left a wife and several children in the U. States, who are now anticipating the pleasure of his return; but whose pleasing hopes must soon be blasted by the news of his death.}

Soon after the boat returned, a breeze sprung up from the northeast, which increased till it urged us along at the rate of about eight knots. Our course was nearly west, for the Island of Flores, on which is a very good light; and about 11 o'clock p.m. we had the satisfaction to see the light at the distance of a few miles on our starboard bow. Being now certain of our position, we pursued our course for the harbour as we supposed, though without the intention of anchoring before day light; when about 3 o'clock in the morning [June 1st], the water suddenly shoaled from seven or eight to four fathoms; and we were on the point of running upon the English Bank. {This was owing to a very strong current setting down the river, which became evident as day light appeared, and we could observe the alteration of our bearing, with Flores, and the Mount, of which we had a distinct view, as well as of some vessels lying at anchor off the town of Monte Video. The depth of water from Lobos, was for some distance from thirteen to fourteen fathoms, and then it gradually shoaled to about seven fathoms, the bottom being all along a soft mud. On approaching the English Bank, the water shoals suddenly, and the bottom is hard.}

Through the day we had to contend with a head wind, and our progress was consequently very slow. At evening, however, the wind became a little more favourable, so that we could steer such a course as would nearly take us into anchorage; and we continued this course till 2 o'clock in the morning, when we anchored in four fathoms water, and in sight of the vessels in the harbour. At 3 o'clock, our first Lieut. left the ship and went in pursuit of the *Lexington*; {and in about three hours he returned, and reported that he had found the *Lexington*, and learned there that the disturbances at Buenos Ayres respecting the Falkland Islands were still unsettled.} At day- light [June 2d], we found ourselves lying about five miles from the town of Monte Video, in a south-west direction, and about two miles from the Mount. Immediately after breakfast the boat was sent to town for a pilot to take us up the River, and also to obtain fresh provisions for the crew. {In the course of the day we were visited by the Captain and officers of the *Lexington*, and heard their statements in relation to the Falkland Islands; which, however, I shall not at present insert.}

Early the next morning, June the 3d. Mr. Haven [Charles H. Haven, steward] who had been sent to town, returned with a pilot, and the wind being fair, we got under way about 8 o'clock, and pursued our course up the River. At first we took a S.W. course a distance of 35 miles, and then W.S.W. seven miles, when we anchored on account of the thick weather, which prevented a sight of Punta del Indio, an indispensable landmark in determining the course past certain shoals which render the navigation above somewhat intricate and dangerous. After lying at anchor about an hour, this important object became visible, and we again resumed our course with a fresh breeze from the north-east, accompanied with heavy rain. Our course now was N. West & N.N.W. about 30 miles, and then W. ten or fifteen miles, when we anchored for the night, on the southern edge, and at the upper end of the Ortiz Bank. The depth of water varied from three and a half to five fathoms, the bottom being every where a soft mud.

June 5. At day-break yesterday morning we got under way and pursued our course up the River; but the wind being ahead, our progress was slow. It was now found, that instead of being only about fifteen miles from Buenos Ayres, as was supposed when we anchored the night before we were at least thirty. We continued to beat through the day under as much sail as the ship could well carry; and at sunset found ourselves in sight of the town of Buenos Ayres, and of the vessels lying at anchor. It was both difficult and somewhat dangerous for us to proceed farther at night with a head wind; we cast anchor for the night as soon as it became dark and at the distance of about five miles from the usual station of men of war.

Soon after we had located ourselves for the night, the Captain took his boat and set out in opposition to a strong breeze, which was blowing down the River, to visit the *Warren*, and deliver the despatches to the commanding officer of the squadron. After he left the ship, the wind increased and the River became quite rough insomuch that we were apprehensive he would not be able to accomplish his object, and would be compelled to return. Lights were kept burning for him during the greater part of the night, but his resolution rendered them unnecessary, as it enabled him to overcome all the opposition he met with from the wind and waves, and to reach the *Warren* much soonner than any of us expected he could.

At 10 o'clock this morning the wind being fair, we again weighed anchor, and shaped our course for the position which we intended to occupy, and which we reached about 12 o'clock. We are now lying, about four miles from town, and within a quarter of a mile of the *Warren* & *Enterprize*.

One of the first persons who came on board after we came to anchor, was the health officer, to inquire whether we had any epidemic disease on board, in reference especially to the Cholera; as the Government had been led to the adoption of the regulation, of examining men-of-war as well as other vessels, from the fear that this disease might be imported, and commit the same ravages here that it has done in Europe. The health-officer is a Prussian attached to the Buenos Ayrean army, and seems to be a very intelligent man. He tells me that he was with Napoleon in his disastrous Russian campaign; was afterwards some time in the Austrian army, and in 1825 came to this country and joined the army where he had been ever since. He has been so kind as to offer me the use of his rooms on shore, and to introduce me to some of the best families in the town.

June 14— Last friday, the 8th. I went on shore for the first time at this place, in company with Lieut. Brent, Mr. Robinson [Horatio N. Robinson, schoolmaster] & Midshipman Carroll. Just as we were about to leave the ship, a very thick heavy fog came on, and continued till some time in the afternoon. By the help of a compass, however, we made our way through the fog; and when we had approached within forty or fifty rods of the shore, we were met by a cart drawn by a pair of miserable half-starved ponies, into which we stepped from the boat, and soon landed among a crowd of spectators. This is the usual way of landing here, it being unsafe, and even impossible, except when the River is very high, for boats to approach near enough to shore for persons to land on the beach. And not only are passengers obliged to have recourse to the carts, but the cargoes of vessels are landed & taken on board in the same way.

It might be supposed by one not acquainted with the River, that a pier might be built out, so as to afford a convenient landing, at least for boats; but this has been attempted, and was found to be impracticable on account of the soft muddy bottom, and of the heavy sea which is sometimes forced in here by a northeasterly wind. {As I expected to spend but one night on shore, I did not think proper to avail myself of my Prussian friend's generous offer, and went to the house of a Mrs. Wells, who, though an Irish woman, calls herself an American, and manages so as to make her house the principal resort of Americans.}

I had been but a few minutes at this house, when I met with two old acquaintances whom I was much surprized, and very glad to see, namely Mrs. Canfield [Thalice Canfield, wife of Arthur Canfield], and her brother, Mr. Ruggles, who had arrived the night before from the other side of the River, and were about to embark for the U. States.[4] Mrs. C. has been in this country ever since 1819, and when I was at Monte Video, in —26 —27 & —28, she was residing there; and when I saw her last in April —28, she was making her calculations to revisit her native country in a few months, and to spend the rest of her life there among her friends. In consequence, however, of her niece [Mary] marrying Dr. Bond [Dr. Joshua Bond], a resident of Monte Video, and going to reside there, together with her mother and sister, Mrs. C. was induced to change her plan, & to consent to remain some time longer in the country. {Soon after the arrival of her friends at Monte Video, she left that place, and went with them about a hundred miles up the River, where she has been living ever since. Her husband and two sons are still there, and expect to remain there some years longer.} I accompanied this lady to the house of Dr. Bond whom I had known at Monte Video, and from whom I received some additional information respecting the government and state of the country, as well as respecting the late proceedings at the Falkland Islands.[5]

According to his statement, the government must be considered extremely arbitrary, and by no means deficient in intelligence and a determination to maintain their rights. As an evidence of the arbitrary and despotic character of the government, a recent transaction here may be adduced, which will be considered altogether conclusive. It appears that considerable disaffection was manifesting itself among the troops stationed at a distance from the city; and to appease this, the Governor ordered several hundred women of bad character to be sent from this place to the army, which was accordingly done. Now, although this measure may have been beneficial to the town, and for the present perhaps, prevented a revolt among the troops; yet no act could be more arbitrary, or more revolting to the feelings of every one who has correct ideas of personal and civil liberty.

With respect to the late transactions at the Falkland Islands, {I shall say nothing more now, as the subject is about to undergo an investigation, than that I am convinced, from having heard the statement on the other side, that Capt. Duncan has at least acted precipitately, and given this Government just cause of complaint.[6] Of his conduct to his prisoners, as it has been represented to me, I cannot speak in too severe terms; for whatever may have been done by the Governor of the Islands, or by this Government, in violation of our rights, Capt. D. cannot be excused from treating the men whom he found on the Island, with inhumanity. And that he did so treat them there can be no doubt, if keeping them in irons, and not only not providing them himself with such clothing as the inclement season required, but refusing to permit others to supply them as their necessities demanded, constitutes such treatment.} It is fortunate, however, that we had then a commander on this station, whose heart was not insensible to the sufferings of others, even although they might have been employed as the agents in doing injury to his countrymen, and who disapproved entirely of the cruel measures adopted by Capt. D. towards his prisoners, and did all in his power to avert the unhappy consequences that were likely to result from them. This man was Commodore Rodgers, whose kindness to those prisoners after they came into his power, deserves as much praise, as the unkindness of Capt. D. deserves censure. The excitement produced among the citizens here, by the news of Capt. D's proceedings at the Islands was great, and especially by the report of the manner in which he had treated his prisoners; and if nothing had been done to allay this excitement, there is reason to believe that very serious consequences would have followed. This was happily effected to a considerable degree, by the judicious course which the good sense and humane disposition of Commodore Rodgers led him to pursue. He particularly testified his disapprobation of Capt D's conduct towards his prisoners, by supplying all their wants, and releasing them from confinement, as soon as they came into his power; and as soon as circumstances would permit, they were set at liberty and sent ashore. This humane conduct of the Commodore, had a great effect in allaying the excitement of the people, and probably saved the lives of several Americans. Such was the favourable effect, indeed, produced by this mild conciliatory course of the Commodore, that not only private citizens, but the Governor himself and other public officers, attended his funeral, and testified the highest respect for his character.

Such is the present state of the public mind here, according to the best information I can obtain, in relation to the difficulty that has arisen respecting the Falkland Islands. If Commodore Rodgers had lived, and been permitted to influence the negociations by the advice which he was qualified to give, I have not the least doubt, that every misunderstanding might have been adjusted without difficulty or delay. {But as circumstances now are, there is reason to apprehend that, although a negociation will finally result in an amicable settlement of the difficulties, it will be attended with considerable embarrassment, and be made to occupy a much longer time than would otherwise have been necessary. Respecting the qualifications of Mr. Baylies, for the situation in which he is placed, there can be no doubt, nor can there by any of his disposition to have every thing amically settled as expeditiously as possible; but, when it is considered that he has heard so much said respecting the proceedings at the Islands, by those who were disposed to approve of every thing that had been done on our part, and to condemn every thing that had been done on the other side; and when it is considered farther, that Mr. Slacum, the former Consul here, who has been suspended from the exercise of his functions, in consequence of his interference in the affair of the Islands, has manifested the utmost attention to Mr. B. & his family, and has taken them into his house; when all this is considered, I say, there appears to me reason to believe, that Mr. B. will be led to take such a view of the subject on which he is to negociate, as will render this Government less ready to comply with such terms as may be proposed, than they otherwise would be.[7]

Whether Mr. Slacum is actuated by any other motives than those of kindness and hospitality towards Mr. Baylies and his family, is not for me to say. It has been suggested, however, that his attention to Mr. B. has proceeded from a desire to enlist him on his own side, and to induce him to adopt such measures as he may dictate. But whether there is any truth in this or not, Mr. B. is not a man who will allow himself to be influenced in his public conduct by any private considerations, unless I am greatly mistaken in his character; and whatever Mr. Slacum's motives may have been in offering him the use of his house, it is certainly a great favour to him as he is by this means provided with better accommodations, than he could have procured for himself in so short a time.}

Some preparation being necessary before the house was in a condition to receive its new occupants, and Mr. B. not wishing to manifest a great hurry to land; it was not till the 9th. that they took leave of the ship, and became residents of Buenos Ayres. They were to have landed in the morning, and arrangements had been made to receive them; but a thick fog came on which rendered invisible the signals that had been agreed upon, and consequently deferred the landing till the fog cleared away. This took place about 3 o'clock in the afternoon, when they left the ship under a salute of fifteen guns, and then moved on towards the shore where a considerable number of spectators, principally Americans, had assembled to see them land. In this, however, they were disappointed; for instead of landing in the usually way, that is by means of carts, and then getting into the coach which Mr. Slacum had provided for them, the coach took them directly from the boat, at the distance of twenty or thirty rods from shore; and then proceeded on towards the residence of Mr. Slacum without stopping; so that the curiosity of those who had been waiting some time to have a view of the Minister and his family, was in a great measure defeated. Capt. Cooper [Commander Benjamin Cooper, USS *Warren*], the commanding officer on the station, and Capt. Geisinger, followed in another coach. The afternoon was very favourable for their landing, the surface of the River being unruffled by wind, and the weather being clear and pleasant.

In the evening, I called at Mr. Slacum's and found the ladies in a spacious, well-carpeted and comfortable parlour, where they must have experienced much the same feelings, that prisoners do when released from a long and close confinement, and restored to their liberty. I cannot speak for others, but for myself I can say in sincerity, that I part from this excellent family with much regret. During the three months that they have been with us, their deportment had uniformily been such as to gain the esteem and good will of all who have had an opportunity of associating with them; and I have no doubt that this part of our cruise will long be thought of by us all with peculiar pleasure.[8]

{June [n.d.] The next day being Sunday [June 10], and there being an English Church here, where there is regular service, I was desirous to go; but as an opportunity offered early in the morning to return on board the ship, I thought it best not to let it pass, lest another might not soon offer, and accordingly took a passage in the Captain's boat and reached the ship about 10 o'clock. Having seen as much of the town as I wished to, and expecting that we should sail in three or four days, I concluded that I should not go ashore again;} but finding that we should not sail soon as the time fixed upon, and having received an invitation to dine at Mr. Zimmerman's [John C. Zimmermann], a principal merchant here, I paid a second visit to shore yesterday, the 13th.[9]

I landed about 12 o'clock, and went to the usual place of rendezvous for Americans, namely Mrs. Wells, where I met with Capts. Cooper & Geisinger, besides several of the officers both of the *Warren* and our own ship. During the time that I spent at Mrs. Wells's waiting for the dinner hour to arrive, I had an opportunity of learning something satisfactory respecting future movements, and the time of our departure from this place. {This information I obtained from a conversation which took place in my hearing between Capt. Cooper and Mr. Roberts;} and the amount of it is, that we are to leave here next Monday, and proceed, after a short stay at Monte Video, to a port on the west side of the Island of Sumatra, where we are to wait for the Schooner *Boxer*.[10] I was very glad to learn that Capt. Cooper, who is authorized, as I understand, to detain the ship on this station, has come to the conclusion to let us proceed on our eastern voyage without delay; {for I would rather sail twice around the world, than remain two years on this station, and most of the officers belonging to the ship possess the same feelings.}

At three o'clock we repaired to Mr. Zimmerman's. A considerable number of officers had been invited, but only four were present, namely, Capt. Cooper, Lieut. Command. Downing [Lt. Commander Samuel W. Downing] Lieut. Fowler & myself. There were four ladies at the table, namely, Mr. Zimmerman's mother, wife, and two daughters.

Mr. Z. has been considerably in the U. States, and is quite partial to Americans. He has two sons now at school at Bloomingdale near N. York. While we were setting at table, he received a letter from one of them, which he showed to us, and in which his son, who is about 12 years of age, expresses himself so well pleased with his new residence, that rather than return to Buenos Ayres, he would have his father go to the U. States.

From Mr. Z. I learn, that there has been no addition of consequence made to the city for some years, in consequence of the almost uninterrupted state of war.[11] Considerable improvement, however, has been made within a few years, in the interior of the houses, which renders them much more comfortable as well as more decent in appearance, than they formerly were. Until a few years ago, he says there was not a papered room or a carpeted floor in Buenos Ayres; but now, it is almost as common to see rooms handsomely papered, and the floors, whether of brick or wood, covered with rich carpets here, as it is in the U. States.

This is a kind of improvement that is certainly very well, and shows that the inhabitants have a disposition to promote their own comfort, and to present a decent exterior; but I am sorry to say, that there is another kind of improvement which is much more important to them, as it would conduce much more to their happiness and respectability, but in which they appear not to have made any progress. The improvement of which I now speak is in moral and intellectual worth, in which, I have the strongest reason to believe, these people are lamentably deficient. I do not pretend to speak on this subject from my own knowledge, for that is entirely too limited to serve as the basis of a correct conclusion; but the representations of those who have had ample opportunities of knowing the truth, are such as lead me to conclude that nothing is more rare here than those qualities of the heart and the head, which constitute the highest excellence of the human character, namely, virtue and intelligence. After making every reasonable allowance for exaggerated reports, there is still conclusive evidence, that there is so little restraint here from the principles of virtue and morality, that it is not considered disgraceful even for wives to obtain the means of gratifying their fondness for dress, by the violation of those obligations, which constitute the basis, not only of domestic happiness, but [even in] a great degree, of the welfare of the community. These gross moral defects belong principally to the native citizens, as I have reason to believe; but there is a strong tendency in the foreign residents to conform to the practices of those among whom they live, so far as they can do it without being guilty of the flagrant violations of moral rectitude mentioned above. {An instance of this I met with, much to my sorrow, in a young lady of my acquaintance, three or four years from the U. States, who had been taught to pay outward respect at least to religion and all its observances, and especially to the Lord's day; but who can now talk of dancing and attending parties on that day, without manifesting the least sense of the impropriety of spending the day in a manner which she considered highly sinful, until the experience of evil example changed her views, and led her to adopt the practices which she would once have condemned.

The time passed very pleasantly at Mr. Zimmermann's until about half past 7 o'clock, when a message came to Capt. Cooper from Capt. Geisinger, informing him that Capt. G. was very sick at Mrs. Wells's and wished to see him immediately. Supposing that my services might be required, I took leave of the party, and went with Capt. C. expecting to find Capt. G. suffering under some sudden and severe attack of disease; but we had no sooner entered his room than we discovered that it was all a trick played off upon Capt. Cooper.[12] I should not mention an unmanly and foolish transaction of this kind, if it were not for the purpose of introducing some remarks which I intend to make respecting the conduct of naval commanders. It is certainly to be expected, by those who have not had opportunities of knowing the contrary, that every commander of an American ship of war, is a man of some dignity of character, whose general deportment is in conformity with the common rules of civilized society. But I am sorry to say, that I have recently observed instances of a gross departure from these principles, and many others of the same kind might be mentioned. I have witnessed conduct since my arrival at this place, which would have been considered censurable in a high degree, and on some occasions would have given serious offence, if those to whom I allude had not been invested with an office, which is supposed to be entitled to respect. But why is drunkenness more excusable in a naval commander than in a private citizen? And what gives the former a license to use profane and obscene language, and to conduct with a rudeness and disregard of all decorum, which would forever exclude the latter from all decent society? For my own part, I look upon these excesses in commanders as even more culpable than in a private citizen; inasmuch as their example exerts a greater influence, and is therefore productive of worse consequences. To judge from what I have recently had too frequent opportunities of seeing, however, I should conclude, that a naval commander supposes that by becomming intoxicated, and saying whatever may happen to come into his mind, and especially by being profuse in the use of oaths and imprecations, he is exhibiting himself to the best advantage. Even ladies must be supposed to like an officer the better for conducting in this manner; and it is but a short time since I saw a naval commander have recourse to these means, to recommend himself to the ladies on board our ship. Perhaps I am not right, however, when I say that the person to whom I allude, became intoxicated and conducted in the manner that a man usually does while under the influence of liquor, for the purpose of appearing to better advantage before the ladies; but I am positively right in saying that the presence of ladies, and of those too, whom he had never seen before, was not a sufficient check upon him, to prevent his committing those violations of decorum, which every well-bred man must condemn, and especially when they take place in defiance of the presence of ladies.

I do not mention these violations, not only of those rules of sobriety and decorum, which every man is bound to observe, but also of the rules and regulations of the Navy, because I bear any personal ill-will towards the individuals who have been guilty of them or wish to exhibit them before the public in an unfavourable character; but on the contrary, I appreciate as highly as any one their kind and amiable qualities, which they have never failed to manifest when ever an occasion offered to call them into exercise; and as to myself, their deportment has been uniformly such as to deserve my favourable regard. Personal considerations alone, however, ought not to govern one in expressing his opinion of those who occupy public stations, and whose conduct, whether right or wrong, must exert an influence on others as well as themselves. It is on this ground, that I feel myself at liberty, and even called upon by a sense of duty, to take such notice of their conduct as it seems to me to deserve. In doing this, I am well aware, that I subject myself to the ill-will, not only of the persons to whom my remarks immediately apply, but also to the censure of a large number of the officers of the Navy. This shall not deter me, however, from doing what I conceive to be my duty. The general welfare and respectability of the Navy, are objects of far greater importance in my estimation than the favourable opinion of any number of officers, whatever their rank may be, and especially if that opinion is to be obtained by giving countenance to excesses and irregularities, which would ruin the reputation of any one in a private station. But how are the welfare and respectability of the Navy to be promoted, if commanders are allowed to be guilty of every species of excess and indecorum? How is it possible to maintain that discipline which is considered indispensably necessary to the well-being of the Navy, when commanders allow themselves to commit those very acts, for which they would consider themselves required by the regulations of the service, to inflict severe punishment on others? For example, under what pretense can either of the commanders of whom I have particularly alluded, punish the crime of drunkenness in any one under their command; when they have not only been repeatedly seen in a state of intoxication by all those under their command, but are even heard to talk of these excesses with a sort of exultation, as if they had performed achievements deserving of the highest praise? And farther, what respect can a commander be entitled to or reasonably expect, either from those under his command, or from others, who is known to be almost in the daily habit of disguising himself with liquor to such a degree as not to know what he says and does, and therefore says and does what he is ashamed of in his sober moments? What must a lady think of a naval commander, who, with an inexcusable rudeness, insists on her dancing with him at a party on board his own ship, and who is so unconscious of what he is doing that he has not the least recollection of it the next day?

Now, so long as commanders can thus violate all the principles both of morality and decorum with impunity, it is perfectly idle to expect that the Navy will ever attain that high standing in public estimation, which its best friends earnestly desire. There can be no real permanent respectability, either of individuals or public bodies, that is not founded on moral worth. If the Navy, therefore, ever acquires that standing for real honor and respectability, it can only be done by suppressing every species of criminal excess, as well in those who occupy the highest stations in the Navy as in those who have no rank to protect them.}

June 19. {After a much longer detention than was expected, and for several days entertaining doubts whether we should not be kept on the Brazilian station, and our eastern expedition entirely broken up in consequence of the difficulty respecting the Falkland Islands; all obstacles to our departure were at length removed, and we took leave of Buenos Ayres, about 12 o'clock, and with a favourable breeze, commenced our voyage to the East. At the time the sails were loosed and the ship began to move forward, a salute of thirteen guns was fired in compliment to Capt. Cooper, which was immediately returned. We passed so near the *Warren* that we could exchange adieus and good wishes, and the crews of the two ships having cheered each other as we passed, we made all sail and soon lost sight both of the shipping and the town.}

Having now seen all that I probably ever shall see of Buenos Ayres, I shall here conclude the remarks that I have to make on the town and its inhabitants. With respect to the town, I have but little to add in addition to what I have already said. Its site is pleasant, being elevated about a hundred feet above the surface of the River, and from its highest elevation having a gradual descent in every direction. A large proportion of the buildings are but one story high, and exhibit externaly a decaying and ruinous appearance. Some of the private dwellings present a decent exterior, but there is nowhere to be seen any thing like architectural taste or elegance. The style of building here is the same as in the other Spanish towns that I have seen. Every house of any considerable size, is a sort of castle, and so constructed as to be easily defended against any hostile attack that might be made upon it. The windows are grated with large iron rods, and have besides, ponderous shutters secured within by heavy bars and bolts. The doors are thick and heavy like those of a prison, and filled with large iron spikes to render them secure against any violence that might be attempted from without. Almost every house has an open space in the centre, the entrance to which is by a large arched portal and around which the different appartments are arranged. If the house has two stories, the lower appart- ments are appropriated to store-rooms, stables, etc and the upper are oc- cupied by the family. There is usually a terrace running around in front of the second story, which furnished a cool and comfortable retreat from the heat and dust. The tops of the houses are generally flat, where it is very pleasant to walk in the evening of a hot summer's day.

The only public buildings that I went into were the churches, of which there is a large number in Buenos Ayres, as in all other Spanish towns. The largest of these is of course the cathedral. It is an irregular misshapen mass of brick and mortar, exhibiting a rough forbidding appearance externally, and within, rows of huge columns supporting numerous arches, some of which seemed to be crumbling to pieces and almost ready to fall. The objects most worthy of notice in the cathedral, were the paintings, some of which were very good. Among them were the descent from the cross, Christ receiving the little children, and Abraham offering up Isaac, which seemed to me to be well executed and well deserving of a place in every christian church. There was less magnificence displayed in this church, as well as a smaller number of images than I have ever before seen in any Spanish Catholic church, that could be compared with this in size. And to judge from what I saw, I conclude that the congregation who assemble here, bear but a very small proportion even to the small display of wealth and deco- ration which the interior of the church presents. I happened to be passing the Cathedral on the Saturday before Whitsunday, and hearing the organ playing, and the priests chaunting, I went in expecting to find a large congregation assembled; but to my surprize, there were not more than half a dozzen, besides those employed at the altar, and they were apparently of the lowest order of the people.[13]

This leads me to remark, with regard to the character of the inhabi- tants, in addition to what I have already said on this subject, that since toleration was permitted to protestants, the catholics seemed to have thrown off religious restraint almost entirely, and from seeming to be bigots and persecutors, they have become indifferent to all religion. The forms and ceremonies of religion are indeed kept up in some degree, but it is very evident, from the information I have received, that the true spirit of religion, that living principle which governs the heart, and life, exerts but a very feeble influence here. And I regret, that truth compels me to say, that this remark applies to foreigners, and even to my own countrymen, as well as to the natives. Indeed, I have reason to conclude, from the observations that I have made, both here and elsewhere, that the protestants from the U. States who become residents in catholic countries, where the restraints of religion are but little regarded, become even more irreligious, and manifest a greater contempt for every thing that bears the name of religion, than even the most unrestrained of the catholics themselves. It is rare, I believe, to find a catholic so entirely lost to all sense of religion, and so far to have lost the impression which must have been made on his mind by the religious in-struction which he received in early life, as not [to] pay some kind of respect, at least to the externals of religion, however remote his heart and life may be from its proper influence; but many foreign residents are to be met with, and especially from the U. States, who do not even deign to bestow the least external mark of respect on religion, or any of its institutions. They very rarely, if ever attend church, and if they do, it is for the purpose rather of gratifying an impertinent curiosity, than of receiving that instruction which might tend to their everlasting welfare. The Lord's day, instead of being spent as it ought to be, in an attendance of religious worship, when that is practicable, or at least in quiet retirement, is to them a day of noisy mirth and amusement. To follow their own inclinations, wherever these may lead them, is the only rule by which they are governed; of which a declaration of one of my mess-mates may be taken as an example, and this was, that whether right or wrong, he would dance on Sunday whenever an opportunity should offer. {As religion is the basis, and the only basis of every thing that is deserving of esteem in the human character, it must be concluded from the remarks that have been made respecting the religious character of the people of Buenos Ayres, that they must be in a great measure deficient in those moral and intellectual qualities, which alone can give them any claim to the respect of other nations, or render them worthy of the blessings of liberty and independance.}

The climate of Buenos Ayres has always been considered one of the mildest and most salubrious in the world, and that the place justly deserves the appelation which it bears; but while we were there, we had no reason to form such an exalted opinion of it. There was not much rain, it is true, and the weather was not in reality cold; but the air was very damp, and the temperature though not below 53 or 54°, caused almost as great a sense of cold, as a freezing temperature in the U. States. So humid, indeed, was the atmosphere, that the sidewalks in the town were as wet at night from the dew, as if there had been a heavy shower of rain. It was the beginning of winter while we were there, and perhaps the climate was more unpleasant than it is in the summer season; though it is principally in the summer that those violent tempests called "pamperos", are experienced. The pampero is a wind which blows from the cold region of Patagonia, in a southwest direction across the pampas or plains, which extend several hundred miles to the southward of the River Plate, and from the ocean to the Andes. This wind comes sometimes with such sudden and tremendous violence, that nothing hardly can withstand it. Vessels are often driven from their anchors or part their cables, and sometimes upset, and their whole crews lost. There have been many instances of boats being surprized by these pamperos, while passing between vessels in the harbour and the shore, and all on board having perished. They are most severe, as I have observed, in the summer, and it happens not unfrequently, when there has been no rain for a consid-erable time, and the surface of the ground has become very dry, that they raise such a cloud of dust in and over the town, as entirely to obscure the light of day, and to render candles as necessary in the streets and house at mid-day as during the darkest night. If rain succeeds as it usually does, before this cloud of dust is dispersed, it falls in a shower of mud and adhering to the walls of the houses gives them the appearance of having been newly plastered.[14] The violence of these winds is usually of short duration, though it sometimes continues for two or three days. They are always followed by clear, cool pleasant weather, which produces a most agreeable effect on the human system, in giving tone and vigor to the body, and exhiliarating and renovating the spirits.

The year at Buenos Ayres, as within the tropics, is divided into two seasons, namely summer and winter, or the dry and rainy seasons. The former is the most pleasant season there, but is not the safest for navigating the River, in consequence of the pamperos being more frequent, as well as more violent in the summer than in the winter. But although the winter is the rainy season, during which a sufficient quantity of water usually falls, to answer all the purposes of vegetable and animal life; yet it sometimes happens that there is a long interval without rain, and much loss and suffering is the consequence of it. Such has been the case recently. For nearly three years until a short time before we were there, but very little rain had fallen; in consequence of which millions of cattle had died, and as they constitute the sole property of most of the country people, many have been reduced from wealth to the extreme of poverty. But however severely the country may suffer from drought, the citizens can never be in want of water, since the water of the River there is always fresh, and can be easily conveyed to every part of the town. It is always more or less muddy and requires filtering but when filtered, it is as good water as I ever drank. Vessels in the harbour, always take in their supply from along side, and indeed this is done fifty miles below Buenos Ayres, unless the wind has been prevailing from the eastward, and drives the sea water farther up than the tide usually carries it.

The River even at Buenos Ayres, two hundred miles from its mouth, is like a sea, being twenty seven miles wide, and no land being visible on the other side, except when the atmosphere is unusually clear. It is shallow, however, there being only about three fathoms water, any where within several miles of Buenos Ayres, and in many places, not more than five or six feet. The bottom consists of a soft light mud, which, with the shallowness of the water, renders the anchorage there very unsafe. It is not considered as safe for vessels to moor there, as to ride by a single anchor, with a long scope of cable. Our Pilot, who has had fifteen years experience in navigating this River, said that a vessel rode out a severe pampero better with one good anchor, and eighty or ninety fathoms of chain cable, than with two anchors and the usual length of cable.

Having now concluded all I have to remark concerning Buenos Ayres, I shall proceed to narrate the events as they occurred, on our voyage to the east. We sailed from Buenos Ayres, as I have already mentioned, on the 19th. of June, and proceeded down the River with a favourable breeze. Our progress was soon interrupted, however, by a change of wind, and we were obliged to anchor for the night. During the following day, we lay most of the time at anchor, the wind continuing still adverse. Thus we continued contending against a contrary wind, the greater part of the way to Monte Video, and did not arrive there till the 22d. at three o'clock in the afternoon. {It being the Captain's intention to stay as short a time here as possible, I went ashore immediately after we had anchored, to provide supplies for our mess on our long voyage to Sumatra. My time being short, I saw but little of the town; but from what I did see I was led to conclude that it is in a much worse state than it was when I was there before [1828]. And indeed, this corresponds with the declaration of the foreign residents there, who have had an opportunity of comparing its past with its present condition.} The three years drought, from which the interior of the province of Buenos Ayres has suffered so much, has also been severely felt here; in consequence of which the market is very badly supplied, and provisions of all kinds are very dear. Fowls are nearly a dollar a piece, and eggs from 60 to 70 cents a dozzen. {These articles were therefore dispensed with, as none of us are such epicures, as to gratify our palates at such expense.} Beef and mutton which used to be exceedingly cheap, the former not more than a dollar a hundred, and the latter about a quarter of a dollar a piece, cost us now about the same that they would in the U. States.

On the following day, June 23d. a party of the officers went a gunning in the neighbourhood of the Mount, and returned at evening, with about forty five patridges or quails. These were larger than the same kind of bird is in the U. States. Another party, consisting of Midshipmen, spent the next day, notwithstanding it was Sunday in the same amusement; but met with little success. This single fact shows sufficiently plain, how the Lord's day is regarded by us; for notwithstanding we comply so far with the observances of our country, and with the regulations of the Navy, as generally to have divine service on Sunday, it is perfectly evident, from the fact just mentioned, that this is a mere formality, and that we entertain no religious respect whatever for the day.

As we expected to sail early the next morning [June 24], it became necessary for me to decide on the case of Lieut. White [Lt. John White], and make such a report as would either warrant the Captain in permitting him to leave the ship there and return to the U. States, or to remain on board, and perform such duty as the infirm state of his health would permit. {This is another instance to be added to the long catalogue of cases, in which an intemperate use of intoxicating drink, has produced effects which must excite pity in every one who is a friend to his fellow-man and who can rejoice in his usefulness and respectability, and grieve at his sufferings, whether voluntary or unavoidable.} For the last twelve years, Lieut. White had been labouring under an affection of the lower limbs, which has almost entirely disabled him for active duty, and during a considerable part of this time, has confined him to his bed. {This complaint, I was told, on first learning that Mr. W. was ordered to the *Peacock,* was Elephantiasis, a disease which he contracted in Cochin China; and until a short time before we sailed, I had no reason to doubt the correctness of the information that I had received. But at my first examination of the diseased limbs, I was satisfied at once that the complaint was not Elephantiasis; and that, although it might first have shown itself in Cochin China, it was nevertheless occasioned by intemperance.[15] Such was the opinion, that I was lead to form of the origin of this complaint, some time before we sailed; and I had no doubt but that the cause which first produced it, would continue to operate, and that Mr. W. would grow worse, and either be compelled to leave the ship, or die before the end of the cruise. He was so anxious to undertake the cruise, however, and his situation in the Navy seemed to render it so necessary that he should embrace the present opportunity of performing the requisite amount of sea-service to entitle him to promotion; that I forebore to express my opinion, and determined to do all in my power to prevent his becoming worse, and to keep him in a condition that would enable him to be useful, notwithstanding he should be unable to perform any active duty. We had been but a very short time at sea, not even twenty-four hours, before I had the most conclusive evidence that my opinion respecting the cause of his complaint was correct; and long before we reached our first port, I was fully convinced that if he determined to make the cruise, he would be the whole time on the sick-list, and consequently unable, if he should live to render any important or useful service. If the Commodore had been at Rio, it was my intention to have taken measures for his leaving the ship there and returning home; but he seemed so reluctant to return home on account of his health, and it being impracticable for him to do so then, in consequence of the absence of the Commodore, I came to the conclusion, that unless he should become much worse, I would advise his remaining on board, and endeavour all in my power, to induce him to pursue such a course, as would be most likely to prevent an increase of his malady. Former habits, which had been long indulged, were too strong, however, for his resolution; and after observing some degree of prudence for a few days, he gave the accustomed liberty to his appetites, and} became so bad while at Buenos Ayres, as I learned the day after we left there, that I resolved at once to recommend his leaving the ship at Monte Video. This I did on the 24th. and on the following day he took leave of us, apparently with much regret, which was reciprocated on our part, notwithstanding it was evidently best for him as well as ourselves that his cruise should terminate here; {and that while he had health enough remaining, he should return to his family, by whose cares he may have some chance of prolonging his life, and of experiencing some improvement in his health.}

June 25th. By employing all our efforts in hastening the business which we had to transact at Monte Video, it was completed at 5 o'clock in the afternoon; and the wind being fair, we weighed anchor, and proceeded on our destined course. We now considered ourselves as fairly entered upon the expedition to which our attention had been directed from the time of our leaving the U. States; and although we had a distance to traverse before reaching our destined port of ten thousand miles, and had reason to expect much unpleasant weather, still we were very glad to take leave of the River Plate, and none of us had any desire ever to see it again.[16]

Having now probably taken my last leave of Monte Video, I shall make such remarks upon it as its magnitude and importance may render in some measure interesting. This is a small town containing from seven to ten thousand inhabitants, originally belonging to the Province of Buenos Ayres and settled by Spaniards. It is situated on the north side of the River Plate, and about a hundred miles from its mouth. Its situation is pleasant, the ground which it occupies being elevated about a hundred feet above the surface of the water in the River. Like Buenos Ayres, it was built on a regular plan, its streets being straight, and crossing each other at right angles. The buildings are after the same fashion as those of Buenos Ayres, but larger and of a better appearance. The cathedral stands on the highest ground occupied by the town and is much the most conspicuous object there. It is a huge mis-shapen pile, however, and out of all proportion to the population of the place. A very large congregation might assemble there, but the number who do go there from other motives than those of curiosity, is very small. The towers of the cathedral are visible ten or twelve miles from the town, and serve as a landmark to vessels steering for the harbour, or proceeding up the River.

The harbour is on the northwest side of the town, and is formed by an arm of the sea, which sets back about a mile, and affords a tolerably secure anchorage for vessels of a moderate draught of water. This harbour being open to the southwest, it is exposed to the violence of the pampero, and there have been several instances of a considerable number of vessels being driven ashore there and lost. Merchant vessels usually lie in the harbour, but ships of war always anchor outside, from one to four miles from the town. The landing at Monte Video from boats is very good, there being a mole built out into the harbour, and provided with steps, where boats can go with perfect safety in the roughest weather.

Formerly there was considerable trade at this place, and business was active and prosperous; but now the trade is much diminished, and there is consequently but little business done, and every thing exhibits an appearance of poverty and decay.

About two miles from the town to the westward, is the Mount from which the town takes its name, and which is the most elevated ground of any within a space of fifty miles, being from three to four hundred feet above the surface of the River. It is really a beautiful eminence, as its name imports, its form being almost perfectly regular, its sides sloping very grad-

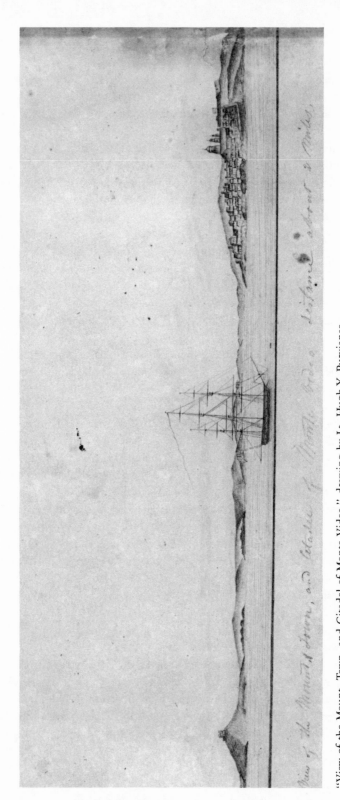

"View of the Mount, Town, and Citadel of Monte Video," drawing by Lt. Hugh Y. Purviance. (Edmund Roberts Papers, Library of Congress.)

ually in every direction, and its surface being covered with an uniform coat of verdure. On its summit is a light-house, which, however, owing to the dimness of the light, is of but little use until vessels have approached within a few miles of the anchorage.

The country about Monte Video, as seen from the tops of the houses, presents a verdant, slightly undulating surface, without a single tree except here and there a fruit tree or garden shrub, as far as the eye can reach. The ground is but very little cultivated, agriculture being an employment to which the guachos or inhabitants of the country, are exceedingly averse. These people in their appearance, customs and mode of living, seem to bear a strong resemblance to the Tartar race, and I am inclined to think that they are a branch of the same stock. In one respect, however, they are different from the Tartar race, so far as I am acquainted with it; and that is, in the use of the lazo [lasso]. This is a cord made of raw-hide, from twenty to thirty yards in length, which they use with astonishing adroitness in taking cattle, horses, and even those small animals, which it is difficult to kill with fire-arms. It has an iron ring at one end through which the cord is passed, and a noose formed, which the Guacho holds in his hand together with so much of the lazo coiled up, as he may judge sufficient; and when near the object of his pursuit, he whirls this coil several times around his head, and then darts it at his object with almost unerring certainty. Cattle are generally taken by the horns, and horses by the neck; but both are sometimes taken by the legs. The noose is always proportioned to the size of the object over which it is to be thrown, and such is the skill of these people in throwing it, that the noose is made to assume a circular form by the whirls around the head, and this form and size it retains till it encircles its destined object. The Guacho is always on horse-back when he throws the lazo, one end of which is fastened to his saddle, or around the body of his horse. The horses are so well trained to this employment, that they seem to understand it as well as their riders do. When a large animal is caught there is always a violent struggle between him and the horse; but the latter by his skilful manoeuvering, is almost always victorious. The moment the lazo is thrown, the ensnared animal starts of[f] with all his might to free himself from his toils, and at the same instant the Guacho wheels his horse in an opposite direction; and as soon as the horse finds the length of the lazo is run out, he braces himself as firmly as possible to avoid being thrown down, and retains his position, till the force of his antagonist begins to yield a little, when he renews his efforts to advance, and in a short time has the struggling animal entirely in his power. There may be a satisfaction in witnessing the dexterity and intrepidity of these people in the use of the lazo; but there is much that is revolting to the feelings of every one who is capable of sympathizing in the sufferings of inferior animals, in their method of slaughtering cattle, and those who have once seen it, cannot, I am sure, ever desire to witness it again.[17]

With respect to the political state of Monte Video, and the Province, of which it is the capital, I can say nothing more, than that disaffection is beginning to manifest itself, and that there has been some fighting in the interior; {from which there seems reason to conclude, that the Government is not settled upon a firm and lasting basis. Our departure from Monte Video, as has been noted, was on the 25th. of June, in the evening. During that night the wind was very light, and our progress down the River very slow; but early the next day the breeze freshened, and we moved along as rapidly on our destined course, as a [dull] sailing ship could be made to go. For six days the wind blew from the north with but little variation, and the weather was most of this time thick and heavy, with occasional showers of rain. As the wind had a great extent of ocean to sweep over, it raised a high sea; which kept the ship incessantly tumbling and tossing about, so that for several nights, those of us who occupied births, were almost entirely deprived of rest. At last, however, a change of wind from the north to southwest brought pleasant weather, and a smooth sea, which enabled us to enjoy some repose, as well as the comfort of a dry ship. But we enjoyed this respite from the discomfort of a rough sea and unpleasant weather, only a short time; for on the following day, which was the 3d. of July, the wind again blew from the north, accompanied with dark cloudy weather, and a heavy swell.}

July 4. Notwithstanding the unpleasant state of the weather, we were not unmindful of the respect which we owed to the aniversary of an event to which our country is indebted for her liberty and independance; though we could not observe it in the manner that we wished. If the weather had been pleasant, it was intended that the officers and crew should have been mustered on the quarter deck, and the Declaration of Independance read; but the bad weather rendered this impracticable. A salute, however, was fired at sunrise, and at twelve o'clock a collation was prepared in the cabin, of which all the officers were invited to partake. Here as well as at dinner in the Ward-Room, to which the Capt. Mr. Roberts, and two of the young gentlemen were invited, our country's prosperity was pledged in the usual manner, and probably with as much real feeling of patriotism, as if we had been seated at the festival board on her own happy soil, instead of being separated from her by a distance of nearly ten thousand miles. And while wishing a long duration to the happiness and prosperity of our country, we did not forget the friends we have left in the enjoyment of their share of that happiness, and of the blessings of home; while we are doomed to wander for years over stormy seas, and under a burning sun, where we are subjected to many & great privations, and exposed to dangers seen & unseen on every side.

July 8. This day being Sunday, and the sea tolerably smooth & the weather pleasant, we had prayers on the quarter-deck; after which the Rules & Regulations of the Navy were read. This was the first time after the second Sunday in June, that circumstances had permitted us to have divine service on board; a duty which it is very desirable we should faithfully perform during the cruise. Notwithstanding I have heard the Rules and Regulations of the Navy read a great many times, and have always been struck with the manifest violation of many of their injunctions by the profane language and immoral conduct of officers; yet I was never more deeply impressed with this gross defect in our discipline, than the last time I heard them read. {It is positively enjoined upon "all commanders of vessels in the public service, to show in themselves a good example of virtue, patriotism & subordination, etc, and to guard against & suppress all vice & immoral conduct; to forbid all profane swearing etc." Now, any one not acquainted with the facts, would conclude, from a perusal of these Regulations, that commanders would not dare to depart from them, and not only tolerate all kinds of vice and profanity, and others, but also indulge in the same practices themselves. A short time in a ship of war, however, would be sufficient to convince such an one of his mistake, and to lead him to the conclusion, that all the Regulations which were designed to promote morality and maintain a correct deportment among officers, are nothing but a dead letter, and never exert the least influence in restraining any one from following the bent of his inclination. And in no vessel, perhaps, in the public service, would he be sooner led to this conclusion, than in this, for in no one, I believe, has the example of the commander been less calculated to enforce an observance of that part of the Regulations which I have cited, than the commander of this ship, and especially with regard to profanity.}

It was with good reason, therefore, that I was peculiarly struck, at the last reading of the Regulations, with their entire inefficiency, as it respects the moral conduct of officers, and the idle mockery of pretending to be governed by them in having them publicly read to the crew, when every one of them must have known that they were violated every hour in the day. Such inconsistency, as might be supposed, has evidently been productive of very bad effects on the young officers & crew; {and I am fully persuaded, that it would be far better to have no regulations respecting moral conduct, than to have them, and not pay them that obedience which they enjoin. And, indeed, however desirable it may be, that officers should observe the strict rules of morality and decorum, not only when at home among their countrymen, but also when at sea and in foreign ports; I am nevertheless induced to consider it a fault in our Navy Regulations, that they pretend to any controul over the moral conduct of those who are subject to them, any farther than to enjoin punishment for such offences as are considered punishable by the laws of our country. It is utterly impossible, by the wisest and most efficient legislation, to make men moral, and especially to controul the license of the tongue. Virtue and morality depend on the state of the heart, which no laws can reach, with whatever authority they may be enacted, or with whatever sanctions they may be enforced. It is therefore worse than useless to pretend to influence the moral conduct of the officers and men in the Navy by Rules and regulations. If this end is to be attained at all, it can only be done by the Government acting uniformly and decidedly upon the principle, of rewarding all those who have distinguished themselves by their strictly moral and upright deportment, as well as those who have manifested unusual bravery or nautical skill; and on the other hand, of either dismissing from the service all such as have been notoriously guilty of a violation of any moral duty, or at least, withholding from them every mark of favour, however daring they may have shown themselves in times of danger.} Courage is undoubtedly to be ranked among the virtues, but it is certainly not the first, even among those whose profession may lead them to consider it as of the highest value, and as deserving of the highest reward; and I am decidedly of the opinion, that an officer renders more important service to his country by his temperance, sobriety, and by avoiding the use of profane language, as well as by restraining himself from other vicious indulgencies, than he could possibly do by the display of a courage equal to that of Julius Caesar.

{This opinion, I am well aware, is at variance, not only with the sentiments and practice of a large proportion of the officers of the Navy, but also with the practice of those who have the controul of the Navy; since the former pay no farther regard to the virtues which have been just mentioned, than to avoid such a gross violation of them as shall injure their reputation as officers, and the latter make no distinction in bestowing their favours, between those whose conduct has been regulated by the strictest rules of virtue and morality, and those who have violated them all without restraint. In this exists one of the greatest evils in our Navy, and one which must be corrected before the Navy can ever attain that high standing, to which its real importance might otherwise justly entitle it.}

July 11. It being desirable that we should ascertain whether our chronometers were entitled to confidence or not, and as Tristan de Acunha with its adjacent islands was very near our route, we had shaped our course for it from the time of leaving the River; and early this morning we had the satisfaction of seeing it. We passed it in the night, and when we first had a view of it in the morning, we were probably fifty miles from it. This Island is situated in 37°-7′ south latitude, and 11°-48′ west longitude; and is nearly equidistant from the Cape of Good Hope, & the coast of S. America. It rises to such a height, that in clear weather, it can be seen at the distance of ninety miles. Its top, & sides nearly half way down, were covered with snow, which had a very perceptible influence on the temperature of the air for a distance of nearly [a] hundred miles. We passed to the northward of it, and the wind being fresh from the southward, the cold was piercing during the whole of that night, and a considerable part of the next day. The Island is not now inhabited, and from what I can learn, there is nothing to induce vessels to stop there except water. The anchorage, however, is so bad, and squalls are so frequent and sudden in the neighbourhood of the Island, that vessels rarely venture to stop there even for water. The British frigate *Lion,* with Lord Macartney [Sir George Macartney] stopped there on her way to India, for the purpose of watering; but a heavy gale of wind came on in the night, and she was obliged to weigh anchor and proceed to sea immediately, before she had taken in any water.[18]

{Our chronometer was found to be very nearly correct, the error not being more than twenty miles, and even this was ascertained before we left the River; so that from the River to this Island, a distance of about two thousand miles, no additional error was detected, and it was therefore considered safe to place entire confidence in it for keeping our longitude. Notwithstanding the correctness of the chronometer, however, lunar observations were always taken when practicable, and the longitude deduced from them was compared with that of the chronometer, between which the difference was usually small, and thus each served to establish the correctness of the other. While passing the Island, a vessel was seen at a little distance from us; but not near enough to enable us to ascertain what she was, or whither she was bound.

The islands that I have mentioned as lying near Tristan d'Acunha, are named Nightingale and Inaccessible. These we did not see, and therefore I can say nothing about them.}

July 14. After passing Tristan d'Acunha, we had a light breeze, and made but little progress for a few hours, when a fresh breeze set in from the north, which carried us along at the rate of eight or nine miles an hour. At about nine o'clock in the evening of this day, we passed the meridian of Greenwich, and entered the eastern hemisphere.

July 20. The wind continued fair and our progress rapid, until we had passed the Cape of Good Hope, on the 19th, making a passage of twenty-three days from Monte Video, in which time we must have run nearly four thousand miles. During the whole of this passage, flocks of Cape pigeons had accompanied us; and for nearly three thousand miles, albatrosses also kept us company, and seemed to take delight in showing us with what power and gracefulness of motion (if the term may be so used), they could urge their rapid flight against the wind, and skim along the surface of the foaming and raging sea. This bird is of immense size, and of all aquatic birds, is probably the largest. It sometimes measures between the extremities of its wings, fourteen or fifteen feet. Their plumage is principally white interspersed with grey, but some are entirely of a brown colour. The Cape pigeon is a small bird, with a speckled plumage of black and white.

On the 20th. the day after we passed the Cape, we saw a ship to the southward of us, at the distance of eight or ten miles, and standing to the westward. Being at this time on the Bank of Lagullas, which extends a great distance to the southward & eastward of the Cape, and shortening sail for the purpose of sounding, this vessel changed her course to run down for us, supposing probably that we were in distress, and had stopped for the purpose of obtaining assistance from her. But before we were apprized of her apparent intention to run down to us, our sails were again filled, and we were pursuing our course, which being observed by her, she resumed her course, and thus we missed an opportunity of speaking her, and probably of apprising our friends at home where we were, and of our good fortune thus far.

Until we had doubled the Cape, we experienced very little delay from contrary winds, and this part of our long voyage was accomplished in a shorter time, by at least seven days, than we had expected. And contrary to our expectation too, the wind which favoured us most was from the north, for we had calculated on a prevailing westerly or southwesterly wind, accompanied with a heavy sea, and a degree of cold that would be very uncomfortable. We had indeed, rather a rough sea most of the time till we had passed the Cape, though generally less so, than we had reason to expect in the winter season; and as to temperature, we were much more comfortable than we had been in the River, the temperature was not disagreeable. The ship, however, was generally wet, from which we suffered much greater inconvenience and discomfort, than from the cold.

During the prevalence of the northerly wind, the atmosphere was generally loaded with humidity, and frequently so thick & foggy, that we could see but a little distance from the ship. Showers of rain were frequent during this state of the weather and sometimes the rain descended in torrents. There was also lightning every night, but it was not accompanied by thunder. When the wind shifted to the west & southwest, which it invariably did, after a longer or shorter time, the weather cleared up, and the air became dry and invigorating, as it is in the U.S. during the prevalence of the northwest wind.

These changes in the weather were always indicated by the barometer, the mercury falling from one to three tenths of inch a short time before the commencement of the northerly wind and continuing so until it was about to change to the southwest, when it rose to its former height.

This change in the barometer, however, was less than sometimes takes place when the changes in the weather are less considerable, and therefore gave some reason to the officers who were not in the habit of observing it attentively, to conclude that it did not afford correct indications. And I must confess, that I began to lose confidence in the instrument, or finding that, during the five or six days of dark rainy weather, with the wind almost blowing a gale at times from the north, after leaving the River, it did not fall below 30; but subsequent observation soon taught me, that although it always fell considerably below 30° in the River, when it indicated bad weather, we were not now to expect it to fall so low, when indicating the same degree of change in the weather. The gravity of the atmosphere seemed to increase as we advanced to the eastward, as we found, by the mercury rising higher in the barometer during the first clear weather after leaving the River, than it had done before; which accounts satisfactorily for its not having fallen so low during the preceding five or six days of unpleasant weather, as it had always been observed to do before. Until this time, the greatest height to which I had observed the mercury to rise, except the 15,

16, & 17 of March, was 30 inches & 3 tenths, and this but seldom; but now it arose higher, and about the time we passed the Cape of Good Hope, it was as high as 30 & 65 hundredths.

{I have been thus particular in my remarks upon the barometer, because I am satisfied that the facts which I have mentioned prove the correctness and utility of the instrument, which its supposed failure in one or two instances, would have led the officer of the ship to deny, with farther inquiry.}

With a fresh and favourable breeze, and pleasant weather; we passed the southern extremity of Africa, and entered the Indian Ocean on the 19th. of July; and a little before twelve o'clock that night, we sounded on the Lagullas Bank, and found bottom in 60 fathoms water. The lead brought up a coarse gray sand. The next morning we had soundings in 70 fathoms. {Our position at 12 o'clock this day, July 20th. was lat. 35.°30′, & east long. 22°-45′.}

July 24. We had advanced but a short distance to the eastward of the Cape, when the breeze which had favoured us for several days, left us; and during the three following days, we sometimes had no wind at all, and what there was, came directly from the point toward which we wished to shape our course. On the night of the 21st. we were carried by an unexpected easterly current, very near to, if not directly over the supposed situation of the "Telemaque Shoal"; but we saw nothing of it. Our position on the 21st. was lat. 36°-20′- & east long. 23°.16′; and on the 22d, lat. 38°16; & long. 23.°43.′*

July 25. This was the most uncomfortable day that we had experienced, from the time we left Boston, on account of the heavy sea, and the consequent rolling and plunging of the ship. The wind was from the north, and though hardly fresh enough to be called a gale, yet I have seldom known a higher sea; and as we had it on our beam, we felt it much more than we otherwise should have done. During the preceding day there had been but very little wind, and the sea had been unusually smooth; but in the evening the breeze began to freshen, and the sea began to rise, and before morning the ship became so uneasy, that it was impossible for those who occupied births, to get any sleep.

At such a time as this, eating is a business that is attended with a

---

*The longitude is by chronometer, and 20 miles are to be deducted for error.

good deal of difficulty, and some danger; and whenever we succeeded in making a meal, without the occurrence of any important accident, we considered ourselves fortunate. On the occasion that I am now speaking of, however, we received no injury ourselves, nor sustained any material loss in our crockery. But this was not effected without much caution and effort, in watching the motions of the ship, and keeping ourselves from being thrown down with one hand, and holding our dishes fast with the other, until a momentary respite succeeded, and then disposing of our meal with all possible expedition. Many such efforts were required, however, to get through with a single meal; and when it was finished without accident, it was considered an important achievement, and an occasion for mutual congratulation. But our neighbors the Midshipmen, were not quite so fortunate as ourselves in this respect; for they had their table entirely swept while set for breakfast, and every thing broken with the exception of one or two articles.

It was supposed, that this very high sea, which seemed greatly disproportioned to the wind, was owing to the influence of the Mozambique passage, which then bore about north from us; and through which there is frequently a strong current setting to the southward.

August 6. The rough weather which has just been described, continued only about twenty four hours, when it was succeeded by pleasant weather, which continued till the night of the 6th. During this time, however, there was a very heavy swell, which kept the ship incessantly tossing from one side to the other, and consequently wet and uncomfortable. But the wind was favorable, and our progress rapid beyond what we had reason to expect. So swiftly indeed did we glide through the water, that although our ship had hitherto been considered quite a dull sailer, it seemed scarcely possible for any vessel to move at a more rapid rate than she did, during a part of the period of which I am now speaking. In one day she run 259½ miles, the greatest distance that I had ever sailed in a day before, {although I had sailed more than a hundred thousand miles in ships that were reputed good sailers.}

On the day above mentioned, we passed the Island of Amsterdam, which is situated in south latitude 38°-42′, and east longitude 77°-14′. The Island appeared in sight from the deck about 2 o'clock in the afternoon, and we passed it on the south side, at the distance of about four miles, at 6 o'clock in the evening. It rises from the water by a very steep ascent, to the height of 1500 or 2000 feet, and presents a dreary and forbidding aspect.

Its length from W.N.W. to E.S.E. appears to be three or four miles, and its breadth one or two miles. On its eastern side, and at a little distance from it, is a cone in the form of a sugar loaf, and as I should judge, three or four hundred feet high.

This Island is said to be volcanic and vessels passing to the leeward of it, if reports are true, have sometimes had their decks covered with ashes; but when we passed it, no signs of its volcanic character were to be seen.

While in the neighborhood of the Island, we were surrounded by flocks of albatrosses, and Cape pigeons; but they found no inducement to follow us far, and by the next morning, very few of them were to be seen, especially of the former. Most of the albatrosses seen here, were brown and of a smaller size than those about the Cape of Good Hope.

A few days before we made this Island the best of our two chronometers stopped in consequence of some injury to the work, which, however, could not be accounted for; and the other not being entitled to much confidence, there was considered uncertainty respecting our reckoning. It was found on comparing our reckoning with the position of the Island as it is laid down, that the chronometer was a little more than a degree too fast. By the lunar observations, however, which had been taken two or three days previously, the error in the reckoning was considerably less.

It had been the Captain's intention to make the Island of St. Paul, if he could do it without the loss of much time; but the wind being unfavourable for the accomplishment of this purpose, we proceeded on our course without seeing it. It is situated about fifty miles to the northward of Amsterdam, from which, in clear weather, it is distinctly visible.

August 10. Having reached these Islands, we considered our voyage as nearly accomplished, at least the most unpleasant part of it; as we were now to pursue a northeasterly course which we supposed would soon take us from a rough to a smooth sea, and into a warmer climate. But this transition was not to take place without our experiencing again the war of the elements, and we had but just passed the Island, when the breeze, which had been rather light during, the preceding day, began to freshen, and the sea, which had been comparatively smooth, began to grow rough, and before morning, we were contending with the severest gale that we had yet experienced. It increased during the following day, and before night we were obliged to lie to. The gale continued with little abatement for about three days; but during the latter part of it, the wind having become more favourable, we were enabled to pursue our course, under a close reefed main-top sail & fore sail. The direction of the wind was from N.N.E. to N.W. There were occasional heavy showers of rain, especially before the wind shifted to the westward. The sea was higher now than experienced seamen had almost ever known before; but our ship laboured as little, perhaps, as any one could in the same circumstances. No other damage was sustained than the loss of a boat, the Captain's gig, which was occasioned by a very heavy sea striking the ship on her side and throwing her over so far as to fill the boat, which was swung on the opposite quarter, and by the rolling of the ship to the other side, a weight was thrown upon the davits to which the boat was swung, too great for them to support; and they consequently broke, and the boat went to pieces. The same sea that caused this damage, was also the occasion of the fracture of rib in one of the men, by throwing him with great violence from one side of the deck to the other against the corner of a mess-chest.

The barometer fell lower during this gale than it had ever done before, it being so low as 29.25, where it remained some hours. This was on the second day of the gale, and was followed by heavy showers of rain, but without any increase of wind. In the course of the day the barometer arose to 29.70, where it remained till the next day. This rise in the barometer was immediately followed by a change of the wind to the westward, and by more pleasant weather; though the wind continued to blow with considerable violence occasionally, for some time longer.

I am thus minute in my remarks on the changes in the state of the weather, in connection with the changes in the barometer, in consequence of the mistaken notion, which some of our officers entertained of a very useful instrument. According to the opinion which they had formed of the instrument, an opinion too, not founded on observation, it ought always to indicate wind as well as rain, whether the wind was accompanied with any other atmospheric phenomena or not; and if it failed to do this, they pronounced it to be entirely useless. But as the barometer is affected only by the gravity of the atmosphere, it must be evident, that it can only indicate wind, when that is accompanied with a change in the degree of atmospheric pressure. Now, so far as we know, the gravity of the atmosphere is more affected by humidity than by any other cause, and hence when it is most charged with aqueous vapour, and a heavy rain is approaching, the barometer falls most; and on the other hand, when the atmosphere is most free from humidity, the barometer rises highest. Whether wind accompanies this state of the atmosphere or not, the barometer is equally affected, and consequently gives the same indication; and likewise on the other hand, there may be a violent wind while the atmosphere is dry, and the weather pleasant, and the barometer stands as high as if there were no wind at all, the pressure of the atmosphere not being in the least affected by the wind. It is only therefore as wind accompanies those states of the atmosphere, in which its gravity is diminished, that the fall of the barometer indicates it; but as these states of the atmosphere are almost always accompanied with some change both in the force and direction of the wind and as it is important, at sea especially, to know beforehand when to expect such changes, an instrument that will, in a great majority of instances, give this information, must certainly be a useful one, and deserving of careful observation.

August 21. For several days preceding this date, we had been directing our course for Christmas Island, which is situated within about a day's sail of Java Head; with the view, of shaping our course directly from thence to Bencoolen, in case our chronometer should prove to be correct, and thus save the time of running one or two hundred miles out of our way in order to make Java Head, before proceeding to Bencoolen. Supposing ourselves on the 20th. within less than a hundred miles of the Island, our sails were reduced during the night, and watchful eyes employed in earnest endeavors to discover the object of our pursuit. About 2 o'clock the next morning, we were a few miles to the eastward of the situation of the Island, as it is laid down on the chart; and even at day light were near enough to have had a distinct view of the Island, if there had not been a considerable error in our reckoning. But no Island was to be seen, and hence it was to be concluded that our chronometer was at least 40 or 50 miles too far to the eastward, as the Island is said to be high, and visible at the distance of thirty miles.

We had been favoured with a fresh southeast trade for the last four or five days, and our progress had been at the rate of more than two hundred miles a day. When we first took the wind, which was in latitude about 23°- and longitude 101°-, it was nearly southwest; but it gradually veered to the southeast, from which point it varied but little for several days. The weather for the first two or three days after we took the trade wind, was very pleasant, and the atmosphere dry; but after we had approached within about 15°- of the equator, the atmosphere became hazy, humid, and there were occasional showers of rain. The thermometer rose gradually as we advanced to the north; and at the date under which I am now writing, we found ourselves in a temperature of 78, and were glad to exchange our winter garb, which we had worn, with the exception of a few days, for about ten months, for a summer dress. The barometer gradually fell during this period, and the 21st. it stood at 30.00.

August 23. After being disappointed in our attempt to make Christmas Island, our course was shaped for Bencoolen, and to eastward of the Island Engano, which is situated about a hundred miles to the southwest of that place. The wind now became very light, and our progress was consequently much slower than it had been, which, {while it caused some uneasiness on account of our desire for a supply of the poultry, eggs & fruit which we expected to find in great abundance at Bencoolen,} it enabled us nevertheless to enjoy the comfort of sailing on a smooth sea, which we had scarcely experienced at all from the time of our leaving the River Plate. {On the 22d. the rain fell in great abundance for several hours during the forenoon; but in the afternoon the clouds gradually dispersed before the freshening southeast breeze, and by night the weather had become quite pleasant. The thermometer had now risen to 80°- and we were obliged to reduce the amount of exercise, which we had been in the habit of taking in the cool weather which we had experienced both in the River Plate, and for about 8000 miles of our passage to the east.}

On the 23d. we passed the Island of Engano before mentioned; and found an error in our chronometer of fifty-eight miles. It was too fast, and consequently our true position was this distance farther west than we had supposed it to be. This Island appeared to be fifteen or twenty miles in length, but of its breadth I could form no opinion. The southern part of the Island, or that nearest to Sumatra, is quite low; but toward the north, it rises into mountains of considerable elevation. The Island appeared to be covered with verdure, and is said to be inhabited by a people more hardy than those of the neighboring Island of Sumatra. There is said to be good anchorage and water on the eastern side, and also an abundance of good fish.

We passed to the eastward of the Island, and at the distance of ten or twelve miles from it. At sunset it bore about west from us, and we continued our course towards Bencoolen during the night with a steady gentle breeze; and at day-light the next morning, the lofty mountains of Sumatra, presented themselves to our view. During the night, a heavy thunder shower hung over these mountains, and vivid flashes of lightning darted frequently from the clouds, accompanied with heavy peals of thunder; but we were at too great a distance for the shower to reach us.

August 28. From all the information we had received respecting the direction of the winds at this season of the year, on the west coast of Sumatra, we expected to meet with no difficulty in running to Bencoolen, provided we made the Island to the southward of the harbour; but in this we were mistaken. For after having passed Engano, and approached within sight of Sumatra, the wind died away, and during the three succeeding days, we were not favoured with a fair wind for a single hour, and at the end of this period, we found ourselves as far from our port, as at the beginning of it. {There had been more or less wind during this time, and occasionally it was so fresh that if it had been favourable, we could have run into the harbour in a few hours; but it was constantly ahead, and being accompanied with an adverse current, it was impossible to gain any thing by beating. A great quantity of rain fell on the 24th & 25th. especially at night, accompanied with lightning and thunder.}

On pursuing our course into the harbour we passed two low points of land, namely, Buffalo Point and Poulo Point, which form the southern boundary of the harbour, and extend out some distance to the southwest. The former of these Points, extends farthest out. They are about five miles apart, and are both covered with trees. Our course till we had passed these points was about N.W. and then it was gradually changed to N.E. which was continued for a distance of eight or ten miles. Having advanced this distance, we had Buffalo Point bearing S.S.E. distant about 10 miles, and Rat Island, a small low island covered with palm trees, being W. distant 5 or 6 miles. A shoal is laid down between this Island & Poulo Point, but near to the former, and the passage is consequently between the Point and the Shoal. After passing the Shoal, our course was gradually changed to N. & N.N.W. till we reached the anchorage. The depth of water was generally 12 or 13 fathoms, till we reached the anchorage where it was 11 fathoms. We anchored at 11 o'clock a.m. with Rat Island bearing S.W. distant 2 miles, and the Town & Flag-Staff bearing E.S.E. distant 4 miles. Thus we reached our first port in the East, after a passage of 63 days, and traversing a distance of 9,215 miles, without having experienced near as much rough weather as we had been led to expect.

CHAPTER IV

Bencoolen and Anjer

Trip to Rat Island; Visit to the Resident; School at the
Resident's; Character of the Resident; Commerce of Bencoolen;
Departure from Bencoolen; Arrival at Crackatoa; Arrival at
Anjer; Visit on shore; People of Anjer; Departure from Anjer;
Pass through the Straits of Banca; Arrival at Manilla.

[August 28] We had not been more than an hour at anchor, when a boat
came off from the town with a man in the service of the Resident [governor],
from whom we learned that the place was in possession of the Dutch, and
had been so for about seven years.[1] A Lieut. [Acting Lt. Arthur Sinclair]
was immediately sent ashore to the Resident* with a message from the
Captain; who returned about sun-set, and gave a very flattering account of
his reception, the Resident having treated him in a most hospitable manner,
and kindly offered his services in furnishing the ship, with such supplies as
she might require.

During the visit of this officer to the Resident a party, consisting of
Mr. Roberts, Lieut. Cuningham [1st. Lt. Robert B. Cunningham], the
Marine Officer [2nd. Lt. Fowler], and myself, made an excursion to Rat
Island, where we were told resided a Raja Mundo, who would readily supply
us with such articles of provision as we wanted. Our information, however,
was erroneous, for although we found Raja Mundo, he seemed not only to
be quite as destitute as ourselves of such articles as we wanted, as nothing
grew on the Island except coconuts, but to be even incapable of procuring
any. This island is of small dimensions, its surface not comprizing more

---

*Whose name was Knoeler [J. H. Knoerle]

than two or three acres, and so low, that when a high sea rolls in, as it sometimes does, in the N.W. monsoon, the spray sweeps over from one side to the other. Extensive coral reefs surround the island, which in process of time will probably be covered with vegetation, in the same manner, no doubt, that the present verdant surface of the island has been formed; and thus in time an island may be formed of sufficient extent and fertility to support a considerable population. Besides the family of Raja Mundo, consisting of himself, wife and daughter, there were several other families residing on this island; all of whom exhibited an appearance of great poverty and wretchedness. With the exception of two or three individuals, they were all Malays, and Mahometans. The Raja could speak some English, and although 73 years of age, was quite an active robust man. The house which the Raja and his family occupied, was an old frame building two stories high, and of considerable size, erected many years ago by the English for a store-house. All the other dwellings on the island were made of bamboo, and seemed to be designed rather as enclosures for birds and beasts, than the habitations of human beings. The sides of these dwellings are formed by fixing pieces of bamboo five or six feet long perpendicularly in the earth and interlacing them either with reed or narrow strips of bamboo. The roofs are formed of bamboo-rafters, and a covering of palm leaves; and they descend within four or five feet of the ground.

It was among these people that I first saw the effects of a practice which is almost universal throughout the East, and of which I had heard much, namely, chewing the arica [areca] nut & betel-leaf; and these effects were such as would have excited my astonishment at the continuance of a practice which produced them, if I had not seen in almost numberless instances, the continuance of a practice from which much worse consequences result.[2] The effects produced by the practice of which I am now speaking, are a blackening and eventually, an entire destruction of the teeth, an inflammative swelling, and excoriation of the lips; all of which give to the mouth the appearance of a large sloughing ulcer, and consequently excites an extreme degree of disgust in one who beholds it for the first time. This odious practice is followed by the women as well as the men, and the wife of the Raja exhibited all the effects that I have just described. She seemed, besides, to be afflicted with a disease of the skin, a kind of leprosy, which added considerably to her otherwise sufficiently forbidding apearance.[3] The daughter appeared to be still exempt both from the natural and artificial blemishes of her mother, and with proper culture, might have been made to appear to very good advantage.

Appearance of Rat Island of Bencoolen Dist. 3 Miles
with the North & North Breeses

Rat Island — Bay of Bencoolen

Rat Island, Bencoolen, drawing by Lt. Hugh Y. Purviance. (Edmund Roberts Papers, Library of Congress.)

The effects of which I have been speaking, produced by the betel-nut, are in my opinion owing principally to the chunam or quick-lime, which is always a constituent part of the masticatory, and imparts to it that quality, which seems to be most highly prized.[4]

We were surprised at seeing several large anchors lying on the coral reef a little distance from the island on its north side, and could imagine no other use for them than that of affording a secure mooring to vessels that might be at anchor on that side of the island when the N.W. monsoon renders the greatest degree of precaution necessary, to avoid being driven on the coral reefs. Subsequent inquiry confirmed this conjecture, and led to information, which, if we had possessed it before we anchored, would have induced us to anchor nearer the island than we did. There is a channel on the northeast side of the island between two coral reefs, where there is eleven fathoms water within a little distance of it, and where vessels of any size may be with perfect safety at all seasons of the year, under the protection of the coral banks. {At flood tide there is sufficient depth of water in this channel for vessels of small size, quite to the island, and this is their usual place of anchorage, while lading and unlading their cargoes.}

When we were there, however, the commerce of Bencoolen had declined so such, that it was rare for a vessel of any description to be seen at anchor near the island, or indeed any where in the harbour.

After spending an hour or two on this island we returned to the ship, and soon afterwards, the officer who had been sent to the Governor or Resident, arrived with the favourable report which has been already mentioned, and with an invitation from the Governor, for the Capt. and some of the officers to take breakfast with him the next morning [August 29]. This invitation was cheerfully accepted, and at 8 o'clock the next morning, a party consisting of the Capt. Mr. Roberts, Lieutenant Purviance & Brent, the Marine officer, and myself left the ship, and after rowing about an hour we reached the landing, where we found the Governor's servants waiting to conduct us to his residence. A carriage was also waiting, but as it afforded accommodations for only two, the Capt. & Mr. Roberts took passage in it, and the rest of us walked.[5] The Governor's residence being only about half a mile from the landing, we reached it in a few minutes, and were received and entertained in a most hospitable and friendly manner.

He is a German by birth, but has been many years in the service of the Dutch Government. Although it was evident, that our party was larger than he had expected to breakfast, yet the table was amply supplied, and our appetites having become very sharp, we made it manifest before we left the table that we relished in a high degree the entertainment which he had provided for us. The table was furnished with a variety of dishes cooked in the chinese style, consisting of stews of meat or fowls, etc, besides a considerable variety of vegetables, some of which were dressed with oil and curry, & others were in their natural state, or had only undergone the process of boiling. Instead of coffee or chocolate, wine was drank as at dinner, and indeed the whole meal was rather a dinner than a breakfast. At the conclusion of it, however, we were served with a cup of tea, and the best, although made in the usual manner, that I ever tasted.

While seated at the breakfast-table, we heard the voices of a number of children in a distant part of the building, and on inquiry we learned, that the Governor had established a school in his house for the children of Englishmen by native women, who had been left unprovided for, when the place was transferred to the Dutch. After breakfast, the Governor took us to see this school, with which [we] were most highly gratified, and from which, if maintained for a sufficient time, the best consequences must result. Here from twenty to thirty destitute and unprotected children were receiving that instruction which may be the means of transforming them from a state of deplorable barbarism to one of usefulness and intellectual and moral improvement. The school was conducted on the Lancastrian plan,[6] and so far as we could judge, the pupils were making such progress in the acquisition of knowledge, and at the same time manifested such perfect obedience to their instructors, as must afford the Governor the highest satisfaction. Some were learning to write, and the rest were receiving instruction in the rudiments of their native language. This language was the Malayan, but the characters were Arabic. Among the elementary books employed in this school, I observed St. John's Gospel, in the Malay language,[7] and although in the hands of those who are taught to regard the Koran as their standard of faith and practice, all the Malays being Mahometans, yet there can be no doubt that it will make an impression upon those young minds, which will exert a salutary influence on their conduct through life, and by means of their example on the conduct of many others; and thus a foundation may be laid for the erection of a Christian Church among these people, which shall eventually triumph over idolatry and Mahometanism, and the light of divine truth shall dispel from their minds that pagan darkness in which they are at present enveloped. I allude here particularly to those inhabitants of Sumatra who are not Malays and who from ignorance of the true God, are still worshipping images of wood and stone, the work of their own hands. These constitute much the greater part of the population of the island, and are still addicted to some of the most odious practices of idolatry, notwith-standing Europeans have for a long period had establishments on different parts of the island.

After leaving this school, we took a walk accompanied by the Governor, in the environs of his residence, and were gratified in a high degree with a sight of the towering palm with its tufted top of dark green foliage waving gracefully in the breeze, and with the fragrance of the nutmeg and clove trees, which border the avenue, in the vicinity of the Governor's residence and perfume the air with their grateful odour.

The nutmeg-tree is about twenty feet in height, and has a large bushy top. The leaves are small, of an oblong shape, and a dark green colour. On every tree we observed the fruit in its different stages, from the blossom to the full grown nut. The nut is immediately envelloped with a thin coat, which is the mace, and when ripe, is of a bright red colour. This is surround-ed with a thick rind, like that of a walnut which cracks open when it has arrived at maturity, and disclosed the nut within, enclosed in its red covering of mace. The quantity of fruit obtained from a nutmeg-tree, is said to average about one nut a day, throughout the year. It requires about a hundred nuts when fit for market, to make a pound, and they were sold when we were there at about fifty Spanish dollars the pecul [picul] of a hundred and thirty-six pounds [133 ⅓ lbs.]. The mace sold for nearly twice that sum.

We returned from this walk about twelve o'clock, and found a table spread, and furnished with a variety of sweet-meats, fruits, and liquors, of which we were required by the hospitable Governor to partake, although not more than two hours had elapsed from the conclusion of a breakfast, which might well have sufficed for a whole day.

The time had now arrived, when we had intended to take our leave and return to the ship; but our host would by no means consent to it, and insisted on our staying to dinner, to which we assented; and at five o'clock, sat down to a table furnished in a style which exhibited the specimen of the sumptous fare of the East, among those who are in a condition to gratify an appetite for luxurious living. As I place but little value, however, on these things, I shall not spend any time in enumerating or describing the different dishes displayed on the Governor's table. The party which now surrounded the table, was considerably larger than at breakfast, as the Governor had not only invited some of his countrymen to honor us with their company at dinner, but also three of the Rajas or native chiefs.

These were men of great consequence among their countrymen, and it was therefore the interest of the Governor to treat them with such attention as to conciliate their favour, and attach them firmly to his service. Accordingly they were placed next to the Governor at table, and were treated by him with every possible mark of respect. They could neither speak or understand any language that was spoken at table; but the Governor who understood Malay, took pains to inform them of every thing that was said, in which they could feel the least interest. As they were Musselmen, they were prohibited the use of wine; but two of them, notwithstanding, threw off the restraints of their religion, and drank as freely of the juice of the grape, and with as keen a relish apparently as any one at table. One of them, however, was more conscientious than his brethren and did not put the wine to his lips; and so true was he believed to be, to the injunctions of Mahomet, that the Governor told us, he supposed he would sooner suffer death than drink a glass of wine. So far as we could judge, these Rajas possessed very good natural talents, and were capable of becoming most important agents in promoting the cause of science, morals and religion, not only among those who are immediately under their control, but also throughout the island.

During our stay at the Governor's, we had an opportunity of acquiring some knowledge of his character, and also of the general policy, and effects of his administration. He exhibited great amiableness of temper and manners, in his deportment towards his numerous servants, and others under his authority; and yet it was very evident, that he was very much feared, as he received the most prompt and respectful obedience, from every one to whom he gave an order. Indeed, he had found it necessary on his arrival there, to adopt severe measures with the natives, and to enforce them with the utmost strictness. At the time of his assuming the government, murders were very frequent among the natives, and were committed with impunity, there not being energy enough in the government to try and punish the criminals. He entered upon the discharge of the duties of his office, with the fixed determination, which he made known explicitly to all the natives within the limits of his jurisdiction, to inflict exemplary punishment for every crime that should be perpetrated; and in order to impress the natives with a deeper sense of his disposition to maintain strict justice, and to render his measure, the more effectual in preventing crime, he adopted the trial by jury in cases requiring capital punishment, and the jury was composed of the natives themselves. The wisdom of this policy was soon made manifest by the beneficial effects which resulted from it; for while the life and property of no one were safe, previous to the energetic measures of the present

Governor, he had been but a few months in office, before murders and other crimes wholly ceased, and it became perfectly safe to walk the streets unarmed by day or night. To produce this favourable change, however, it had been necessary to execute five of the natives, all of whom had committed murder, and were tried and found guilty by a jury of their own countrymen.

But while the Governor advocated the necessity of pursuing measures with the half civilized people under his jurisdiction, which might be considered severe by those unacquainted with the circumstances in which he was placed; he nevertheless reprobated the policy which the Dutch had usually pursued in their eastern possessions. He said they had treated the natives with great cruelty, and had thereby rendered them implacable enemies; whereas, if they had pursued a different course, and shown severity only to those whose crimes evidently deserved it, they would have conciliated the good-will of the better part of the natives, and kept the rest in abject subjection by a fear of the punishment which would certainly follow the commission of any crime against the Government.

In the course of the afternoon we paid a visit to Fort Marlborough, constructed by the English nearly a hundred years ago; and were much gratified with every thing we saw there. It is situated on elevated ground near the water of the harbor, and on the north side of the town, a few rods from the landing place. Its form is very irregular, and so far as I was capable of judging, is calculated to afford the most effectual resistance to any enemy who might approach either by land or water. The garrison consisted of a hundred men, and the number of mounted guns was about thirty, all of which were iron, and none of a larger caliber than twelve pounders. Every thing within and about the fort, appeared to be in perfect order, and the few officers whom we saw, impressed us with a very favourable opinion of the wisdom of the Dutch Government in selecting officers for its foreign service.

Within the walls of the fort, we were led to notice the graves of two Englishmen, a Resident and his Secretary; the former of whom was assassinated by the natives, and the latter lost his life in consequence of his exertions to protect the wife and children of his friend.[8]

From the fort we took a walk through the bazar, or market place, where most of the population of the town are crowded together; and I have scarcely ever seen any place that exhibited a less inviting appearance than this. A few narrow dirty streets branched off in different directions from a kind of central square, and after running a few rods between rows of bamboo huts, they terminated, on one side, at the water of the bay, and on the others, at the hill on which the fort stands, and in the open country. A large proportion of the population who occupied these miserable dwellings, were Chinese, most of whom were shop-keepers; but nothing was to be seen in their shops, except a very few of the most ordinary articles of European and Chinese manufacture. The central square was occupied by [an] enclosure which was thronged with half naked Malays and Chinese, to the number of some hundreds, who spent the whole day in gambling and cockfighting. Provisions here were scarce and dear, there being so little demand for them, that very few were produced for market. Fowls were $3.25 a dozen, eggs $2.50 a hundred, yams $3. a pecul of 136[lb] & other productions of the country cost at about the same rate.

In the course of this day, a vessel commanded by an Englishman arrived from Padang, a Dutch settlement a small distance to the northward of Bencoolen, who not only confirmed the report which we had received the day before from the Governor,[9] respecting the proceedings of Commodore Downes at Poulo Battoo [Kuala Batu], but he added considerably to it. According to the report as communicated by this trader, the Commodore had killed a hundred and seventy of the natives, and entirely destroyed their town.[10] This summary vengeance for the outrage committed on the *Friendship*, had produced great sensation among the natives, not only in the immediate vicinity of Poulo Battoo, but also throughout the island, and the greatest dread was every where entertained of the Americans. With respect to this transaction, I shall at present make no other remark, than that, however just it may have been to inflict punishment on those who had been concerned in the affair of the *Friendship*, and however expedient it may be considered, according to the rules of interested policy, to involve in the punishment of the few guilty, a large number of those who could not have had the least participation in their crime, for the purpose of striking the natives with the greater terror of American vengeance; I cannot bring myself to believe, that the advantages which will result from this severe measure, although they may be realized to the utmost that could possibly be expected, can possibly be such as to justify so great a sacrifice of human life.[11]

The number of foreign residents at Bencoolen, at the time of our visit was small, and of these, we had an opportunity of becoming acquainted with only three or four. They gave a favourable account of the climate, and judging from dwellings, and the surrounding scenery, a residence there provided life and property were secure, must be far from unpleasant. Their houses are mostly constructed of brick, and are white-washed both inside and out, which gives them quite a neat pleasant appearance. The roofs consist of a thatch of palm-leaf, and project several feet from the body of the building, over a piazza which surrounds the second story, and forms a comfortable retreat from the sun in the hotest weather. The second story is generally the only part of the building occupied by the family, the lower being used as a store house, shop, or carriage house. These dwellings occupy cool airy situations in the open country, and are surrounded by the different kinds of palm, the nutmeg and the clove tree, which cool the air with their shade, and perfume it with their fragrance.

With these measures of enjoyment, it might be supposed that a residence at Bencoolen would admit of as great a degree of happiness, so far at least, as it depends on external circumstances, as could be realized any where; but there was wanting, nevertheless, an indispensable constituent of human happiness, without which men would be miserable, though placed in a paradise, and that was society. It is very rare for the Europeans to have wives; but they have families by the native women, who, though faithful to those by whom they are kept, are by no means qualified to contribute any thing towards the formation of society, or to exert that influence over the other sex, which constitutes one of the greatest blessings of civilized life. This connexion between the Europeans and native women being only temporary, it has frequently happened, that the confiding and unfortunate female has been left with her children entirely destitute, when the interest of the unprincipled foreigner on whom she had depended for support both for herself and children, has led him to change his residence, and break those ties without reluctance, which even an uncivilized native had considered sacred.

I have already taken notice of the humane and praise-worthy measures which the Governor was pursuing with those children who had been thus left by their English fathers, at the time of the transfer of the place to the Dutch. No measure could be adopted, which would more effectually counteract the effects which might be expected to result from so many children being left without guidance and support, and surrounded with temptations to every sort of wickedness, which it would hardly be possible for them to resist. After these boys (for the school was composed wholly of them) had become sufficiently instructed, they were to be sent out into different parts of the island to find employment as writers [clerks], in which others trained in the same manner had readily succeeded, and were thus enabled not only to obtain an honest livelihood for themselves, but might confer the same benefit on others, by communicating to them the instruction which they had received.[12]

Although the Governor was unmarried, yet from what he had seen of the evil consequences of forming such connections as I have spoken of, I am disposed to consider him free from that crime, for a crime and one of no inconsiderable magnitude, it certainly is.[13]

His whole time seemed to be occupied with the duties of his office, and with the execution of the plans which he had devised for improving the condition of the natives, and by that means, rendering them more useful to the Dutch, as well as more capable of promoting their own best interests. He exhibited as much firmness and decision in carrying his plans into execution, whenever they clashed with the prejudices of the natives, as sound judgement, and wise policy in devising them. One adventure of his will sufficiently show his fearless intrepidity, and that was crossing the island of Sumatra from Palambong [Palembang], on its eastern side to Bencoolen. This was a most perilous undertaking, and he was the first white man that had ever accomplished it. He passed through some tribes of natives who were extremely savage and ferocious, and he narrowly escaped losing his life among them; but he finally succeeded in reaching Bencoolen in safety.[14]

The house which he occupied was the same which the English Residents occupied, and was large and airy; but entirely destitute of elegance in its structure, and almost equally so in articles of furniture. Hospitality, however, supplied every deficiency, and it will be long before we shall forget the kind treatment that we received from the Resident of Bencoolen.

But while discharging the duties of an important office with so much wisdom, and such benefit both to his own government, and to the natives under his jurisdiction, he was suffering under a disease of the liver, which would probably render it necessary for him to leave the island; and indeed he told me that he intended in a few weeks to go to Batavia and from thence to Bengal, where he intended to remain during the next cool season.

Having enjoyed the Governor's hospitality in the manner I have described, from early in the morning till eight o'clock in the evening, we were at last compelled to take leave of him and return to the ship, which we reached a little before ten. The Rajas who had favoured us with their company at dinner, attended us to the boat, and gave such demonstrations of their good-will towards us, as left a very favourable impression on our minds, and it is to be hoped, that the specimen which they saw of the American character, was such as to induce them to exert their influence with their countrymen, to treat all Americans who may visit their island in a friendly manner.

On the following day Aug. 31. [Aug. 30] we were visited by two

Englishmen, Mr. Hay, & Mr. Grant, from whom we learned some farther particulars respecting the island. According to the statements of these gentlemen, the commerce of Bencoolen has been declining for some years, and very little remained at the time of our visit. One cause of this, was said to be the high duties imposed both upon imports and exports; which were still continued notwithstanding the bad effects that were obviously resulting from them. Another cause, which had contributed considerably to this reduction of commerce, was the lowering of the prices of the articles of export, and especially of pepper, which had formerly been the most valuable production of that part of the island. The price of this article, as well as of nutmegs, cloves, and mace, had fallen more than one half from what it had formerly been; and the consequence was, that very little of either, and especially of pepper, which is cultivated with much more labor and expense than the others, was produced for market. At the time when the pepper trade was in a flourishing state, it was common for ten or twelve large India ships annually to take in their cargoes there; but for some years previous to our visit, it was rare for a vessel to enter the harbour oftener than once in six months.[15]

In the vicinity of Bencoolen were several spice-plantations, which we were told were well worth seeing; and that the ride to them was very pleasant; but time did not permit us to gratify ourselves with a view of them. From these gentlemen we received a confirmation of what writers have said, with regard to the low estimation, in which the chastity of unmarried females is universally held by the natives. So little, indeed, is it valued, according to their representation, that it is very common for fathers to offer their daughters, for a trifling compensation, to the use of foreigners; and even the old Raja, whom we saw at the island which we visited on the day of our arrival, made a tender of his daughter's services to every foreigner who might seem willing to accept them.[16]

The jurisdiction of the Resident of Bencoolen, is quite limited in its extent, and embraces only a few square miles of the level ground in the vicinity of the bay. Beyond this to the eastward, the island appears rugged and mountainous, and some of the mountainous ridges, are of considerable elevation. Among the most conspicuous objects of this kind, and one which serves as an important land-mark, is a peak called the "Sugar-Loaf," which is situated to the northward of the town, and bore N.E. from the ship as she lay at anchor. It was probably about twenty-five miles from us, {and though appearantly covered with vegetation, it exhibited a rugged aspect, as if composed of rocks.} Its hight, as I judged, was nearly three thousand feet, and its ascent very steep.

One of our English visitors told me that the natives entertained some superstition respecting it, which led them to suppose that an attempt to ascend it would be fatal. Five Englishmen made the attempt some years ago, and were told by the natives, that although they might succeed in their bold undertaking, yet they would pay dear for it, as two of their number would die soon afterwards. And it happened according to the prediction; for by great fatigue, and sleeping at night in the jungle, two of the party were immediately attacked with fever, which soon proved fatal, and thus tended to confirm the natives in their superstition.

Although the number of foreigners at Bencoolen was very small, yet the Dutch Government had not been unmindful of the importance of maintaining christian worship there; and a Chaplain [Rev. W. C. Slingerland Conradi] was stationed there, who officiated regularly every Sunday. He resided with the Governor, and besides discharging his clerical duties, he assisted the Governor in the management of the school. He seemed to possess considerable classical learning, and we managed to carry on a little conversation in latin, which he spoke with considerable readiness and accuracy; but our pronunciation was so different, that it occasioned a good deal of embarrassment, and prevented our maintaining any very satisfactory discourse.

The objects for which we visited this port being now accomplished, at least, so far as practicable, we were ready to leave the harbour with the first favourable breeze. A principal object, it appeared our touching at this port, was to leave information for the Schooner *Boxer,* which was expected soon to follow us; or rather to wait for her so long as circumstances would permit, this port having been considered the most convenient for the assembling of our squadron, consisting of the *Peacock* and the *Boxer.* [17] Before we arrived there, however, it became evident that if we waited the arrival of the Schooner, we should be unable to cross the China Sea before the change of the monsoons, and our passage would be much prolonged, and the safety of the ship perhaps endangered; as it frequently happens that very violent gales of wind called typhoons, accompany the change of the monsoons. It was therefore determined to make as short a stay as possible, and then proceed on through the China Sea.

Until a few days before we arrived there, it was expected there would be no occasion for the ship to anchor; but only to lie too off the town, and send a boat in with a letter for the Commander of the Schooner. It was ascertained, however, a short time before our arrival, that our supply of bread was likely to fail, and it was therefore necessary to remain long enough in port, if possible, to obtain an additional supply of this most indispensable article. But with every effort that could be made both by ourselves, and the Governor, only a very small quantity of bread could be procured; and we were obliged to supply the deficiency with yams. This was found to be an excellent substitute for bread and was obtained in great abundance and at a moderate price, that is, at about $2.50 a pecul of 136 pounds. We also partly filled up our water, which was found there very good, and was obtained with out much trouble on our part, as the people of the place brought it off in boats provided by the Governor. By this means our men were saved from much labour and fatigue, which would undoubtedly have occasioned more or less disease, and probably have destroyed some lives. When practicable, wooding & watering within the tropics, should always be done by hire whatever the expense may be; for no expense that would be incurred in this manner, would equal the hazzard to which the lives of a ship's crew would be exposed, if compelled to perform this duty themselves.

Besides the articles that have been mentioned, a few bullocks of caraboo kind, were taken on board for the use of the ship, and the Captain received one or two more as a present from the Governor, which he also shared with the officers and crew.

Every thing being thus in a state of readiness, and a favourable breeze springing up, we weighed anchor at nine o'clock in the evening of the 31st. of August, and stood out to sea. In leaving the harbour, we pursued the same rout as in entering it; and although there are many coral reefs in the harbour, which render the navigation in rough weather, difficult and dangerous; yet as we had a light breeze and a smooth sea, we made our exit from the harbour without the least difficulty.

Sept. 6. The favourable breeze with which we left the harbour of Bencoolen, continued through the night, and the next morning we found ourselves advanced about thirty miles on our course towards the straits of Sunda. It had been recommended by the Governor and others at Bencoolen, to keep near the island in running to the southward, so that we might have the land-breeze at night, as the southeast trade wind blows almost uninterruptedly at a distance from the island. But after attempting this for two days, it was found impracticable, without running so near to the island, as to endanger the safety of the ship, in case the wind should blow fresh toward the land, or a heavy swell should set in that direction, without a breeze that would enable the ship to resist it. After the second day, therefore, we abandoned the design of taking advantage of the land-breeze, and endeavoured to make the best of our way with the adverse southeast wind by beating. {In this manner we spent two days, during which we made but little progress, the wind being light and there being constantly a heavy swell setting against us. At last, however, a large volume of black clouds collected over the island to the northeast of us, which moved gradually towards us, with most threatening appearances, and after a few hours, began to pour down their stores of rain in overwhelming torrents. A favourable breeze accompanied this shower, which continued with little interruption for about twenty-four hours, at the end of which time, we were within a few miles of "Flat Point", the southwestern extremity of Sumatra, which bounds the Straits of Sunda on the north.}

It was about sunset on the 6th. when we had thus arrived at the entrance of the Straits, and preparation began to be made for anchoring at the island of Crockatoa, where we had determined to stop for water.

But at this moment the breeze which had been so propitious to us, died away, and was succeeded by a calm, which continued some hours. During this calm the ship was carried by the heavy swells which set across the Strait towards Sumatra, so near the shore that she was supposed to be in some danger, which occasioned no small degree of hurry and tumult. The evidence of danger, and certainly a very conclusive one, was the sudden decrease of the soundings from sixty-five to twenty fathoms. Though this rapid approach to a lee-shore, and one with which we were entirely unacquainted, was sufficiently unpleasant of itself; yet the scene was rendered much more portentous by the threatenings of an approaching tempest. {For some time a body of black clouds had been collecting, from which darted occasional flashes of lightning, followed by the low rumbling of distant thunder; but the flashing of lightning had now become extremely vivid and were followed in an instant, by loud peals of thunder. Such was the threatening aspect of the heavens, when we unexpectedly found ourselves, in twenty fathoms water, and consequently near the shore, with a heavy swell carrying us directly towards it; but at this critical moment, when the scene around us seemed truly terrific,} the storm which had been some time threatening, burst upon us, and instead of increasing the danger of our situation, as had been apprehended, it was the means of our escape from

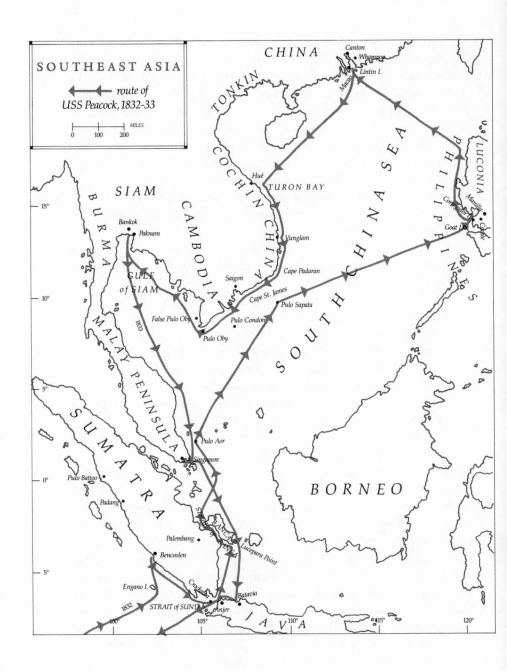

SOUTHEAST ASIA

→——← route of
USS Peacock, 1832-33

MILES
0   100   200

CHINA

Canton
Whampoa
Lintin I.
Macao

TONKIN

COCHIN CHINA

Hué
TURON BAY

Vunglam

Cape Padaran

SIAM

BURMA

CAMBODIA

Bankok
Paknam

Saigon
Cape St. James

GULF
of SIAM

False Pulo Oby
Pulo Condore
Pulo Sapata

Pulo Oby

MALAY PENINSULA

1833

SOUTH CHINA SEA

PHILIPPINES

LUCONIA

Corregidor I.
Manilla
Cavite
Goat I.

Pulo Aor

Singapore

SUMATRA

BORNEO

Pulo Battoo

Padang

Palembang

Bencoolen

BANCA
Minto Reef
Lucepara Point

Engano I.

Crockatoa
Batavia

1832
STRAIT of SUNDA   Anjer

JAVA

15°

10°

5°

0°

5°

100°   105°   110°   115°   120°

it. For though it came upon us with rather a severe blast, yet the wind being in our favor, we were enabled to stand off from the land, and in a short time all danger was past.

Sept. 8. The next morning after we had escaped from a situation of some danger, in the manner that has been described, we found ourselves out of sight of land, and carried by an adverse current, much farther to the westward than we had supposed. The weather, however, had become pleasant and the regular southeast trade-wind had prevailed over the land breeze which had enabled us to make our escape from a lee-shore. {We had now no prospect of a fair wind, and therefore depended on making our way into the straits by beating. In this we succeeded quite as well as we had reason to expect, and by sunset of the 7th, we had passed "Flat Point", and as was supposed, were within thirty miles of Crockatoa, which we expected to reach early the next morning. But an adverse current again disappointed our expectation, and at sunrise the next morning, we were almost as far from the island as we had supposed ourselves the evening before, notwithstanding we had been favoured during the night, with a tolerable fresh breeze.} The breeze, however, becoming more favourable as we advanced in the strait, we made very good progress on this day, and at 12 o'clock at night we anchored within three or four miles of the island to which our course had been directed. During the run of this day, we passed several islands all of which appeared to be clothed with a rich and luxuriant verdure. We also had a view of the Southern extremity of Sumatra, which rises, here and there, into mountains of very considerable elevation.

Early the next morning, Sept. 9th. Lieut. Sinclair was sent ashore to look for the town and watering place, which we had expected to find, from the representations of books and charts, on the northeast side of the island. But after a search of several hours, he returned and reported that he could find neither watering place or town. The Capt. and Mr. Roberts also made an excursion on shore,[18] and after they returned another party, consisting of Lieutenants Cunningham, & Sinclair, the Marine officer, Dr. Gilchrist, and several Midshipmen, made a visit to the island in which they spent the whole of the afternoon. {In the mean time a favourable breeze sprung up, and having ascertained the impossibility of obtaining water here we weighed anchor and directed our course towards Anjer on the island of Java where there was known to be a very convenient watering place, though the water was said not to be good.}

The island of Crockatoa[19] is of small extent, being only about four miles in length, and about one mile in breadth. Its height seemed to be disproportioned to its size, which appeared to me to be a striking feature of all the islands that we had yet seen in the straits. This island, like the others that we had seen, was clad with a luxuriant vegetation of a dark green hue, {which presented an inviting aspect as affording a cool and comfortable retreat from the scorching rays of a vertical sun. Very near to this island, are two smaller ones, which at a distance appear to belong to it, and to constitute but one island. One of these is situated on the northwest side of Crockatoa, and the [other] on the northeast, which, from its shape is called "Long Island".

About six miles to the north of Crockatoa is "Tamarind Island", which appeared to be of rather greater extent, as well as of greater elevation, than that island.}

The depth of water where we anchored off Crockatoa, was thirty fathoms. During almost the whole of the time that we remained at anchor here, which was about sixteen hours, there was a strong current setting to the westward; so that, although we failed of procuring water, yet we lost no time by anchoring, as we should have been unable, with the light breeze that prevailed during this time, to make any heading against the current. Having waited some time for the return of the boats from the excursion to the island, we got under way about four o'clock in the afternoon, and stood to the eastward. We had advanced but a small distance, when the boats were discovered under sails coming around the northern extremity of the island, and a little after sunset they reached the ship.

The party had explored the shores of the island for a distance of several miles, and that part of it which was represented as having been the site of the town and the watering-place; but not the least vestige of either could be discovered. Smoke was seen to rise in several places from among the trees; but there was reason to suppose that it proceeded from volcanic fire. A very conclusive evidence of this, was the heat of the water near the shore, which was so great, that when the hand was immersed in it, it had to be instantly withdrawn, and a bubbling motion was observed like that of boiling water.

As we advanced towards Anjer, on a course about E. by S. the breeze freshened, and the distance being only about thirty-miles, we had approached as near to the harbour as was safe at night, by twelve o'clock, when we came to anchor in about 19 fathoms water. A short time before we anchored, we passed a ship within hailing distance, and as she did not return an answer to our demand of "what ship is that", we were called to quarters, and for a few minutes were engaged, with great hurry and bustle, in making preparation for a battle.[20] These hostile movements, however, very soon ceased in consequence of the stranger informing us, that she was "H.B.M.S. *Magician*," just from Batavia, & bound to Ceylon.

It was found the next morning, Sept. 10th, that we had anchored within three or four miles of the usual place of anchorage; and so near the town that by six o'clock, the ship was surrounded with boats, and the decks were thronged with the natives, who were offering their goods for sale with an eagerness which it was difficult to resist. They were all Malays like those of Bencoolen, and most of them, from their intercourse with Americans and Englishmen, who stop there for water, had learned so much English, as to carry on their trafic without embarrassment, and they had also become very familiar with the practice, which they had probably learned from Europeans and Americans, of asking twice as much for their articles, as they would finally consent to take. It was amusing to see the eagerness with which these people offered their various articles for sale consisting of poultry, eggs, monkeys, birds, shells, etc, etc,; and how rapidly they would lower their prices, when they perceived us rather backward to purchase. It was evidently their design to dispose of their goods at their own prices before we could have any communication with the shore, and before any additional supplies should be brought off. The utmost competition therefore took place among the numerous applicants for purchasers, and for about three hours, our upper deck seemed to be transformed into a Malay bazar; where the naturalist, as well as the epicure, might have found a great variety of articles adopted to his taste.

About 9 o'clock, however, a light breeze sprung up, and our unfortunate customers were obliged to leave the ship. We now got under way, and run into the usual place of anchorage, which was about a mile N.W. from the landing place, where we had a depth of water of fifteen fathoms.

Immediately after coming to anchor, the first Lieutenant was sent with a message from the Capt. to the commanding officer on shore, informing him who & what we were, and that we had touched there for the purpose of obtaining water and articles of provision. At the same time, Lieut. Sinclare was sent with a watering party, and a boat on shore was also employed to assist in watering, that our detention here might be as short as possible.

The first Lieut. returned about four o'clock in the afternoon, with an impression rather unfavourable towards the commanding officer, whom he represented as being quite difficult in those attentions, which are usual on such occasions, and which are considered essential to true politeness. This officer was a Dutchman, and had the rank of Deputy-Resident, Anjer being under the jurisdiction of the Dutch Government.

But notwithstanding the seeming unpoliteness of this gentleman, Mr. Cunningham passed an hour or two at his residence very pleasantly; for he found there an English lady with her husband, who was a Russian, but who spoke English well, and was a man of intelligence. From this gentleman he learned that the plauge [plague] was raging at Muscat, and Mocha, places which we expected to visit, and that the foreign residents were moving out as fast as possible.

It frequently happens that the faults which we attribute to others, may with much more reason be attributed to ourselves, if not with precisely the same circumstances, yet with others that are equally deserving of reprehension; and so it proved to be with regard to the Dutch Resident at Anjer. He did not hold such communication with the first Lieut. as the rules of politeness would seem in ordinary circumstances to require; and the reason on his part was, that he could not converse well in English, and on the first Lieut.'s part, that he could not speak a word of either Dutch or French, which was certainly quite as culpable as the Dutchman's inability to speak English.

An opportunity occurred the same afternoon, for the Resident to show that he was not wanting in politeness, but on the contrary, that he was very desirous to manifest it in the best manner he was able; for the Capt. Mr. Roberts, and several of the officers went ashore and were invited to his house, where they were treated in the most polite and hospitable manner. In return, the Resident was invited to visit the ship the next morning, and the Capt. was to send a boat for him, at as early an hour as would suit his convenience.

Sept. 11. Early this morning I went on shore for the purpose of making some purchases, and taking a survey of the town. With respect to the town itself, there is nothing deserving of particular description. The houses were mostly constructed of bamboo, like those at Bencoolen, and afforded shelter, not only to the family, but also to poultry, pigs, and such other animals as the occupant might possess. I could not learn the population of this place, but I should suppose that it amounted to two or three thousand.

There was no regularity in the arrangement of the streets and buildings, but wherever convenience directed, there the frail shelter, was erected, without any reference, as it appeared, either to the streets, or to other houses. Not a pane of glass was to be seen in the place, and very few of the houses so far as I had an opportunity of observing had any other floor, than a small platform of bamboo raised a foot or two above the ground, on which the indolent native dozed away a considerable part of the day, and which served the whole family as a lodging-place at night.

In the course of our rambles about the town, we stopped at a dwelling of a better appearance than ordinary, where there had been a wedding party the day before, which had afforded our officers who were on shore a good deal of amusement. Great preparation, it appeared, had been made, as is the custom with the Malays, and the entertainment, which had already continued three or four days, was to continue two or three days longer. We found here quite a large band of musicians, all seated on the ground, and earnestly engaged in playing to a crowd of eager listeners. On our approach the master of ceremonies, who could speak a little English, invited us in, and then entertained us with music and dancing. Mats were spread on the ground for the dancers, who were masked, and accoutred in a most fantastic manner. The dance was a sort of pantomine, consisting of a variety of antic gestures, which seemed to be so well executed, as to deserve great applause; and the master of ceremonies asked me with an appearance of exultation, if we had any thing like that in America. As I had no disposition to mortify his feelings, I told him that we had not; but I could have told him with the most perfect truth, that I had seen exhibitions on the American stage, which could almost rival that in the ridiculous; and that in the Italian opera, which is supposed to be the most perfect in the world, I had seen exhibitions far transcending theirs in every thing that was indecent and disgusting.[21]

Their musical instruments were of a very simple construction, so far as I could judge by a distant view of them, and their music would be considered by the lovers of modern Italian jargon, coarse, vulgar, and not even deserving the name of music; but for my own part, I must say, that coarse and unrefined as it was, it possessed nevertheless much more harmony for my ear, than any Italian orchestra that I ever listened to. The instruments used by these uncultivated Javanese, consisted principally of blocks of wood hollowed out, with pieces of metal, probably iron or steel, seven or eight inches long and an inch broad lying across, which were struck by two little hammers [a percussion instrument called a gambang]; as the different pieces of metal emitted a different sound, according to their position over the excavation, the performer was enabled to produce a considerable variety of sounds, and to combine them in such a manner as to constitute rather an agreeable harmony. There was another kind of instrument, which was louder but less agreeable. It also consisted of the excavated block; but instead of the narrow pieces of mettal, metalic vessels in the form of cups or basins, of such a size as probably to contain about a pint, with metalic covers, were placed over the cavity and the covers were struck by hammers, in the manner already described [an instrument called a bonang or kromo]. Besides these instruments, there were several gongs, which seemed not to be adapted, however, to the present occasion, as they were but very little used.[22]

After spending about half an hour in witnessing this exhibition, and bestowing such small change as we happened to be provided with, upon the principal performer in the dance, who signified to us after the performance was ended, that he expected to be paid for the pains he had taken to entertain us; we visited the tomb of Col. Cathcart [Lt. Colonel Charles Cathcart],[23] the brother of Lord Cathcart, who died here while attending his brother on a mission to China, and whose death put a stop to the mission.* The monument was about thirty feet high, and from six or seven feet above the ground, of a pyramidal form. On one side of the base was a latin inscription, which was highly flattering to the character of the deceased. He died in 1788, at the age of 29. The monument occupies the most elevated ground in the vicinity of the town, and is the most conspicuous object that is seen on approaching the anchorage. Within the enclosure in which it stood, was a garden in a fine state of cultivation, in which I observed several of the productions of our own gardens, as peas, cabbage, beets, etc. The monument is about a hundred rods from the town, and between them the ground is low and wet, and in a climate so hot, must be productive of disease.

After returning from the visit to the monument, we went into the fort, in which the Governor had his residence, and which though small, we found in fine order, and much the most comfortable place we met with on shore. The walls of the fort embraced an area of about an acre, in the centre of which was the place of parade, which was so clean and well shaded, as to be a most inviting place of retreat in the heat of the day.

When we first visited the fort, the Resident was absent on his visit to the ship; but before we left the town he returned, in company with the Capt. and Mr. Roberts, and we were invited to repeat our visit, which we did, and were treated with much politeness and hospitality. He was very urgent that we should stay longer in port, that we might have an opportunity of taking a ride into the country, in which it would afford him much pleasure, he said, to accompany us, even to Bantam, if we chose to ride so far. Bantam is on the east side of the island, and probably about thirty

---

*Anderson[24]

miles from Anjer, between which places there is a very good road. There is also a good turn-pike road from Anjer to Batavia, a distance of eighty miles, on which it was perfectly safe to travel, not only by day, but also at night. A public conveyance affords very good accommodations for travelers, and the Russian gentleman and his wife took passage in it for Batavia, the next morning after our arrival. The fare, however, was very high, it being eighty dollars, that is, a dollar a mile. The journey is performed in ten hours.

This road, I have been informed, was made by the English, while they were in possession of the island, and not only did they accomplish this work, which is certainly of very considerable importance; but they also made a road through the whole length of the island, a distance of about seven hundred miles.

In the character of the Malays who inhabit this island, there seems to have been considerable improvement within a few years. They were formerly a savage murderous race of people, more ferocious, if possible, towards the unfortunate foreigners who might fall into their hands, than the tigers with which the forests of their island abound. And no longer ago than 1826, an English officer and a boat's crew, who had been to an island a few miles distant from Anjer, were attacked by these barbarians and all murdered. The officer's body was found and interred at Anjer, where a monument was erected, attesting the circumstances of his death. But at the time we were there, they seemed to have lost, in a considerable degree, the worst features of their character, and unless provoked, or influenced by the prospect of rich plunder, were not addicted to robbery or murder. Although the Malays are said to be all Mahometans, yet these Javanese Malays, so far as I could learn, were not; for I questioned one of them on the subject who could speak English tolerably well, and who had been in England, but he seemed to be utterly ignorant, not only of Mahomet and his religion, but also of every other kind of religion.[25] Images of different descriptions were seen in their houses, and hence it may be concluded that they are idolators; but of the particulars of their idolatry, I could not, of course, obtain any information.

The individual to whom I have alluded, spoke in very flattering terms of Englishmen and Americans; but the Dutch, he said, they did not like, and when the Dutch vessels came into the harbour, none of his countrymen went on board of them. He gave the preference, however, to Americans, because they were most ready to trade, and most in the habit of paying for what they purchased in money.

Polygamy is freely allowed among them, every man, whatever his rank and condition may be, being permitted to have as many wives as he chooses.

The person to whom my inquiries were addressed, told me that he had three wives, two of whom lived with him in the same house; but the other had conducted [herself] so bad, that he had sent her away. It was rare, he said, for any man there to have more than three wives, though there were a few individuals who had four or five. The expense of supporting them, however, cannot be any great obstacle as the whole expense of this man's family, including house-rent, was only sixty dollars a year. One important item of female expence was here almost entirely dispensed with, & that was, the expense for dress; for they seemed to require nothing more than two pieces of cheap calico, one of which they wrap around the waist, and the other around the upper part of the chest, so as to conceal the breasts. The only difference between the dress of the men and women consisted in the latter using a partial covering for the upper part of the body, whereas the men were entirely naked above the waist.

In their general features the Malays, so far as I had yet an opportunity of observing them, are very similar to the Indians of N. America. They have the prominent cheek-bones, the small brilliant eye, and the long, coarse black hair, of the red men of America; but they are of a smaller size, and, the complexion of their skin, approaches more to the yellow than to the copper colour. In their natural appearance, these people are by no means unagreeable; but their practice of chewing betel-leaf and arica nut, to which the women are equally addicted with the men, gives them always a disgusting, and frequently a very hideous first view, {that they should persist in a practice which they must be sensible renders them objects of disgust to all beholders, and which moreover must be attended with a good deal of suffering, from the corroding qualities of the composition; but our surprize will cease when we direct our observation among our own country men and witness the effects of practices among both sexes, which are far worse in their appearance, and in their influence on the mind and body, incomparably more deplorable.}

Anjer is a good deal resorted to as a watering place, it being very convenient watering there, and the water good. The water is brought from a distance on the surface of the ground, in a narrow channel formed of brick and lime; and within fifty or sixty rods of the landing-place. This aquaduct crosses a narrow arm of the sea, where boats go, and by means of a hose, in a few minutes take in a load of water, without any labour or fatigue to their crews.

The ground in the neighborhood of Anjer is low and flat, and the soil is of a sandy quality. It seemed to be fertile in those productions which were adopted to it, especially the coco-nut tree, of which I had never seen such numbers before. Yams and sweet-potatoes were also abundant, and we found there an ample supply of poultry, eggs etc, which we procured at moderate prices. {For fowl we paid fifty-cents a dozzen, and eggs a dollar a hundred.}

At a little distance back of Anjer the island of Java presents in some places a rugged and sterile appearance, and its surface is broken into hills and mountains, some of which have an elevation of two or three thousand feet.

On the same day that I made this visit on shore, Sept. 11th. at 3 o'clock in the afternoon, we weighed anchor and proceeded on our voyage. A short time before we got under way, however, an American vessel passed us, which we boarded, and learned that she was from Boston by way of Rio Janeiro, which she left on the 15th of July. She was bound to Batavia, and was a few miles ahead of us when we got under way.

{Although we were favoured with a fair and tolerably fresh breeze for several hours, yet we experienced so strong an adverse current, that our progress was very slow; and when the breeze died away, which it did before twelve o'clock, we were obliged to anchor, and remain there during the night. A light breeze sprung up the next morning, and we weighed anchor, and moved on at a very slow rate for a short time, the current being still against us; when the breeze died away, and we remained at anchor through the day. It being perfectly calm, and the sun shining clear, the heat during this day was more oppressive than we had yet experienced.}

Sept. 13. Having been favoured during the preceding night with a fair and rather fresh breeze, our progress had been quite rapid, for we had now no adverse current to contend with; and by nine o'clock this morning we were near the entrance of the Straits of Banca. {The course which we had run from our last anchorage, which was about four miles to the S.W. of two small rocky islands called "The Brothers," had been nearly north, and the depth of water had been eleven or twelve fathoms.} While thus proceeding on with a favourable breeze, and expecting to meet with no impediment, the soundings suddenly decreased from nine to three and a half fathoms, which occasioned a good deal of alarm, and no time was lost in shortening sail, and letting go anchor. Boats were immediately sent out to sound, and it was found that in the direction which we ought to take the water soon began to deepen; so that after a detention of about an hour, we weighed anchor and resumed our course. The shoal on which we anchored, is described by some writers, but no one I believe, represents the water as being so shoal as we found it. From our position while lying at anchor, the island of Lucepera bore N.E. by N. distant about ten miles; and the distance to the coast of Sumatra, was probably about the same.

Having passed this shoal, we considered our course free from danger, and the wind being still favourable, every sail was set, and we entered the Strait about 12 o'clock going at the rate of eight or nine miles an hour. In this manner we continued to advance all the afternoon, having a distinct view of the island of Banca on one side and of Sumatra on the other.

The island of Banca is about sixty miles long, and generally low, though hills of considerable magnitude are occasionally to be seen.

This island is said to abound in tin. The coast of Sumatra which bounds this Strait on the west, is low and flat, and appeared to be covered with a thick growth of timber.

We met with no interuption to our progress till about eight o'clock in the evening, when the soundings again decreased, and we were obliged to anchor. Boats were again sent out to sound, and it was found that we had approached rather too near the shore of Banca, from which shoals extend out four or five miles, and render the navigation of that side of the Strait somewhat dangerous. As the surf on the beach could be seen from where we lay at anchor, it was judged that we could not be more than three miles from it.

We remained in this situation about two hours, till the moon rose, when we were enabled to pursue our course with safety, and accordingly the anchor was weighed, and we continued our progress through the night without any farther impediment.

By daylight the next morning, Sept. 14th, we had nearly reached the northern extremity of the Strait, and had in view the point of Sumatra which forms the northern boundary on that side, and is called "Fourth Point", there being three other points to the southward of this, which are numbered according to their situation, the first being near the southern entrance of the Strait. The "Fourth Point" forms the southern boundary of the mouth of Palambong River, on which, about thirty miles from its mouth, there is a Dutch factory.

{In the situation which I have just described, our soundings again indicated approaching danger, having suddenly decreased from eleven to five fathoms. An anchor being immediately let go, arrested our farther progress, until the boats were sent out to sound, and there was not found any where a less depth of water than where we lay. No time was then lost in getting under way, and with a fair wind we proceeded on our course during the remainder of the day, and the following night. Our course during this time, was nearly N.E. and we passed several groups of islands, the first of which, are called from their number, "Three Islands," the next "Four," and the others "Seven." Although we passed the two last of these groups at night still we were near enough to see them. Most of them possessed that feature which has been noticed of the islands in the Straits of Sunda, namely, an elevation which seemed to be disproportioned to their magnitude, which rendered them visible even at night, to a very considerable distance.}

Sept. 15. At 12 o'clock this day, we found ourselves by a meridian observation, fifty-five miles to the northward of the equator. Our course was now changed from N.E. to N.N.W. with the view of making a small island, called "Pulo Aor," agreeably to the advice of the best writers on the navigation of the China Sea. During the remainder of this day and the following night, we moved onward before a steady breeze, and by day-light the next morning [Sept. 16], the island toward which our course had been shaped, was in sight. It was so high as to be visible forty or fifty miles. From this island we took our departure, and pursued a course N.N.E. for the island of Sapata, which it was desirable to make, before keeping away to the eastward for Manilla.

Sept. 22. We passed Pulo Aor with a fresh breeze from the southward, which we supposed was the regular south-west monsoon, and on which we might depend for a short passage to our destined port. In this supposition, however, we were mistaken, for within 24 hours after we had passed the island that has just been mentioned, the wind died away, and for many days, there was scarcely wind enough to cause a ripple on the water. The sun being verticle, and most of the time unobscured by clouds, the heat was oppressive, not only during the day, but also throughout the night, especially in our state rooms below. Day after day, we looked with anxious expectation for a return of the S.W. monsoon, it being yet too early in the season for the change of these periodical winds to take place; but every day we were doomed to meet with a painful disappointment. What rendered our situation at this time particularly unpleasant, and made us so anxious for a fair wind, was the state of our provisions, which were so far exhausted as to cause some fear that we might be reduced to a short allowance, and possibly to a state of starvation. In order to guard as much as possible, against such an extremity, an account was taken of all the provisions on board, and it was ordered that they should be served out in such a manner, as to make them hold out as long as possible, and at the same time to be most satisfactory to the crew. It was particularly with the bread-stuffs, and their substitutes, however, that it was necessary thus to economize; because the supply of these was considerably less than of the other articles belonging to the ration.

About the time that this measure was adopted, that is, on the 22d. of Sept. we were gratified with a sight of Pulo Sapata, from which we were to take our final departure for Manilla. We were not a little surprized to find ourselves so far advanced to the north, while, according to our dead reckoning, we supposed ourselves nearly a hundred miles to the southward of the island; and considered ourselves indebted to a strong north-easterly current for this unexpected progress. {The view that we had of the island of Pulo Sapata was a distant one, and therefore I can say nothing more of it than that it seemed to be high.} Our latitude on the day that we passed this island, was, lat. 9°27′ north and longitude about 109° east. {Until we had passed this island, we had scarcely been off from soundings after entering the China Sea, the depth of water being from the Straits of Boneo [Borneo] to Pulo Aor, from fifteen to thirty six or seven fathoms; and from that to Pulo Sapata, from thirty to seventy or eighty.}

We continued in the situation that has just been described about two days longer, that is till the 24th of Sept. when we began to experience something like a steady breeze, and to make a constant though slow advance towards our destined port.

No one who has never been placed in the situation, in which we were at that time, can conceive with what anxious feelings every rising cloud is watched, and with what delight the sails are seen to swell with the freshening breeze, and the noise of the ship is heard urging her way through the water. {Such were our feelings at the time I am speaking of;} and we had the satisfaction to find our progress continually increasing, with a rising breeze, which commenced at the north, and gradually changed its direction to the westward, and finally to the southeast, where it remained until the 28th. when we made the Goat Island, at about two o'clock in the morning.

{Our course for some days after passing the island of Sapata, was about N.E. in order to avoid the extensive shoals which lie to the eastward; and we were greatly favoured in having been enabled to advance far enough to the north, before we met with the northerly breeze, to clear these shoals with a fair wind. We changed our course from N.E. to E.N.E. when we were in twelve degrees and about ten miles north latitude; and we varied but little from this course till we made Goat Island which is about thirteen leagues from the entrance of the harbour of Manilla.

On making this island we found an error in our longitude, which showed the great importance of having a good chronometer, especially in navigating at sea, where strong currents are frequent, and so irregular that it is impossible to make any calculation respecting them, that is entitled to confidence.} At 12 o'clock on the 27th. our distance from Goat Island, according to the dead reckoning, was 180 miles, and consequently, although we were favoured with a fresh breeze, we could not expect to see it before 10 o'clock the next day. So much confidence was placed in the correctness of this reckoning, that the ship was kept under as much sail as she could carry, and was going at the rate of seven or eight knots, till about two o'clock the next morning, when, to the surprize of all on board, land was discovered a few miles from us on the lee-bow. We tacked immediately, and stood from the land till day-light, when it was discovered that this land was an island a little to the south east of Goat Island, which was now distinctly in view. {The wind still continued fair, and having run to the north three or four hours, so as to pass the northern extremity of Goat Island at the distance of ten or twelve miles, as recommended by Hansburgh [Horsburgh][26] we pursued an easterly course for the entrance of the harbour.} An island called "Corregidor," is situated at the entrance of the harbour, at the distance of thirteen leagues from Goat Island, as has been already mentioned, and eleven leagues from the anchorage at Manilla. This island appeared in sight about noon; but the wind then died away, and for two or three hours we lay becalmed, and had about given up the expectation of advancing any farther till the next day, when a breeze sprung up from the westward, which continued till we had reached the entrance of the harbour, on the north side of Corregidor, when it left us, and we were obliged to anchor.

Sept. 30. Discovering at day light this morning, a small village on the island of Corregidor opposite to us, a boat was despatched to it, for the purpose of procuring eggs, milk, fruit etc; but after an absence of two hours, it returned, without having been able to obtain any thing except a bottle or two of milk, and a small quantity of bread, and a few cucumbers, which the Governor of the place sent off as a present to the Captain.

There being no wind to enable us to get under way, the Capt. Mr. Roberts, & the Marine officer, paid a visit to the village above-mentioned, where on the beach looking for shells, they remained two or three hours. In the mean time a light breeze from the westward began to ruffle the surface of the water, which was an indication for us to prepare for moving onward to the harbour; and the anchor was weighed, and the sails set, {but we were prevented taking advantage of the favourable breeze, for some time, by being obliged to wait the return of the Captain. At last he returned, and the breeze having freshened considerably by this time, we advanced towards the anchorage at a rapid rate.}

After passing Corregidor, we entered one of the largest and finest bays that I have ever seen, and indeed one of the finest in the world. It is of very great extent, and is so enclosed by the island of Luconia, and its entrance is so protected by the island of Corregidor, which is situated nearly in the middle of it; that it affords secure anchorage at all seasons of the year. The day was clear and pleasant when we entered this magnificent bay, and we had as distinct a view as the distance would permit, of the scenery which surrounds it. To the southeast we had a view of the town & harbour of Cavita, fifteen or twenty miles distant; and far beyond, the hills of Luconia presented themselves to the sight, with their variegated surface of cultivated fields, and native forests. Farther to the north and to the eastward of Manilla the hills rise to a hight which may entitle them to the appellation of mountains, but still farther to the north, the land is so low and level that we had a very imperfect view of it.

About 4 o'clock in the afternoon, the spires of Manilla were first seen emerging from the water, and soon after, the town and the vessels in the harbour presented themselves to our view. At half past five o'clock, we let go our anchor in six and a half fathoms water, and thus terminated a voyage of ninety seven days from the River Plate, having sailed in this time, the distance of 11,439 miles, making the whole distance from Boston 19,154 miles.

CHAPTER V
Manilla

Visit on shore; Farther particulars respecting Quallah Battoo;
Second visit on shore; Religious Procession; Dinner party on
shore; Account of Manilla; Capt. McDonnell & the Sandwich
islands; Letter to the Capt; Last visit on shore at Manilla;
Cholera; Departure from Manilla; Arrival at Lintin.

We found an English Sloop of War, the *Curacoa* lying in the harbour, and
we had scarcely let go our anchor, before her first Lieutenant came on board
to pay the usual compliments which pass between the public vessels of
different nations, when they meet in foreign ports. {As soon as this gentleman took his leave, a conference with closed doors, took place in the cabin,
between the Capt. & Mr. Roberts, not of an amicable nature, as was very
evident, though the precise tenor of it was not known to any but themselves.
It was not difficult to satisfy ourselves with respect to the subject of this
angry dialogue, and the causes which led to it; since it was not the first of
the kind that had taken place between them, and we had observed for
several days previously, that the Capt. had become so excessively testy and
irritable, that every thing seemed to offend him, and excite a gust of passion.
In this irascible, moron humor, he had no doubt assumed an imperious
dictatorial air with Mr. Roberts, which no man of independant feelings
would submit to, and which was particularly reprehensible as directed towards Mr. R. since the office with which he was vested by the Government,
placed him entirely beyond the control of the Captain.[1]

Such conduct on the part of a commander is altogether inexcusable
and should wholly preclude him from ever being entrusted with a command
afterwards. This was not wholly the result of natural temperament, though

121

he was obviously of a very irritable character; but it was owing in a considerable degree, to the excessive use of intoxicating drinks. He did not, indeed, drink every day to the degree of intoxication; but he was every day, for a considerable time previous to our arrival at Manilla, so much under the influence of liquor that it was very apparent in his conduct and conversation. This propensity to excessive drinking, I had observed very soon after we left the U. States, and augured the worst effects from it. In the River Plate, it had nearly proved fatal, and if we had remained there two months longer, and he had continued to associate with the same persons, that he did during our short stay of two weeks, in which time his health declined very fast, I do not believe that he would ever have left the River.

It is painful to me to make these remarks; but as it is as much my object, to describe men as inanimate things, I should fail of performing the task that I have undertaken, if I were to omit giving a sketch of the principal traits, in the characters of those men whose situations and offices give them an important influence on others. Though the individual whose conduct gave occasion for these remarks was at all times easily offended, and for the merest trifle, would fly into a rage with his servants, and use the roughest language to them which the tongue of man can utter; yet when he had not made too free with the bottle, he was kind, affable, and generous almost to an extreme, with his officers, and was ready to do every thing in his power to promote their comfort. Could he have pursued the course, to which his good feelings at such times would prompt him, he might have enjoyed the satisfaction, of which he was very desirous, of seeing the officers and men under his command, as contented and happy, as any in the service. But, allowing his capricious and irritable feelings to predominate, and taking offense at trifles that were utterly unworthy of his notice; he had the mortification to see that all the officers avoided him as much as possible, except on duty, and that when he would have been glad to pass an hour or two in conversation with them, he was left to his own solitary reflections.

I have often had occasion to observe with sorrow, the exceeding deficiency of Navy officers in mental resources, and their great aversion to those studies, from which a reasonable reflecting man might be supposed to derive any satisfaction; but I have never met with an instance where these faults were more apparent, than in that now under consideration. To attribute any natural mental defect to a man as a fault, would be impious; and to consider a man culpable for not acquiring that knowledge for which his mind is not adapted, would be unreasonable; but it is surely the duty of every man, and especially of one occupying the important situation of commander of a ship of war, to do all in his power to remedy the natural defects of his mind and not by a misapplication of the powers which he does possess, to make his deficiences still more apparent, and more productive of bad consequences. And as to reading, although the structure of his mind may be such as to incapacitate him in a great measure for engaging advantageously in those studies which are proper and useful for all men, and especially so, for one holding the important office of commander in the Navy; yet it is certainly in his power, to avoid that kind of reading which tends to incapacitate him still farther for useful studies, and to increase his distaste to all works of science, and plain unadorned literature. How much more in character would a commander appear, engaged in those dignified pursuits, which give him a claim to respect from all who know him, and especially from those under his command, than in such employments as cleaning shells, nursing birds, and others of a similar kind? And instead of spending his time in reading the most extravagant, and useless works of fiction, how much better would it be, not only for himself, but also for his country and those under his command, if he would employ his leisure hours in making himself familiar with all those branches of science which belong particularly to his profession, and in studying history, and the laws of nations? While the conversation that has given occasion to the preceding remarks, was going on in the cabin,} a Spanish boat came off from the town with an officer, who made inquiry respecting the ship, the health of the crew etc; and requested in the name of the Governor, that no boat should go ashore from the ship, till she had been visited again the next morning.

Oct. 1. Early this morning we received a visit from the Capt. of the port, accompanied by Mr. Edwards [Alfred H. P. Edwards] the American Consul, and Mr. Sturges [Henry Parkman Sturgis], another American gentleman, who had been residing at Manilla several years. Soon after these gentlemen came on board, we were visited by the Health officer, whose inquiries were answered in such a manner, as to satisfy him, that there would be no danger in our being permitted to hold communication with the town. The visit of the two Spanish officers was short, but the two American gentlemen, remained till after breakfast.

As soon as possible after the formalities of this visit were over, a boat was sent to town with Lieut. Sinclair, who waited on the Governor with the Captain's compliments, according to the usual custom on visiting foreign ports. He returned in due time, and made a very favourable report of his reception. A salute had been agreed upon, and was accordingly fired immediately after his return, consisting of seventeen guns, and was answered by the fort with an equal number. The consul accompanied Lieut. S. to the Governor's and returned with him to the ship, and soon afterwards, the Capt. & Mr. Roberts accompanied the two American gentlemen on shore, where they remained till the next day. The Consul very generously made us all welcome to his house during our stay there, and tendered his services to us in a most frank and friendly manner. Mr. Sturges also seemed equally disposed to perform offices of kindness and hospitality towards his countrymen.

Oct. 2. This morning I paid my first visit on shore; not for pleasure, but for the more important purpose of procuring supplies, of which we were greatly in want. I found the distance to be considerably greater than I had supposed; and instead of being only half an hour, as I had calculated, in reaching the landing, we were at least two hours. After rowing about three miles, we entered the mouth of the River [Pasig] between a fort on the right-hand side, and a light-house on the other. A wall on each side of the river, which was not more than the eigth part of a mile in width, gave it the appearance of an artificial canal. There is sufficient depth of water in this river for ships of a large size, and we passed several such in our progress up.

The town is situated on both sides of the river, and about half a mile from its mouth is a bridge communicating with the two parts of the town, which was constructed principally of stone, and in a very substantial and durable manner. A part of it, nevertheless, was thrown down by an earthquake in 1826, which has been since rebuilt with wood.

The view of the town that first presented itself on ascending the river, was such especially on the north side, as to give us quite an unfavorable opinion of it; the houses being all made of bamboo, and exhibiting an appearance of great poverty and negligence. As we advanced up the river, however, the aspect of the town improved considerably, and the river was lined on both sides, with large, well constructed buildings.

We ascended this river against a strong current, nearly a mile, when we landed at the residence of the consul, which was situated immediately on the left bank of the river. Here I found the Capt. Mr. Sturges, and two or three other American gentlemen. The Consul was about to accompany the Capt. on a visit to the Governor, and during their absence, I accompanied Capt. Pierce [Captain Pearce, an American skipper of the *Jeanette*], one of the gentlemen mentioned above, in a ride about the town. We crossed the bridge into the old town, or that is generally called by the people themselves, Manilla, in contra-distinction from the other part of the town, which is called the suburbs, though containing a much larger population, than the city itself.

The old town was enclosed by a wall, and surrounded by a moat or ditch, which was partly filled with water, and was ten or twelve feet deep. Over this was a draw-bridge at each of the gates of the city; but whether these were drawn up at night, when the gates were closed, I did not learn.

As we were driven rapidly through the city, I had but a very imperfect view of it; but from what I did see, I was led to conclude, that it does not differ in any important particular, from the other Spanish towns that I have seen. The houses are mostly two stories high, with balconies projecting out a few feet from the second story. There was an appearance of neatness and comfort in these houses, which gives a stranger a favorable opinion of the condition of their occupants. The street along which we passed, was very clean, and well paved.

After passing through the city, we directed our course to the calzada, or common, which is a plain of considerable extent, just without the walls of the city, and is a general place of resort in the evening, for all those who wish to enjoy the cool refreshing breezes of the evening, and to profit by that exercise, which the heat of the day had rendered impracticable. It being a little after mid-day, however, when we crossed this plain, we saw nobody there, except here and there a native pursuing his way to & from the city, and a few grazing buffaloes.

In returning, we entered the city by a different gate from that through which we had passed out, and crossing the bridge unto the suburbs, we went to the residence of Mr. Sturges, where we made a short stay, {and were very politely treated by Mr. Moore [Josiah Moore], a young gentleman belonging to the house.}

Mr. S. was from N. York, and having been several years established in business at Manilla, most of the American business passed through his hands.[2] The house which he occupied was of immense size, and served both as a dwelling & ware house. {The upper story was occupied also, as a counting house, and was so arranged as to answer most effectually, the different purposes for which it was designed.}

Having spent half an hour here, we returned to the Consul's, where we found the Capt. and Consul just returned from their call on the Governor.

The Capt. gave me a very flattering account of his reception by the Governor, who occupies the most important station, I believe, of any individual at present, under the Spanish Government.

Having accomplished the business that took me on shore, I left the Consul's a little past 2 o'clock, to return to the ship. When we went ashore in the morning, there was no wind of consequence, and the water was smoth, both in the bay & in the river; but there was now quite a fresh breeze, blowing directly against us, which raised considerable sea, even in the river, and outside, it was so high as to render boating extremely uncomfortable and even in some dangerous. At a little distance from the mouth of the river is a reef of rocks, which lay directly in our course to the ship, and which I had not noticed in the morning, there being no breakers, to point out the danger. {I steered the boat there being no other officer in it, and not being aware of any danger, I took the most direct course for the ship; and had reached the edge of the brakers, before the danger was discovered.} The sea was high, and breaking with great violence just ahead of us, and the probability is, that if we had advanced the length of the boat farther, the sea would have broke over us, and we should all have perished. The only means of escaping from this situation, was to keep the boat's head to the sea, and let her drift toward the shore; it being too rough to attempt to put her about.

In a few minutes, we drifted so far from the breakers, that we could venture to alter our course, and make head way so as to get around them. Having then passed the reef, and escaped from a situation, of considerable danger, we again shaped our course for the ship. We had been now about an hour struggling against the wind and waves, and we continued our efforts about two hours longer; when the men had become so nearly exhausted with rowing, that we scarcely made any progress, and were thoroughly drenched with the spray, which every moment broke over us. Fortunately, we were now so near the ship, that the fatigued condition of the boat's crew, was seen and a large boat, with a fresh crew was sent to our relief; and about sunset, I got safely on board.

About two weeks elapsed before my next visit on shore, during which time nothing of very material importance occurred. Three American vessels arrived from the U.S. during this period, and brought papers as late as the 9th of June [1832], but they afforded us very little news.

We learned from the Mate of one of them, however, some particulars respecting the transactions at Pulo Battoo, which gave quite a different aspect to the whole affair, from that in which we had been led to view it.

This man, who was said to be entitled to belief, stated that he was mate of an American ship at Pulo Battoo, sometime before the outrage on the *Friendship;* and that the ship to which he belonged, as well as a French vessel that was lying there at the same time, took in a cargo of Pepper and sailed without paying for it, which so enraged the natives that they determined to be revenged on the first American or French vessel that came into the harbour. It happened unfortunately, that the *Friendship* was the first vessel that visited the port after this disgraceful transaction, and underwent the threatened vengeance.

Thus it appears, if this statement is true, of which I have not the least doubt, that a most base and culpable fraud on our part, has led to the slaughter of several of our own countrymen, in the attack on the *Friendship,* and to the destruction of a large number of the natives by the *Potomac.*[3] How such conduct on our part is to be justified, and made to accord with our professions of strict regard to the rights of others, I know not; but probably in the same manner, that the stronger has always justified measures of tyranny & oppression toward the weak, namely, by making power the criterion of right, and the sole rule of action.

Indeed, if the information, respecting the cause of the outrage on the *Friendship,* and of the subsequent proceedings, is correct, I know of no instance in which power has been more unequivocally made the sole measure of right, and in which the interests of the stronger, have been pursued, with less regard to the rights and interests of the weaker, than in this. A most gross fraud had been committed on our part, such as would have led to a demand for ample reparations, if we had been the injured party, and if this had been refused, a declaration of war would have followed; but, because the despised people against whom this fraud has been committed undertake to retaliate, as might have been expected, and some of our countrymen unfortunately lose their lives, an armed force is sent out, with orders, {not to investigate the case from the beginning, and to adopt such measures as strict impartial justice would require;} but to demand in positive terms the surrender of the individuals who had been concerned in the affair of the *Friendship,* and in case of refusal, to attack & destroy the town. {These orders were strictly complied with.} The demand for the surrender of those who had been the principal agents in the unhappy affair of the *Friendship,* was not complied with, on the ground, that it was not known who those individuals were; and consequently the town was attacked, and a hundred and fifty of the natives were killed.[4]

Now, if here is not an arbitrary display of power, and a full exemplification of the principle on which those who possess superior power, act towards those who are not in a condition to defend themselves; I know not where an instance of it can be found.

And with regard to the policy of this summary mode of inflicting punishment upon those who are accused of having invaded our rights, I think there is reason to apprehend that it will be found to be the worst that could have been adopted. So far as concerns only the Sumatrans, perhaps the policy which led to the destruction of a whole village, as the punishment of a few individuals, may succeed to the satisfaction of those who adopted it; inasmuch as the tremendous vengeance with which they have been visited for daring to use the only means in their power, to obtain redress for the injury they had received, may have so terrified the natives, that they will not dare, hereafter, to complain of any fraud that may be committed upon them by Americans, or to retaliate any ill treatment which they may receive from us, however gross & unprovoked it may be.[5] But the consequences of this severe treatment of the inhabitants of Pulo Battoo, will no doubt extend beyond the limits of Sumatra; and instead of fear will excite a feeling of hostility towards Americans, which may be expected to manifest itself in similar outrages to that committed on the *Friendship*. {The news of what the *Potomac* has done, has no doubt been communicated to the Chinese Government, as well as to the Governments of Cochin-China, & Siam, and it is surely not to be expected that they will approve of such proceedings, or be deterred by fear, from pursuing measures of retaliation, whenever an opportunity may offer. And to this cause I am disposed to attribute the conduct of the Chinese authorities at Canton, towards the *Potomac,* while lying in that port, as it has been reported to us here at Manilla. According to this report, the armed boats were ordered down from Canton to Macao, where she was lying, with instructions to inquire for what purpose she came there, and the reason of her remaining so long, (she had then been sometime there) and to order her away immediately. This took place, it is stated, on the 8th of Sept. and the *Potomac* sailed on the 15th.}[6]

Oct. 15. On this day I made another visit on shore, for the purpose of attending the Consul & the Capt. in a call on the Governor; it being the birthday of the King of Spain, and the Governor holding a levee for receiving the salutations of all who chose to call upon him. We happened, however, to be a little after the hour appointed, though by no means too late, the Capt. had become impatient, and had gone before we reached the Consul's where he & Mr. Roberts had been staying from the time of our arrival in the port.

In a short time they returned, without having seen his excellency; {and to my regret, I found that a paroxism of ill humor had seized the Capt. which urged him to the use of such language, and the exhibition of such feelings as are exceedingly improper in any man, and especially so in a commander. The cause of this, was the course which had been pursued respecting a man who had died of the cholera, the night before.

It being important, as it appeared to the first Lieut. and myself, to prevent any report of the cholera being on board, reaching the town; we thought it best to bury the man in the harbour, at the distance of a mile or two from the anchorage, and so early in the morning; that it would not be observed by any of the vessels in the harbor. This course was adopted by the first Lieut. in pursuance of my advice; but not till he had sent word to the Capt. of the man's death, and requested directions respecting his burial. Being confident, that the course pursued would be that which he would direct, it was thought best not to wait for the boat to return with his directions; especially as several of the natives would be on board before the boat could return, and seeing the body, as they probably would, it was apprehended, that they would carry such a report on shore, as would occasion us a good deal of trouble, and perhaps lead to our being ordered immediately to leave the port. For these reasons it was thought best to have the body taken out as early as possible, a mile or two from the ship, and committed to the deep; which was accordingly done before sunrise, by the first Lieut. himself. Soon afterwards a message came from the Capt. that he wished the man to be buried on shore, and should request the Consul to take the necessary steps to have it done as soon as possible.

Upon the receipt of this message, the first Lieut. addressed him a note, stating that by my advice, he had buried the man in the harbor; presuming at the same time, that if he had been on board, he would have pursued the same course. This note he had just received, when I met him; and as may be supposed his resentment was aimed principally at me. It appeared that he had been put to the trouble of rising from his bed a little earlier than usual, and the Consul had also been put to the greater trouble of going first, to the Alcalde & the undertaker, to make arrangements for the burial, and again, to counteract the orders that he had given. This was the whole amount of the evil that had been done, and as this had resulted from our being actuated by what seemed to be the best motives, there was no reason whatever, for the Capt. to get angry about it. He nevertheless, was very much excited, and showed all the petulance of an ungoverned child when something has happened contrary to his wishes. I cared not at all for his rage but stated to him plainly, the motives which had led me to give the advice I had done to the first Lieut. and which I was satisfied were perfectly proper, considering all the circumstances of the case; and having done this, I left him, and the conference ended.

I mention these particulars, which to one not immediately interested, must appear very trifling, for the purpose of showing what an irascible man we have for a commander, and how much trouble and vexation the merest trifles may occasion, when operating through the medium of such a temperament. This was the first time that he had addressed me in the language of anger, and I hope it will be the last; but whatever course he may choose to take, I shall endeavor to discharge my duty to the best of my ability, and whenever circumstances may require, I shall give such advice to himself or others, as a sense of duty may seem to render expedient.

I had the mortification also to find, that the Capt. had communicated a portion of his resentment to the Consul, and I consequently met with rather a cold reception from him. A statement of the particulars, however, which have been already mentioned, was sufficient to restore him to his usual good humor.

As usually happens with persons of a very excitable temperament, the flame which had so rapidly kindled in the Capt. quickly subsided; and then his conduct became exceedingly conciliating and polite. It is impossible, however to derive any satisfaction from associating with a man who suffers his passions to govern him on every occasion, and who is constantly upon the watch, lest he should be treated with less respect than he considers himself entitled to.} I therefore spent the day with very little satisfaction; and if there had been a boat on shore that I could have returned to the ship immediately after my interview with the Capt. I should have done so, and relieved myself from the disagreeable necessity of spending the day in his company. With respect to the Consul, it gives me pleasure to say, that he did all in his power to make the day pass pleasantly, and to have the occurrence of the morning forgotten. He had expected that five or six of the officers of the ship would accompany the Capt. on his visit to the Governor, and had provided dinner for them, and also invited several others of our countrymen to join the party at dinner.

After dinner, he procured carriages, and we took an excursion to the calzada, and returned through the city, or the old town, where a procession was about forming in honor of the day, which we stopped to witness. Finding the streets very much thronged, so that our carriages could not readily pass, we left them and made our way through the crowd some distance on foot, and then stopped at the house of a Spaniard, where we could very conveniently view the procession as it passed. After waiting here about half an hour, the procession began to move along. First came several hundred soldiers, in two columns, one on each of the sidewalks of the street, and each soldier carrying a lighted taper. Next came a hooded friar in the middle of the street, preceding an image as large as life, of some saint, borne on four men's shoulders, and very gorgeously arrayed. This was succeeded by a band of music, and after the music came the image of another canonized bishop, as appeared from his mitre and crozier. Next followed a college of young canons, or divinity students, with their green frocks, and red bands, each bearing a lighted taper, and then came the image of the Virgin most splendidly arrayed in gold & jewels. The bishop, walking under a canopy supported by four bearers, closed the procession.

The crowd that followed the procession was very great, so that it was some time before we could venture out to look for our carriages. And when the crowd had dispersed, and we were about to go, we found to our surprize, that a table had been set for supper, and furnished with every thing that was inviting to the taste, of which we were most politely requested by the proprietor of the house, to partake. As we had just dined, we excused ourselves and took leave; the hospitable Spaniard, making us a tender, according to the Spanish custom, of his house, and all it contained.

Having found our carriages, we commenced our return to the Consul's but finding the narrow passage through the gate of the city, and in its neighborhood, still thronged with people, our progress for some time was very slow. At last, however, we got clear of the crowd, and reached the Consul's residence between 8 & 9 o'clock.

On reflecting upon the scene which we had witnessed, I was led to the conclusion, that it was calculated rather to gratify the populance, and by that means, to maintain their attachment to the Romish Church, than to promote the cause of true piety, and the best interests of the religion of the Bible. Indeed, it appears to me, that most of the external display of the Romish Church in processions, ceremonies, etc, is designed to influence principally that class of people who are governed rather by what they see & hear than by the dictates of reason and conscience. And however childish, and even ridiculous, such exhibitions as that which I have described, may appear to those whose minds are sufficiently enlightened to be able to form correct opinions on the subject of religion, and who require nothing advent[it]ious, no gilded trappings, to recommend it to their attention; yet, I have not the least doubt, but that the influence of such displays on a larger proportion of those who witness them, is salutary; and probably nowhere more so, than in Manilla.

The whole of that class of the population, on whom exhibitions of this kind could be expected to exert much influence, is composed of the natives of the island, who of course, are extremely ignorant on all subjects, and especially on the subject of religion, as it is contained in the Word of God. These people have been prevailed on to abandon their idolatry, and to attach themselves to the Romish Church; but as their conversion from idolatry to the Romish religion, could not be the result of investigation, in as much as very few of them possess sufficient knowledge to read & judge for themselves, and even those few are not permitted to do so; it is reasonably to be supposed, that their attachment to this Church is weak, and requires all the art and management that can be employed, to maintain it. Hence it is, that a large number of the natives, have been induced to enter the clerical profession, which is said to be highly gratifying to the great body of their countrymen; and hence also the policy of employing those adventitious aids, which are calculated to strike the imagination & feelings of those who are governed rather by their senses than by reason & reflection.

Such a policy, and such measures, may seem to us Protestants, to be highly reprehensible, and abstractly considered, perhaps they are so, but if all the circumstances connected with the subject as it respects Manilla, are taken into view, I am disposed to think that a different conclusion will be drawn. It is evident, in the first place, that the people of the island are in a much better condition under the present government of Spain, than they would be, if left to govern themselves; it is therefore for the interest of the natives, that the present government should be maintained. But the government cannot be main[tain]ed, unless the great body of the people belong to the established Church; for let idolatry become the universal religion of the people, as it formerly was, and the Spanish authority would immediately cease, and probably all Spaniards, as well as other foreigners, would be either murdered or driven from the island. It is therefore best that the attachment of the people to the established religion, should be maintained. And this, as I have already attempted to show, cannot, in the present unenlightened state of the public mind on the subject of religion, be effectually accomplished, without the aid of the extrinsive means which I have mentioned.

Thus, it appears, that until the minds of those who are most under the influence of the ceremonies and pompous display of the Romish Church, become sufficiently enlightened to be acted upon through the agency of reason, and common sense, the policy of which I have been speaking, is by

no means to be condemned; but on the contrary, is deserving of the approbation and support of all who have an interest in it.[7]

Oct. 18. An invitation having been given by Mr. Strachan, a Scotch-merchant
of Manilla, and his lady, for the officers of the ward-room to dine with them
on this day; as many of us as could leave the ship, accepted the invitation,
and went to the dinner. We left the ship at 2 o'clock, and landed at the
Consul's little past 3 where we joined the Capt. Mr. Roberts, & the Consul,
and about 4 o'clock proceeded to the house of Mr. Strachan. The party from
the ship consisted of Lieutenants Sinclair, Brown [Lt. William H. Brown,
acting Master of the *Peacock*] & myself. The Marine officer, who was on
shore, was also one of the party at dinner. At the house of Mr. Strachan, we
had the pleasure of meeting two ladies, the first we had seen for several
months, namely Mrs. Strachan, the lady of the house, & Mrs. McDonald,
the wife of Capt. McDonald [Capt. McDonnell], of the English merchant
service. We had also the satisfaction to meet there the Capt. & some of the
officers of H. B. M. Ship *Alligator*, which ship had arrived in the harbor a
day or two before. {Besides the persons whom I have mentioned, were our
countryman, Mr. Sturges, and a Scotch resident by the name of Butcher.}
At five o'clock we sat down to the table, and rose from it a little past seven.
{During the entertainment hilarity prevailed, as usual where the bottle is
made to circulate freely, and the utmost cordiality and good feeling were
exhibited in the conduct of the officers of the two nations towards each
other.}

This was the first time that I had ever had an opportunity of meeting
English officers on terms of social intercourse; and I was much pleased to
witness such a reciprocal display of kind and friendly feeling. I was particularly pleased with the sentiments of Capt. Lambert [Capt. George Robert
Lambert] in the toasts which he gave; not only on account of the regard
which he expressed for the U. States, but also on account of the very
handsome language in which his sentiments were conveyed.

I happened to be seated at table next to Mr. Butcher, who had resided
at Manilla from 1826; and I took the liberty to propose many inquiries to
him respecting the place and people, which he was undoubtedly well qualified to answer correctly. His communications to me were full and free on
all the subjects proposed to him; but I discovered in the course of the
evening, that freedom of speech in relation to the measures of the Government, is not fully enjoyed there. From the representations of this gentleman
it appears, that the course of measures pursued by the Government both

with regard to the natives, and to foreigners, including even Spaniards themselves, is as erroneous as could well be conceived. It seems to be the design of every measure that is or has been, adopted within a long period, to prevent improvement of every kind, as much as possible, by imposing such restraints on commercial, and agricultural enterprize, as in a great degree to check every kind of exertion.

The civil authority of Manilla, as indeed of the whole island of Luconia, of which it is the capital, and also of all the other Philippine islands, is vested, almost exclusively in a Governor, whose title is, "Governor & Commander in chief, of the land and naval forces of the Philippine islands". But I was informed, and no doubt the information was correct, that the reins of government are almost entirely in the hands of the clergy. If clerical rule is any where to be preferred to civil, I believe it is at Manilla, where the great body of the people are much more easily wrought upon by the promises and threatenings of the Church, than by the denunciations of the Laws.

The clergy are said to be very numerous, at the head of whom is an Arch-Bishop, who in nominal rank is equal to the Governor, and is the only individual, besides his excellency, who is permitted to ride in a carriage drawn by four horses. There is also a Bishop there, and both these dignitaries, as well as a few of the subordinate clergy are European Spaniards. The Capt. called, with the Consul, on the Arch-Bishop, and they found him to be a very affable intelligent man.

Monachism seems still to prevail to a very considerable extent at Manilla, there being five convents of different orders for men, besides some for women, though the number of nuns is much smaller than that of the monks.

There are no public seminaries of learning for males; but for females I was informed that there are several, where a useful course of instruction is pursued. Of this, however, there is reason to entertain some doubt, since a branch of knowledge so important as that of geography is so much neglected, that the best informed both among the men and women, scarcely understand the meanings of the simplest terms made use of in that science.

The interests of science and literature appear to be objects of very subordinate consideration with the Spanish Government, in comparison of its pecuniary interests; at least with respect to the inhabitants of its foreign possessions. And notwithstanding it might be supposed that the measures pursued at Manilla, are such, as almost entirely to defeat the object of revenue; yet such is the fertility of the island of Luconia, and the consequent extreme cheapness of its principal productions, that in spite of all the obstacles thrown in the way of trade, the revenue derived from it amounts to about half a million of dollars annually, besides the expenses of the Government.

The principal articles produced for export are sugar & hemp. Of the later, about twenty thousand peculs, of a hundred & forty pounds each, were exported in 1831, and in 1832, about twice that amount. The amount of sugar exported I did not learn.

Coffee is beginning to be cultivated for exportation, but the quantity exported is yet very small. With the view to promote the production of this article, a liberal bounty is said to have been offered by the Government, to the first man who should form a plantation of fifty thousand trees. This bounty has been lately awarded to a Frenchman near the lake Passig, who has completed a plantation of sixty thousand trees.

The population of Manilla, is much greater than I had supposed, being at least two hundred thousand. This includes, however, the population of the suburbs, which properly constitute a part of the city; though the citizens themselves, when they speak of the city of Manilla, mean only the old walled town, the population of which is about twelve thousand. The suburbs are divided into several parishes, which are distinguished by different names, as the different wards of one of our large cities, are distinguished by their numbers. The old town, or Manilla proper, is situated on the south side of the river Passig, which may be about two hundred yards wide; and the suburbs or new town, occupy the other bank. Here most of the business is transacted, and foreign merchants, I believe, have their residences here.

With respect to climate, my intelligent informant assured me, that there was as little disease in Manilla which could be attributed to the influence of climate, as he had ever known in any place where he had resided. No epidemic disease had ever been known there except the cholera in 1821, and the place is almost wholly exempt from fevers, and consumption, the diseases which prove fatal to so many both in Europe and the U. States.

A few cases of cholera occur there every year, and in some years the number of cases had been considerable; but the disease has always been confined, almost exclusively to the lower class of people, to those who are exposed to the heat of the sun by day, and to a cool damp air by night, and who live most irregularly. This disease is much less dreaded here, than it is in Europe & the U. [States], it admitting generally of a cure, if medical aid is obtained in season. It was represented to me as being less destructive since 1821, even when most prevalent, than the Typhus fever has been in the large cities of Europe. But it is, nevertheless; a terrible disease, and I had unfortunately too much opportunity to learn from my own observation; and although it may be more easily cured than typhus fever, if remedies are administered in season, yet it is only within a very few hours of the attack, that remedies can avail any thing; the system becoming very soon so extremely prostrated, that nothing can act upon it.

It has been mentioned that Capt. McDonald of the English merchant service, was at this dinner; of whom I shall now make some farther remarks. He was from the Sandwich islands [Hawaiian Islands] about three months before, and seemed to be well acquainted with our missionaries there, and spoke of them very freely. I am sorry to say, however, that the terms which he used to represent their character and conduct, were such as to exhibit them in the most unfavourable light. He did not scruple to say, that instead of teaching the natives, as well as by their example as by precept, to abstain from all dissolute and licentious practices, they committed themselves, almost as openly as the natives had ever done, those very acts, which have constituted the principal vices of the natives. This gentleman stated farther, that he had read Mr. Stewart's Journal,[8] and pronounced it to be as complete a falsehood, so far as respected the Sandwich islands, as ever was published. He spoke particularly of what Mr. Stewart says of our Consul there, Mr. Jones [John C. Jones, Jr.], whom he represented as one of the most generous & hospitable men in the world; about whom, nevertheless, Mr. S. has most grossly abused. Capt. Finch [Capt. William Compton Bolton Finch], was also included in this charge of ill treatment to Mr. Jones.[9]

Now with respect to the truth of these assertions of Capt. McDonald, it is of course, out of my power to decide; but, without supposing this gentleman to have intentionally misrepresented any thing, I can very easily believe, that his representations are very far from the truth.[10] Indeed, it is altogether easier for me to suppose, that he was mistaken, in consequence of having viewed every thing at the islands through the medium of self-interest, than that both Capt. Finch and Mr. S. should repay with deliberate ill-treatment, the kind and hospitable attentions which they had received from Mr. Jones. And as to the licentious conduct of the Missionaries, I am disposed to believe, that Capt. McDonald founded his assertion upon the malicious report of some person at the islands, who was interested in traducing their character. {But however this may be, I must declare, that while I have no reason to doubt Capt. McDonald's regard for truth, I cannot give credit to his report respecting the missionaries, until I have more conclusive evidence of the facts alleged against them.}

Capt. M‹Donald had been trading some years to the Sandwich Islands, and might therefore be supposed to feel deeply interested in all the transactions there by which trade could be affected; and it may be likewise reasonably concluded, that almost in proportion to the success of the missionaries in enlightening and christianizing the natives, would be the diminished facility with which foreigners could take advantage of them in trade.

Hence the almost uniformly unfavourable reports of traders to those islands, respecting the improvement that has resulted from the labours of the Missionaries. And that Capt. M‹D. was not an exception from this charge, was evident to me, from the reply that I received from his chief mate to an inquiry which I made of him respecting the state of things at the islands.

On the same day that I dined with Capt. M‹D. and before I went ashore I was called upon by his chief mate, to visit one of the crew; and on my [way] to the ship, I remarked to the mate, (who by the bye, was a Connecticut man, and had been trading some years to the Sandwich Islands) that I presumed great improvement had been made in the character and conduct of the natives; but to this remark he made no direct reply, though from what he did say, and his manner of saying it, he gave me reason to conclude, that a change had indeed taken place among the natives, which he could not deny to be an improvement, but of which he was unwilling to speak favourably; because this had proved prejudicial to his pecuniary interests. The sentiments of this man in relation to the Sandwich Islands, are undoubtedly those of a very large proportion of all those who trade there, and from what I have witnessed myself, and learned from others, I have not the least doubt, that those persons would much rather that the natives of those islands should remain forever in their original state of ignorance and barbarism, than that their minds should be enlightened by divine truth, and their conduct regulated by the precepts of the gospel; because, in their original state, they knew so little of the value of property, that a string of beads, or a knife would purchase as much from them as ten dollars will now.[11]

I am sorry to have reason to speak in such terms of any class of my fellow men, and especially of my own country-men; but since I have been led to speak on the subject, I must relate the truth, however hard it may bear upon those individuals implicated in the charge contained in the preceding remarks.

It has been mentioned that the wife of Capt. McDonald was one of the party at Mr. Strachan's. This lady had accompanied her husband in his voyages during the last three years; and it had happened, that all their children, three in number, were born at sea. The youngest, about a month old, was born off Van Dieman's Land [Australia], on their passage from the Sandwich Islands. In answer to my inquiry how she liked being at sea, she replied, that as she was with her husband, she liked it very well, implying that she would rather submit to the privations, and encounter the dangers of the seaman's life in the company of her husband, than remain at home without him. She was probably not singular in this, there being many wives, {and my own, I will venture to say, of the number,} who would rejoice to be permitted to accompany their husbands in all their wanderings, however distant and hazardous they might be.

{Such is the sum of the information which the entertainment at Mr. Strachan's gave me an opportunity to acquire, and such are the remarks which were suggested by the communications that were made to me, by the gentlemen whose names I have mentioned. Being desirous to return on board as early in the evening as possible, I left the house of our hospitable host very soon after rising from the table; and a boat being ready, we reached the ship about 9 o'clock.}

Oct. 23. {On this day I had again to encounter the petulance and folly of the Capt. and on no other account, than because I had endeavoured to perform my duty, in recommending measures for the preservation of the lives and health of the officers and men belonging to the ship.} Two cases of Cholera had occurred the day before, one of which had terminated fatally, and the other was about to terminate in the same manner; and becoming at this time, notwithstanding the case of cholera which had previously occurred, one of which had terminated fatally, he persisted in his determination to let the crew go ashore on liberty, {and this without saying a word to me on the subject.} I addressed him the following letter, which was the cause of his anger.

U.S. Ship *Peacock*
Manilla, Oct. 22, 1832

"Sir:

Having been just informed by Mr. Cunningham, that you have directed him to allow the men to go ashore here on liberty; I am induced by a sense of duty, to address you on the subject, and apprize you of the danger with which such indulgence will be attended. You will perceive by the sick-report of this day, Sir, that two cases of the Cholera have occurred since last evening, one of which has terminated fatally, and the other will probably terminate in the same manner before night. These as you know, Sir, are not the first cases that have occurred on board, and there is no reason to believe that they will be the last.

With respect to the causes of this disease, my opinion is, that they exist to a considerable degree, in the atmosphere; but it is certain that there are other causes which frequently induce it in those who would otherwise be likely to escape it, and which always greatly aggravate it. Of these, the principal are all kinds of irregularity, & excess, especially in drinking.

Now, Sir, knowing, as you do, the habits of sailors, it must be perfectly obvious to you, that there would be great danger of this disease being increased to a most alarming extent, if the permission which you have given, for the men to be allowed liberty on shore, were to be acted upon. You will therefore perceive, Sir, the reason & propriety of my recommending, as I do in the strongest terms, that this liberty be withheld, until we arrive in a port, where it can be allowed with less danger than would attend it here.

And I take the liberty farther to recommend, Sir, that, as the cause of the Cholera exists principally in the atmosphere, as I have already observed, and as the other cases of disease that have occurred on board have been gradually assuming a more severe character, we leave this port as soon as possible".

I am very respectfully,
Sir, your obed^t Servt
B. Ticknor
Surgeon"

Capt. D. Geisinger
Manilla

This letter reached him in the evening, and early the next morning he came on board, and most unexpectedly expressed a high degree of displeasure, at my having written him such a letter; complaining particularly of my having written in stronger terms than the occasion required; in such terms, as he petulantly said, as I would have used in writing to a Turk. I replied to him, that the letter was respectful in its style, and as to my having written in strong terms, I felt it my indispensable duty to do so, as I had reason to believe, that he had resolved to let the crew have liberty on shore whatever the consequence might be. He then observed that the letter might be transmitted officially to the Navy Department, and would represent his conduct in an unfavourable light; to which I replied, that I was perfectly willing the letter should go to the Department to be judged of these or by any body else, being fully assured that taking all the circumstances into consideration, no one would say that I had exceeded my duty.[12] {I shall repeat no more of this conference, which was terminated as soon as possible by my leaving the cabin; though not till the storm had considerably subsided, and he began to appear sensible, that, if he had no reason to thank me for what I had done, he certainly had no reason to be angry, knowing perfectly well, that I had been actuated by which I believed to [be] the best motives. Soon after this interview ended, he left the ship and returned to town; but in the mean time, he came to me, and in a very placid manner, told me, that any thing I thought proper to recommend for the health of the crew, should be promptly attended to.

Now, with respect to these disagreeable occurrences, it became perfectly evident to me, that the Capt. in order to gratify the men, and by that means to obtain popularity among them, had determined at all events, to let them go ashore; and that, notwithstanding he told me during our conference, that a mere hint from me on the subject would have been sufficient, he would never have consulted me about it, even after having been apprized by the Consul and others, of the fatal consequences which frequently resulted from sailors going ashore there on liberty. Such, I have not the least doubt, was his determination at the time he received my letter; but after being thus warned of the danger of persisting in his purpose in such terms as the case obviously required, he dared not incur the responsibility of carrying his purpose into execution; for he knew very well that if he did, and any bad consequence had followed, a representation would have been made to the Government, which would probably have cost him his commission.}

Oct. 31. On this day the sixth fatal case of cholera terminated, after a continuance of about twenty-four hours. The subject of it was the Ward-Room Steward [Lewis Johnston], who had been some time suffering under a complaint of the bowels, but without having reported himself, or omitting the performance of his duties. At two o'clock in the morning of the 30th. while I was watching with the sick, he came to me complaining of feeling very bad; and I saw at once that he was labouring under all the symptoms of cholera in its worst form. The pulse was like a vibrating thread, the skin was cold & covered with a clammy sweat; the countenance was sunken & ghastly, and the prostration was so great that he was scarcely able to stand. {I administered immediately a large dose of laudanum & peppermint, and directed him to get into his hammock, and keep as still as possible. Directly afterwards he was seized with spasms in the extremities,} and notwithstanding the diligent use of all the means that seemed most likely to afford relief, {as laudanum, ether, cajeput oil, & brandy in large doses; sulph. of Morphine carb. Ammon. & Camph. in such doses as the stomach would bear; and strong frictions with volat. linam. containing large proportions of tinct. opii, together with sinapisms to the stomach & extremities;} he continued to sink till 5 o'clock the next morning, when he expired.[13]

During this man's illness, and that of another man who died in the evening of the 30th. the Capt. came on board, and accidently saw them, and was most forcibly struck with the sight. He now became sensible, that the cholera, of which he had been disposed to make light after the first case occurred, was in reality a most terrible disease, which ought by all possible means to be prevented. Now he was convinced, as was full manifested in his conduct, that the strong language of my letter, which had given him such umbrage, was not stronger than the occasion called for; {and he was ready to do every thing in his power, to hasten our departure from the port, and to prevent the occurrence of any more cases of a disease, which had exhibited to his casual view, a greater degree of malignity, than he could possibly have conceived of.}

On the same day that our steward died I made my last visit on shore, I stopped in my way to town, on board the American ship *Romulus* [Capt. Harding], to visit some of her crew, who had been sick for some time, and been visited the day before by my assistant. This ship arrived two days before from N. York, after a passage of 152 days. She received some damage on the passage, which caused her to leak so much, that it became necessary to throw a part of the cargo overboard.[14] Her crew began to get sick about the time of passing the straits of Sunda, and before she reached Manilla, one had died. Besides six or seven cases of dysentery, one of which was very bad, and seemed to be going on to a fatal termination, I found one poor fellow labouring under organic disease of the heart, which was attended with much distress, and must inevitably terminate fatally, and that probably in a short time. Notwithstanding his sufferings, however, of which some idea may be formed from the fact, that the motions of the heart were so violent as to be seen distinctly to the distance of twenty-feet; this poor fellow had been kept hard at work, from the belief, on the part of his commander, that his complaint was in part feigned, or at any rate, that it was no worse then than it had been for several years.

I do not mention this with the view of attaching any blame to Capt. Harding, who seemed to be a humane, and professed to be a pious man; {but to show with what suffering this man must have performed his duty from the time that his heart became thus diseased, which he said was about four months. The patient himself seemed to be as little aware of his real situation as the Capt. but I endeavored to undeceive them both, and assured the patient that the disease under which he was labouring, would certainly carry him off, and probably in a short time too, unless he discontinued every kind of labour, and kept himself as quiet as possible; and Capt. H. was told unequivocally, that there was no deception in this case, which was of a most serious character, and must totally exempt the man from every kind of labour.

Having performed the service that was required of me on board the *Romulus*, I proceeded on my way to town and arrived at the Consul's about 1 o'clock, where I found Mr. Roberts; the Consul & Capt. being absent on a visit to the Governor. They returned in a short time, however, and I was pleased to find that the impression which the sight of the two dying men had made upon the Capt. the day before, still remained in such force, as to cause him to make every effort in his power to leave Manilla the next day. His conduct towards me was now courteous and conciliatory almost in the extreme; and he made it perfectly manifest to me, that he regretted having remained so long in port, after having been warned of the danger of doing so.

After remaining a short time at the Consul's I went to the residence of Mr. Sturges, where I dined, and remained till about 5 o'clock in the afternoon. Here I met with the supercargo of the *Romulus*, and Capt. Hamet of the American ship *Fanny* from N. York, both of whom left the U. States about the first of July [1832], and brought later news than any we had received. It appeared from the reports of these gentlemen, as well as from the latest papers, that the alarm excited in some of our cities, N. York especially, by the Cholera having appeared in Canada, had considerably subsided.}

Since I have mentioned the subject of Cholera, it will not be considered improper, I trust, if I give an account of the disease as it appeared on board our ship. The first case that occurred, was that of an infirm old man, and proved fatal in fifteen hours.[15] He was attacked soon after making a hearty dinner, with the usual symptoms and before I could get to him, although called immediately, he had become unable to stand, and could scarcely raise his head from the deck, on which he was lying. His general appearance was then, within fifteen minutes of the attack, that of a dying man. The pulse could scarcely be felt, his whole surface was cold and bedewed with a profuse clammy sweat; and of a livid color; his eyes were sunken & countenance livid & ghastly; spasms were commencing in the lower extremities, which soon affected, not only all the limbs, but also the muscles of the abdomen, and caused such excruciating agony, that it required several men to keep the patient in his hammock. The evacuations were at first copious & watery; but they soon ceased, and did not recur. The treatment consisted in the exhibition of laudanum, ether, cajeput oil & brandy, in doses proportioned to the urgency of the case—that is, from ziss to zij of laudanum, zi of ether, & 40 or 50 drops of cajeput oil, with half a wine glass ful of brandy. Strong frictions with tinct. of opii were used at the same time to the limbs & body. But notwithstanding the diligent use of all these means, the powers of life gradually failed; the patient fell into a state of perfect insensibility, in which he continued till he expired. Such were the principal features of the first case of this terrible disease that I had ever seen, and I had no hesitation in pronouncing it a case of genuine Asiatic Cholera, and expected that it would be succeeded by others of the same character.[16]

This expectation was realized, to my sorrow, for scarcely a day passed after the occurrence of the first case, that one or more of the crew was not labouring under the disease in such a form, as to keep me in a constant state of anxiety, both day & night. On the occurrence of the second and third of the fatal cases, which came on within a few hours of each other, I sent my Assistant on shore, not being able to leave the ship myself, to consult with a Portuguese Physician, who had been long resident in Manilla, and who had seen much of the Cholera both there & else where and was said to be very successful in his treatment of it. This gentleman very frankly communicated to Dr. Gilchrist all the information respecting the disease & its treatment that we desired and I was surprized, as well as gratified to find, that his mode of treatment was precisely that, in every particular, which I had pursued. So exactly alike indeed, were our modes of treatment, that if one had been copied from the other, they could not have been more so.

It is not my intention, however, to write a treatise on this disease here;

and I shall therefore conclude my remarks on the subject, with observing, that there was a strong predisposition to the disease in all on board, which was manifested by a sense of oppression at the stomach, accompanied with more or less nausea, and a great degree of lassitude. {This may have been partly owing to mental causes, as all were more or less under the influence of alarm which always tends to derange the stomach, and through the medium of that, to impair all the powers of the system;} but it was owing principally to some other cause, and that cause existed, no doubt, in the atmosphere.

Nov. 2. Every thing being at last ready for our departure from Manilla, we took advantage of a favourable breeze that sprung up in the afternoon, and at five o'clock weighed anchor and stood out to sea. In leaving the harbour, we passed very near to the British ship *Alligator,* and the officers of the two ships exchanged adieus and good wishes, with as much seeming cordiality and good feeling, as if all had belonged to the same nation. From the time the *Alligator* arrived in port, there had appeared a strong disposition on the part of her commander and officers, to cultivate a good understanding with us; and I hope that our conduct towards them was such, as to make it manifest that we were actuated in an equal degree by the same desire.

Having thus taken leave of our English friends, and parted with the Consul, and two other Americans who had come on board to see us off; we spread all our canvass to the wind, and proceeded rapidly out of the harbour.

Never before did I experience greater satisfaction on leaving port, than at this time; for I had never left a port before, where I had suffered more from anxiety, and a hot suffocating climate, than at Manilla. My anticipations with regard to this place, had been entirely disappointed; for I had expected to find the climate good, and to be able to enjoy some satisfaction in going ashore there. But instead of this, the climate was about as hot and uncomfortable as any that I had ever experienced; and besides being confined most of the time to the ship, in consequence of the Cholera being on board, I met with nothing on shore, when I did go, that could compensate the trouble of going & returning. {I was therefore greatly rejoiced, as were all on board, to turn our backs upon this miserable place, and none of us had the least desire ever to visit it again.}

By 9 o'clock in the evening, we had reached the island of Corregidor, at the entrance of the harbour, and soon afterwards entered the China Sea, and shaped our course for Canton.

Nov. 5. On this day we buried another man [Artemas Holt, Seaman] who died of the Cholera, after an illness of about thirty hours. This poor fellow probably fell a martyr to his imprudence in eating and drinking. He had been long labouring under disease of the stomach and bowels, which had been brought on and continued by an imprudent indulgence of his appetite, notwithstanding he had been repeatedly warned of the danger of persisting in such indulgence. Caution and advice, however, were disregarded, and he continued to drink his daily allowance of spirits, and to satiate his morbid appetite with the most improper kinds of food, until the Cholera seized him; when he became almost instantaneously prostrated to such a degree, that the most powerful means produced no sensible effect.

{Soon after this man was attacked, another was taken down with the disease in its worst form; but as his health had previously been good, and as remedies were immediately employed, his life was saved.

We had experienced a very sensible change of climate on leaving the harbour of Manilla, and had flattered ourselves, that no more cases of cholera would occur, and that those already sick, would soon regain their health. Great disappointment was therefore felt, when new cases of this terrible disease continued to occur; and when, besides, instead of the sick-list diminishing, it became considerably larger than it had been at any time before.

For about twenty-four hours after leaving port, we lay nearly becalmed, being so near the island of Luconia, which was here of considerable hight, that the N.E. monsoon, which was now blowing, could not reach us. As we receded from the island, however, the breeze, as it descended from the mountains of Luconia to sweep over the China Sea, began to fill our sails; and our progress soon became as rapid as we wished. Our course, until we reached the 18th. degree of latitude, was nearly north, in order to avoid being carried too far to the south, by the current which we expected to meet with on passing the northern extremity of Luconia.}

Nov. 7. {When we had coasted along the western side of Luconia nearly to its northern extremity, which is in about 18 degrees of north latitude, we took a northwest course, or one nearly so; and at the same time the monsoon began to freshen, and soon became so strong as to carry us along at the rate of eight or nine miles an hour. The weather was now sufficiently cool, and we all began to feel the renovating influence of a pure and temperate atmosphere.} We had not yet done with the Cholera, however, notwithstanding the great change of climate that we had experienced; for before we reached the port of Canton, another case occurred, and one of the worst too, that we had met with. But notwithstanding the disease for about twenty-four hours, resisted all the means that were employed and the patient appeared at last, to be actually in the agony of death; yet a favourable change took place, and he recovered. A more unexpected & extraordinary instance of recovery than this, I had never known.[17]

Nov. 8. We had entered the Bay of Canton in the evening of the 7th. and having advanced as far as was deemed prudent, we anchored between eleven and twelve o'clock. When we were at the distance of fifteen or twenty miles from the entrance of the bay, a Chinese boat came along side of us, and inquired if we wanted a pilot; and being told that we would take one, two men came on board, {who seemed to belong to the very lowest order of the people}, and were evidently no more pilots, than all their countrymen are who spend their lives in fishing, in the waters of the bay and its vicinity.

These aquatic people are exceedingly adroit in the management of their boats, and it was surprizing to see with what expertness they would bring their boats along side the ship, while she was moving quite rapidly through the water. So ready and quick were they in performing the manoeuvers necessary for boarding while the ship was under way, that while we were wondering at their inconsiderate rashness in coming in contact with the ship with their large boats and high masts, and supposed that their efforts would certainly fail without assistance from the ship; they had secured their boats by means of hooks to the ship's side, and were already climbing up the rigging to come on board. The boats which we saw here, though large, were light, and provided with masts and mat-sails. They were furnished with a mat roof, extending from side to side, and covering six or eight feet of the middle of the boat, and forming a secure retreat from the sun & rain. The form of these boats was that of a wedge, being quite broad at the stern, and tapering gradually to the bows.

{Before we reached the entrance of the harbour, we had several offers of pilots, and some came on board to offer their services, who appeared to be much better qualified for that employment, than the one we had taken; but as it was unnecessary to have a pilot at all, and the Capt. had taken one only because the regulations required that he should do so, if one offered, the one we had would answer our purpose as well as any other.} He could scarcely speak a single word of English, however, so that all his directions had to be communicated by signs. His demand for his services was at first twenty dollars, but he consented at last to take fifteen; which was sufficient to maintain himself and his family, if he had one, a whole year.

Early in the morning of the 8th, we weighed anchor, and stood towards Macao, on the west side of the bay; and at about 8 o'clock anchored within four or five miles of the town. After breakfast, Mr. Roberts & Lieut. Fowler went ashore there, and spent the day. They returned in the evening, but without bringing us any news.

Nov. 9. It being unsafe lying at anchor at Macao during the N.E. monsoon, that is, from October to April or May, we removed this morning to Lintin, on the other side of the bay and nearer to Canton. We anchored there about one o'clock p.m. in 10 fathoms water, and about a mile from the island on its west side.

CHAPTER VI
Lintin

Smuggling at Lintin; Party on board an English ship; Cholera;
Mrs. Heber; Party on board the *Lintin;* Walk on shore at
Lintin; Visit to Lintin Peak; Visit to Canton; Reach Whampoa;
Passage from Whampoa; Water-population; Arrival at Canton.

There were lying here eight or nine sail of American vessels, and about the
same number of English, besides several others; making the whole number
nearly thirty. All these vessels I afterwards learned, were more or less concerned in smuggling, and most of them in smuggling opium. This article
is entirely prohibited by the Chinese laws, from admission into the empire;
and yet millions of pounds are smuggled in every year, which is well known
to the mandarins or officers of the Government; but as they are much
addicted to the use of the prohibited article, they take no pains to enforce
the laws against its introduction. The price of opium, at the time we were
there, was at the rate of about four dollars & a half a pound; but it had
formerly been much higher, & sometimes as high as fourteen or fifteen
dollars a pound.

We had but a short time at anchor at Lintin, when we were visited by
several of our countrymen, masters of vessels in the harbour, and also by
several English Captains; all of whom testified much satisfaction at our
arrival, which they had been for some time expecting. Before night we were
almost surrounded by Chinese boats, with provisions & other articles for
sale, which they urged upon us with a clamorous importunity which it was
difficult to resist. So eager, indeed, were they to dispose of their articles,
that it required threats, and even actual force to prevent their coming on
board; and when they were permitted, as some of them were, to come on

149

board, they never ceased urging us to deal with them, until they were told in the most peremptory manner, that we would have nothing to do with them. Merely telling them that we did not wish to purchase the articles which they offered for sale, was not sufficient; they would pretend not to understand, and still persist in urging us to buy, till, they found by a language which they could not fail to understand, that farther importunity would be useless. Among the other boats that crowded around us in the course of the afternoon, were several with women, who had been attracted by curiosity, or very possibly by motives of a less innocent character. These females, it was evident, were of the lowest class, and therefore did not exhibit the symbols of gentility for which the Chinese ladies have been famed, namely, the small feet & long nails. {The feet of these females were of the common size, and were not encumbered by either shoes or stockings; and as their hands had to be used in the most laborious employments, their finger nails could not attain an extraordinary length.} The dress of these women was so like that of the men, that by this alone the two sexes could not be distinguished. It was chiefly in their manner of dressing their hair that the exterior of the men differed from that of the women. The former had the fore part of their heads shaved, but the hair of the back part was suffered to grow, and hung down their backs in braids, which frequently reached nearly to the ground. The latter had no part of their heads divested of this ornament of nature; but it formed a black & glossy covering which parted on the forehead, and being carried back, was formed into a braid resembling that of the men.

The dress of both sexes, consisted of a loose cotton frock, which descended about half from the hips to the knees; and of very large, loose trousers of the same material, which reached about half way from the knee to the ancle. The legs & feet of both were generally naked.

Notwithstanding these females appeared to belong to that station in life, which must in a great measure preclude enjoyment, and notwithstanding they were crowded together in their boats, like cattle huddled together in a yard, so that they had scarcely room to move; yet they seemed to be perfectly contented and happy, and amused themselves, while they were allowed to remain along side of the ship, with playing at a game resembling some of the games of cards, but with pieces of wood or ivory, which they handled with surprizing dexterity. It seemed probable that they spent the greater part of their time in these boats, although they were not of that class of Chinese, who live altogether on the water.

Among the Americans who visited us on our arrival at Lintin, was Capt. Maccondry [Capt. Frederick W. Macondray], who commanded a ship called the *Lintin*, and had been there several months engaged in a business, which though honest and probably lucrative, was nevertheless forbidden by the commercial laws of China.[1] This gentleman had his lady with him, and therefore was as contented and happy on board his ship, without any other society than such as the occasional arrival of vessels might afford, as if he had occupied a palace, and been surrounded with a multitude of people. In the evening, the Capt. Mr. Roberts and first Lieut. [Cunningham] paid a visit to the *Lintin,* and there they met some other ladies besides Mrs. Maccondry, and spent the evening in a most agreeable manner.[2]

Nov. 12. Having received an invitation two days before from Capt. & Mrs. Durant [Captain William Durant and his wife Euphemia] to spend the evening of this day on board their ship (the *Good Success*);[3] a party of us went, consisting of Lieutenants Cunningham & Fowler, and my Assistant, Dr. Gilchrist & myself, and spent the evening very pleasantly. The party there consisted of four ladies, namely, Mrs. Durant, Mrs. Lathrop & her daughter, Mrs. Rickets, & Mrs. Maccondry; and of gentlemen to the number of ten or twelve. A band of music had been collected from the vessels in the harbour, and dancing commenced soon after the company assembled, and was kept up with but little interruption till after 12 o'clock. About 11 o'clock, the company were invited to supper on the lower deck, where a table was set in as good style, and as well furnished with every thing that the appetite could desire, as we should have found on a similar occasion, at any gentleman's house on shore.

The company, with the exception of Capt. Maccondry & his lady, and the officers of our ship, were English; but the same cordiality and good feeling were manifested, as if all had belonged to the same nation. Indeed, it is impossible to meet with more polite and friendly treatment than that which we received from the English, not only at Lintin, but wherever else we had been together in port, for a sufficient length of time to permit us to become acquainted with each other. Our hostess on this occasion, was a native of India, and a very amiable, affable, and agreeable lady. Mrs. Lathrop, though an English lady, had spent several years in the U. States, and married there. Her daughter, Mrs. Rickets, was a native of Boston; and they were both very intelligent and agreeable. Mrs. Maccondry, was a native of Taunton in Massachusetts, and deserves to be spoken of in terms of high commendation. Such were the ladies, whose society we had the pleasure of enjoying this evening, and pleasure which none of us expected to enjoy in China, nor indeed any where to the eastward of the Cape of Good Hope.

In the course of the evening I had some conversation with Mrs. Maccondry respecting the Missionaries, Mr. Bridgman [Elijah Coleman Bridgman], & Mr. Beale [David Abeel], the latter of whom was in Cochin China. Of him she spoke in high terms, and thought he was calculated to do much good among the natives, with whom his amiable manners had rendered him quite popular. She also spoke of Dr. Morrison [Dr. Robert Morrison], whose services she had frequently attended at Macao; but her account of him was not such as I expected. He did not officiate regularly, as I had supposed, to large congregations, or at least, to a considerable number of hearers; but his services were occasional only, and performed with little apparent interest, and attended by a very small number of hearers.[4]

As several of the gentlemen whom I met this evening, had been long in India, employed either in the service of the East India Company, or belonged to what is called the Bombay Marine, and were familiar with every part of India, I had an opportunity of acquiring some useful information, and among other subjects, on that of Cholera. This disease, it appeared by their accounts, had committed much greater ravages among the English seamen and soldiers at Bombay than I had supposed, from any published accounts that I had seen. They mentioned several instances, where the progress of the disease had been rapid, and the mortality great, beyond any thing that I had ever heard or read, of that or any other disease. In one instance, a vessel sailed from Bombay with a crew of about a hundred & forty men, and the first night after she left the port, the Cholera made its appearance, and by the next morning thirty-five had died. In another the deaths occurred in such rapid succession, that there were seven dead on board at one time. And on shore among the troops, the disease was equally terrible.

With respect to the treatment, so far as I could learn from these gentlemen, bleeding was very generally employed, and as I should judge, was not confined within very moderate limits, as to quantity. I draw this conclusion, from their telling me, that in the first instance which I have mentioned, that where thirty five died in one night, the deck of the ship the next morning was covered with blood; so many having their veins opened at the same time, that for want of vessels to receive the blood, it was suffered to flow on the deck. With respect to other particulars, of the treatment, if indeed other means were employed, I obtained no information; and as to that which I have mentioned, the very great & rapid mortality, affords conclusive evidence that it was not efficacious, whether it was really indicated or not.[5]

Before I conclude my remarks on the proceedings of the evening, I will mention some particulars respecting Mrs. Heber [Amelia Shipley Heber], which were communicated by Mrs. Durant, and which fully confirms the opinion I had previously formed respecting Mrs. H. The lady from whom these particulars were learned, was acquainted with the Bishop [Reginald Heber] & his lady, and said that while the Bishop was on his visit to Bombay, he became apprehensive that he should never see his family again; and wrote a farewell & most affecting letter to his wife, advising her with great solicitude, as to the manner in which he wished their children to be trained up, never once intimating the thought, that she would ever marry again. This letter she shewed to Col. Cutting, the worthy friend of her late husband and herself. But notwithstanding she seemed at first to be overwhelmed with grief, and her friends supposed that she would remain long inconsolable; yet to their great astonishment {and grief}, they saw her within two short weeks, at a party of pleasure, and dancing a quadrille. {From this fact but one conclusion can be drawn, and that is, she never loved her husband.} The same gentleman whom I have mentioned, on seeing her at this party, observed that, as far as it depended on herself, she would be a bride in two months; and her conduct since, has proved that he was right.[6]

Nov. 14. We were visited today by two English gentlemen, who were engaged in the East India Company's service, namely, Capt. Grant [Captain Alexander Grant],[7] and Mr. Cahoon [Calhoon]. The former was the senior Capt. at Lintin, and acted as a kind of Commodore, as he could issue his orders and make signals, to any of the other commanders of the Company's ships, which they were all bound to obey. The latter was a resident of Calcutta, probably a merchant, although a little tinctured with dandyism; yet he was very intelligent, and seemed to be well versed in commercial and mercantile transactions, especially with the transactions of the E.I. Company. He told me that with respect to the China-trade, our country was a century in advance of England; because with us the trade with China was not only not a monopoly, but it was as little restricted by duties as possible, whereas with them it was a strict monopoly, and was likely to remain so. {The charter of the E.I. Company was to expire in 1833, but notwithstanding the reform in parliament, he had no doubt he said, that it would be renewed, at least with respect to the China-trade. The effect of this would be, as it always had been, to benefit the individuals composing the E.I. Company, and those employed in their service, and also to benefit the U. States; but with regard to the English nation at large, its effect would be prejudicial. That such effects must result from the monopoly of a trade so important as that with China, was sufficiently obvious, from the following facts.

In the first place, as the Company encounters no competition in this trade, they charge an enormous profit on their teas, which the people of England are compelled to pay, or attain their teas from the U. States. Hence the Company is enriched at the expense of the people who pay probably at least four times as much for all the tea that is furnished by the Company, as they would if the trade with China were free. And in the second place, with regard to the U. States, the duty on teas being abolished, or so much reduced, as not to operate as a restriction, there would be a vastly greater quantity imported into the U. States, than could be consumed there; and consequently a good deal would be sent to England, where it would be sold much cheaper than that imported by the company. Hence, the U. States would be benefited by the monopoly of the Company being continued, while the great body of the English population would be injured by it.}

Having received an invitation from Mrs. Maccondry, to spend the evening of the 14th. on board the *Lintin,* a party of us went, consisting of Lieutenants Cunningham, Sinclair, & Fowler, & myself. We arrived there a little before 8 o'clock and found the company assembled on the quarter deck, which was very neatly fitted up for the occasion. The ladies who favoured us with their company this evening, were Mrs. Maccondry, Mrs. Durant, and Miss Low [Harriet Low]. The latter was the niece of a Mr. Low [William Henry Low], who had been some years a merchant at Canton, and who had a family at Macao, where all the families of foreigners are obliged to reside. Miss Low had spent about three years in the family of her uncle, and seemed to be very well contented with her situation, notwithstanding she was confined, as all foreigners were, to the limits of Macao except when she visited Mrs. Maccondry at Lintin, about fifteen miles from Macao. This young lady was one of the very few foreign females, who had ever visited Canton, the jealousy of the Chinese having always excluded European & American ladies from the empire, and suffered them to approach no nearer than Macao. But as is usually the case, the prohibition increased the curiosity of the ladies, and a party was formed at Macao, who determined at every risk, to break over the prohibition, and gratify themselves with a view of Canton.

Of this party Miss Low was one, and they succeeded in carrying their purpose into execution; but so far as I could learn, without enjoying the satisfaction which they anticipated. For although they went in disguise, yet the Mandarins were immediately apprized of their arrival at Canton; and in consequence of it, not only were they obliged to confine themselves strictly within doors during the day, and though they ventured out in the evening, their curiosity was only partially gratified; but the business of the House of Russel [Russell] and company, the principal American House in the place, was suspended by an order of the Mandarins, until the departure of the obtrusive visitors. This induced them to make a shorter visit than they otherwise would have done, though as it was, they managed to spend three weeks there; and when they returned to Macao, they went down what is called the inner passage, which has generally been carefully closed against all foreigners. This was the first party of foreign ladies, I believe, that ever entered the Celestial Empire, and will probably be the last, until an entire revolution takes place in the character and customs of the Chinese.[8]

The evening was spent on board the *Lintin* in dancing, by those at least, who could dance; and to all it passed away very pleasantly. About midnight we sat down to supper in the lower cabin where we were entertained with every thing that could be desired on such an occasion. After supper, a few songs were sung, and then the dancing recommenced, and continued about an hour; when the party broke up and dispersed. It was half past two o'clock when we reached our ship; much too late an hour for the friends of sobriety and regular habits, to return from an evening party.[9]

Nov. 16. In the afternoon of this day, I made a short excursion on shore in company with Capt. Lockwood [Captain Benoni Lockwood] of the ship *Panther* & Mr. Whitmore, a young gentleman who came out in the ship *Lion* of Providence.[10] At a small distance back from the beach where we landed, is a small Chinese village, where we found an assemblage of men, women & children, hogs, cattle & poultry grouped together in front of the dwellings, which seemed to belong almost equally, to the human & brute portions of this assemblage. I had here a demonstration of what I had been told of the dirty and disgusting habits of the Chinese. The men, women & children were all seated in the dirt when we went up to them, each with his dish of rice in one hand, and his chop-sticks in the other, with which he was throwing the rice into his mouth, so adroitly as to astonish one who had never seen it. But although excessively filthy in their persons and mode of living, yet these people were very neat in the cultivation of their gardens & fields, as we had an opportunity of observing in the course of our rambles.[11] They cultivate principally the sweet-potatoe & rice. The rice had been harvested a short time before, and the fields were just planted with the sweet potatoe. In order to derive the full benefit of irrigation, the ground had been made as nearly level as possible, by means of stone walls of a sufficient hight on the lower side to equal the descent from the upper. {Earth being brought and raised to the top of the wall, a level plot was formed, which in some places, where the descent was very gradual, was of considerable extent; but in others, where the declivity was more considerable, they were very small. This was the case especially, on the side of the mountain, for so straitened were these people for land to cultivate, that they had constructed fields or embankments, as they may more properly be called, in a ravine on the side of the mountain, and had carried them almost to its top.} They rose one above another in regular succession, and exhibited quite a verdant & pleasant prospect. To prepare the ground for the sweet potatoe, it was thrown up into ridges, about three feet appart, into which the plant was inserted; transplantation being the mode, as I was told, in which this useful vegetable was cultivated there.

In going from the beach to the village, we passed by their threshing floor, which was without shelter, and appeared to be formed of lime, and was as hard as stone, and perfectly smooth. The whole extent of this floor, comprized, as I should judge, about thirty square rods; but it was separated into several compartments, by partitions of the same material that formed the floor, and three or four inches high. There several divisions of the floor, belonged probably to the different families composing the population of the village. {Around this threshing-floor, we saw a large quantity of hay bound up in bundles of about a hundred pounds each; for which I suppose their is a market in the winter season.}

The island of Lintin exhibited on its west side where we lay, a naked and barren surface, except those places that I have mentioned; which were of very small extent compared with the whole island. The length of the island is about a mile & a half, and its breadth about one. It is high, like almost all the other islands to the eastward of the Straits of Sunda; the most elevated point being, as I should judge, at least two thousand feet. All the islands that I saw in the bay of Canton, which were very numerous, resembled Lintin, {in their appearance of barrenness, and aridity, as well as in their elevation; all of them possessing a height disproportioned to their other dimensions.}

I have mentioned that I was accompanied in this visit on shore by Capt. Lockwood & Mr. Whitmore. The latter was recently from the Sandwich

Islands, and I made inquires of him respecting the state of things there, expecting, or rather wishing, as I had no reason to suppose him unfriendly to the Missionaries, to receive from him a favourable representation. In this I was mistaken, however, for his account was quite as unfavourable as that of Capt. McDonald at Manilla. He mentioned several facts to show the correctness of his statement, and that it was not at all the result of prejudice; and among others, he adduced two, which, if really facts, prove conclusively, that the conduct of the Missionaries is deserving of censure. These were, first, selling religious tracts at a high price to the natives; and second, compelling certain individuals who professed to belong to the Roman Catholic Church, to renounce their faith and become protestants, or suffer such penalty as they chose to inflict. The individuals alluded to, were French females, and on their refusing to abjure their religion, they were compelled to labour hard all day in erecting a wall around the dwellings of the Missionaries; and according to Mr. Whitmore's account, were treated in all respects with a degree of severity, which indicated a spirit of extreme intolerance & persecution on the part of the Missionaries.[12]

Now, although I am a friend to missions, and am therefore disposed to view their conduct in as favourable a light as possible; yet, from the facts which I have mentioned, for such in substance, I must consider them, and from the other representations that have been made to me on the subject, I am constrained to believe, as I do most firmly after making every deduction for prejudice and exaggeration, that the conduct of the Missionaries has been such, as justly to subject them to censure. Perhaps it would be impossible for any men, however wise, prudent, and pious they might be, to occupy the situations which those Missionaries do, and be subjected to all the opposition and vexation, both from the foreign residents, and the natives, and at the same time to pursue a course of conduct, that should be in all respects right. But surely it is practicable for them, and it is therefore their indispensable duty, whatever their trials and vexations may be, to pursue a course of conduct, which shall in a great measure, if not entirely secure them against unfavourable reports, and lead even those who do not favour the cause in which they are engaged, to speak well of them. There is a meek, benevolent, charitable, and tolerant disposition inculcated by the Gospel, which all men must admire and praise, however hostile they may be to the Gospel itself, and to the office of those who teach it. Let such a disposition be uniformly exhibited in the conduct of the Missionaries at the Sandwich Islands; and although there might, and probably would be a few individuals who would speak evil of them, yet by a large majority, even of those who might dislike the cause which they were endeavouring to promote, they would be spoken of in terms of esteem and respect.

Nov. 20. About 12 o'clock today I received an invitation from Capt. Maccondry to join a party on an excursion to Lintin Peak, the highest point on the island. The party consisted of one lady, namely, Miss Low, and of six or seven gentlemen, besides, porters, servants etc. We left the *Lintin* at one o'clock P.M. and at half past two, reached the summit of the Peak. By pursuing an oblique winding course along the side of the mountain, and proceeding very slowly, we ascended with but little fatigue; and no one with less than Miss Low. On the summit of the Peak, we found a flat rock, of sufficient dimensions to serve us for a table; and here a cloth was spread, and a most excellent repast prepared, consisting of poultry, fish, ham, pastry etc. A variety of wines was likewise displayed on our table, and contributed their share to the pleasure that was enjoyed.[13]

From the position which we now occupied, we had a very extensive and distinct view of the bay of Canton, and of the almost numberless islands with which it is filled. The day was fine, and though the heat was rather uncomfortable while ascending the Peak, yet on its summit we enjoyed a cool refreshing breeze. {Besides the sources of enjoyment which I have already mentioned,} we had a small band of music, with which we were entertained while eating, and during the several stops that we made on our return.

Having spent about an hour on the top of the Peak, enjoying the view of the surrounding scenery as well as the good things with which our table was provided, {and for which our exercise had well prepared our appetites;} we commenced our descent about half past three o'clock, and took a different rout from that by which we had ascended. The descent was very steep, and the mountain being coated here with a short dry grass, it was difficult to keep upon our feet. Two of us supported Miss Low and succeeded in keeping her from falling.[14]

Our descent was much more rapid than our ascent, and with one exception, we reached the landing place without injury. {Capt. Daily, who was rather feeble from intermittent fever, received two falls in the course of our descent; by the first slightly injuring his knee, and by the other his nose, which caused for a short time a profuse flow of blood. A rivulet being near, however, the application of cold water soon checked the bleeding, and we proceeded without farther accident.}

Just before we reached the bottom of the Peak, we passed one of the

Chinese dwellings, where we saw and old Darby & Joan,[15] {who kindly invited us to enter and partake of some rice, the only refreshment, it was evident, which they had to offer. This invitation was declined, but the old woman observing that Miss Low appeared to be fatigued, brought out a stool, and insisted on her setting down and resting herself. For this politeness of the old lady, Miss L. was obliged to submit to the scrutiny of her curiosity;} she appeared never to have seen a white woman before. Miss L. had on a pair of white kid gloves, which first attracted the old lady's notice; and when Miss L. took them off, & handed them to her, she seemed to be doubtful whether she had not actually stripped the skin from her hands. To be satisfied whether the white and red of Miss L's complexion was not artificial, she put up her hands to examine her face; but this was rather too close a scrutiny, and leaving her gloves with the old lady, Miss L. escaped farther annoyance by our resuming our progress. Boats were waiting for us at the landing, and about sunset we arrived on board the *Lintin,* where I took tea with the ladies, and then returned to the *Peacock,* where I arrived at eight o'clock.[16]

On the 22d. of November, a party consisting of Lieutenants Cunningham, Sinclair & myself, and four Midshipmen, took passage in the American ship *Panther* for Canton. This ship was commanded by Capt. Lockwood, who had invited us to take passage with him, and by whom we were treated with a kind and generous hospitality. Besides the party from the *Peacock,* there were two other passengers, viz: Capt. Sheldon, and Capt. Benjamin; making the whole number of passengers nine, for whom Capt. Lockwood managed to provide both food and lodging in such a manner, as to render our passage up more pleasant than we could have anticipated. It was about 6 o'clock in the evening when we left the Lintin anchorage, and the wind being light, our progress was slow. This was of but little consequence, however, as we could not pass the Bogue, as the Bocca Tigris is usually called, till the next day. The tide being in our favor, and the wind, though light, assisting our progress some, we reached the Bocca Tigris, a distance of 30 miles, about midnight, where we anchored. The Bocca Tigris, or tiger's mouth, is the entrance into the Canton River, and is formed by the island of Chuen Pee on the right or east side, and Tiger Island on the other. On both these islands near the water's edge are fortifications, which if well provided with guns and men, might prevent any force from entering the river. But in the state in which we saw them, they would be able to make but a feeble opposition to any foreign foe, who might attempt to ascend the river, for the purpose of making an attack on this city. A little distance to the southward of the Bocca Tigris, are two small islands on the left hand, the southern most of which is called Sung-EEt [Long-eet], and the other Sam-Pan-Chow.

Before passing the Bogue, vessels are obliged to obtain a chop or permit from the {Chop or} Custom House on shore, which is sometimes attended with considerable delay. Our detention, however, was short, and by nine o'clock the next morning, we were ready to proceed. The weather was very fine, and the tide and wind being both in our favor, our passage up the river was as rapid as we wished, and very pleasant. Until we had passed the Bogue, all the numerous islands that we saw, presented a naked and barren surface, but as soon as we had passed the islands, which bound the entrance of the river, appearances of fertility began to meet the eye; and on the banks of the river, we began to have a view of the plains on which rice is cultivated, and which increased in extent as we advanced. At the distance of twelve or fifteen miles from the Bogue we passed a bar in the river, which is called "Second Bar," and which can be passed by large ships only at high tides. Just above this bar, were three large ships lying, belonging to the E.I. Company, waiting for an opportunity to go down. As we approached Whampoa the prospect on each side of us, became more cheering, as the rice fields became more extensive, and the distant hills exhibited a clothing of verdure {much more pleasing to the eye, than the naked, sterile surface, which constituted a principal feature of all the islands that we had seen, since entering the bay of Canton.}

Nearly equidistant from Second Bar & Whampoa, and on the summit of a hill of considerable height, on the left hand, is a Pagoda, the first that is seen in ascending the river. It was too far off to admit of my having a distinct view of it; but it probably did not differ from those which I afterwards saw, and of which I shall give a description. A little above this Pagoda is the First Bar; but this causes less obstruction to the navigation, than the other, which I have already mentioned.

By the time we had arrived within ten miles of Whampoa, we began to be surrounded with boats; in which were men, women and children, apparently as contented and happy in their floating habitations where they spend the whole of their lives, as the occupiers of the most stately mansions. These boats were mostly small, but so arranged within as to form quite a comfortable residence. This kind of boat is called Sam Pan, and is managed principally by the women. They are generally propelled by two or three oars, one of which is fixed to the stern, and is used by one of the women in sculling, at which they are remarkably dextrous. These boats have all mat roofs which afford a good protection against the sun and rain, and in the middle they have a flooring of bamboo, which is also covered with a mat. On each side of the floor is a low seat, and between that and the higher part is a partition which forms two apartments, a parlour and a kitchen, in the latter of which the cooking utensils are kept and the necessary work of the family is performed. There is more cleanliness and comfort in one of these boats, than could be supposed; and I should prefer living in one of them to living on shore in the manner that the lower class of Chinese do.

A good deal of trouble is frequently met with from these boats, by vessels passing up and down the river; for they will run along side of a ship and make fast so dextrously, that before they can be warned off, which is always done when their design to board is discovered in season, men, women and children are already on board, and commencing their thieving practices, at which they are extremely expert. Several of them attempted to board the *Panther,* but Capt. Lockwood being well acquainted with their character, kept so strict a watch over them, that they were unable to accomplish their purpose; and after hovering about the ship for sometime, they took leave of us, and made for the shore.

A little before sunset we reached the lower anchorage at Whampoa, where some of the large E.I. Company's ships were lying waiting for their cargoes. There was lying at Whampoa a fleet of from 40 to 50 vessels, of which about one half were American. They extend up & down the river a distance of about three miles, the river being narrow, and admitting of only a few vessels lying abreast. The English ships constituted the lower part of this fleet, and the American the upper. But very few vessels of other nations were to be seen there.

By the time we reached the lower part of the fleet, the wind died away; and the tide began to run down, which rendered it necessary for us to anchor, although we had not reached the position which Capt. Lockwood wished to occupy. Directly after we came to anchor, Capt. Pierce, whom I saw at Manilla the first time I went ashore there, and with whom I took a ride through the city, came on board, and gave an invitation for some of us to spend the night on board his ship, the *Jeanette,* offering at the same time to provide us a conveyance to Canton the next morning. Midshipman Mooney [Midshipman John Mooney] & myself accepted his invitation, and were very hospitably entertained.

Early the next morning, Nov. 24th. the *Panther* moved up to her proper anchorage, a little distance from Capt. Pierce's ship, and by ten o'clock, we were all ready to set out in the boats which had been provided for us, for Canton. In the mean time, I had an opportunity of surveying the surrounding scenery, which was here more variegated, and interesting than we had yet met with. On the north side of the river, the course of which was here nearly east & west, we had a view of a level and fertile country where Chinese industry appeared to have been employed to the best effect, in the cultivation of rice, and other articles which serve the inhabitants for sale or consumption. Beyond this plain, mountains and hills of every degree of elevation presented themselves to the view, some of which appeared to be clothed with verdure, and to admit of cultivation, while others presented a naked and cheerless aspect. On the left hand, and but a little distance from us, was French Island, the surface of which was quite uneven, rising in some places into hills of considerable height, and in others sinking into plains, almost on a level with the water of the river. The whole of this island so far as I could see, appeared to be fertile and was cultivated even to the tops of the hills. Behind the hills which bordered on the river was a village of considerable size, a part of which was visible between the hills, and exhibited a neat and pleasant appearance. On the side of one of the hills towards the river, was the cemetery for foreigners, where all foreigners who die either at Canton or Whampoa, are interred. Here several foreigners have found their final resting place, and among others was an American by the name of Magee [Major William Fairchild Megee], who had spent many years in Canton, and had attained so high a standing among the Chinese, on account of the services which he had rendered them against the pirates, that he had been made a Mandarin, and invested with all the powers and priviledges which belong to that office.[17]

Our party having assembled on board the *Jeanette,* and the tide and wind being in our favor, we set out about noon for Canton. There were three boats provided for our accommodation by our countrymen, in which we were equally distributed, and had a very pleasant passage to the city, a distance of about twelve miles. About a mile from the place of departure, we passed the town of Whampoa, which is situated on the right hand side of the river, on an island to which the Dutch gave the name of Bankschall, from its being used by them as a place of deposit. We could see but little more of the town of Whampoa, than that part of it which bordered the river, and this consisted principally of small bamboo huts, erected on piles over the water. They exhibited an appearance of a great degree of poverty and wretchedness.

The next object that we passed deserving of notice, was a pagoda, occupying an elevated position on the right bank of the river, and about three miles from the anchorage below. This structure consisted of nine stories, and as near as could be estimated, was a hundred and sixty or seventy feet high. It was of an octagonal form, and at the base probably thirty feet in diameter, decreasing very gradually to the top. At the top of each story it was surrounded with a cornice, which appeared to project about a foot from the body of the tower, and from which, as well as from the top, long grass was growing, giving evidence of the antiquity of the structure. On the four sides facing the four cardinal points, were openings like windows, in each of the stories from the bottom to the top. This pagoda was in a ruinous state, as I was informed by a gentleman who had just made a visit to it; and no use appeared to be made of it.

About half way from Whampoa to the city, we passed another pagoda on the left bank of the river, which was similar in form and height to that which I have described, but evidently a much more recent work. Respecting the object for which these structures were erected, I have no satisfactory information. It is evident that they were not designed exclusively for religious purposes, as they are not used for those purposes now, so far as I could learn, and there are other buildings of a very different structure from the pagoda, dedicated to the deities of the Chinese in which their religious worship is performed. It appears to me probable, that they were designed principally as observatories; not merely as astronomical observatories, but partly intended for that purpose, and partly also to serve as sentry-posts, from whose high summits an extensive range of the surrounding country could be seen at one view, and timely notice given of any occurrence that might threaten such consequences as it would be desirable to prevent.[18]

As we ascended the river towards the city, the plain on each side became more extensive, and exhibited a greater degree of fertility, and a higher state of cultivation. Such was the prospect presented to the view on either hand, till we had arrived within about four miles of the city, where the Junks, canal-boats, and sam pans, which had been increasing in number from the time we left Whampoa, became now so thick on each side of us, that we could see nothing else. Besides the almost innumerable multitude of these vessels that were moving up and down the river, there were so many lying at anchor on each side of us, as to form a compact floating wall, through which the sight could not penetrate. A considerable number of the junks were men-of-war, stationed there to prevent any illicit trade, or any violation of the laws of the empire. They seemed, however, to be poorly

"Whampoa from Dane's Island," print by Thomas Allom, ca. 1840

calculated for warlike operations, as most of them appeared to be in a state
of decay, and to be inadequately provided with men. A considerable number
of the merchant junks were new, and some of them were quite large; being,
as was judged, of four or five hundred tons burden.

The form of this kind of vessel is probably the same now, that it was
a thousand years ago, or at the period when it first began to be used. Its
structure appears to be extremely clumsy and awkward, the fore and after
parts being several feet higher than the middle, so that a line running along
the deck from the bow to the stern, would describe nearly a semi-circle.
They have two masts, one of which is large, and is placed near the centre
of the vessel; the other is small and stands near the bow. The sails are made
of matting, which appears to be a very good substitute for canvass. The
mainsail of a large junk is of immense size, but instead of being managed,
{as is universally practiced now by people who have made any progress in
navigation, that is,} by being attached to a yard that remains stationary
while the sail is let down from it when set, and drawn up to it when taken
in; the yard itself is lowered down with the sail, {when it is furled or taken
in,} and raised with it when it is set. {The rudder of these vessels is very
large, and is perforated with a great number of holes, to lessen its resistance
in the water.} There is a contrivance for lifting the rudder out of the water,
which is always done while the vessel is lying at anchor. On each side of the
bow of a junk, a large eye is painted, {which makes quite a ludicrous
appearance.}

The canal-boats bear some resemblance both in size and form to our
canal-boats, being large, and covered over with mats so as to afford perfect
security against sun and rain. Each of these boats is the residence of one
family at least, where they spend the whole of their lives without scarcely
ever setting foot on shore. The number of people who spend their lives on
the water in the neighborhood of Canton, in the canal-boats and sam-pans,
must be very great; and they constitute{, as I was informed,} an entirely
distinct class of the population. Employments and modes of living among
the Chinese are hereditary, and descend through a long series of generations
from father to son without the least variation. If the ancestor, therefore,
chose an occupation which required him to be a good deal on the water, he
was obliged to relinquish all claim to a residence on shore, and content
himself with a junk, canal-boat or sam-pan, as his only place of habitation;
and his descendants to the latest generation must not only follow the same
avocation which he did, but they must also take up their residence on the

water, without the least thought of ever being permitted to possess a habitation on shore.

There may seem to be a good deal of cruelty and oppression in thus compelling a numerous class of people to spend their lives on the water, and denying them the priviledge of ever owning a dwelling place on land; but the measure is undoubtedly founded in reason, as must be obvious to any one who knows how great the population of Canton and its vicinity is, in proportion to the means of obtaining subsistance from the earth; and from what I saw, I have no doubt, that the water population of Canton live more comfortably and contentedly, than those of the same rank do on land. Their food consists almost wholly of rice, which the wife boils in a little pot or kettle over a small fire in the bow or stern of the boat; and their matted deck or floor, serves them all for a bed. In these respects they are at least on a level as to comfort, with their countrymen of the same rank who have their residence either in the city or its neighborhood; and with respect to breathing a pure air, and being free from many annoyances that are experienced on shore, those who live on the water certainly have the advantage over their terrestrial fellow-countrymen.

About three miles below Canton on the right bank of the river, we passed an old Dutch fortification which is denominated the "Dutch Folly". This appelation originated in the following manner. Soon after the Dutch obtained permission to trade at Canton, they applied to the Chinese Government for leave to establish a hospital in the neighborhood of the City, for the accommodation of their sick and disabled seamen. Permission being obtained to erect a hospital, a scite was selected about three miles below the city, in a commanding situation; where, instead of a hospital, they began to construct a fort for the purpose of taking possession of the city. The work progressed rapidly and without interruption till the walls were about completed, and ready to receive the guns. These were enclosed in casks and landed under the name of medical stores for the hospital; but it happened unluckily for the designing Dutch, that one of these casks of medical stores fell, as they were hoisting it up, and being dashed to pieces, an instrument for destroying human life, instead of the means of saving it, presented itself to the astonished sight of the Chinese. They exclaimed on seeing that the contents of the cask were designed rather for their destruction than the cure of sick Dutchmen, "how can sickman eat gun"? and from that moment a stop was put to the building of the pretended hospital, which has ever since gone by the name of the "Dutch Folly", the Dutch were compelled to relinquish their trade with China.[19]

We had passed the Dutch Folly but a few rods, when one of our boats struck upon a rock in the river, and very narrowly escaped being upset. She was fortunately got off, however, without much detention, and without any material damage. By this time the river had become so entirely covered with the different kinds of craft that were plying in every direction, that it required skillful management for us to work our way along among them, without coming in collision, and receiving or causing injury. After pursuing this intricate navigation for some time, however, we reached the landing-place, and made our way through a dense crowd of Chinese to the Factories, about thirty rods distant. Our first inquiry was for the residence of Mr. Latimer [John R. Latimer], at which the Capt. was staying; and after some delay {in consequence of being directed wrong}, we met with Mr. Latimer himself, who conducted us all to his house, and immediately made arrangements for our accommodation. It was very soon settled, that Lieutenants Cunningham, Sinclair and myself should remain with him, while the four Midshipmen were quartered at two other American houses. We were provided with excellent accommodations at Mr. Latimer's, and during the whole of our stay there, {which was eight days,} we were treated with a kindness and hospitality which I shall never forget.[20]

This gentleman was originally from the state of Delaware, but he had spent many years in Canton, where he had established a character that stood unrivalled by that of any resident in Canton, both as a man of business, and as one of honesty and integrity. Such implicit confidence had the Chinese, who are generally suspicious of foreigners, in his honesty and fair dealing, that the trunks, boxes, etc that were sent to or from his house, were never examined, his word being considered sufficient; while a strict scrutiny was made of all the goods that passed through any of the other factories.

We arrived at Mr. Latimer's about 3 o'clock in the afternoon of Saturday the 24th. of November, having been about two days on the passage from Lintin, a distance of seventy miles.

On Sunday the 25th. I attended church at the chapel of the English East India Company, where Mr. Wimberly [Rev. Charles Wimberley], the Chaplain of the Company officiated. He performed the service very well, and preached an excellent sermon. There was but one service, which commenced at 11 & ended at 1 o'clock; the afternoon being devoted to feasting and recreations. Mr. Wimberly had but recently arrived, and he had a family at Macao. {I was accompanied to the chapel by Capt. Geisinger, and Dr.

Bradford [Dr. James Bradford],[21] both of whom called themselves Episcopalians, and joined in the service.} The chapel was a small but very neat
building connected with the English Factory, and provided with seats for a
hundred persons; a larger number, I presume, than ever assembled there.

CHAPTER VII

Canton

Vaccine Establishment; Dr. Morrison & Mr. Bridgeman; Rev.
Mr. Stevens; Another visit to Dr. M.; Chinese Dinner; Walk in
Canton; Honam Temple; Plan of the Temple; Reflections;
Factories; Opium Trade; Departure from Canton; Mr. Dana &
Qualla Battoo; Death of Wm Buker; Prepare for departure.

Monday Nov. 26. I went this morning with Dr. Bradford to the vaccine
establishment, where the poor assemble every Monday morning with their
children, who are vaccinated gratuitously by the Chinese physicians. Vaccination, as I was informed, was introduced into Canton a few years ago, by
Dr. Pearson [Dr. Alexander Pearson], the physician to the British Factory.[1]
He encountered much opposition at first from the prejudices and fears of
the Chinese; but his philanthropic efforts were at length successful, and he
could indulge the grateful reflection, that he had been instrumental in
saving many thousands from falling victims to the small-pox, a disease which
had frequently prevailed in Canton with terrible mortality. The mode in
which the business of vaccination was managed by the Chinese physicians,
appeared to me well calculated to ensure its greatest efficacy. In the first
place, the operation was so performed, that it could hardly fail of communicating the disease, the matter, which was taken fresh from the pustule,
being inserted in three places in each arm; and then to ensure the success
of the operation, and the genuineness of the disease, the child's name was
inserted in a register kept for the purpose, together with the time when the
operation was performed, the name of the operator, and the name of the
child from whom the matter was taken; and on the eigth day an examination
was made of every child thus vaccinated, at which time the disease was

pronounced either genuine or spurious, and the proper entry made in the register. In case it was found to be spurious, or that the operation had produced no effect, it was repeated in the same manner that I have described.[2] The number of children assembled at the time of my visit, was very considerable, and their incessant cries, together with the loud and confused voices of their parents; made a very unpleasant scene, and one from which I was glad to make my escape, as soon as my curiosity was gratified.

After returning from the vaccine establishment, I called on Dr. Morrison, the celebrated Chinese scholar, who had appartments in the British Factory.[3] I was well pleased with the short interview I had with the Dr. who although quite grave in his aspect and deportment, was nevertheless affable, and made inquiries apparently with much interest, respecting the state of religion, both in the U. States, and in our public ships. Religion seemed to be the subject which principally interested him, and which he appeared anxious to promote by all the means in his power.

I had heard insinuations both at Lintin and at Canton prejudicial to Dr. Morrison's character, and had been told particularly, that he was exceedingly prejudiced against the Government and people of the U. States, but I saw no reason to believe that these insinuations & reports were well founded. On the contrary, he manifested the same regard for our country, and countrymen, when he was led to speak of them, that he did for his own; and he appeared equally desirous for the advancement of the best interest of both.

On this visit I was accompanied by Dr. Bradford, and he also accompanied me from Dr. Morrison's on a visit to Mr. Bridgman, the American Missionary, whose residence was in the factory occupied by Oliphant, King & Co. [Olyphant, King & Co.][4] We found him in his room engaged in his studies, which he prosecutes with great industry and perseverance. He had been then nearly three years in China, during which time he had made such progress in the Chinese language, that he could both speak and write it. His devotion to the cause of introducing the Christian religion among the Chinese, appeared to be very great; and so far as I could judge, the course which he was pursuing, was that which seemed the most likely to accomplish the great purpose which he had so much at heart. He had a small school of Chinese to whom he was imparting the most useful instruction, and with such success, I had reason to believe as must have afforded him a high degree of satisfaction.[5] At the residence of Mr. Bridgman, I was introduced to another Missionary, a Mr. Stevens [Rev. Edwin Stevens], who had been recently sent out by the Missionary Society, for the purpose principally, of officiating among the seamen at Whampoa.[6] He appeared to be quite a young man, but of his qualifications for the station which he was expected to fill, I had no opportunity of judging. He had preached a few times at Whampoa, and so far as I could learn, his services had been well received. The field which he was intended to occupy, was certainly one in which a clergyman suitably qualified may do much good. A number of seamen from the U. States & Great Britain, to the amount of several hundreds at least, are assembled at Whampoa during several months of every year, who are in a great measure destitute of clerical services; but on whom the Gospel might be made to produce its renovating and saving effects, as well as on others, if communicated to them by a person possessing the requisite qualifications. From what I heard of Mr. Stevens, I was led to believe that he was such a man, and I therefore anticipated with much satisfaction, the effects which his services might produce.

Tuesday Nov. 27. Until this morning I had visited none of the China shops, nor made any purchases; but I now commenced exploring the shops for curiosities, of which a great variety was presented to the view at every step. As my curiosity, however, had some regard to utility in the articles that I wished to purchase, as well as to what was novel and curious, {either on account of the article itself, or of the ingenious workmanship which it displayed;} I found it necessary to impose some restraint on my inclination to buy, and to select only a very few of the great variety of the curiously wrought articles that were urged upon me and which, if means had permitted, I should have purchased for the gratification of my young friends at home.

There are but two streets in Canton where foreigners are permitted to trade, namely, old & new China streets; but in these almost every thing is to be found that a foreigner can wish to purchase, with the exception of teas, which are obtained only from the Hong Merchants. The articles which principally fix the attention of a foreigner, {especially at this first visit, and induce him to part with his money,} are the various kinds of carved work in ivory, turtle-shell and mother of pearl, laquered ware, silk handkerchiefs, and crape shawls. In carving in ivory etc the Chinese display great ingenuity, and their dexterity must be equal to their ingenuity, or they could not possibly afford to sell so cheap as they do, those articles, {as work-baskets, card-cases, etc.} on which a great amount of labour must have been bestowed.[7]

The extent of the two streets that I have mentioned, does not exceed sixty rods; and their width, which is greater considerably than that of any other street in the city, at least in that part of it which foreigners are permitted to see, is about twelve feet. The shops are small, and lighted principally from the roof. No display is made of his goods by the China merchant as is done by ours, nor does he recommend them in such extravagant terms, and urge one to buy with a vexatious and impertinent importunity. When an article is called for he shows it, and states the price, which is sometimes higher than he will finally consent to take; though it seemed to be a general rule with them, so far as I observed, to have but one price for an article from which they would not be prevailed upon to deviate.

Every dealer in the two streets that have been mentioned, had learned so much of English as to enable him to transact business; but the English which they spoke, was such an uncouth jargon, that it was almost as unintelligible to me as Chinese itself. The name of every merchant and shopkeeper is written in Roman letters over his door, and his calling is also expressed in English, as "Silk-Dealer," "Carver in ivory" etc. etc. In my several shopping expeditions, I was accompanied by a Capt. Jennings [master of the *Lancaster*], who had dealt much with the Chinese, and was perfectly familiar with their lingo. This gentleman, though by birth an Englishman, was in all other respects an American; and had been trading some years under the American flag between China and St. Blas on the coast of Mexico at the entrance of the Gulf of California.

He was rapidly accumulating a fortune, and expected soon to abandon the sea and locate himself in some part of the U. States, and there to spend the remainder of his life.

On returning from shopping about one o'clock, I met Dr. Morrison coming from Mr. Latimer's, where he had been, in company with Mr. Bridgeman, to return my call. He invited me to take a tiffin [luncheon] with him the next day at two o'clock, {saying that he was desirous to have some conversation with me; for which I was of course very willing to give him an opportunity, and therefore accepted with pleasure, his invitation. I found Mr. Bridgeman at Mr. Latimer's; but his stay being short, we had an opportunity to do but little more than pass the usual compliments.}

Wednesday Nov. 28. The morning of this day was spent as the preceding had been, among the shops in the two China streets. A little before two o'clock, I went to Dr. Morrison's where I spent an hour very much to my satisfaction. I found the Dr. in his study, with three or four Chinese, and a

"A Street in Canton," print by Thomas Allom, 1843

great quantity of Chinese Books around him; and he seemed to be as diligently employed as the most laborious student could be. After a few minutes conversation we set down to the tiffin, which consisted of soup, flesh, and fowl; and on which he told me he usually made his dinner, as the company [East India Company] dined at seven o'clock, a later hour than was agreeable to him to dine. As I was already engaged to dinner, I partook but sparingly of the tiffin; and after spending a short time at the table, we returned to the study. The conversation again turned on the subject of religion which seemed principally to engross his thoughts. On learning that I belonged to the Episcopal Church, he asked me whether I was bred up in that church, or whether it was the preaching of the Gospel that induced me to join it; and being told that it was the latter, {as my parents belonged to the Congregational Church,} he made particular inquiries with respect to the preaching of the Episcopal clergy of the U. States, compared with that of the congregational clergy, intimating that the latter were more zealous and evangelical in their preaching than the former. He seemed pleased, however, when I assured him, that so far as I had an opportunity of knowing, the Episcopal clergy were equally zealous in declaring the great doctrines of the Gospel with their congregational brethren.

I had been informed, contrary to what I had supposed, that the Dr. was a dissenter from the established church of England, and I was therefore not surprized at his seeming to entertain rather an unfavorable opinion of the piety and zeal of the Episcopal clergy, when compared with the clergy of the denomination to which he belonged.[8] He seemed as free from an undue partiality for his own order, and as ready to exercise charity towards those who differed from him, as any man that I have met with; as satisfactory an evidence as can be given of the genuineness of his own piety. In answer to my inquiries respecting the success of his labors in introducing the Christian Religion among the Chinese, he told me, that the harvest which the good seed had produced, was still small; but sufficient to afford encouragement to perseverance. He showed me the Bible which he had translated into Chinese, as well as several other books and pamphlets in that language, designed to promote the cause of virtue and religion. All the efforts, however, that were made for the purpose of introducing the Christian Religion among the Chinese had to be disguised under a veil of secrecy, as they were in opposition to the laws of the empire. He seemed anxious for the religious instruction of seamen, and inquired whether I had observed any evidence of piety among the officers and men of our ship. To these inquiries, I was compelled to reply, that I did not know a single individual in the ship who had experienced the influence of religion {and that, although we generally had religious service on Sunday, yet I had too much reason to believe, that it was a mere formal observance, if not a wicked mockery, at least as respected the individual whose example had more influence on the men than that of any other person; since he would turn from a paroxism of violent cursing and swearing to join in the service with apparent devotion, and the moment that was ended, the Prayer-Book was laid aside, & the tongue which had just been offering prayer and thanksgiving to the Deity, was again employed in blaspheming his name, and in the use of all other kinds of indecent and improper language. Such being the conduct of the commanding officer, I told the Dr. it was scarcely possible that any good effects could result from the performance [of] a short religious service on Sunday, especially if done by a layman; and I very much doubted, whether we were not aggravating our sins by doing so. He entertained the same sentiments on the subject, and in the course of his remarks upon it observed, that he should suppose any person of religious feelings would be very unwilling to enter a service, where he would meet with so much to give him pain, and render his life unhappy.}

Our conversation was next directed to the state of the Sandwich Islands, of which I told him that I had heard, both at Manilla and Canton, very unfavourable reports. He had also heard the same reports, and had drawn from them the same conclusion that I had done, namely, that in consequence of the labours of the Missionaries there, the natives had become so much enlightened, that it was impossible now for dishonest traders to impose upon them as they had done, and carry on so profitable a trafic. This was confirmed by the inadvertant avowal of the Master of a vessel who had been there, which was, that he could formerly procure as much from the natives for a rusty nail, as he could now for a dollar. The Dr. observed that the same unfavourable reports had been made respecting the English Missionaries; but it was perfectly evident that they all proceeded from the same cause, and that was, the enmity of those men whose whole aim is directed to worldly pursuits, to the Gospel, and to all those who are engaged in its dissemination. In speaking of his long residence in China, the Dr. told me that he had spent five and twenty years at the table at which he was then setting; and on my asking him how long he was employed in compiling his Chinese Dictionary, he told me that he was engaged in it fifteen years; though he was at the same time engaged in other avocations.

The time had now arrived when my engagement to dinner required me to take leave of the Dr. which I did with a sincere regret, that I could not spend a longer time in his company.

After this, my last interview with Dr. Morrison, I heard some hard things said about him by a few of my countrymen, residents in Canton; but so little evidence could they adduce in proof of what they asserted, that I am fully persuaded there was no ground for their unfavourable representations. The principal charges which these gentlemen brought against him was his enmity to Americans, and his fondness for the pleasures of the table. With regard to the first, I am satisfied it went no farther than the conduct of those Americans with whom he was acquainted at Canton, would warrant; and with respect to the second, it was nothing more than such an indulgence of the appetite, as a robust frame, and a vigorous state of health required.

In assigning the conduct of my countrymen as the ground of Dr. Morrison's alledged hostility towards Americans generally, I wish it to be distinctly understood, that I do so only for the purpose of defending the character of a worthy man against what I believe to be unjust aspersions; and without the least desire to represent the conduct of my countrymen as deserving of censure. As a professor of christianity, and a clergyman too, I know not how Dr. M. could consistently do otherwise than express a decided disapprobation of the conduct of those who manifest a total disregard of the Christian Religion and its institutions, by following their worldly avocations with as much eagerness on the Lord's Day, as on the other days of the week, and by allowing an unrestrained indulgence to all their sensual passions and appetites. And as an Englishman, and a member of the East India Company, who first opened the door to foreign trade with China, and therefore considered themselves justly entitled to the preference in that trade, and the principal advantages resulting from it; taking all these things into consideration, I say, it is certainly natural that Dr. M. should entertain a feeling of jealousy towards those who were evidently maintaining a successful rivalship with the Company to which he belonged, and should sometimes express these feelings in language that might be considered hostile.

Now, with regard to the first reason that I have assigned for the Dr's supposed hostility towards Americans, I must declare, that while I most cheerfully, and so far as I am personally concerned very gratefully, award them all the praise that can possibly be considered due to a most kind and generous hospitality; {I must at the same time charge them with the violation of the Lords Day which I have mentioned, since I was obliged to witness it myself; and although I have not the same evidence with respect to their other violations of the laws of virtue and morality, yet the evidence was too strong to admit of my entertaining any doubt on the subject.}[9]

And as to the other reason that I have adduced to account for and excuse the Dr's unfavourable opinion of Americans, namely, the rivalship existing between them and the East India Company to which he belongs; I require no other evidence of the correctness of what I advance, than the fact, that it is but a short time since the E.I.C. petitioned the Chinese Government for the adoption of measures, by which their interests might be promoted, while the interests of the Americans should be obstructed as much as possible. Such a proceeding on the part of the E.I.C. certainly proves an unfriendly disposition towards Americans, as it was very natural to expect, from both parties aiming at as large a share of the China-trade as could possibly be obtained; and this disposition was not diminished by the failure of the petition.[10]

From all these facts and circumstances, I find no difficulty in the supposition, that Dr. M. may have been led, by what he had witnessed himself, to express an unfavourable opinion of the religious character of Americans; and also to consider and speak of them as men so entirely devoted to their own interests, that they regarded but little the interests of others; to such conclusions, I say, I can readily suppose Dr. M. to have been led by what has fallen under his own observation, with respect to Americans, and yet without deserving to be considered criminal in doing so; or as doing otherwise than an American, and a clergyman too would do with respect to Englishmen in the same circumstances. With regard to the Dr's situation and employment at Canton, I found myself mistaken; for besides being Interpreter to the British Factory, I had supposed that he acted as their Chaplain, and also as a Missionary to the Chinese. But it appeared that the only appointment which he held, was that of interpreter to the British Factory; and that all his labors for the Chinese, which had certainly been great, had been bestowed without any formal missionary appointment.* His salary as Interpreter was a thousand pounds sterling annually, besides his expenses at Canton; and of this sum a large proportion was spent in charitable contributions. An Anglo-Chinese College was established at Malacca some years ago, towards which the Dr. contributed, as I was informed,

---

*From subsequent information I learned that I was mistaken with respect to Dr. Morrison's Missionary appointment. His son told me, that he received an appointment from the London Missionary Society, in 1807, to China, under which appointment he has ever since acted; but for several years past, he has relinquished the salary, which he had been allowed by the Miss. Soc.

four thousand pounds. He was appointed President of this institution, which promises to be of the greatest utility in promoting a knowledge of christianity, and of the arts and sciences among the Chinese.

After returning from my visit to Dr. M. I partook of a dinner at Mr. Latimer's served up in the Chinese style, for the purpose of giving us an opportunity of seeing the manner in which a Chinaman entertains his friends with a dinner. To describe, if I could do so, all the dishes which constituted this multifarious entertainment, would be an unprofitable task; I shall therefore only observe, that the number of dishes, of which flesh, fish or fowl formed a constituent part, was thirty three or four, most of which were so well prepared, that an American palate would have [been] content to make a meal on any one of them. With one or two exceptions, they were in the form of soups and stews; and among them was the Birds Nest which the Chinese are said to value so highly. I found it to be really a nutritious and savory dish, and after eating of it was not surprized that the Chinese should be fond of it.

In order that his entertainment should preserve as much as possible its Chinese character throughout, knives & forks were prohibited, and we were all required to use chop-sticks, {which were small rods of ivory about eight inches long}; and instead of wine and wine glasses, we were provided with a liquor distilled from rice which we drank hot from small China cups. Tea was also served several times during the entertainment which was drank, according to the Chinese custom, without either milk or sugar.[11]

Such was the specimen of a Chinese entertainment, which Mr. Latimer furnished us at an expense, I presume, of a hundred dollars. The party who partook of this expensive dinner, consisted besides our host, of Mr. Roberts, Capt. Geisinger, Lieutenants Cunningham & Sinclair, Dr. Bradford & myself. Mr. Latimer deserved, and I doubt not, received all our thanks for the pains and expense to which he subjected himself, in order to gratify our curiosity with a specimen of Chinese luxury.

Thursday Nov. 29. After spending an hour or two among the shops in China street, I took a walk with Dr. Bradford through the city as far as the gate, and for some distance along the wall. In this excursion I was disappointed in not meeting with rough treatment from the Chinese; for I had been frequently told that foreigners rarely escaped abusive treatment, whenever they ventured in to any part of the city, from which Chinese jealousy had excluded them.[12] We did not meet, however, with the least interruption, or the least appearance of incivility; and I have no doubt but that I could walk through all the streets of Canton without the wall, and meet with less annoyance from the rude conduct of the inhabitants, than I should in some of our large cities.

The streets through which we passed, were so extremely narrow, and the houses so compact, and their inhabitants apparently so numerous, that I had no difficulty in comprehend[ing] the immense population of a Chinese city. The usual width of the streets through which we passed, was about four feet, and they were so crooked and irregular, that to follow one of them was something like following the windings of the paths which cattle make in the woods. Each street appeared to be appropriated to a particular employment; and hence we found in one only dealers in silk goods, in another only dealers in carved work etc. etc. One street appeared to be appropriated wholly to the preparation of the birds nests, which I observed to be a much more onerose and tedious process than I had supposed. Another seemed to be appropriated, in like manner, to the preparation of the Biche le Mer, or sea-slug, an article of Chinese luxury quite as much in repute as the Birds nests.

I had an opportunity of observing the manner in which they carry on several of the mechanical arts; and was highly gratified with the simplicity which seemed to characterize all their mechanical operations. If ingenuity consists in the small number of instruments with which any work of art may be effected, then the Chinese are certainly entitled to the praise of ingenuity; for I cannot conceive it possible that the mechanic arts could be carried on with a smaller number of instruments, or that manual labour could by any means be rendered more effective.

The shops both of the merchant and mechanic are generally small; and as every shop had an advertisement in front, in large Chinese characters, which are generally either red or yellow, the narrow streets presented quite a gay & lively appearance. In consequence of the extreme narrowness of the streets, neither carriages or horses are used; but their place is supplied by palanquines, which are used by all the citizens who can afford the expense of this mode of conveyance. A foreigner, on meeting one of these vehicles, is obliged to make way for it, which it is sometimes difficult to do in a crowded street only four feet wide; and he consequently meets occasionally, with pretty severe rubs, as the palanquin bearers never stop or turn aside, to avoid running against the people in the street, and especially against foreigners, who are considered as intruders and treated with contempt, by those who are honored with the service of a Mandarin, or any other person of distinction.[13]

The gate-way which forms one of the entrances in to what is properly denominated the City of Canton, and through which foreigners are not permitted to pass, was a broad arched passage, which appeared to be no otherwise guarded than by a few soldiers; so that it would have been very easy for a very small armed force to overcome all the resistance that would have been met with, and advance into the city. This was actually accomplished a few years ago by a number of young men, who under pretence of obtaining redress for some alleged grievance, forced their way through the gate and continued their progress into the city, until they were met by a message from the proper authority assuring them that the satisfaction which they sought should be granted.[14]

The wall of the city along which we passed some distance, appeared to have been constructed of brick and lime, and bore marks of great antiquity. Its height I judged to be about thirty feet, and its breadth was probably about the same. It appeared to be crumbling to pieces in many places, and not many more years will elapse, before it will probably be nearly levelled with the ground.

The streets of Canton where they intersect each other, have gates which entirely close them, and which are shut on any disturbance occurring; by which means a stop is speedily put to it, and the authors of it readily detected.

Having concluded my rambles through the city, I went at two o'clock in the afternoon with Mr. Bridgeman, to visit the Temple, or rather Monastery of Honam.[15] This place of idolatrous worship is situated on the island of Honam, directly opposite to Canton, and is well deserving of a visit from every foreigner who goes to Canton. This Temple belongs to the Buddhist sect, and is the principal place of the Buddhist worship in that part of China. We crossed the river, which was about a quarter of a mile wide, in one of those small boats called sampans, which was navigated by a man and his wife, whose only home and probably only property it was. We found it to be very neat and comfortable and to constitute a more agreeable place of residence, as I have already observed of these boats, than the lower class of Chinese possess on shore.

Immediately on landing at the island of Honam, we entered the limits of Buddhas teritory, which comprised, as I should judge, about ten acres. After walking about twenty rods on a broad flag pavement, we came to what may be called the vestibule of the Temple, which was an edifice one story high, and through which was a broad, arched passage, leading to the proper residence of Buddha. Two immense wooden images of a very grotesque appearance occupied the vestibule, one on each side of the passage, whose office it seemed to be to guard the sacred precincts. After leaving the limits of these gigantic, but unfaithful centinels, we entered an appartment which appeared to be the residence of several of Buddha's priests, where we found a number of them assembled and spending their time in smoking and sleeping. Mr. Bridgeman entered into a negociation with them for a conductor to attend us in our proposed rambles through the sacred enclosure, and after some debate on the price that was to be paid for his services, it was agreed that we should pay him two dollars. Having thus obtained a conductor we commenced exploring the various and complicated mass of temples, cells, gardens, intricate passages etc, of which this idolatrous establishment consists.

Our time permitted us only to take a rapid view of the various objects that we met with; so that it would be impossible for me to give a minute description of what I saw, if I were inclined to do so. A general account of such objects, however, is all that can be interesting; and that is all that I can pretend to give.

I had proceeded thus far with my account of the great Honam Temple or Jos House, when a pamphlet was put into my hands, published by Dr. Morrison, and giving an account of Canton and its vicinity; and among other things, containing a plan and description of the Temple at Honam. For the purpose of conveying a more accurate idea of this Temple, than a mere verbal description could do, I copy the plan from Dr. Morrison, with such additions, as my own observations enable me to make, in order to render it more perfect.

Explanation of the plan

1&. The stone pavement leading to
2. The Hill Gate. "The Buddha priests in China affect to separate themselves from the rest of mankind, and to live in hills & mountains; hence, although a monastery be on a level plain, the first gate leading to it is always called the Hill-gate."
3. "The name of the Temple written over the gateway."
4. "The Angler's Eminence", a name given to this elevated shelter in all public halls & buildings.
5. Inscriptions relating to Buddism.
6.

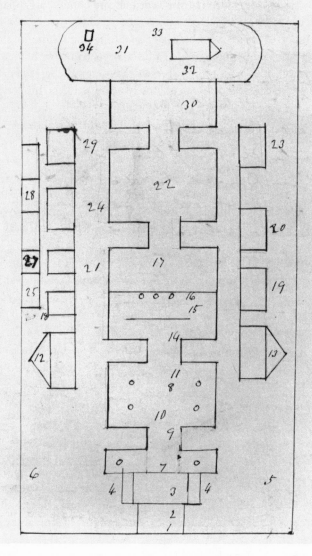

"Ground plan of the Temple at Honam," page 410 of Journal II B. (Benajah Ticknor Papers, Manuscripts and Archives, Yale University Library.)

7. The vestibule of the temple in which are the two centinels, representing ancient wariors of which I have already spoken.

8. "The pavilion or palace of the four great celestial kings, certain ancient wariors. In this pavilion they reckon thirty–two pillars."

9. Represents an incription.

10. Also represent inscriptions.

11.

12. Pavilions containing the images of ancient military demigods.

13.

14. "The principal hall or pavilion, called 'The Great, Powerful, Precious Palace'".

15 "An inscription, denoting, 'The Golden coloured region'".

16. "The three precious Buddhas," 'the present, past & to come'. On each side of the hall are represented eighteen disciples of Buddha, which will be more particularly described hereafter.

17. "A single image of Amida Buddha".

18. "Room for receiving visitors."

19. "Place for keeping alive domestic animals, pigs, fowls, ducks, & geese, agreeably to the leading doctrine of the sect, that no animal should be deprived of life". Adjoining

20. "The Book–Room," in which are religious and moral books for sale". "Adjoining this is a Chinese printing office, where the curious may see the mode of printing from blocks of wood, or wooden stereotype, in China."

21. "An idol of the Tau sect, the kind of hades."

22. "A pagoda of white stone, with several idols carved on it."

23. "An upper room containing a number of idols."

24. "A large bell that is struck night and day."

25. "The treasury."

27. "The dining–room."

28. "The cook–house".

29. "The chief priests apartments. Here Lord Amherst's embassy[16] was lodged; and in one of the rooms, the chaplain of the embassy, Mr. Griffith, preached and administered the communion, Jan. 1817."

30. "Palace of a female Buddha". "In this hall are reckoned forty two pillars".

31. "A kitchen garden".

32. "A pavilion in memory of a deer attached to its master".

33. "Mausoleum in which the ashes of the burnt priests are deposited once a year."

34. Place where the bodies of the priests are burnt.

The first apartment to which our conductor took us, was the palace of the four ancient wariors (8); which were represented by four gigantic images, with a gilded covering, and very much resembling those of Buddha. These images were in a siting posture, inclining a little backward. Their height, if standing, would probably have been about twenty feet, and their other dimensions in the same proportion.

From this apartment, we next proceeded to that of Buddha, (14) which was about thirty-feet square, as I should judge, and had a floor of stone. The three images of Buddha were in the human form, and resembled both in size and features those which we had just seen. They also presented a gilded exterior. They were seated in a row on a kind of throne, which was surrounded by a railing to guard them from the too near approach of profane intruders. Their countenances were expressive of great complacency and good nature; qualities which must indeed be of the first importance in an imaginary deity.

The eighteen statues arranged along the walls of this palace, on each side of Buddha, and said to be those of his followers, were all in a standing posture, and about the medium stature of a man. They were arrayed in different costumes, expressive, I suppose, of the different pursuits in which they spent their lives. One was clad in a coat of mail, and had a helmet on his head to signify that the individual whom he represented, belonged to the military profession; another bore in his hands the implements of husbandry, intimating that the individual thus personified, devoted his life to agricultural pursuits; and others were provided with the implements of the several mechanic arts, as practised among the Chinese.

From Buddha's temple or palace, we went to the residence of the sacred animals, which appeared to be about as comfortable, and to receive about as much attention in order to its cleanliness, as the abode of the priests themselves. We saw there several kinds of animals, as pigs, geese, and goats, the pious offerings of Buddha's devout followers; which were treated with as much ease and tenderness as if they had been human beings. Our notice was principally attracted by the swine, on account of their extreme fatness, and the marks of age which some of them, exhibited.[17]

We next proceeded to the printing office, where we saw the wooded stereotype which, though clumsy and rude, was nevertheless, better adapted, as it appeared to me, to Chinese printing, than moveable types would be. This was probably a specimen of the first kind of type ever used in the art of printing; which has received but little improvement among the Chinese since its inventions; while in the western hemisphere, it has gradually been so improved, that from viewing it in its present state, we are almost led to conclude, that its origin could not have been so rude as it was among the Chinese.

We next visited the garden (31) comprising some two or three acres of the domain appropriated to Buddha; which was in a good state of cultivation, and contained all those articles, so far as I could judge, that constitute the diet of Buddha's followers. There were several men at work in the garden, with whom Mr. Bridgeman spent a few minutes in conversation, while I went to view the place (34) where the bodies of the priests are burnt. It consisted of a trench in the ground about eighteen inches deep, and of a length and breadth sufficient to admit the body [of] a man; which was lined with stone; and over it was a structure of stone, eight or ten feet square, ten or twelve high, and surmounted with a kind of dome. Here the body of every priest belonging to the establishment who dies, is burnt to ashes, which are deposited in the Mausoleum (33) till the stated time for committing them to their final abode.

Having now reached the farthest limit of Buddha's territory, we commenced our return, and on our way back, visited the residence of the female Buddha (30) where we fortunately had an opportunity of witnessing the mode of worship which the Buddhists practice. The female deity was seated on a throne like her brethren, and was arrayed much in the same manner as I have frequently seen the image of the Virgin among Roman Catholics. Her stature was that of a female of the usual size. On a stone floor before the idol a young lad fourteen or fifteen years old, was kneeling, and holding a pot of smoking incense in his hand. Behind him were three or four priests, who were alternately engaged in chaunting from their sacred books, and in kneeling and bowing with their foreheads to the ground. The exercises of the priests appeared to be governed by musicians who occupied a station at the right hand of the throne, and played, one on a fife, another on some other kind of wind instrument, and a third beat a gong.

There was an apparent solemnity in the worship which these ignorant people paid to their senseless idol; and it corresponded in several particulars, with the worship of the priests of the Romish Church. The occasion of this address to their deity, for it was not their usual hour of worship, was the death of the young man's father, who was kneeling before the idol; and the object was to propitiate their deity in favour of his departed spirit.

At a little distance from this temple, we noticed a palanquin standing by the wall, and six or eight paper figures representing men standing by it. These were the bearers of the palanquin, which had been brought there by the young man for the accommodation of his father's spirit.

From this place we were conducted to the setting room (18), where we were presented with tea & sweetmeats, and then took leave of our conductor, and made our exit from Buddha's domain by the same rout which had led us to it. We found the boat in which we had crossed the river, waiting for us; and in a few minutes we reached the city, where I parted with Mr. Bridgeman, and did not see him again.

In reflecting on what I had seen in the temple of one of the principal false deities that are worshiped at the present day, and comparing the worship which the Buddhist pays to his imaginary deity, with that which the christian offers to the true God; I could not help thinking that the man who falls down in acts of worship before an idol of wood or stone, must either be endowed with a very small portion of reason, or he must be guilty of a most criminal abuse of the reason that has been given him. For it seemed impossible that men possessing the usual share of reason, could remain so ignorant of the true objects of worship, as to pay their adorations to the work of their own hands; or knowing the true God, could refuse to pay him the worship that is due to the Supreme Ruler of the universe. But in pursuing this train of reflections, the inquiry suggested itself, whether there were not many who call themselves christians, who are not as much the objects of commiseration, on account of their idolatry, or of their ignorance or contempt of the true God, as the Buddhists or any other sect of professed idolaters are? and I saw at once that no other than an affirmative answer could be made to this inquiry.

Idolatry does not consist alone in paying devotion to an image of wood or stone, but it consists in paying religious homage to any other object than the one true God; so that the man who makes wealth, fame, or pleasure, the object of his homage, is as much an idolater as the worshiper of Buddha. Now, how large a proportion of every christian community must be considered idolaters, notwithstanding they have always enjoyed the light of true religion, and claim the name which signifies their belief in the divine author of christianity! Their knowledge of this all important truth, is not practical, but barely theoretical; such, indeed, as a Mahomedan or Buddhist might possess, and still remain as sincere a worshiper of Mahomed or Buddha, as if he had never heard of Christ or his religion. There is another portion, however, of every community that is called christian, who are guilty of a more gross perversion of reason, than the Buddhists are; for they wilfully withhold from the true God, who has revealed himself to them in his word, the obedience and worship, which they are compelled to acknowledge are justly due to him, and which the more dutiful Buddhist freely pays to his deity. This constitutes quite a large class of every community in every christian country; and however much we may commiserate the ignorant and deluded followers of Buddha, and however anxious we may be for their conversion from heathenism to the true religion; we have reason still more to pity that numerous class of whom I am speaking, who refuse obedience to the true God, and treat his laws and precepts with as much contempt, as they do the sites of a heathen deity. The Buddhist acts according to the best of his knowledge, and worships his deity in the manner which he believes most acceptable; but those christians of whom I have been speaking, possess a knowledge of the only proper object of worship, and of the duty which he requires of them, but this knowledge had no influence on their conduct. While the poor Buddhist prostrates himself in humble reverence before his idol, and does every thing which he supposes will obtain his favor; the nominal christian is too proud to bow to the Supreme Majesty of heaven and earth, and too self-sufficient to acknowledge his dependance on an omnipotent Deity, or to offer a single supplication to him for the purpose of obtaining his favor and protection.

I lament to say, that I know many of my own countrymen, and have been closely associated with them, who have been taught the great truths of revelation by christian parents, and could not therefore be ignorant of the true God, and of the duty which they owed him; but who, nevertheless, were as unmindful of him as if he had no existence, and thought no more of paying him an act of homage, than of prostrating themselves before an idol of Buddha. The bible was treated by them with even more contempt, than they would have manifested towards any book of idolatrous worship; because they would condescend to notice the latter so much as to look into it, but the bible they threw aside without deigning even to cast a glance on its sacred page. How much more deplorable, then, must the condition of such christians be, and how much greater their guilt in the sight of Heaven, than that of the Buddhist, or any other idol worshiper; since the former wilfully refuses to serve the God whom he knows, while the latter endeavors faithfully to serve a Deity whom he does not know.

Friday. Nov. 30. This day was spent in making preparation for leaving Canton, which I intended to do on the following day. As I had now seen as much here as I had expected to see, and as much almost, as any foreigner is permitted to see, I had become quite anxious to conclude my visit and return to Lintin. I shall close my account of what I saw there with a short description of the foreign Factories.

These are sixteen in number, extending about fifty rods in a line nearly east and west; being [bounded on the east by a canal, &] on the west by one of the narrow streets of the city. They front the river, at a distance of about thirty rods from it; and being two or three stories high, and white-washed in front, with green blinds, they presented on landing a very neat and pleasant exterior. A broad stone pavement runs in front of them, which in the evening forms a very agreeable promenade; and indeed the only comfortable one to which foreigners can have access. The lower stories of the factories are used for the purpose of storing goods, and called Go Downs. The upper stories are used by the merchants as their counting-rooms and places of residence; for as none of them are permitted to have families there, they have their counting rooms, dining and sleeping apartments all under the same roof. These apartments are generally large, well ventilated, and consequently comfortable. The factories are generally narrow in front, and extend back a considerable distance; so as to afford several successive suits of apartments, which are entered from an arched passage running under the second story the whole length of the building. These long passages are lighted at night with lamps, and present the appearance of the narrow streets of a city.

The principal factories are—1, that next to the canal, or the eastern-most, occupied in part by Mr. Latimer {, with whom I staid}; 2, the Dutch next to that; 3, the English, with a verandah in front {projecting out forty or fifty feet, and not only improving the appearance of the building, but being a very agreeable place of resort in a hot day}; 5, the old English, with an arched passage extending far back, on each side of which were the appartments of the several gentlemen belonging to the factory, and among the others, of Dr. Morrison; 6, the Sweedish, in which Mr. Jenkin [Jabez Jenkins], of Philadelphia was doing business; 7, the Imperial, occupied by Russel, Low & company; and 10 [the ninth factory in the row], the American, occupied by Mr. Oliphant, King and company. This is called the American factory, not because it is exclusively occupied by Americans, but because it had been the residence of the American Consul, while we had one there. Mr. King [Charles W. King] held this office until the recent visit of the *Potomac* to Canton, when some difficulty occurred between him and Capt. Downes respecting some trifling ceremonials, which induced him to relinquish the office, and no one had yet been appointed in his place.

With respect to the trade at Canton, it appeared to me, from all the information that I could obtain on the subject, that the Americans enjoyed their full proportion of it. The American business is transacted both by companies and by individuals, while that of the English, who are the principal rivals of the Americans, is conducted wholly by the E.I. Company. The monopolizing spirit which has always actuated this company, has caused considerable collision between themselves and the Americans, which had threatened to prove highly injurious to the interests of both parties. Notwithstanding this rivalship, however, the English Company, owing to their long establishment there, and the manner in which they conduct their business, exerts an influence over the whole foreign trade of China, which, {an American merchant at Canton, and a very intelligent one too, assured me} was highly beneficial. Hence there was reason to conclude, that the abolition of this company which was ardently desired by many, would prove seriously injurious not only to the English trade with China, but also to that of all other foreign nations with that country.[18]

There is a branch of trade, however, carried on with the Chinese, which is not at all under the control of the E.I. Company, nor indeed of the Chinese Government; and while we were at Canton, as well as during several of the preceeding years, it was the most lucrative trade that was carried on. I allude to the trade in opium, which was strictly forbidden by the laws of the empire, but which nevertheless, was carried on to a most astonishing extent. No contraband trade, I presume to say, has ever flourished like this, or threatened more destructive consequences. I was informed {by Mr. Latimer, who was an extensive dealer in the article,} that the quantity introduced into the empire during the last year, had amounted to fourteen millions of dollars.[19]

The best kinds of opium in the estimation of the Chinese, who use it only for smoking, are those of Patna and Benares, {places in India, two or three hundred miles from Calcutta.} The price at which it was sold, varied from five hundred to a thousand dollars a chest, containing a hundred and thirty three pounds, or a pecul.

To prepare it for smoking, it is dissolved in hot water, filtered through brown paper five or six times, and then boiled down in a brass pan to an extract. In undergoing this process it loses about fifty per cent. To smoke it a small pill is placed in the bowl of a pipe constructed for the purpose, and it is then ignited and a dense fume produced, which the Chinaman, lying on his back, draws through the long tube of his pipe into his mouth, and swallows a part of it, and puffs the rest out through his nose. Sleep soon succeeds, accompanied probably with all the pleasing reveries which opium usually produces when taken into the stomach. This is the highest species of luxury in which a Chinaman can indulge, and there were few, I was told, who could afford it, that did not so far disregard the laws of the empire as to participate in it. The trade in opium has speedily enriched almost all the foreigners who have been engaged in it; and while I was staying with Mr. Latimer, he made upwards of twenty thousand dollars in one day, in consequence of the sudden rise in the price of the article.[20]

With respect to the Chinese themselves, I can say but little; but that is more in their favour than the opinions which foreigners have generally expressed of them.[21] So far as I had dealing with them, I found them to act as honorably as the same class of people in the U. States. Their complexion is darker than I had supposed, being quite as far removed from white, as that of our indians, but partaking rather of a yellow than of a copper colour. The dress of both sexes consists of short, loose trousers, and of a wide frock, which descends below the knees. These garments in the lower classes are of cotton, but in the higher of silk.

I had several opportunities of seeing the celebrated small feet; and wondered how the Chinese ladies could submit to a fashion so ridiculous, {and which must have cost them so much suffering, until it occurred to me, that the fashion of tight-lacing which my fair countrywomen follow as obsequiously as the ladies of China of that of cramping and deforming their feet, is at least quite as ridiculous, and far more injurious.} The foot of a Chinese lady of fashion, is about four inches long, with all the toes, except the great one, doubled down and immovably imbeded into the sole of the foot. The ancle, however, is disproportionately large and clumsy. The walking of one of these ladies, is tottering and unsteady, like that of a child when first beginning to use its feet.

Sunday Dec. 2. This morning at about ten o'clock, we took leave of our kind and hospitable entertainer, and bade adieu to Canton; a place which I had always been desirous to see, but which I had no desire ever to see again. {My two mess-mates, namely Lieutenants Cunningham and Sinclair, who had been staying at Mr. Latimer's with me, were my companions in returning.} We embarked at Canton in a boat belonging to Capt. Pierce, whom I have already had occasion to mention, which he had sent up by my request for our accommodation. On our passage down the river to Whampoa, nothing new presented itself deserving of notice, {with the exception of a Duck-Boat, which may be ranked among Chinese curiosities. These boats are so named from their being used for keeping ducks for market, of which several hundreds usually belong to each boat. The floating poultry yards, move from place to place along the banks of the river, and whenever they meet with a paddy-field, which affords a supply of food for the numerous flock, the boats are moored, and the ducks are sent out into the field, and suffered to remain there till they have satisfied their appetites; when at the call of their keeper they all hurry back to the boat with the utmost speed. The one that is so unfortunate as to be the last receives chastisement from its keeper, which appears to have quite as much affect in preventing a repetition of the offence as the same method has with beings of a higher order. We saw one of these boats anchored near a paddy-field, in which several hundred ducks were busily employed in gathering their food.}

The tide being in our favor, we descended the river at quite a rapid rate, and before one o'clock, reached Capt. Pierce's ship, the *Jeanette*, where we took dinner. Finding on our arrival here, that the ship in which we had expected to take passage to Lintin had sailed, we had to look for another opportunity; and fortunately we met with one without experiencing any delay. The ship *Israel*, Capt. Crocker [W. Crocker], was to sail the same evening for Lintin, and we were kindly offered a passage. About nine o'clock we went on board, but the wind being unfavorable, the ship did not get under way till the next morning. As soon as the tide began to ebb on Monday morning, we got under way and proceeded down the river; but the wind being still ahead, we were obliged to anchor when the tide turned, and remain at anchor during the flood. In this manner we proceeded, until we reached Lintin, which was early on Wednesday morning. [Dec. 5]

For myself, I had no occasion to regret that our passage was so long, as I found Capt. Crocker to be not only a generous, kind-hearted man, but moreover, a man of real piety; at least his conversation and conduct, gave me reason so to consider him.

During this passage in the *Israel*, I had an opportunity of learning some farther particulars respecting the outrage on the *Friendship* at Qualo Battoo, of which I have already had occasion, more than once to make some remarks. The supercargo of the *Israel*, Mr. Dana told me that he was on board the *Friendship* soon after the outrage was committed; and he related to me facts which prove conclusively, that such provocation had been given to the natives as would fully justify, according to the law of retaliation, the only one by which such people are governed, the measures which they adopted. He had witnessed himself the fraud committed on those ignorant people by American traders, in having false weights which they used in taking in cargoes of pepper, and by which the natives were cheated out of at least one sixth part of the cargo. This in an article so valuable as pepper, must have amounted to a very large sum. An attempt was made, it is true, to justify this nefarious proceeding, by assigning as the reason for it, that the natives were in the habit of mixing sand with their pepper, and also of wetting it with salt-water, of which it will absorb a good deal, for the purpose of increasing its weight; but the truth is, I have not the least doubt, the natives never had recourse to this fraudulent practice, till they found themselves cheated by foreigners, and then only in self-defense. The gentleman who stated to me this fact, acknowledged that he was interested in it; and he seemed desirous to justify the conduct of his countrymen on the ground that I have mentioned; but he did not succeed in convincing me, that the natives were the first aggressors.

In the course of our conversation on this subject, he stated another fact, which, though not immediately connected with the transaction that has led to these remarks, tends nevertheless, to confirm the opinion that I have expressed, of the fraud being first committed by those who ought to have set before the poor natives of Sumatra, an example of fair and honorable dealing. The fact to which I allude, was an instance of the same species of fraud, committed by an American Captain in the port of Leghorn, with which the Sumatrans have been charged, and which has been assigned as an excuse for cheating them in return, until they were provoked to commit acts of murder and robbery, for which they have been visited with a severe punishment. Mr. Dana was again a witness to the dishonesty of his countrymen, which consisted in wetting with sea-water the pepper that was about to be sold, so as to add at least a sixth part to its weight. {No attempt was made to justify this iniquitous conduct, by pleading the dishonesty of those who were the objects of it.}

Now taking all these facts and circumstances into consideration, we cannot come to any other conclusion, it appears to me, with respect to the measures of our Government towards the people of Qualo Battoo, than that they were in a high degree precipitate, unjust, and cruel.

December 5. At about seven o'clock in the morning we reached Lintin, and immediately went on board our ship, where we found that nothing very important had occurred during our absence. {Several of our men had run away, it is true, but they were such as could well be spared, being all of them the least useful of the men composing the crew.} During our absence, however, a ship {the *Franklin*,} had arrived from the U.S. and brought accounts from N. York to the 14th. of July [1832]; by which we learned that the Cholera had made its appearance in that city, and occasioned the greatest consternation. {Among the several particulars stated by the Capt. of the *Franklin*, which gave me uneasiness, there was one that caused me peculiar distress. This was the death of two ladies, who left N. York in good health for Connecticut, and died the next day. From the Capt's statement, this must have taken place just at the time when my wife expected to be in N. York; and although there might be hundreds of ladies who left that city for Connecticut at the same time, yet I could not free myself from the distressing fear, that my dear wife might be one of those two ladies, who thus suddenly fell victims to the Cholera.

When I left the ship for Canton, there were two men on the sick list with dysentery, who had been labouring under it a long time, and had become so bad, that I saw no prospect of their recovery. On my return, I found them both worse, and it was evident that their lives were rapidly drawing to a close.}

December 20. At three o'clock this morning, the last of the two men whom I have mentioned above Wm Buker was released by death from his sufferings, which he had borne with much patience and fortitude. {The other man died five days before. His death was sudden and unexpected, and although he had been led to consider his recovery as very uncertain, yet he seemed to view death with great indifference, and exhibited no evidence that he was prepared to meet it. With the other, however, it was different.} He [Buker] became convinced, several days before he died, that his life was fast drawing to an end; and his conscience, which had never before caused him any uneasiness, was aroused, and he began to look back on a wicked life, and forward to the eternal world, into which he was sensible he must soon enter, with dreadful apprehensions. His life had been short, and he had spent the whole of it, as he freely acknowledged, in those practices of vice and dissipation, to which sailors are almost universally addicted. He had been watched over, and often and earnestly admonished by a pious mother, until he was seven or eight years old, when she died; and he spoke of her with much feeling, and lamented that her pious instructions had not been followed. A pious uncle had also taken great pains with him; but all to no effect. He had passed through many dangers both by land and sea, and his life had been preserved almost as by miracle; but he remained unmoved notwithstanding these alarming warnings, and it was only till a lingering disease had reduced him to the last state of suffering, that he began to turn his thoughts towards a future world. But the prospect there was terrible, for his sins had been too many and great, as he supposed, to admit of pardon, and he despaired of the happiness which he would give the world to obtain. He wished anxiously for instruction on this all-important subject, and I did all in my power to give a right direction to his thoughts, and to point out to him the only source from which he could hope for pardon and future happiness. The bible was read to him, especially those passages which seemed peculiarly applicable to his case; but the bible he had hitherto entirely neglected, and now its doctrines and precepts were dark and difficult, and he could not understand them. He was told of a God and Savior against whom he had sinned during his life; of the indispensable necessity of repentance, and faith in the Lord Jesus Christ; and that he must rely entirely upon the merits and intercession of the Savior, for pardon and salvation. To all this he seemed readily to assent, and professed to feel the most sincere sorrow for the sins which he had committed, and expressed a confident belief, that if his life were to be spared, it would be spent in an entirely different manner from what it had been, but he found it impossible to bring his mind to that exercise of faith, and to that unreserved surrender of himself to the divine disposal, which he now saw to be necessary, and most anxiously desired. He tried to pray, for his awakened conscience urged him to offer his supplications to the God whom he had so often offended, and in whose presence he expected very soon to appear, but this exercise was so entirely new to him, that he could not engage in it with such feelings as he desired, and he did not derive that comfort and satisfaction from it which he had ardently hoped for. In this distressful situation he continued, his strength gradually failing, but with the perfect exercise of his reason, until death terminated the painful scene. When he perceived that death was near, he expressed a perfect willingness, or even a desire to die; but at the same time he declared that his feelings afforded him no evidence, that his sins were pardoned, and the salvation of his soul secured. Such was the melancholy close of a life {consisting of four or five and twenty-years} which had been wholly spent in sinful practices; and it taught to all who witnessed it, in the most impressive manner, the all-important truth, that religion alone can enable one to meet the king of terrors with a peaceful resignation, and to look forward to the future world without alarm.

December 22. On this day the capt. and Mr. Roberts arrived from Canton, where they had been from the 10th of November. This was a signal of our speedy departure, which was highly gratifying to us all; as our stay had already been protracted much beyond the period which had been assigned for it, and the weather was becoming quite cold and uncomfortable, which made a warmer climate highly desirable. Mr. Roberts, however, had some business to transact at Macao; and after a short stop at the ship, he continued on to that place in the vessel which had brought him and the Capt. down from Canton.[22]

December 25. Mr. Roberts returned from Macao this afternoon, in company with Lieut. Brent & Dr. Gilchrist, my Assistant, who had been there on a visit from the preceding Sunday. Mr. Morrison [John Robert Morrison], a son of Dr. Morrison, a young gentleman one or two and twenty, was also one of the party, and had been employed by Mr. Roberts as interpreter, and also as private secretary.[23] Every thing being now ready for our departure, we only waited for a fair wind, to weigh anchor and bid adieu to the Celestial Empire.

CHAPTER VIII

Vunglam

Departure from Canton; Arrive off Turon Bay; Run to Phuy
Een; Arrival at Phuy Een; Visit from a Priest; Excursions on
shore; Other Mandarins visit the ship; Discussion with the
Mandarins; Renewal of the discussion; Present from the King;
Another deputation from Hué; Departure from Cochin China;
Remarks on Cochin China; Character & habits of the people;
Provisions etc.; Passage from Cochin China to Siam.

December 29. From the 25th. until this day the weather had continued so
unpleasant, that notwithstanding the wind was fair, it was deemed advisable
to remain in port. On this day, however, the weather partially cleared up,
and about twelve o'clock we got under way and stood out to sea. {The wind
being fresh and fair, we found ourselves in a few hours, tossing on the
troubled bason of the China-Sea.} An English ship the *Ann* of Bombay,
Captain Allen,[1] left the anchorage at Lintin about the same time that we
did; but she stopped at Macao to take on board some passengers, and we
passed her there and saw no more of her. I had made several visits on board
this ship, to see one of the officers who was quite ill with Bilious Remittent
fever,[2] and my last visit was made while she was getting under way. I had
the satisfaction to find my patient better, and notwithstanding he would
receive no farther medical attendance, there being no medical officer on
board, although the ship was nine hundred tons, and had a complement
of a hundred men; there was reason to believe that he would ultimately
recover.

An American ship, the *Tremont*, Capt. Sturgis, sailed from Lintin a
few hours before us; but we passed her during the following night, and the

next morning she was so far astern of us, that she was scarcely visible. This was an achievement which caused considerable exultation among the sea-officers, and obtained for the *Peacock* a good share of praise. Hitherto she had been considered by most of the officers, who professed to be competent judges on the subject, as rather a dull sailer; {but she now proved herself to be entitled to a better name than she had received, since as she had gained so much of a ship which had borne a tolerable reputation for sailing.}

January 1, 1833. We found ourselves today within sight of the high lands about Turon Bay, the port to which we were bound, and the nearest to Hué, the capital of Cochin China, and the residence of the King. From the time of our leaving Lintin, until we had arrived in the neighbourhood of our port, the weather had been cloudy and rainy, with the exception of a few hours on the 30th. when the clouds broke away, so that we were enabled to get an observation, and ascertain our latitude. Expecting that the N.E. monsoon prevailed as well in Turon Bay as in the China Sea, we had flattered ourselves with the prospect of an easy entrance into the harbour, on the same day that we arrived within sight of it. As the event proved, however, we had calculated very erroneously; for we had no sooner obtained a view of the most elevated land-marks about the harbour, than the wind changed its direction to N.W. which was directly ahead for entering the harbour; and was accompanied with thick heavy weather, {which entirely obscured the land, and with occasionally heavy showers of rain.} In these circumstances it became necessary to stand from the land, till the weather cleared up so that we could see our way into the harbour; {and the current being strong to the southward, care was taken to avoid being carried to the leeward of the port.}

Jan. 3. Notwithstanding all that could be done, however, to maintain our position to the northward of the port, until a change of wind and weather should permit us to enter; we found ourselves on this day, when we were enabled for the first time for four days to ascertain our latitude by observation, about forty-five miles to the southward of the harbour. Our prospect of reaching this port was now quite discouraging, as we had to beat a distance of forty-five miles, against an adverse wind, as well as against a strong current and heavy swell; for the wind had now resumed its usual direction from the N.E. which would have been fair, if we could have maintained our position to the northward of the port. Notwithstanding there seemed scarcely a possibility that we could contend successfully against

such powerful obstacles; still it was deemed advisable to make the effort and
see whether, in the course of twenty-four hours, we could make any progress
towards our destined port.

{Jan. 4. The weather on this day, was fortunately clear, so that a meridian
observation was obtained, from which it appeared, that we had not advanced
a single mile towards our port. It now became evident, that small as the
distance was that separated us from Turon Bay, we should never diminish it
by beating against a strong current and heavy sea; as the attempt which we
had already made, has been attended with as favourable circumstances as
could be reasonably expected; and since this had failed, we could not expect
that any farther efforts would be more successful. It was therefore determined
to abandon the design of going into Turon harbour, and to direct our course
for a harbour, which was represented as being a very good one, about two
degrees to the southward of Turon. This was called the harbour of Phuy-
Een [Phuyen], and at five o'clock in the afternoon we commenced our
progress towards it; but moved at a moderate rate lest we should be again
carried to leeward, before we might have an opportunity of determining
our situation.}

Jan. 5. During the preceding night we had been favoured with a moderate
breeze, and found ourselves at day-light this morning within a few miles of
the coast of Cochin-China, and as we supposed forty or fifty miles to the
northward of our port, after making a large allowance for the force of the
current. The current, however, had a good deal exceeded the calculation
that had been made for it, {and instead of being forty miles from the port
to which we were bound, we were not more than ten; and had not the wind
been light, and the atmosphere clear, so that every object along the coast
was distinctly visible to us, we should certainly have been again carried to
the leeward of our port, and probably been compelled to abandon the
mission to Hué, till the change of the monsoons in April or May.}

The objects by which an approach to the harbour of Phuy-Een from
the north may be known, are; first, several, dark coloured, pointed, conical
rocks, standing apparently at a small distance from the coast, and rising
fifteen or twenty-feet above the water; second, a bed of very white sand,
which rises from the sea in an oblique direction up the side of a hill, and
being rather narrow, and bounded on each side by verdure, exhibits the
appearance of a white belt on a ground of green; and third an island a mile
or two in length, situated near the coast, and running parallel with it; the

northern extremity of it, which is but a little distance to the southward of the belt of sand which has just been mentioned, being probably two hundred feet high, and there being a gradual descent to the other extremity. This island, as well as the adjoining coast, was covered with verdure. At the distance of a few miles from the coast runs a chain of mountains, broken into peaks of various elevation, some of which were at least three thousand feet high.

We were first led to suspect {an error in our reckoning on account of the unexpected velocity of the current, by the conical rocks and the island which have been mentioned, and also by a conical mount of considerable elevation, which presented itself nearly ahead, at the distance of twenty or thirty miles; but} our near approach to Phuy-Een was rendered certain by the appearance of a great number of boats at the distance of a few miles from us. In order, however, to be certain of our situation with relation to the entrance of the harbour, the first Lieut. was sent, with Mr. Morrison as interpreter, to those boats, for the purpose of obtaining the requisite information. A signal was soon made directing our course into the harbour, where we arrived and anchored at twelve o'clock.[3]

We had been an hour or two at anchor when we were visited by an old man with a long white beard descending to his breast, and clad in a most miserable garb; who proved to be one of the lower order of mandarins, and had come to make inquiries respecting our character, and the object of our visit. As our interpreter was unable to speak the language of Cochin-China, and our visitor being unable to speak Chinese, they could communicate with each other only by means of the Chinese characters, which are used in the written language of Cochin-China, as well as in China itself. By this means a correspondence was maintained without difficulty, till all the old man's inquiries were answered, when he took leave of us, having given us rather an unfavourable impression of the people of Cochin-China.[4]

Jan. 6 This afternoon we were again visited by the old mandarin, who was accompanied by two or three others of a rather higher order, and also by a Chinaman as interpreter, and five or six others, apparently of the lowest class of the people. Mr. Roberts being absent when this party arrived, they were detained till he returned; and in the mean time were introduced into the cabin and ward-room, and treated with brandy, of which some of them drank so freely as to manifest signs of intoxication before they left the ship. The object of this visit, was to obtain farther information respecting ourselves, and the design of our entering the port. Having received such answers to their inquiries as Mr. Roberts deemed it proper to make to persons of their rank, they left us a little after sunset, much to our satisfaction; as they were becoming so familiar as to be quite troublesome.

Jan. 8. [Jan. 7][5] Until this day, nothing had been definitely arranged with regard to the mission, as the mandarins, who had yet visited us, were not considered competent to take upon themselves a business of so much importance; but an officer of higher rank than any we had yet seen came on board today, who engaged, after considerable discussion, to receive the communication which Mr. Roberts had prepared for the King, and forward it to him immediately. He manifested considerable reluctance, however, to do this in consequence, as it appeared, of the refusal of Mr. Roberts to answer certain inquiries which he made, and which Mr. R. considered impertinent, and therefore not deserving of an answer. These inquiries, or rather demands, as they may more properly be considered, related to the powers with which Mr. R. was vested, and to the presents that he had brought for the King. Not being satisfied with the assurance of Mr. R. that he was duly authorized for the mission on which he was sent to the King of Cochin-China, or with the evidence which he might have derived from the fact, of his being in a public ship of the U. States; he demanded a sight of his credentials. To this demand a prompt and positive refusal was very properly made, and he was told, moreover, that they would not be shown even to the Governor of the province. Mr. R. was next required to inform him whether he had brought any presents for the King; but this demand was also met with a decided refusal, on the ground that it was made by one who was not duly authorized to make it. Not being able to obtain any satisfactory information on these important points, the mandarin seemed resolved to have no agency in forwarding the mission; but on being asked by Mr. R. in direct terms, whether he would engage to forward his communication to Hué as soon as it should be ready, he reluctantly consented; and before night the despatch was prepared in due form and sent ashore to him, where he waited to receive it.

Jan. 9. [Jan. 8] About nine o'clock this morning another party from shore came on board consisting of six or seven persons; one of whom appeared to be of a higher rank than the rest, and exhibited quite a decent exterior. Mr. Morrison being absent, his efforts to make us understand the object of his visit, were unavailing, until he pronounced a word or two of latin so as to be understood, and made signs for a pen; when the following dialogue commenced between him and myself in latin, and was carried on by writing, his pronunciation of latin being so different from what I had been accustomed to, that I could not understand him.[6]

He began thus: "I am a Catholic Priest, and am sent by the Governor, to learn of what nation you are, and whether you are Catholics"?

Ans: We are from North America, and a few of us are Catholics.

Priest: "Is your business here with our King, or is this a merchant ship"?

Ans: Our business is with your King, and this is a ship of war (navis regia) a public or King's ship, and not a merchant ship.

Priest: "Is it your intention to remain here, or go to our King at Hué"?

Ans: We expect to visit your King at Hué when we hear from him.

Priest: "Have you any presents"?

Ans: I cannot answer that question.

Priest: "I am sent by the Governor (Praefectus) to learn of what nation you are and what business you have with our King."

Ans: We are from the U. States of N. America and a message had been forwarded to your King, respecting our business. Have you any knowledge of N. America?

Priest: "I do not know any thing of N. A. Has your King sent presents to our King, or do you come empty-handed"?

Ans: This is a question which I cannot answer.

Priest: "Have you an envoy (nuntium) to our King, (ad nostrum regem) duly qualified to be admitted into his presence (ad visitandum et cognoscendum)"?

Ans: We have an Envoy on board to your King, to be received and acknowledged by him.

Priest: "How many cubits long is your ship"?

Ans: About a hundred.

Priest: "I wish now to return to the Governor who sent me."

There the dialogue ended, and the Priest with his attendants soon afterwards left the ship. He was a native of Cochin China, and appeared to be a very mild amiable man; that was very deficient in general knowledge, notwithstanding he had been educated, (as he said) at a Catholic college. His ignorance of the usages of nations, as well as of geography and general history, was manifested by a remark that he made on the answer to another question which he asked and which I forgot to insert in its proper place. The question, with my answer and his remark were as follows—

464

a decent exterior. Mr. Morrison being
absent, his efforts to make us underst.
and the object of his visit, were unavailing, until he pronounced a
word or two of latin so as to be understood,
and made signs for a pen; when the
following dialogue commenced between him and my self in latin, and was
carried on by writing, his pronunciation
of latin being so different from what I had been accustomed to, that
I could not understand him. He began
thus: "I am a Catholic Priest, and am sent
by the Governor, to learn of what nation
you are, and whether you are Catholics"?
Ans: We are from North America, and a
few of us are Catholics.
Priest: Is your business here with our
King, or is this a merchants ship"?
Ans: Our business is with your King, and
this is a ship of war (Navis regia) a
public or King's ship, and not a merchant ship.
Priest: "Is it your intention to remain here,

Dr. Ticknor's Latin dialogue, page 464 of Journal II B. (Benajah Ticknor Papers,
Manuscripts and Archives, Yale University Library.)

Priest: "Is this a ship of war or a merchant ship, and do you come with friendly views"?

Ans: This is a ship of war, and not a merchant ship; and we come here with the most friendly motives.

On receiving this answer, he said with a smile, and an air of incredulity, "a ship of war come here with friendly motives"? thus intimating his belief, that an armed ship could enter their port with no other than hostile intentions.

Jan 17. From the last date until this day, nothing hardly occurred deserving of particular notice. For several days none of the native boats came off to the ship, and we were unable to obtain any supplies from the shore, as the people seemed fearful of us, and unwilling to admit us to any intercourse with them, until they had become satisfied with regard to our character and designs. After four or five days, however, their reserve so far yielded to their interests that they began, not only to furnish us with supplies by our sending on shore for them, but even to bring them on board themselves. At first the supply was scanty, and the articles were dear; but finding that the demand for them still continued, and rather increased, they were induced to increase the supply as well as to lower the prices; so that we obtained without difficulty almost every thing that we wanted and at as reasonable a rate as we expected.

During the interval of which I am now speaking, parties were on shore almost every day for the purpose of recreation and collecting shells. On two or three occasions, I joined these parties, and perambulated the shore of the bay over rocks, and through the sand, for a distance of several miles. In these excursions we passed several little villages or groups of bamboo huts in the vicinity of the bay, and were frequently surrounded by large numbers of the natives, both male and female. They gazed on us with eager curiosity, having probably never seen a foreign face before. Their conduct was generally very civil, and with the exception of a few of the soldiers, whom we occasionally met with, they gave us no other trouble than by their urgent importunity for us to exchange the buttons on our clothes for the shells which they offered us. Nothing seemed so valuable in their eyes as our gilt buttons, and to obtain them they seemed ready to part with every thing they possessed. Their appearance was exceedingly disgusting, on account of their neglect of cleanliness, their practice of chewing betel nut, and of a cutaneous disease resembling the itch, with which many of them were affected. They appeared, so far as I could judge, to lead an indolent inactive

life; and notwithstanding the land in the neighbourhood of the bay exhibited marks of fertility; still it was so inefficiently cultivated that it produced
only a small part of what it might have been made to produce, if agriculture
had received due encouragement.

Civilization appeared to have made very little progress among these
people, and they manifested in several instances, a want of those natural
affections which are generally found even in the breast of the most uncivilized
of the human family. I allude particularly, however, to a want of maternal
affection, which is found as deeply implanted in the heart of an uncultivated
native of the forest, and to exert as great power there, as it does among the
most enlightened and refined. One of the first persons that I met with on
my first visit to the shore, was a mother with an infant in her arms; and as
she saw me, she reached out her child towards me signifying that she wished
me to take it away and keep it; and when she found her offer rejected, and
that she must still be burdened with the care of her own offspring, she
manifested by her looks that she knew not what would become of herself
and her child. That condition of life must certainly be wretched in the
extreme, which can compel a mother to give away the infant that she is
holding in her arms, and that receives its nourishment from her breasts to
a stranger whom she had never seen before, and would never see again.

When the despatch of Mr. Roberts to the King at Hué was sent on
shore to the Mandarin to be forwarded, it was expected that twelve days
would elapse, before an answer would be returned. But about sunset of the
ninth day after the despatch left the ship, that is, the 17th. of the month,
a message arrived from Hué. A little before sunset, two large boats, accompanied by a small one were observed to be slowly advancing from the shore
towards the ship; and when it was ascertained that they had persons on
board who wished to visit the ship, one of our large boats was sent to bring
them on board. They proved to be four Mandarins, who had come to
superintend the business of the mission.[7] Two of them were from Hué, the
residence of the King, but the others were from one of the provinces. These
were a higher grade of Mandarins than any who had yet visited us, though
they were also of a subordinate rank; and their appearance was much more
genteel than that of our former visitors.

They were clad in silk, the outer garment being a kind of frock, which
descended to the ancles, and had wide loose sleeves. The colours of these
garments were green and blue, but whether they indicated a difference of
rank in the wearers, I did not learn. They wore no hats, but had their heads
encircled with rolls of crape in the form of turbans. They had on no

stockings, but wore a kind of sandal on their feet with thick wooden soles, and which were so made, as just to admit the toes, a very clumsy awkward substitute for shoes. They had long white beards, which gave them quite a venerable aspect.

But little time elapsed after they were seated in the cabin, before they made known the object of their visit, and they entered upon the business with which they said the Minister at Hué had entrusted them. This was, as it very soon appeared, to apprize Mr. Roberts of an error which he had committed in the direction of his despatch to the King; and also to direct him, both as to the contents and the address, of another letter. The letter which had been addressed to the King, was returned, on the ground, as they alleged, in the first place, that it ought not to have been address[ed] to the King at all, but to the Prime-Minister; and in the second place, that if it had been proper to address the king himself, there was an error of one or two characters which would have prevented its being received.[8] These were the reasons which they assigned, of the letter being returned, but it soon appeared that there were others to which they attached greater importance, and which at first threatened to defeat the mission, and occasion our immediate departure from the port. Notwithstanding they had expressed themselves in very flattering terms respecting our country, at the beginning of the conference; saying that they had been informed what a great and glorious nation ours was, and were very happy to see one of our public ships in their waters; yet, when the subject of a communication to the Prime Minister came under consideration, and they were requested to give his address, their suspicion, that the Minister of this "great and glorious nation", was about to propose terms, to their Government which would involve it in difficulty, would not suffer them to give the address which Mr. R. asked for, until they had seen the contents of the letter. But this condition, improper as it was, did not satisfy them and they proposed others which were even more objectionable. These were, that they should be made acquainted with the communication which Mr. R. was authorized to make to the King; and that he should address the Prime Minister in the terms which they dictated, and which solicited in the most humble and supplicating style, that he, the Prime Minister, to whom Mr. R. acknowledged himself inferior, would be pleased to introduce him to the King.[9] Such arrogant demands kindled Mr. R.-'s resentment, and rising hastily from his seat, he assured them that if these terms were insisted upon, he had nothing farther to do; but should immediately proceed to sea, and when he reached the U.S. should report to his government the obstacles which they had thrown in the way of his mission. The communication, he told them, which he was commissioned to make to the King of Cochin-China, was from the President of the U.S. and he was directed to deliver it to the King in person; and consequently they could not be permitted to see it. And as to the humiliating and supplicating letter which they wished him to write to the Minister; the letter was his own, and he would suffer nobody to dictate it to him, and much less should he consent to use the language of supplication, as if begging a favour of an acknowledged supperior; since he had no favour to ask, but only propositions to make, which were as much for the benefit of Cochin-China as the U.S; and he acknowledged no superior in Cochin China, except the King himself. Such prompt and decided language confounded them, and they begged Mr. R. not to consider them as throwing any obstacles in the way of his mission. Still, however, they refused to give the address of the Minister, and they tried every indirect method in their power, to ascertain the particular object of the mission, but without effect; Mr. R. being determined to keep them in ignorance on a point, with which he was satisfied they had no right to be made acquainted. The subject of presents for the King was also agitated in the course of the conference; but here they were equally unsuccessful, no answer at all being made to their inquiry. Mr. R. declined answering their questions in relation to presents, on the very proper ground, that, on the one hand he would give no occasion to the Government of Cochin China to proclaim him a tribute-bearer, as the Chinese Government did Lord Amherst, by letting it be known that he had presents for the King; and on the other, he would not defeat the mission by declaring that he had none.[10] In such fruitless discussions the evening was spent till eleven o'clock, when the conference broke up, and the Mandarins with their attendants left the ship, having agreed to resume the negociation the next day.

Jan. 18. About twelve o'clock today, the Mandarins and their attendants, (among whom were two who came as interpreters, one speaking Portuguese, and the other a little English, and both natives of Cochin China) came on board, and after a little delay, the unfinished business of the preceding evening was resumed. Mr. Roberts not being quite ready to receive them when they came on board, they were taken into the Ward-Room, where they spent about half an hour in making inquiries respecting our country; of the extent and situation of which, they evidently possessed no correct knowledge. They knew that our country was once under the Government of England, but was now independant, and they asked how long it was since we became independant, and what were the powers and prerogatives of our King. In answer to these inquiries they were told, that we had been an independant nation fifty six years; and that our King was elected by the people every four years. Before the latter answer was made, however, the first Lieut. to whom the questions were addressed, began to tell them through the interpreter, that we had no King, but selected from among the people the wisest and best man for our chief ruler or magistrate; and in this way he was proceeding to delineate to them the form of our Government, when he was checked, by being told that inasmuch as our republican form of Government could not be so explained to them that they would understand it, it would probably be productive of bad effects on the mission, to tell them that we had no King, from whom alone, according to their ideas, an Envoy could derive the necessary powers. It was therefore deemed proper, to give to our President the title of King, and to tell them that he was elective; as they could readily understand this method of bestowing the regal title and powers, it being the practice in their own country, to depose one king and place another on the throne, whenever such a measure is supposed to be beneficial to the country.

This information was perfectly satisfactory to them, with regard to the powers of the President, a title which they were led to consider as synonymous with King; but they were desirous to learn his age, and whether he had any children.

In addition to the inquiries respecting our country, they made some respecting Europe, which showed that they were not entirely ignorant of the events which have recently taken place there. They not only knew of the abdication of the late king of France, and of the disturbances in Portugal & Spain; but also of the Reform Bill in England, and proposed questions on all these subjects.

In this manner the time was spent, until Mr. Roberts was prepared to receive them; when they were introduced into the cabin, and the business of the mission was resumed.

Mr. Roberts had written a letter to the Prime Minister which he would show them on condition that they should previously give him the address which he had asked for; but he declared to them at the same time in unequivocal terms, that they should not make any alteration in the letter, which could materially alter its import. At this declaration they seemed rather confounded, and refused to give the required address. They again renewed their efforts to draw from Mr. R. the information which he had refused to communicate at the preceding interview, respecting the particular objects of his mission; but finding him determined rather to leave the port without proceeding any farther in the negociation, than satisfy their inquiries, they consented at length to the proposition that he made, and gave him the address. The letter was now put into their hands, which merely informed the Minister, that the writer of it, was sent as an Envoy by the Government of the U. States to the King of Cochin China, to propose to him terms of a free and friendly intercourse between the two nations; and that he desired an introduction to the King, for the purpose of communicating to him the terms which the President of the U.S. had authorized him to propose. They suggested several alterations in the letter, and among others, that the term friendly intercourse should be substituted by that of neighbourly intercourse, intimating that the former implied a closer connection than they wished their King to enter into with the U. States. At this Mr. Roberts laughed heartily, the idea of a neighbourly intercourse between nations twenty thousand miles apart, appearing exceedingly absurd; and although they seemed at first surprized that he should receive their proposition with a burst of laughter, yet when they were told of the cause of it, they joined heartily in the laughter occasioned by their own ignorance, and seized Mr. R. by the hand, in token of their readiness to reciprocate a friendly feeling. The proposed alteration was of course abandoned, and none other of material consequence was proposed.[11] The letter to the Minister having thus received their approbation was signed, sealed, and delivered to them for immediate conveyance to Hué. This being the only business of the present conference, it terminated as soon as the letter was ready, and the Mandarins with their attendants took their leave about three o'clock in the afternoon.

It is customary with the people of Cochin China, to make presents to foreigners who have any dealing with them, and to receive presents in return, and on their last visit to the ship, the Mandarins brought a present to Mr. R. consisting of a bullock, three sacks of rice, a pig, nine fowls, and three jars of liquor made from rice, which is a very tolerable substitute for wine. {Whether they expected a present in return or not, I do not know;} but none was made, and probably for the same reason that no answer had been given to the question of presents for the King.

{In transacting the business of the two interviews of which I have given an account, Mr. Morrison was the medium of communication between the two parties; and the conference was carried on wholly in writing, and by the use of the Chinese characters. This young gentleman appeared as familiar with the Chinese written language, as the Mandarins themselves, and translated with such facility, that the parties experienced but little delay in communicating with each other. The interpreters who accompanied the Mandarins had consequently very little to do,}

Before the Mandarins left the ship, they said that they should remain at the village nearest to us which was called Vunglam, during our stay in the port, and would see that every thing was provided for the ship that we required.

Jan. 20. When the Mandarins left the ship at the close of the interview on the 18th. they invited the Capt. and Mr. R. to visit them the next day at their residence on shore. For some reason unknown to me they did not go; but Mr. Morrison went, accompanied by Dr. Gilchrist and Lieut. Fowler, and they met with a very friendly and hospitable reception. On the following day [Jan. 20] they returned the visit, and staid on board about an hour. They came in a barge rowed by thirty men, and were attended by their usual retinue of interpreters and servants. On leaving the ship, they manifested some signs of dissatisfaction; but on what account, nobody knew.

{Jan. 22. Men vested with similar power and authority can never remain long together without disagreement, unless a constant and watchful guard is kept over their passions, and there is an exercise of mutual forbearance. To men jealous of the power which they possess, and quick to discern every supposed encroachment upon it, the most insignificant causes are sufficient to produce the most violent explosion, and to transform those who were apparently friends, into the most implacable enemies. The truth of these remarks was verified by the occurrences of this day, which I record only to show how unhappy men render themselves by allowing indulgence to their angry passions, and how necessary it is, that they should be kept under the strictest control.

It happened that the officer of the deck, Mr. Brown [William H. Brown], an acting Lieut. left the deck in charge of a Midshipman and went below to his dinner, just as the first Lieut. [Robert B. Cunningham] was coming along side from the shore, where he had been to superintend some work which the mechanics were doing for the ship. According to the regulations of the service, Mr. Brown ought to have been on deck to receive the first Lieut., but having held the office of Lieut. only a short time, he was not aware that he was treating the first Lieut. with disrespect, by leaving a midship. on deck to receive him. It was construed into disrespect however, by the first Lieut. and instead of speaking to Mr. B. and showing him his fault, which would have rendered any farther steps entirely unnecessary, he reported him to the Capt. and demanded his arrest. On investigating the case, and learning the Mr. B. did not intend any disrespect to the first Lieut. the Capt. refused to arrest him. This led to a conference between the Capt. and First Lieut. which commenced and was maintained by crimination, and recrimination, and terminated with feelings of the most determined hostility.

To report the reproaches and accusations that were made and retorted in rapid succession, during this angry interview, is what I shall not spend my time in attempting to do. As almost always happens in contests like this, both parties were in fault, and perhaps equally so. The Capt. feeling himself very uneasy under the responsibility which naval commanders usually consider as belonging exclusively to themselves, and which they never transfer to others, of superintending and directing the discipline of their ships; had transferred the greater part of this responsibility to the first Lieut. and authorized him to pursue such measures with regard to the internal concerns of the ship, as he might think proper. This constituted the principal fault of the Capt. in relation to the disagreement of which I have been speaking; and the great fault of the first Lieut. consisted in his not being satisfied with the powers which he already possessed, and in his presuming upon the weakness and incompetency of the Capt. to arraign his conduct in such reproachful and dictatorial terms as he would not otherwise have dared to use. The one, in freeing himself from the responsibility which properly belonged to him, but which he found to be too great for him to sustain, had lost in a considerable degree, the authority which he was now desirous to exercise; and the other, by being allowed more power than belonged to his station, was uneasy and dissatisfied because he had not the entire control, both of the ship and the commander. Both were anxious for popularity, and each asserted over the other a superiority in this respect when in fact, neither of them possessed much popularity with the officers and crew, as he might have done, by pursuing to its full extent the proper line of duty. The Capt. had perhaps relaxed the reins of discipline rather too much; but the first Lieut. was disposed to hold them too tight.

A regular course of discipline is certainly necessary in public ships; but there are many minutiae of discipline, which are of no real importance, and which may therefore be dispensed with, without the least injury to the service. To these, however, first Lieuts. are apt to attach very great importance; because by so doing, they have an opportunity of making their power felt to its fullest extent. Indeed it may be said of all officers, so far as I know, who have the control of discipline, that the minutiae are attended to, while the more important particulars are neglected. Of such persons it may be said with the greatest propriety, that they "strain at a gnat and swallow a camel", because they consider it a great offence to neglect any of the trifling particulars of discipline, as going on deck without uniform, setting down on deck etc; while they bear the most profane and indecent language used every hour in the day, without taking any notice of it, and are even themselves, frequently guilty of the same practice. A violation of the regulations of the navy which Congress has established, is committed every day, and indeed every hour in the day, by officers of every grade and not the least notice is taken of it; but a violation of the internal rules of a ship, which have only the sanction of commander, must be punished with the utmost severity. The former prohibit the use of profane or reproachful language, and are intended as well to promote morality, and to suppress all contention among the officers and men belonging to the navy, as to maintain wholesome discipline; whereas the latter are designed wholly to enforce the discipline, and by so doing, to maintain an authority which would often be but little regarded, if it depended upon reason and utility to recommend it. Hence it is, that profanity, dissension and even duelling, are considered much less reprehensible by officers, at least by those who have the chief control of what I call arbitrary or ceremonial discipline, than the least departure from the customary usage and etiquette of the service; and hence also it is, that scarcely a day passes without the occurrence of some angry collision among the officers with respect to discipline.

These contentions might pass without receiving any particular notice from me, if they affected no body but the parties themselves; but it almost always happens that the effects of these disputes extend to more or less to all, and are extremely annoying. I have endeavoured to keep as far removed as possible from such contentions and to take no part in them whatever; but I have notwithstanding, been obliged to listen to the representations of the contending parties, until my patience has been exhausted, and I have wished most heartily that I could be released from holding any farther intercourse with my fellow-men, or could be associated only with those who would so far govern their angry passions, as to live together in peace and harmony.}

Jan. 23. Today we were honored with another visit from the Mandarins, at least the two from Hué; who came in their thirty-oared barge as before, and were attended by their Portuguese interpreter, and their usual number of servants. The object of this visit appeared to be, to obtain more precise information respecting our country, and the mission of Mr. Roberts. Mr. Morrison being absent, when they arrived, the conversation was carried on until he returned, by means of the Portuguese interpreter, and the W.R. [ward room] steward. Many inquiries were again made respecting the form of our Government; of which they seemed to have acquired no clear and correct ideas, notwithstanding all that had been said to them on the subject at their former interviews. The periodical election of our King, as they were still permitted to call our President, and the limitation of his eligibility to eight years, or two terms; seemed the most difficult features in our Government for them to understand. I believe, however, that these points were finally explained to their satisfaction. But their solicitude was manifested principally respecting the mission of Mr. Roberts. They were desirous to know whether he had brought any letters to the Chinese Government; and on being told that he was sent on business directly to the King of Cochin China, they asked whether he knew what were the contents of the letter from the president to the King. To this inquiry they were answered in the affirmative, and told, that the contents of this letter could be communicated only to the King himself. At this they seemed a good deal surprized, and observed, that this could not be done, as Mr. R. could not speak the language. This obstacle was soon removed, however, by their being told, that the letter would be translated into Chinese, so that the King might read it.

The question of presents again came up, but was soon dismissed. They made many inquiries relative to Europe, of which they appeared to consider the U.S. as forming a part; thus showing their great ignorance of geography. In this manner the interview passed, which occupied about an hour, when our visitors left the ship; and with every appearance of satisfaction and good humor.

Jan. 26. This morning another deputation from Hué visited us, for the purpose of delivering a present which the King had ordered, and which we considered as affording a favourable augury. The present consisted of provisions for the table, of which he supposed we must be in want after a long voyage. There was a great variety of dishes, of flesh, fish, and fowl; besides many preparations of vegetables, the whole of which amounted to more than fifty.[12] The preparation seemed to have been in the best style of the country, and some of them would have been quite acceptable to an American palate, had we known nothing of the dirty habits of the people. Besides the ready-made dishes, a variety of other articles were brought on board, as poultry, rice, bullocks, samshoo etc. Nothing, however, was more acceptable than the fruit, of which they made a very liberal present, consisting of custard apples, bananas, & pomgranates.

The prepared dishes were all arranged on the table in the cabin, and all the officers were invited to partake. After drinking the health & prosperity of the King of Cochin China, in the liquor that he had sent to us, we made an effort to prove to the Mandarins, who were still present, that we had a high relish for the dishes which had been prepared for us with a good deal of labour, and presented with the belief, that nothing could be [more] acceptable. Having just finished a hearty breakfast, however, we were unable to do that justice to the King's entertainment, which we should otherwise have done; notwithstanding the ideas of the long nails, & unwashed hands, which had been employed in preparing it. As soon as we had thus manifested our sense of the King's favor, the Mandarins returned to the shore apparently satisfied with the reception which the present of their Master had met with.

This being the eighth day after the departure of the last communication to Hué, it was time to expect an answer; and a little before night, the barge was seen coming off, and when she had approached within speaking distance of the ship, the interpreter gave information that there were Mandarins on board from Hué; who had set out to visit the ship, but finding that there was so much motion, as would make them sea-sick, they would defer their visit till the next morning.

Jan. 27. There being still too much motion of the ship to admit of the Mandarins coming on board, and Mr. Roberts being anxious for the business of the mission to progress as fast as possible; Mr. Morrison visited them on shore, notwithstanding it was Sunday, to receive such communications as they might have to make. He returned about two o'clock, and reported that nothing definite had yet been done, towards forwarding the mission. They still insisted, as those who had preceded them had done, on being made acquainted with the particular objects of the mission, and would not say any thing satisfactory respecting the visit of Mr. R. to Hué.[13] After dinner, Mr. Morrison went ashore again with instructions to inform the Mandarins, that the general object of the mission had already been communicated to the minister so far as was deemed proper, which was to establish a free and friendly intercourse between the two nations; but the particulars would only be communicated to the King. The afternoon, however, was spent in the same ineffectual discussion as the morning had been; and Mr. Morrison returned on board a little after sunset, without having accomplished any thing. The Mandarins promised to come on board the next morning, and it was hoped that a satisfactory arrangement would take place.

Jan. 28. A little after sunrise this morning, the Mandarins came on board in their barge, and the business of the mission was immediately entered upon. They reiterated the same preposterous demands which had been frequently made and replied to before; and would listen to no proposal relative to a visit to Hué, until these should be complied with. It appeared that the King had not been officially informed of the arrival of an American Envoy, and that the Minister would not make an official report on the subject to his Master, until he had extorted from the Envoy all the information that he desired. Mr. R. however, was firm in his purpose of not gratifying the minister and his agents; and after spending two hours in useless efforts to bring Mr. R. to their ridiculous terms, they left the ship, without giving us any reason to suppose that any farther steps would be taken respecting the mission.

Jan. 29. With the view of giving the Mandarins an opportunity of making farther communications, if they had any to make, and to signify to them our determination to leave the port without making the concessions which they had insisted upon; Mr. Morrison was sent on shore to offer them the pay for the articles which had been received as a present from the King. It now appeared that a deception had been practiced upon us with regard to the present for, instead of being made by His Majesty of Cochin China, as had been asserted, we were indebted for it to the Governor of the province. No pay, however, would be received, and with respect to the mission, they used such langue [language] to Mr. Morrison; (at least such was the language which he reported, when he returned on board) as appeared to be designed not only to stop all farther intercourse between themselves and us, but also to convey the most gross and provoking insult.[14] Indeed, they went so far as to declare, that they had never entertained any real intention of forming a treaty with our country; a country, whose highest officer was elected from among the people, and whose Envoys, could not be clothed with power adequate to treat with the King of Cochin China. We might therefore leave the port as soon as we pleased, as they wished to have nothing more to do with us.

Such was the substance of the conference between Mr. Morrison and the Mandarins; and when he returned and reported the insulting language which they had used, a good deal of excitement was felt, and if the Mandarins had been within our reach, I am not certain but that they would have received the personal chastisement which they deserved. The insult, however, was not allowed to pass without notice, and a demand of satisfaction. Mr. Morrison was again despatched with a message to the Mandarins, and to render the demand for satisfaction more effectual, as well as to guard against any violence that might possibly be attempted on the part of the Mandarins; the Lieut. of Marines in full uniform, with {his sword by his side, and} two of his stoutest men, accompanied Mr. Morrison.

Whether the arrogant Mandarins were intimidated by the martial appearance of Lieut. Fowler and his soldiers, or whether they had reflected on the very improper language which they had used in the morning, and were sorry for it, I shall not pretend to say; but they positively disclaimed all intention of using the language of insult towards the American Envoy, and were desirous that we should not leave the port. They were very polite in their treatment towards Mr. Morrison and Lieut. Fowler during the interview, and at the close of it, parted from them with much apparent cordiality.

Jan. 31. One of the Mandarins who was first despatched from Hué, to dictate to Mr. Roberts the language that he should use in addressing the Emperor's Minister, and to instruct him in the code of politeness of Cochin China, made us another visit on this day; and was led at last, to make so full a disclosure of the concessions which he was instructed to insist upon from Mr. Roberts, as seemed to put an effectual stop to all farther proceedings. Mr. Morrison had spent the greater part of the day before [Jan. 30] on shore with them, in order to ascertain precisely the terms on which they were willing that the mission should proceed to Hué; but all that he obtained from them was, that they had received positive instructions to allow no communication to pass from the American Envoy to Hué, without having examined it, and seen that the language was sufficiently servile and obsequious. They declared that, for their own part, they were willing that the Envoy should proceed to Hué without delay; but that they must adhere to the instructions which they had received, otherwise they signified that they should lose their heads. It was therefore impossible for Mr. R. to go to Hué, until he had shown them the President's letter or a copy of it, and suffered them to make such alterations in its phraseology, as would render it acceptable to the Emperor; not even then, when this requisition had been complied with, could they grant permission for the mission to proceed. All that they could promise was, to inform the Minister at Hué of what they had done, and request his permission for the Envoy to visit the capital. But being conscious, I suppose, that they were making demands of Mr. R. which, if complied with, must not only be exceedingly degrading to himself, but also to his country; they had hitherto forborne to inform him what expressions of servility and homage he would be required to use; and the object of the visit of the Mandarin appeared to be, to teach Mr. R. his lesson so plainly, that he would know precisely what he had to do; to what a degree of humiliation he would be obliged to submit, in order to enjoy the felicity of being presented to the Emperor of Cochin China.

The conference commenced with some remarks on the commerce of the country, and the effects of a commercial treaty with the U. States. The Mandarin asserted that the vessels of foreign nations had free access to their ports, and that as much trade was carried on without a treaty, as there would be with; and it was therefore not desirable that any treaty should be made. This, however, was an unfounded assertion; and when pressed by Mr. R. to state how many foreign vessels had visited the port in which we were then lying, in the course of the past year, he was obliged to acknowledge that there had not been one.

The subject of presents was next brought forward, by the Mandarin inquiring whether there were any, observing at the same time, that he made the inquiry not because the Emperor stood in need of them, for his treasury was full to overflowing; but because it was customary for visitors from the West to the great men of the East, to make them presents, and it was desirable that this custom should be followed on the present occasion. This subject, however, was very soon dismissed, by Mr. R. saying to the Mandarin, that whether he had presents or not, was of very little consequence; and as he had already told them that he should give no decisive answer on that subject, so he should say again. Now came the important disclosure, which showed the vain arrogance of an eastern despot, and the impossibility for any nation who values its honor and independance, to enter into any alliance with one, who, although himself a tributary,[15] exacts from other nations expressions of such homage and awe, as belong only to the Deity. In the first place, the ceremonial of an introduction to the Emperor, or the Coutu [kowtow], came under discussion; and the Mandarin observed that Mr. R. would probably be unwilling to comply with the etiquette of their court in this respect. But before Mr. R. could say whether he would comply or not, in case he were to go to Hué, he must know exactly what the ceremonial was; and upon this the Portuguese interpreter went through with it, and it was found to consist in falling on the knees, and bowing till the forehead touched the ground; which was to be repeated five times. The Mandarin was right in supposing that the American Envoy would not submit to this abject and degrading salutation; and he was told in the plainest terms, that no other mode of salutation would be submitted to than that which was practised in addressing the President of the U.S. which consisted merely in bowing, but this Mr. [R.] said, he was willing to repeat as often as the Emperor desired.

This subject was now dismissed, and that of the President's letter was next brought forward. On being urged to state the expressions in which they wished the President of the U.S. to address their Emperor, the Mandarin used such characters as were equivalent to such servile language as this; "your humble slave, with the most profound awe and reverence, presents you his petition with uplifted hands, and begs the favour of your notice." This was enough: Mr. R. had nothing more to say, than that for the whole of Cochin-China, he would not so far degrade his country, the President, & himself as to use such language in addressing the Emperor; and if that were insisted upon, it was altogether unnecessary to say any thing farther on the subject of the mission.

Before the conference ended, however, the Mandarin was desirous to learn what titles Mr. Roberts bore; and his curiosity was more than satisfied, by being presented with a list of the names of the state, county, town etc. designating the residence of the Envoy, with numerous other particulars; all of which the Mandarin supposed were real titles, and learning that the list was still incomplete, he inquired how many pages more it would require to contain them all, and would proceed no farther with a catalogue of titles more numerous than those of the Emperor of China. This trick was practised upon the Mandarin, as a proper return for his impertinence in questioning Mr. R. respecting his titles.[16]

Feb. 8. The conference that took place on the 31st. ult. was the last that was held relative to the mission, in which any new terms were proposed, or any thing transpired that seemed to warrant a longer stay in the port. Another visit, indeed was made three days after [Feb.3] that which called forth all the ridiculous demands of the Mandarins; but this was merely for the purpose of presenting Mr. Roberts a modification of the phraseology which they had prescribed for the President's letter. The alteration which was now proposed, however, did not in the least vary the degrading and servile meaning of the terms to be used; and consequently they were told in the most unequivocal language, that such terms would never be used, and it was moreover considered insulting to persist in urging them.

Notwithstanding the proceedings relative to the mission seemed to be now fully terminated, and there appeared to be no occasion for us to remain longer in the port; yet, to avoid giving any reason to his Government, to charge him with acting precipitately, Mr. R. deemed it best to wait a few days longer. Friday the 8th. was assigned as the day for sailing.

It having been reported ashore, that we were to sail on the 8th. the Mandarin who had made us the two last visits, again came on board on the 7th. for the purpose of taking leave. Being conscious, I suppose, that the failure of the mission was owing either to his Government or to himself and his colleagues, and wishing to palliate their fault as much as possible; he said to Mr. Roberts, that their ports were open to American vessels now without any commercial treaty, as effectually, and as advantageously, as they would be if a treaty were made. This was all that was said in relation to the mission, and after a short stay, he took his leave, expressing the hope that they parted on terms of mutual friendship & regard.

{Early the next morning, we weighed anchor and stood out to sea, an event highly satisfactory to us all; not only because we were to advance another stage on our long journey towards home, but also because we were leaving a port where we had found very little that was interesting, or that could alleviate the tedium of a long separation from one's family & home.}

Thus terminated the efforts of our Government to form an alliance with the Emperor of Cochin China, and from causes which render it probable that they will not be very soon repeated. The failure, as is evident from the preceding narrative, was not owing to any mismanagement on the part of the American Envoy; but solely to the demands which were made of him by the agents of the Emperor, & with which he could not comply, without degrading, in the most culpable manner, both his country and himself.

Since the mission was undertaken at considerable expense, and consequences of considerable magnitude were probably expected to result from its favourable termination; it was certainly desirable that it should succeed; but I am satisfied, that if any benefits of consequence were expected to result to our country or countrymen from the success of the mission, such expectations would have been disappointed; and consequently as it respects ourselves, there is the less reason to regret its failure.

With respect to the people of Cochin China, however, there is more cause for regret, since they would in all probability, have been the principal gainers. A commercial treaty with the U. States, such as would probably have been formed, if the puerile and ridiculous arrogance of the Emperor and his Minister had not prevented it; would no doubt have opened the door to the introduction of science and religion, among a people who are sunk about as low in ignorance and barbarism, as any in the world who pretend to the least degree of civilization; and there is reason to believe, therefore, that the advantages which they would have derived from such an alliance, in mental & moral improvement, would have been very great, and far more than counterbalanced any pecuniary benefits that we should have received in return.

As to the privilege of trading in the ports of Cochin China, which the Mandarins asserted was granted to vessels of the U.S. to as great an extent without a treaty as it could be with; the truth is, there have never been more than two or three American vessels in any of the ports of Cochin China, and they met with so many obstacles in conducting their trade, and suffered so many impositions from the agents of the Government, that no American vessel will ever engage again in the same enterprize, unless a treaty should be made, which would protect them against the fraud and rapacity of the government and its ministers.[17] The assertion of the Mandarin, therefore, was false, so far as it regarded the present condition of American commerce in the ports of his country, as is evident from the facts which I have mentioned; but as it regarded the influence of such a treaty as his Government would be willing to make, on American commerce, he was probably right. For, there is every reason to believe, that if Mr. Roberts had not been stopped at his first step towards forming an alliance with the Emperor, and had been permitted to proceed to Hué, and lay his propositions before the Emperor & his minister, such terms would have been insisted upon with view to their own exclusive benefit, as was the case with Mr. Crawfurd [John Crawfurd], that if he [Roberts] had not felt himself bound to refuse a compliance with them, and thus to have put an end to the mission without entering into any alliance; but like the English Minister, had agreed to insert in the treaty the clauses required by the Emperor & his ministers for the purpose of giving them the entire monopoly of the trade; if this had been done, I say, there is reason to believe, that the trade would have been so entirely under the control of those who would claim the privileges by treaty of monopolizing the best part of it; that it would present no more inducement to American merchants than it does now.[18] On the whole, therefore, so far as American interests are concerned, I am confident that there is no cause to regret the failure of the mission; but on account of

Mr. Roberts, who had entertained a flattering hope of succeeding, I do sincerely regret it. And I also regret that it failed on my own account, at least that the failure happened before the contemplated visit to the residence of the Emperor; as I expected to have been one of the party to accompany the mission to Hué, and anticipated a good deal of satisfaction from making a journey of two or three hundred miles through the country.

I shall now conclude what I have to say respecting Cochin China, by some remarks on the harbour in which we lay, and the country around it. The name of the bay is Phuyen, after the name of the province to which it belongs. It is of considerable extent; being, as I should judge about three miles from its entrance to its western boundary, and about five miles from north to south. The entrance is about a mile in width, and is free from every obstruction.

There are three principal anchorages in the bay, named from the three villages which occupy the adjacent shores. The first is called Xuandi and is nearest to the entrance on the left hand in going in; the next is Vunglam, in a direction nearly west from the entrance of the bay, and within about a mile and a half of the village of that name; and the last is Vung Chou, about two miles in a northerly direction from Vunglam. The Vung Chou anchorage is the best on some accounts, particularly in being secure from the influence of the swell from the sea which at the others is considerable, especially at the first.

We lay at the Vunglam anchorage, within about a mile and a half of the shore; and until about ten days before we left the harbour, the ship was but little affected by the swell from the sea, but after that time, till a day or two before we sailed, there was constantly so heavy a swell rolling in, that the ship was almost as uneasy as if we had been at sea. The depth of water where we lay was about six fathoms.

About a mile and a half from our anchorage in a northwest direction, was a watering place, from which we readily obtained a supply; but it was not very good. It had a brackish and chalybeate taste, which at first rendered it very disagreeable; but after using it some time, these offensive qualities were scarcely perceived by the taste, though after standing a short time, it emitted a strong sulphurous smell, that was very unpleasant.

The bay is surrounded by hills of various elevation, which rise immediately from the water's edge, except at the scites of the three villages that have been mentioned, where a plain intervenes between the bay and the high lands. With few exceptions, those hills were cultivated to their summits, and exhibited an appearance of fertility, which, with suitable encouragement to agriculture, might be rendered highly productive. The principal article cultivated here was rice; but I have no doubt, that both the soil and climate are well adapted to the growth of coffee, and the sugar cane, and that if the people were allowed to enjoy an interest in the fruits of their industry, a great quantity of coffee & sugar as well as rice might be produced for exportation.[19] The uncultivated hills were covered with trees and a thick growth of under-brush; and inhabited by several kinds of wild animals among which was the tiger. Being in want of wood, our men were sent ashore there to cut it, and in a few days we obtained a sufficient supply.

Beyond the high lands which immediately bound the bay, is an irregular ridge of mountains, which rise in some places to the height of two or three thousand feet. Their ascent is generally not steep, and their sides were cultivated in some places quite to their summits. This mountainous ridge extended in a northeasterly direction as far as we could see, but its height decreased as it advanced to the north.

The climate here during our stay was very fine, the thermometer standing generally at about 77°, and the atmosphere being generally clear and dry. Until two days before we left the harbour, we had a steady breeze from the northeast, which was always cool and refreshing.

From what has been said respecting the country around the bay of Phuyen, it might be supposed that a numerous population would enjoy there the comforts of life to as great a degree as they are almost any where enjoyed, and that their condition would be far removed from every thing that bears the appearance of wretchedness. But in both these respects, such a supposition would be erroneous. For although there is a population considerably numerous, probably amounting to about twenty thousand, inhabiting the country in the vicinity of the bay; yet it is not half as great as it might be if the people were permitted to derive all the benefits from their industry, which they would do under a well-regulated government; and as to their condition being a comfortable and happy one, I have scarcely ever met with people who appeared to be more wretched. Their habits of indolence, and their total unconcern about every thing that regards personal cleanliness, sink them at least to a level with the brutes.[20] Indeed it is scarcely possible to conceive of a more complete want of every thing that constitutes personal cleanliness, than was manifested in the appearance and habits of these people. The best clothes of the common people, consisted generally of a dirty tattered garment of cotton, which was worn apparently not so much for the purpose of comfort, as to answer the most absolute demands of decency. Not only were their bodies almost encrusted with dirt, but they were moreover very generally affected with some cutaneous disease, which rendered them still more disgusting. The finger nails were allowed to grow to the length of half an inch or more, and served the purposes of knives and combs. They never cut their hair or shaved their beards, and no people could seem more averse than these, to molest the vermin with which their heads were most abundantly supplied. And not only was this the case with the common people, but even with the Mandarins themselves, who assume a superiority in all respects over all other people in the world, except the Chinese. It would scarcely be credited, but it is nevertheless a fact, that one of the Mandarins who was sent to teach the American Envoy lessons of courtesy and politeness, while in conversation with him in the cabin, deliberately raised his dirty, crape turban, and seized one of the crawling occupants of his head that had strayed beyond its proper boundary, and laying it on the table, was about to apply his thumb-nail to it, when he observed Mr. Roberts looking at him with an expression of disgust, and he brushed the animal off on the deck, without seeming to be conscious, that he had done any thing in the least improper. This same Mandarin also furnished a specimen of the extreme negligence of these people with regard to personal cleanliness; for while his outside garment was of rich and costly silk, he wore under this, next to the body, a garment that appeared to have been in use for months without having been changed, and was as dirty as if it had been trampled under foot.

After witnessing such an odious want of personal cleanliness and decency even among the Mandarins, I do not hesitate to say, that the idea of making a journey of two or three hundred miles through their country and living several weeks among them, occasioned some qualms of the stomach, and that even on this account, I felt the less disposed to regret the failure of the mission.

In their dealings with us, these people manifested a great degree of selfishness, requiring a full equivalent for every thing they offered us. Even when we went to look for shells on the beach, a host of them would hover around us, and pick up every shell that was worth saving, and then refuse to let us have them unless we would pay for them with the buttons from our clothes, or with some thing else in their estimation of equal value. Besides buttons, scissors and jack-knives were the articles which they seemed most eager for; and with them a profitable trafic might be carried on, so long as the people should have any thing to dispose of.

Notwithstanding, however, the unfavourable traits in the character of these people which I have mentioned, they seemed to be mild and inoffensive; and if they could be permitted to hold intercourse with foreigners, and that intercourse were properly conducted, I do not doubt, but that in a short time an entire change would be wrought in their character and habits. They have minds capable of profiting by religious and scientific instruction, and it is chiefly on account of their being deprived of the opportunities for such instruction, which a treaty between their country and the U. States would have afforded them that the failure of the mission undertaken by Mr. Roberts is to be regretted.[21]

On our first arrival in the harbour of Phuyen, the people seemed unwilling to hold any intercourse with us, and several days elapsed before they would furnish us with any supplies; but after they saw that we manifested no unfriendly intentions, their conduct towards us was changed, and they readily supplied us with every thing which their country afforded. The principal articles were poultry, pigs, and eggs. The fowls, ducks and pigs were very fine, and furnished at reasonable prices. The two former were about two dollars a dozen, and the latter at the rate of two or three cents a pound. Eggs were about a dollar a hundred. Rice and sugar were also to be had, and the former at the rate of about two dollars for a hundred pounds, and the latter at less than five. The sugar was of the same quality as the common sort of W.I. [West Indies] sugar. Beef was procured for the use of the crew, but it was of the buffalo kind, and not very good. The price of a bullock was from twelve to fifteen dollars.

A large number of the people who live in the neighbourhood of the bay spend their time in fishing; but we saw very few good fish there. The boats which they use are generally long, narrow, and carry very large mat sails. Their bottoms are made, not of plank, but of bamboo, wove together like basketwork, and covered with a kind of bitumen which serves the purposes of pitch, and renders them impervious to water.

While we were plentifully supplied with the articles that have been mentioned, during the greater part of our stay at Phuyen, the supply of fruits and vegetables was rather deficient. The only vegetables that we were able to procure, were a very small kind of sweet potatoe, and beans; and the only fruits of which we obtained any thing like an adequate supply, were bannanas and custard-apples. The bannanas were a very small kind, but as good as I ever met with except the long green one at Manilla.

From the conduct of the inhabitants in their intercourse with us, as well as from the information that we had received, it was evident that very few foreign vessels had ever visited that port before, and that ours was the first American vessel that had ever been seen there. Very little trade had been carried on with that port, not more than sufficient to employ two or three junks, which make only one or two voyages in a year. While we were there, one of these junks arrived from the eastern part of the province of Canton, with a cargo principally of silks and teas.

The province of Phuyen is said to be one of the richest and most productive of Cochin China, or Anam, as the natives call their country; and the harbour in which we lay, is one of the best that I have ever seen. The country in the vicinity of the bay, so far as we could see, presented an appearance of great fertility; and there is every reason to believe, that if an enlightened and wise policy were pursued by the Government, a very creative trade might be carried on there, which would be profitable both to the nations and individuals engaged in it. This will never be the case, however, so long as the jealousy and circumscribed views of the Government prevent their entering into any commercial treaty with foreign nations; and while at the same time, they impose such extravagent duties upon all foreign vessels which venture, without the protection of a treaty, to trade in their ports, as must effectually exclude all foreign commerce.

Feb. 13. For the last two days we had been favoured with a fine breeze, and this morning we doubled the southern extremity of Cambodia, and entered the Gulf of Siam. We left the harbour of Phuyen with a light breeze, which died away in the course of the day, and we remained becalmed during the following night at the entrance of the harbour. {The next morning a light breeze sprung up, which partially filled our sails; but it was ahead, so that we made very little progress on the course that we wished to pursue. At the beginning of the third day out, we were still in sight of the high lands bounding the harbour which we had left; and during this day, the 10th. of the month, the wind continued adverse, but it had increased as we seceded from the coast, so that we could make some advance towards our destined port.} In the course of the following night, however, the monsoon, which had been interrupted for several days, an unusual occurrence, again set in; and we pursued our course, at the rate of eight or nine miles an hour, until we entered the Gulf of Siam. On the 11th. in the afternoon we passed Cape Padaran on the coast of Cochin-China, in latitude 11°-30′ - & longitude 109.30. It is a high, rocky, barren hill, on which nothing green was to be seen, except a few blighted shrubs. We passed within four or five miles of it, and consequently our view of it was very distinct. Beyond the Cape, as far as we could see, the country was broken into hills and mountains, which appeared every where barren and uncultivated. A small recess on the western side of the cape afforded a convenient and secure anchorage for such small craft as are employed on the coast, during the northeast monsoon. {A few of them were lying at anchor there when we passed.} On the 12th. early in the morning, we passed within sight of Cape St. James, which bounds the entrance of the river Saigon on the north. It is high land, but we did not approach near enough to have a distinct view of it. About noon the same day, we discovered Pulo Condor, an island of considerable magnitude, and bearing about S.S.E. from us at the distance of 25 miles. A little before sunset, we passed the Brothers, a group of small islands situated about 25 miles from the coast of Cambodia, which is here so low that we could not see it.

{Our course lay about midway between the islands which I have mentioned, and the coast, in the direction of S.W. to S.W. by W. At a little distance to the southward of the extremity of Cambodia, is situated Pulo Uby or Ohy [Pulo Oby], a small round-topped island, which we passed, early in the morning of the 13th. and entered the Gulf of Siam. Our course, after passing this island, was N.W. for two or three hours, and then N.W. by N. At twelve o'clock, our position as correctly determined by a meridian observation, and a good chronometer, was N. Latitude 8°-49' & E. longitude 104.°25'; and at this time the small island of False Pulo Uby or Ohy, bore N.E. ¾ E. distant ten or twelve miles from us. From noon till eight in the evening, our course continued to be N.W. by N. and the distance run was 42 miles. During these eight hours no other islands were seen; and at eight o'clock the course was changed to N.W. and continued so till the next morning, the 14th, at five o'clock, at which time we had run on this course 61 miles.

We now found ourselves almost surrounded by land on all sides;[22] and as we had no chart that could be trusted, it was impossible to determine satisfactorily where we were, or what course we ought to steer. A W. course, however, of six miles, and a course W. ¾ S. six miles, extricated us from the labyrinth in which we unexpectedly found ourselves; so that we could again resume our progress with safety. Our course now, at 7 A.M. became N.W. on which had run 13 miles at 9 A.M; at which time we had several islands, and probably also the coast of Cambodia in sight; of which the bearings and distances were as follows: Three islands on the starboard [head], situated near together, the largest and most distant [Kaoh Pring], being, as I judged, about a mile in length, and bearing E. by N. distant six or seven miles; the next, about half the size of the other, bearing E. distant five or six miles; and the last, which appeared to be only a small bed of rocks just emerging above the water, bearing E. by S. distant four or five miles.

Beyond these islands, and extending both to the southward and northward as far as we could see, we had an indistinct view of what we took to be the coast of Cambodia, which appeared to be generally low and flat, though in some places it rose into hills of considerable elevation. The two longest of the three islands which have just been mentioned were thickly covered with trees, and under-wood. They appeared to rise very abruptly from the water, but their height was less in proportion to their size, than most of the islands in the eastern seas, not being more than two or three hundred feet.

At the same time that the bearings of these islands were noted, there was another small island [Ilot Veer] in sight on the other side, which was ten or twelve miles distant from us, in direction due south. None of these islands were correctly laid down on any chart that we had, and the Gulf of Siam, never having been accurately surveyed by any foreigner, so far as I know; I have been much more minute in noting bearings and distances, than I should otherwise have been, from the belief that my observations may possibly be of some use to those who may hereafter navigate the Gulf without the guidance of correct charts.

The soundings thus far up the Gulf, which had been frequently taken, at least during the night, were eighteen or nineteen fathoms, and the bottom was a thick adhesive mud. The wind gradually changed its direction after we entered the gulf, from N.E. to S.E. and continued a moderate breeze, which carried us along at the rate of from five to eight miles an hour. Our latitude and longitude at noon on the 14th. were 10°-33′ & 102°-42′. We continued to pursue a N.W. course with a light breeze from the S.E. and saw no land till 7 the next morning, at which time we had run from 12 the day before, forty-four or five miles. The land which now appeared in sight, bore about N.E. from us, and appeared to be two or three small low islands. They were probably distant from us fifteen or twenty miles.

From 7 A.M. till 1 P.M. of the 15th. our course continued to be N.W. and the distance run by log, was 33 miles. The latitude this day was 11°-23′ and the longitude 101°-51′. At 1 P.M. the course was changed to N.N.W. ½ W. and we proceeded on this course the distance of 19 miles, when we steered N.W. by W. and made on this course 34 miles, at day break on the 16th. After losing sight of the low land on the morning of the 15th. no more land was seen from deck, till the next morning; but the man at mast head reported it several times in the course of the afternoon, and its bearing appeared to be about N.E. The soundings in the morning of the 15th. were 37 fathoms, and at 8 in the evening 38 fathoms; the bottom at both times being a soft mud mixed with shells.}

[This is the end of the first part of the original Journal II. The diary continues using the revised Journal II, starting with February 17, 1833.]

February 17th. The navigation of the Gulf of Siam was intricate & difficult, owing to numerous islands & shoals & to our having no chart that could be relied on, & our progress was consequently very slow. On this day, however, we had approached so near the south of the Menam river, that we saw a large number of boats, & several junks; and not being quite certain what course we ought to steer, Mr. Morrison was sent to the boat nearest to us, for the purpose of obtaining the requisite information & if possible, a pilot. After an hour's absence he returned, & had been able only to obtain the information that Paknam, a small town near the mouth of the river Menam, was situated to the N.E. of us. A pilot could not be obtained, the natives being suspicious that our designs in visiting their country were hostile, & that if they rendered us any service, they would be severely chastised for it [by] the Mandarins, of whom they always stand in the greatest dread.

Before the close of the day we had a view of the coast of Siam to the westward of the Menam; but it was so low & flat that we could only see the dense forest which covered the ground. We had a view at the same time, of the Shi-Shang islands, situated to the eastward of the Menam, & at the distance of twenty or thirty miles from us.

February 18th. At about 10 o'clock this morning we came to anchor in four fathoms water, & at the distance of four or five miles from the mouth of the river. A sand bar of considerable extent at the mouth of the river, on which there is sometimes only 12 feet of water, prevented our farther progress.

CHAPTER IX
Bankok

Message to Paknam; An officer from Bankok visits the ship;
Departure for Bankok; Account of Paknam; Arrival at Bankok;
Interview with the Prah Klang; Visit from the Portuguese
Consul; Second interview with the Prah Klang; Another visit
from the Portuguese Consul; Professional visit to the Prah
Klang; Visit to Mr. Silveira; Visit to Chroma Kuhn; Siamese
Ball; Visit to the Portuguese Consul; Another conference with
the Prah Klang; Great fire at Bankok; Trip up the river.

About an hour before we anchored, Mr. Morrison & Lieut. Fowler were sent
ashore at Paknam to the chief Mandarin, with a message from Mr. Roberts
respecting his contemplated visit to Bankok, the capital of Siam, & residence
of the King [Rama III]. At 7 o'clock in the afternoon the boat returned, &
it appeared from Mr. Morrison's report that nothing satisfactory had been
done. The mandarin promised to make a more satisfactory communication
the next day.

The distance from the ship to Paknam was estimated by these gentlemen at 10 or 12 miles; and they spoke very favourably of the view as they
approached the town, but of the town itself, and its inhabitants, their
account was quite unfavourable. What they saw tended fully to confirm the
reports which we had previously heard of the excessive filthiness of the
Siamese. They were inquired of with a good deal of interest respecting the
Siamese Twins, who were natives of a place not far from Bankok.[1]

February 20th. In compliance with the request of the Governor of Paknam,
Mr. Morrison made him another visit on the 19th. & succeeded in persuading

him to take the letters sent by Mr. Roberts & forward them to Bankok. The passage from Paknam to Bankok being accomplished in one tide, it was expected that an answer would be received about 12 o'clock today, at which time Mr. Morrison was requested to be at Paknam. Accordingly he set out early in the morning & had arrived within about two miles of the town when he met a boat from Bankok with an officer on board, who had been sent down by order of the King, to ascertain from whence we came, & what was the object of our visit. About 2 o'clock in the afternoon this officer reached the ship, & a conference took place between Mr. Roberts & him that was quite satisfactory, & promised a favourable issue of the mission. The officer, whose name was Piedada [José Piedade], was a native of the country, but his parents were partly Portuguese & he could speak English with tolerable facility.[2] He said that the character of the Americans stood high in the estimation of his Government, & that the King was always glad to have American vessels visit his ports, because they brought money, & occasioned no trouble.

Arrangements were made, so far as they could be at this time, for Mr. Roberts to proceed to the capital & have an interview with the King. Mr. Piedada said he should return to Bankok the same day, & should see the King in the course of the night; and would immediately provide a house for Mr. Roberts & return for him on the 22d. The King he represented as being a plain man, & not much disposed to stand upon ceremony with foreigners.

In speaking of Mr. Crawfurd, the English Envoy sent out by the Governor General of Bengal, & who was treated by the Government of Siam in a very dishonorable manner, Mr. Piedada said it was owing altogether to the Malay interpreter whom Mr. Crawfurd employed. Something on the part of Mr. C. had given offense to the interpreter, & to be revenged, he caused a misunderstanding between the Prah Klang, or Minister of foreign affairs, & Mr. C. in consequence of which every obstacle was thrown in the way of the mission, & every indignity offered to Mr. C. till at last he was obliged to leave the country without having accomplished a single object of his mission. Had it not been for the misrepresentations of the interpreter, Mr. Piedada said that Mr. C. would have succeeded in his mission without difficulty; and as Mr. Roberts would have him for interpreter, who would be desirous to promote, & not like the Malay, to defeat the mission, he had no doubt of its success.[3] Having accomplished the object of his visit to the ship, he left us about 4 o'clock, with the view of returning immediately to Bankok.

The same day, a little before sunset, we got under way & stood out a mile or two farther from the shore, where we anchored in about six fathoms water; there being too little water where we first anchored, to admit of our remaining there with safety.

February 24th. In the afternoon of the 23d information was received that the boats sent down from Bankok to convey Mr. R. & his suite thither, were at Paknam, & would reach the ship this morning. That no time might be lost, all the officers who were to compose the suite were requested to be ready early this morning, & by 8 o'clock, the party was prepared to set out. It consisted, besides Mr. Roberts, of Capt. Geisinger, Lieutenants Purviance & Fowler, Acting Lieut. Brent, Midshipmen Carrol, Thomas [Midshipman Charles Thomas], Crawford [Midshipman D. Ross Crawford] & Wells [Midshipman Alexander H. Wells], & myself.[4] We had a steward, cook, & two servants, as it was expected that we should have to provide for our own table.

About 8 o'clock in the morning a boat with a large number of red flags flying was seen advancing from the mouth of the river towards the ship, & at 10 o'clock she arrived within a little distance of us & anchored. This, it appeared, was one of the boats intended for the Envoy, but Mr. Piedada was detained at Paknam a short time to make arrangements for the party, & nothing could be done until he arrived. At 3 o'clock P.M. he arrived, & at half past 4, we left the ship for Paknam, where arrangements had been made for us to spend the night.

There were two boats for the party, which were of the same size, & from 60 to 70 feet long 8 or 9 feet wide, & each rowed by 42 men. They were also provided with sails, to be used instead of oars, whenever the wind should admit of it. One boat was taken for Mr. R. the Capt. and ward-room officers, & the other for the Midshipmen. The wind being fair, our progress to Paknam was quite rapid, & we landed there at 7 o'clock. As the boats moved away from the ship, a salute was fired by her which was answered by the boats, each of them carrying one gun.

The landing-place was a narrow wooden pier, on which a large number of half naked natives were waiting with torches to receive us, & conduct us to the residence of the Governor. After a short walk we reached his residence, which was constructed principally of bamboo & thatch, & was supported by piles at the height of five or six feet from the ground. The ground being low & flat & extensively flooded at every high tide, it is necessary to build on piles, in order to be above the water during these inundations as well as to be secure against the venemous reptiles & insects, which find there in the mud & rank vegetation a favourite abode.

In the Governor's house was but one habitable room which was about thirty feet by fifteen; and in one corner of that we found him seated cross-legged on a cushion upon a platform raised about two feet above the floor. He received Mr. Roberts & his suite very cordially, & treated us with all the hospitality that his situation would admit of. He appeared to be 45 or 50 years of age, was of the midling size, stout, & well made. His complexion was darker than that of most of his countrymen, being almost as dark as that of the negro. From the questions that he asked it was evident that his knowledge was very limited, & his intellect not above mediocrity. His dress, or rather undress, was not materially different from that of the common people. It consisted only of a piece of red cotton stuff wrapped around the hips & descending half way to the knees, & of a calico sash which encircled the waist. All the rest of the body & limbs was naked.

The Governor having mistaken the number for whom arrangements were to be made, they were not such as they otherwise would have been; but we nevertheless fared much better, & were much better satisfied with the reception that we met with, than we expected to be. The room into which we were introduced & in which we ate & slept, had been fitted up on our account with a carpet, looking-glass, & chandeliers, so as to present quite a neat & comfortable appearance.[5]

As soon as possible after our arrival, supper was prepared, consisting of beef, poultry & fish, all very well cooked; together with vegetables & fruits. Knives & forks being articles of luxury that were not known there, the Governor could not accommodate us with them, but fortunately fore-seeing that we should have need of them at Bankok, we had brought them with us, & readily supplied the only deficiency in the arrangements of the table which his excellency had made for us.

Immediately after supper, he called in his Secretary, who lay down on the floor before him & in a book consisting of long narrow leaves resembling slate, he recorded the answers to the questions that were put by his excellency to Mr. Roberts. These questions were put for the purpose of ascertaining Mr. Roberts' & the Capt's names, & the number of other officers & servants belonging to the party. This record was to be immediately transmitted to the King with the information that the American Envoy had reached Pak-nam, & would proceed the next morning to Bankok. Soon after this business was despatched, a gong was struck two or three times, when the Governor rose, took leave of us & retired.

It being now about bed-time, preparations were made to accommodate us with lodging, & for this purpose, eight or ten settees were brought in & ranged around the room so as to accommodate us all. Mr. Roberts being the "Great Man", was allowed the honor of reposing on a couch prepared for him on the Governor's platform. Each settee was provided with a mat & pillow, but their bottoms being made of bamboo, they were rather hard & caused frequent turning over during the night. The room being entirely open on two sides, there was a free circulation of air, so that we suffered but little from the heat during the night. Fires were made in the yard near the house for the purpose of driving away the musquitoes, so that we suffered but little from this annoyance.

February 25th. Early this morning I took a walk through the village, to see its extent & the condition of its inhabitants. The only objects that I saw deserving of notice, were the temple, & the fortifications. These were quite extensive, & so far as I could judge, were constructed upon scientific principles. They were designed to prevent a hostile invasion by sea, & if well manned, I should suppose that they would so effectually command the river, which is there about three quarters of a mile wide, that no naval force could pass up. I judged that there were about a hundred & fifty guns mounted, which were of a large size, probably twenty-four or thirty-two pounders.

The temple that I have mentioned, was of considerable size, built of brick, & plastered on the outside & stuccoed in the most fantastic manner.

The site of Paknam, as I have already observed, is low & flat, & at every high tide a great part of it is under water. At the driest times the ground is full of water, & the heat being great, a rank luxuriant vegetation is brought forth, which is the abode of a great number of venomous reptiles & insects. From the great amount of decomposition that must constantly be going on there where all the agents of it act with their greatest power, there is good reason to consider it a most unhealthy residence. And the appearance of the inhabitants, the females especially, was a conclusive evidence of this fact. A branch of the river Menam runs through the town, which is navigable for boats, & over which was a clumsy wooden bridge. This stream contained a great quantity of every sort of impurity, & its banks were covered with a thick growth of jungle. The musquitoes here were so troublesome that I was glad to make my escape as soon as possible.

The dwellings of the people were scattered about among the jungle, & were miserable hovels of thatch & bamboo, & raised a few feet from the ground by piles. The population of the town was said to be about three thousand.

After this excursion through the town, I returned to the Governor's, & soon afterwards he made his appearance attended by a train of fifteen or twenty men, some of whom carried swords & constituted his body-guard. As soon as he had taken his seat, his attendants kneeled down, or lay down before him on the floor, it being required of all who attend upon him, or who approach him on business, to assume the most humble & servile attitudes. Breakfast was soon made ready, & as soon as that was disposed of, we took leave of our hospitable entertainer, & embarked for Bankok in the same boats that had brought us to Paknam.

It was half past 8 o'clock when we left Paknam, & the sun was unclouded & shone with great power. We had now a view of the opposite side of the river, where there were other fortifications, capable probably of mounting a hundred guns. These were directly opposite Paknam, & one of them occuppied a small island in the river, & its walls being whitewashed, it made a very neat appearance. A little distance above this island is another small one, on which a temple had been built, rather for ornament, as it appeared, than for use.

The banks of the river at Paknam, & indeed from the sea nearly up to Bankok, are very low & covered with a thick growth of jungle through which it would be impossible to penetrate. The arica-nut palm is to be seen here & there lifting its tufted top of dark-green leaves far above the dense forest of jungle which surrounded them. A few cocoa-nut trees were to be seen along the banks of the river, & loaded with their green & yellow fruit. The yellow cocoa-nut I had never seen before, & they were found to contain a milk of superior flavour to that of the common kind.

Our conductor, Mr. Piedada, did not go in the boat with us, but had a boat, or rather canoe of his own, which moved much more rapidly than our large boats; and as soon as we had embarked, he went ahead of us to provide for our accommodation. The heat being now excessive, & our boats so poorly provided with accommodations, that we were obliged, not only to remain on deck all the time, but had not even room to turn around without interfering with the rowers; our situation soon became extremely irksome & unpleasant.

When we left Paknam the tide was in our favour, & we were also favoured with a breeze which assisted the oars, so that for a while our progress was quite rapid, & we were in hopes, from what had been told us, of reaching Bankok by 12 o'clock. We had advanced but a few miles, however, before the tide changed, & all the rest of the distance we had to make our way against a strong current. Before we had advanced more than half way the breeze also died away, so that we had to stem the tide with our oars alone, & consequently did not gain more than a mile an hour. Our slow progress, however, was partly owing to the awkward manner of rowing. Instead of setting down with their backs toward the bow of the boat, & pulling the oars towards them, these men stood up with their faces towards the bow, & pushed the oars from them; by which means they exerted a much less propelling force than if they performed the operation in the usual way. And besides this, the oars were fastened to the pins about eighteen inches above the gunwale of the boat, which also considerably diminished their propelling power. The boats crew, consisted of Burmese prisoners, who were stout, able-bodied men; and although they did not seem to exert much of their strength in rowing, yet they continued to labour at their oars from half past 8 o'clock in the morning till 7 in the evening with but little interruption. They were at times very noisy, shrieking & halloeing like drunken savages. They drank nothing, however, except water, which they dipped up out of the river, with a piece of bamboo, & their food consisted wholly of rice, as we had an opportunity of seeing; for about 4 o'clock in the afternoon every man left his oar, & brought up from below a pot of rice, of which he scooped out with his hands as much as he designed for his meal, which he devoured with great voracity, throwing it into his mouth with his fingers, & allowing his teeth very little time to perform their office. They were clad in frocks of a coarse red stuff like bombazette, & wore caps of the same bound around with two strips of white.

About six miles above Paknam we passed another village of about the same size called Paklat. Here were extensive fortifications again, which made quite an imposing appearance from the river, & seemed capable of making a very effectual resistance to any maritime force that might undertake to ascend with hostile intentions. On the other side of the river from the town were several sheds for preserving timber.

At Paklat we saw Mr. Piedada's canoe, & in about an hour after we had passed, he overtook us & furnished us with cocoa nuts & plantains which he had stopped to procure for us, & which were very acceptable, as we were beginning to suffer from thirst, which we did not feel inclined to allay with the muddy water of the river.

Until we arrived within eight or ten miles of Bankok, the banks of the river presented the same appearance that has been described; but now they were more elevated, & the dwellings of the natives more frequent. At length, after our patience was nearly exhausted by our constrained & uncomfortable position, the river made a short turn to the eastward, & the capital of Siam presented itself to our view, & shortly afterwards we reached the borders of the city. On the right hand we observed several large junks building, & others lying at anchor; and on the other side, the river was lined with floating houses built on rafts of bamboo, so as to rise & fall with the tide. Advancing a little farther, we found both sides of the river lined with these floating habitations arranged in rows four or five deep, with narrow passages between them, so as to render them accessible by means of small boats. The river was now covered with boats & canoes plying in different directions, & we passed many large junks lying at anchor. Of the city we could see nothing as we passed except that part of it which floated on the river, & which constitutes, as to population, no inconsiderable part of it.

At last our boat drew up at a landing place in front of a building of a very decent appearance on the right, or western bank of the river, which we soon learned was to be our residence. Our conductor was not there to receive us, but he had left orders with a man who could speak Portuguese, to request Mr. Roberts to land with his suite as soon as they arrived, & to have the party accommodated as well as circumstances would permit. Preparation had been made for supper, which was soon served up, & of which we partook with a voracity that must have astonished the natives, (who flocked around us in great numbers) as we had eaten nothing from breakfast, except one or two plantains & the pulp of a coco-nut. The supper was excellent, consisting of poultry, pork & fish, cooked in a variety of ways, besides vegetables & fruits. Bread was not used by the Siamese, & there was not a baker in Bankok; but we had brought a supply of sea-bread with [us], so that we escaped a privation which we should otherwise have felt quite sensibly.

Immediately after supper, Mr. Roberts was visited by a son of the Prah Klang, or Minister of Foreign Affairs, & also by another agent of the Government, called a Moorman, who afterwards proved to be a Secretary of the Prah Klang; whose object appeared to be, not only to inquire into the business which had brought the American Envoy to Siam, but also to inspect the strangers, so as to be able to report respecting our appearance to their Master. The son of the Prah Klang [Luang-Nai-Sit] was about twenty-five years of age, & had two or three wives, & several children. The

Moormen, of whom there were several in the service of the Siamese Government, were generally natives of India; but the one who visited Mr. R. was a native of Siam, though a descendant of Indian ancestors, & being the Prah Klang's Secretary, he was an individual of no small importance. Before they took leave, they wished to know of Mr. Roberts whether he had any message to send to the Prah Klang, or whether he wished any thing farther to be done with respect to the accommodations for the party, as the Prah Klang, whose duty it was to provide for strangers, was desirous to do all in his power for the accommodation of the American Envoy & his suite.

It being now late in the evening, & such provision having already been made as would answer for the night, nothing more was then required, & our visitors took leave apparently satisfied with what they had seen & heard. On retiring to our sleeping rooms, we found the accommodations there rather deficient, most of us being provided with nothing but a mat & pillow; the want of time being assigned as the reason that better provision had not been made for us.

February 26th. After passing an uncomfortable & restless night, in consequence of the heat, musquitoes, & hardness of my bed, I rose early, & walked out & took a survey of our residence. The building had been erected but a short time, & was intended for a factory.[6] It was situated on the right bank of the river, & only five or six rods from it, & occupying a site that was rather elevated, it was as pleasant a residence as any that could have been selected. The building consisted of a main body fronting the river, two stories high, & about twenty-five feet by fifteen; and of two wings extending back one hundred & forty feet, each of which was divided into eight rooms of equal size. The wings were two stories high, & a corridor ran the whole length of the second story, & formed quite a pleasant place for promenade. We occupied the main building & the second story of the right wing, the other wing having been used as a prison for the confinement of some Malay prisoners, though while we were there, it was unoccupied. The rooms which we occupied in the wing were dark & not well ventilated, there being only one door & two narrow windows in front, & four narrow chinks in the rear, each six inches wide & eighteen inches long. In front of the main building was a yard with a high wall in front; and at each end of the yard was a shed which appeared to have been designed for the guard, with which it is necessary that every factory should be provided. Between the two wings was a large yard, at the back part of which was a shed built up against the wall, & there was the fire place, where all the operations of the kitchen

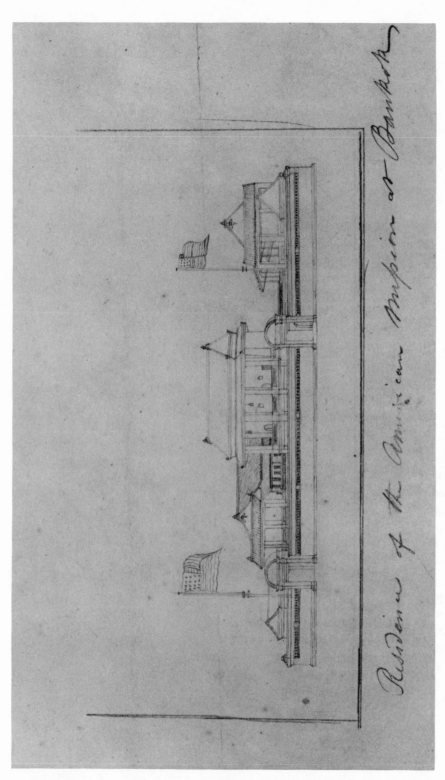

"Residence of the American Mission at Bankok," drawing by Lt. Hugh Y. Purviance. (Edmund Roberts Papers, Library of Congress.)

were carried on. In this yard were two trees of considerable size, considered sacred by the Buddhists, which afforded a resting place to great numbers of crows & buzzards that hovered about the kitchen, & were very bold in the pursuit of their food, in so much that they would sometimes almost take it out of the cook's hands. The several parts of our residence which have been described, were constructed of brick, & plastered & white-washed both within & without, which, when the sun shone bright, as it usually did, caused a reflection that was quite painful to the eyes. Before breakfast we received a visit from the Master of an Arab ship under English colours that we had noticed in passing up the river, for the purpose of making inquiries about Mr. Hunder [Robert Hunter], a Scotch merchant who had been long resident in Bankok, but was then absent at Sincapore. Of this gentleman, I shall have occasion to speak hereafter.

In the course of the forenoon Mr. Piedada called on Mr. Roberts, to inform him what he had done in relation to the mission. He had been sent to the palace, he said, the evening before, & was kept there till 2 o'clock in the morning. He had just seen the Prah Klang, & it was arranged that Mr. Roberts should call on him that afternoon.

Accordingly about 5 o'clock, Mr. R. with his suite, embarked in the two boats which had been provided for the purpose, & in a few minutes were land[ed] near the Minister's residence. We advanced by pairs along a narrow brick pavement a short distance, when we passed through a gate-way, ascended a flight of steps, & found ourselves in the presence of the Minister [Suri-wrung-kosa, Chaopraya Phraklang],[7] who appeared to assume more state & dignity than a European Monarch. Mr. Roberts & Capt. Geisinger were conducted to chairs which had been placed for them on the left of the Prah Klang, & farther back were chairs for the rest of the party. The Prah Klang was seated cross-legged on a platform about a foot & half high, & reclining on cushions covered with damask and spangled with gold. He seemed to be employed when we arrived, in smoking, drinking tea, & chewing the arica-nut. At his right hand, & towards the front part of the room, were two platforms, nine or ten inches above the floor, & on them were lying prostrate, or resting on their knees & elbows, fifteen or twenty men, who were the subordinate agents of the Government, & of whom our superintendent, Mr. Piedada, was one. A scene now presented itself to our view entirely new, & as disgusting as it was novel. Every person in the presence of the Prah Klang, except ourselves, was either prostrate on the floor, or resting on the knees & elbows, with the body bent forward so that the face almost came in contact with the floor. When any one was ordered to help the Prah Klang to his tea, or materials for smoking, he crawled along on his hands & knees pushing the article before him, till he was near enough to present it; and then clapping his hands together, & raising them to his forhead, & bowing his head to the floor, he retreated backward on his hands & knees till he had reached his former position. Among this group of human reptiles was a son of the Prah Klang, a lad ten or twelve years old, who manifested the same degree of abject awe in the presence of his father that the others did. This lad was ordered by his imperious father, to offer us materials for smoking, which he did in the same humble attitude in which he approached his father. Another brought us tea in the same manner.

Mr. Roberts had been requested by the Prah Klang, to take his papers with him, & a servant had been sent with a silver dish for them to be placed in; but the dish not being large enough to contain them, they were carried in a small desk, & when they were called for by the Prah Klang, the desk was placed on the silver dish, & the person who had charge of them crawled along shoving them before him, till he arrived within three or four feet of his Master, where he left them & retreated backward to his former place, with his head bowed almost to the floor as if afraid to look up. This same man was requested by Mr. Morrison to hand him a chair, in doing which he would have to pass in front of the Prah Klang, & he signified that this was an offense which he dared not commit. He ventured, at last, however, to do it, & in the same manner that he had conveyed the papers to his Master. No one dared speak in the presence of the Prah Klang, except when spoken to by him, & then only in the lowest possible tone of voice. It was considered so hazardous to repeat the same question a second or third time, that the interpreter said he dared not do it, especially if the question were such as was not altogether agreeable to the Prah Klang. Whenever any one was spoken to by him, he made the salam, which consisted in raising his joined hands to his forehead, & bowing with his face to the floor; and the same was done whenever any one had occasion to look towards the Prah Klang, or to move from the position which had been assigned to him.

On surveying this exhibition of despotic power on the one hand, & of a most abject & grovelling servility on the other, I experienced such mingled sensations of indignation & pity, as it is not easy for me to describe. That any man, however exalted his situation may be above that of his fellow-men by the concurrence of fortunate circumstances & events, should require from those who differ from him only in not being so fortunate as to hold the same office which elevates him, but which he may lose in a moment, the same acts of homage that are due to the Supreme Being, cannot but excite in the breast of every American the strongest feelings of indignation; and that any men, however humble their situation may be, should so far degrade the nature which God had given them, as to pay Divine honour to a fellow-mortal because he happens to be elevated above themselves, must excite sentiments of commiseration in the breast of every one, who has been accustomed to regard all men as by nature equal.

The room in which this strange & impressive scene was exhibited, was thirty-five or forty feet long, & twenty wide. It was entirely open in front, but had a thick wall on the back side, in which were no windows, but several doors closed by screens. The wall was hung around with paintings & mirrors in the Chinese style, & on each side of the Prah Klang was a small clock of European workmanship. The floor was covered with carpets of several kinds, some of which were quite good taste.

The Prah Klang appeared to be about fifty years of age & was quite corpulent. He wore no other clothing than the serong (the cloth around the hips) & a sash around the waist. He appeared to be affable & good-natured, & entered directly into conversation with Mr. Roberts. He inquired in the first place how long we had been from the U. States, & what places we had visited & whether Mr. R. had taken letters to all those places. He then inquired respecting the officers of the ship & being told that I was the surgeon, he asked whether I had any vaccine matter, being desirous, as I learned the next day, to lessen the ravages of small-pox, which almost always prevails at Bankok, by introducing vaccination.

Mr. Roberts was then questioned with regard to the particular object of his mission, & he stated in reply that his sole object was, to make a commercial treaty with the Government of Siam, by which inducements would be held out to Americans, to trade there. Upon this the Prah Klang observed, that American vessels were now permitted to trade there, & sell their goods to whomsoever they pleased, intimating, as we understood, that nothing would be gained by a treaty. He also mentioned several Americans who had been at Bankok, & among them a Capt. Williams, who was there while Mr. Munroe [James Monroe, 1817–25] was President of the U.S. he said, & by whom he sent a letter to our Government, to which he had never received an answer. As Americans were thus permitted to trade with Siam, he asked why no more American vessels had been there; and Mr. R. assigned as the reason, that the King & his Ministers had exercised the right of selecting such articles from the cargo as they chose at their own prices, which destroyed the profits of the trade, & therefore it could not be carried on unless it were placed upon a different & better footing.[8] This plain statement of a disagreeable truth did not appear to give any offence, & after a little deliberation, the Prah Klang said that he had always assisted the Americans when they had been there; that he had made a treaty with Major Burney [Major Henry Burney], an English Envoy,[9] & he was now ready to assist the American Envoy, if he would make known what he wished. Mr. R. said in reply to this, that if he could be permitted to see a copy of the English treaty, he could very soon propose to the Prah Klang the terms of the treaty which he wished to make. He was told that a copy of the English treaty should be immediately furnished him.

The question of presents was now brought forward by the Prah Klang, not because the King wished to receive any, he said, but merely to know whether there were any; and he was informed that presents were to have been sent out to Canton, but as they had not arrived there, it was presumed they were lost at sea. Presents, however, had been purchased in Canton, Mr. R., said, both for the King & the Prah Klang, though but of small value. The Prah Klang wished to know whether they were of Chinese or European manufacture, & was told that they consisted of both.

Such was the sum of the conversation that passed between Mr. R. & the Prah Klang at this interview that is worth recording. Before any farther progress could be made in the negociation, it was necessary that the papers should be translated, & the Prah Klang proposed that Mr. Morrison, & Mr. Piedada should go into another room & do it without delay. This proposal being acceded to, we took leave & returned to our residence with impressions rather favourable with respect to the Prah Klang, & also with respect to the result of the mission.

In the course of this day there had been something done to improve our accommodations & render us more comfortable, by furnishing us with bedsteads, mattrasses, musquito-curtains.[10] We were now much better accommodated than we had supposed we should be, & were therefore disposed to be quite satisfied with our situation.

February 28th. Nothing deserving of notice transpired on the 27th. except a present being sent by the Prah Klang to Mr. Roberts, consisting of 80 ticals, equivalent to more than 50 dollars. It may be worth noticing, however, as an occurrence of the 27th. that in translating the papers of Mr. Roberts, it was found that the letter of introduction from the President of the U.S. to the King was not sealed; which was considered by the Prah Klang so extraordinary that he sent to Mr. Roberts at a late hour of the night, to ask for an explanation. No other explanation was, or could be given, than merely stating the fact, that it was not the custom of our country for letters of introduction to be sealed. Another message was sent on the same subject today, & it was stated at the same time that Major Burney, the English Envoy, brought no letters to the King that were not sealed. To this Mr. R. replied, that in our country, sealing a letter of introduction was never heard of, which was the sole reason that his letter of introduction was not sealed.

About 11 o'clock today, Mr. R. received a visit from the Portuguese Consul, Don Carlos Manuel de Silveira, a gentleman of very respectable appearance, & about 55 years of age. He had resided at Bankok most of the time for 13 years, & was consequently well acquainted with the language of the country, & the character of the people. He was thus well qualified to impart useful information, & he did not hesitate to speak his sentiments freely. With respect to the King, he said that while he was Chroma Chit [Prince Chesda], & for sometime after he ascended the throne, he used to visit him often, & sometimes spent the whole night with him conversing about the Governments & usages of the nations of Europe. He was very anxious to acquire a knowledge of the forms of government, laws & customs of the other nations; and when he had received from the Consul such information as was calculated to expand his views, & to be highly useful to him in the government of his own kingdom, he observed that until this knowledge was communicated to him, he was blind, but now both his eyes were opened. Not long after he ascended the throne, however, the King began to manifest towards the Consul less regard than he had done, & a less desire to receive information from him; and at last broke of[f] all intercourse with him, & never spoke of him except in terms of extreme dislike. This change in the sentiment, & conduct of the King, was owing, the Consul supposed, to two causes; the first was, his freedom in giving information respecting the Government & country of Siam to foreigners, from whom the Government had always endeavoured to conceal its measures as much as possible; and the second was his, the Consul's, refusing to sign the treaty which the King had caused to be drawn up for himself & the Portuguese Government.[11] In consequence of this refusal to sign the treaty, it never went into operation; so that he remained there without any formal treaty between his own Government & that of Siam, though his services were by no means the less necessary on that account. His situation, however, had become quite unpleasant, & he expected soon to leave the country.

In answer to my inquiry whether the reigning King was not a more intelligent man than his predecessor, he replied in the affirmative, but observed that he was not free from faults of considerable magnitude, & of a bad character. The Prah Klang he did not scruple to call a very bad man; a tyrant in disposition & practice; in the indulgence of his vindictive passions, a ferocious savage; and as a Minister, deceitful & unprincipled, ready to promise any thing that might be required of him, but never performing what he had promised; unless interest or inclination led him to do so.

On the subject of the treaty which Mr. Roberts was about to make, Mr. Silveira observed, that although the treaty made by Major Burney was not as favourable as it might have been, yet Mr. R. could not expect to make one upon more favourable terms, & he would have to take that for his model. The most essential article in that treaty so far as it was to serve as a guide to Mr. Roberts, was that respecting duties; which were levied according to the measurement of the vessel, & not on the individual articles composing her cargo. For every fathom (the Siamese fathom is 79½ inches) of the vessel's beam measured on the upper deck, 1700 ticals were to be paid, which are equal to 1046 dollars. No other duties, either import or export were to be paid.

Notwithstanding Mr. Silveira had witnessed a great many times such scenes as that exhibited to us at the Prah Klang's, yet he seemed to regard them with the same feelings that we did; and even the sons of the Prah Klang, by his account, would have been very glad to have all those usages which appear so revolting in the eyes of an American or European, abolished. The two eldest sons of the Prah Klang used to visit the Consul frequently, & were very inquisitive about the customs & usages of Europe, & particularly respecting the manner in which gentlemen passed their time when not engaged in business; and when they were told that it was the custom there for gentlemen & ladies to meet together, & spend their leisure time in agreeable & profitable conversation, they expressed much regret that they could not go to Europe, where society afforded so much enjoyment. They dared not mention the subject to their father, for fear of losing their heads.

We learned from the Consul that Mr. Abeel left Bankok ten or eleven months before for Sincapore, from whence he expected to proceed to the bay of Bengal, & from thence to the U. States. He left Siam on account of his health. The Consul spoke of him in the most favourable terms & regretted that he was obliged to leave the country. Having staid about an hour he took leave & returned to his residence about two miles below us, & on the opposite side of the river.[12]

In the evening [February 28th] Mr. Roberts paid another visit to the Prah Klang, for the purpose of talking over the subject of the treaty, before it should be drawn up & presented in due form. The conference commenced by the Prah Klang observing to Mr. R. that with respect to duties, no more favourable terms would be granted to the Americans than had been granted to the English, & therefore it was unnecessary to spend any time in discussing that subject. Mr. R. was well aware that it would be useless to ask for a lower rate of duties than that specified in the English treaty, which has been mentioned; but he wished for a modification of these duties, which seemed to him important as well as perfectly reasonable, but which Major Burney, it appeared, had been unable to effect. According to that treaty, a vessel arriving in a port of Siam with only a half or even a fourth part of her cargo, was liable to pay the same amount of measurement duty, as if she brought a full cargo; but while Mr. R. would agree to pay the same duty on a full cargo, he thought it was unjust & unreasonable that the same amount should be paid for only a part of a cargo, & he therefore proposed that the amount of duty should be regulated by the amount of cargo. After some discussion, the Prah Klang acknowledged that this appeared to be reasonable, & consented that it should be inserted in the treaty. Mr. R. then called the attention of the Prah Klang to another point, which he supposed would be likely to prove the occasion of misunderstanding between the two nations, as well as of unjust cruel treatment of individuals; and that was, the manner in which Americans should be treated by the Siamese Government, if they failed to pay the debts which they might contract, or be guilty of any offence against the laws or customs of the country. According to the laws of Siam, or rather the custom founded upon the will of the sovereign, a debtor might be sold, together with his whole family, by his creditor, for a limited time, or even for life, if the debt could not be otherwise paid; and any person, not even excepting a Prime Minister, was liable to be flogged like the vilest slave, at the pleasure of the King. Mr. Roberts wished to insert an article in the treaty which should exempt his countrymen, both from being sold & from corporeal punishment; and that the Prah Klang might see how important this point was considered by the American Envoy, he was told that if an American citizen were either sold, or subjected to corporeal punishment by order of the Siamese Government, it would be considered by the American Government as sufficient cause for a declaration of war. This appeared to be a new doctrine to the Prah Klang, & he could give no decided opinion upon it; but said he would mention it to the King.[13]

It was next proposed by Mr. Roberts, that an American Consul should be permitted to reside at Bankok, for the purpose of superintending American commerce, & settling the differences that might arise between American citizens; but to this the Prah Klang positively objected, saying that a Consul would only create disturbance in the country, by giving information to foreigners as the Portuguese Consul had done, whom he therefore called a very bad man. The King he moreover said, was determined that no Consul should ever be allowed to reside in the country; and he therefore desired Mr. R. to say no more on the subject. Such was the substance of the conversation that took place at this interview, as related by Mr. R. after his return.

March 2d. As none of us were permitted to go out until Mr. Roberts had been presented to the King, & as it was thought best that this ceremony should be deferred until the treaty was concluded, or at least, until some progress had been made in the negociation; we felt an interest in every step that was taken towards accomplishing the object of the mission, which will justify me in narrating particulars, that would not otherwise be noticed.

Having obtained all the data that were within his reach, Mr. R. set about drawing up a treaty in due form, & in the course of this day it was completed & sent to the Portuguese Consul, to be translated into Portuguese; it being necessary that it should be in two languages at least, besides that of the country. The rough draft of the treaty was shown to me, & so far as I could judge, it contained every thing which, under existing circumstances, could with propriety or any prospect of advantage, be asked for. There was but little in it, however, of material importance besides the terms which had been previously discussed with the Prah Klang, & of which I have already given the outlines.

Late in the afternoon, the Interpreter came to inquire whether the treaty was ready to be presented to the Prah Klang, & received an answer from Mr. R. accompanied with such evidences of displeasure as it was thought might give offence, & lead to unpleasant consequences. The cause of Mr. Roberts' displeasure was, his being kept in a situation which rendered it impossible to do, what the Prah Klang appeared to suppose, from the inquiry which the Interpreter had made by his direction, he ought to have done. It was impossible, Mr. R. said to Mr. Piedada, in a tone of considerable impatience, to have the treaty ready, until he could get it translated into Portuguese, which could not be done unless he could have a boat to go to the Portuguese Consul, the only person who could translate it; and yet no boat had been provided for him, & he was shut up in his house as if he were a prisoner. This was certainly true, & Mr. R. had some reason to be displeased; but, considering the circumstances in which he was placed, it would have been more prudent, probably, not to have shown any signs of anger, or used language that could give offence.

Having been now five days in our quarters, and something having been done every day for our accommodation, we were made as comfortable by this time as we could reasonably expect to be, & with the exception of the confinement, were disposed to be quite contented. Our table was very well supplied with solids, as poultry, eggs, fish etc from the market, & with wines from the ship.

On our first arrival, we were a good deal annoyed by the crowd of natives who flocked around us, especially at mealtime; but their curiosity being by this time in some measure gratified, & having been driven away a few times, they gave us no farther trouble. We were furnished with a guard at night, who watched the gates, & prevented the intrusion of any unwelcome visitors. It was soon found to be necessary to guard against thieving, as one of the Midshipmen had all the clothes stolen that he brought with him, & some silver spoons were also missing.

Except the son of the Prah Klang, no person of higher rank than that of commandant of artillery, had yet visited Mr. Roberts; and this officer, whose name was Benidito [Beneditto de Arvellegeria], was of Portuguese descent & a Roman catholic. He appeared to be an exceedingly amiable & good man, but was said to be quite unacquainted with military science. His uniform consisted of a green round jacket of light stuff, an embroidered calico vest, & calico trowsers. No hat with waving plume covered & adorned his head, but he always appeared both bare-headed & bare-footed. Such an exterior would be deemed in our country quite unsuitable for a general officer; but in a country where clothes are so little used, a display of dress & ornament, would not only be superfluous, but from the extreme heat of the climate, insupportably oppressive.

March 4th. Last evening the Portuguese Consul paid another visit to Mr. Roberts, & brought the translation of the treaty which he had just completed. Respecting one or two particulars of the treaty, he gave Mr. R. information which led him to the conclusion, that a farther modification of duties would be necessary, in order to put Americans upon the same footing with the English.

Owing to a difference in the valuation of dollars, a vessel that should bring specie & pay the same measurment duty as one that should bring a cargo, would lose about twenty-five per cent; and it appeared therefore but fair & reasonable that the duties on a vessel with specie should be reduced in the same proportion. This was a point on which Mr. Roberts determined to insist, though it was obviously quite as much for the interest of the Siamese, that the duty on specie should be so reduced as to encourage its introduction into the country as for the American traders.

On the subject of a Consul residing at Bankok, Mr. Silveira spoke without reserve, & said that in his opinion, it was indispensably necessary, for he was perfectly satisfied, from his knowledge of the Siamese Government, that if no American were to reside at Bankok, to see that the treaty was faithfully observed, it would be forgotten within three months, & our countrymen would be subjected to the same vexations as if no treaty had been made. He said moreover, that notwithstanding the opposition of the King & Prah Klang, the English Government would soon have a Consul residing there.

In the course of the conversation respecting the English treaty, and the course of conduct pursued by the two English Envoys, namely, Mr. Crawfurd, & Major Burney; Mr. Silveira had occasion to make some remarks respecting the wives of these gentlemen, as both of them were accompanied by their wives. Mrs. Crawfurd had such an extreme aversion to the manners & practices of the Siamese, that when her husband was invited together with herself, to dine with the Prah Klang on the day after their arrival, she refused to go; and when the Prah Klang visited & took tea with Mr. Crawfurd, she refused to appear at the table because she would not, she said, set at table with a naked man. But Mrs. Burney's dislike to Siamese manners did not carry her quite so far, for when the Prah Klang paid a visit to her husband & took tea with him, she did the honors of the table, but without once raising her eyes towards their naked guest.[14]

It being expected that we should soon have the honor of being presented to the King, & being desirous to know in what manner we should be introduced, & what ceremonies we should be required to perform; Mr. Silveira was questioned with a good deal of minuteness on these points, & gave such information as would serve to prevent our committing any material errors. Formerly, he said, it had been the custom for foreign Ministers to appear before the King without shoes, which custom Mr. Crawfurd complied with; but when arrangements were made for Major Burney to have his audience with the King, & the officers of the King told him that he would have to comply with this custom, he replied that it was the custom in Europe, when a person was presented to a King, to take off his hat & bow, but to keep on his shoes. If, therefore, he were required to take off his shoes on being presented to the King, he should keep on his hat; but if he were permitted to keep on his shoes, he would take off his hat & bow as was the fashion in his country. This was agreed to, though with much reluctance on the part of the King's officers, who were no doubt anxious that foreigners should be as much degraded as themselves in the presence of their King; and ever since that time, foreigners have been permitted to behold his Siamese Majesty without taking off their shoes.[15] An attempt was made, however, some time after Major Burney left the country by the same officers, to compel Mr. Hunter, the gentleman whom I have already mentioned, to conform to the old custom; but he peremptorily refused, & remained at the palace-gate in altercation with the officers, while the King was waiting to receive him, until his Majesty became impatient & sent to inquire into the cause of the delay; and on being told that the Englishman wished to go in with his shoes on, he said, "I know the custom of his country very well— it is to take off the hat, but to keep on the shoes—let him come in". This seemed effectually to break down that riduculous custom with regard to foreigners; for since then, the Consul said he had visited the King with his shoes on, & met with no opposition from the Ministers.

With all the faults of the Siamese Government, there is one good trait in its character, & that is, a tolerant disposition which imposes no restraint either upon christians, or upon those who profess any other form of religion different from the religion of the country. Quite the reverse of this had been the conduct of the Government of Cochin China, after we left there, according to information just received at Bankok; for they had either murdered all the christians in the country, or given orders that it should be done, with the exception of the Bishop, who was loaded with irons & thrown into prison.[16] The number of christians at Bankok was about a thousand, all of whom were Roman Catholics. A Bishop resided there, of whom the Consul spoke in terms somewhat equivocal.

In the afternoon of this day the treaty was sent to the Prah Klang for his inspection; but finding it in Portuguese, & concluding probably, that it had been translated by Mr. Silveira whom he hated, he sent it back with the request that it should be put into Chinese. To this Mr. Roberts demurred very strongly, as it would require at least two days to do it, & after all it could not be so accurately expressed in Chinese as Portuguese. He therefore requested Mr. Piedada to take it back to the Prah Klang with these objections, & request him to dispense with the Chinese translation, until the treaty had been acted upon, when it could be put into that language in its perfect form if it were deemed necessary. To this the Prah Klang so far acceded as to have it translated into Siamese, & to order it to be ready for the interview which he had appointed with Mr. Roberts the next day.

A quantity of refreshments was sent to Mr. R. this evening from the Prah Klang, consisting of 15 or 20 different articles, most of which were fruits & sweet meats, & very good. A sack of sugar was also sent at the same time. This present unluckily arrived just as we had finished supper, so that we had to reserve it till the next day.

It had been the custom in Siam, as we learned from Mr. Silveira, for foreign Ministers to be supported at the expense of the Government, & for this purpose a monthly allowance had been made by the King, of three catties of silver, 240 ticals, & half that sum by the second King, when there had been one. This sum, equal to $221, was paid to Major Burney, during the whole of his stay at Bankok of eight months.[17] The second King died a short time before our arrival; but Mr. Silveira said that he understood the three catties which the King had allowed to other foreign Ministers, he had ordered to be paid to Mr. Roberts. Only one catty, however, had been received, & even this Mr. R. would have been glad to refuse.

March 5th. Early this morning, the Prah Klang sent his boat for Mr. Roberts, & as soon as he was ready he paid him a visit & had another conference on the subject of the treaty. Only two or three of the provisions of the treaty were objected to by the Prah Klang; the principal of which were, that for reducing the duty on vessels carrying specie instead of merchandize, so that such vessels might trade there on as fair terms as those with cargoes; and the other was that respecting Consuls. The Prah Klang could not be made to see that it was as much for the interest of his own country to encourage the introduction of specie as for foreigners, & therefore he would not agree to it. And with respect to Consuls, notwithstanding all the arguments Mr. Roberts could use, his views seemed to be equally erroneous, & he would not consent that a Consul should reside there; but he said that an American merchant would be permitted to reside there for the purpose of superintending the American trade.

Upon the whole, however, the Prah Klang made less opposition to the terms of the treaty than had been anticipated, & at the close of this interview the principal difficulties appeared to be surmounted.

When Mr. Roberts returned, I was requested to visit the Prah Klang, on account of pain & lameness of one of the lower limbs, which was believed to have been occasioned by his having been obliged for several years, to remain for a considerable time every day, & sometimes of many hours together on his knees in the presence of the King. I accordingly visited him accompanied by the interpreter, Mr. Piedada, & found him in his audience room, where we had witnessed the disgusting scene which I have described. The chair which Mr. Roberts had just occupied, was left for me near the centre of the room; and while I was seated here my patient was reclining on his platform, & the interpreter was at a distance from me & fronting the Prah Klang on his knees. The investigation of the case was commenced without delay, & was carried on for some time merely by question & answer; but perceiving, I suppose, that I was not altogether satisfied with this mode of examining the case, he signified that I might approach & examine the affected limb & feel the pulse. On a close view he appeared to be about 50 years of age, was of large stature, corpulent, & had a stern severe countenance. Before I left him, he informed me of another complaint under which he was labouring, & which seemed to be the result of his polygamy.[18]

March 6th. When the Portuguese Consul first called on Mr. Roberts, he complained of lameness in one ancle, which had troubled him for a considerable time, & he requested my advice respecting it. This morning I paid him a professional visit, accompanied by Lieuts. Purviance & Brent, & the Marine Officer.

As we had to descend the river about two miles, both sides of which were lined with the floating habitations which I have already mentioned, we had an opportunity of seeing in what manner they were constructed, & also of making some observations on the appearance & customs of the people.

A float of bamboo about two feet thick constituted the foundation of those dwellings, which were also built principally of the same material, & covered with thatch. Each house consisted of two apartments, of which the front one, or that towards the river, was occupied as a shop, while the other was appropriated to the uses of the family. The front room was always open, so as to expose its contents to the public view. As almost all these habitations were occupied by Chinese, most of the goods exhibited in the shops were of Chinese manufacture, & generally of a very ordinary kind. These dwellings appeared to swarm with inhabitants, and as they extended several miles along the river, it is evident that the floating population must have constituted a large proportion of that of the city. A large number of people of both sexes were employed in boats, vast numbers of which were constantly in motion. The women were quite as much employed in the small boats as the men, & they seemed to be as much designed for those employments which in other countries are supposed to belong exclusively to the men, as the men themselves; for they exhibited less of the feminine character in their appearance & conduct than I ever witnessed before. A large proportion of them wore no other clothing than the serong; so that all above the waist & below the middle of the thighs, was perfectly naked. Others who were not quite so destitute of all ideas of decency, wore a piece of cotton stuff, or a piece of black crape about the chest which partially concealed the breasts. Besides exhibiting such a degree of nudity as made them sufficiently disgusting, they were universally in the habit, without a single exception, of chewing the arica-nut compound, which caused ulceration of the lips & gums, blackened the teeth, & together with their shameless nudity, rendered them as completely disgusting as can possibly be conceived.

On our way down the river to the Consul's we passed a floating theatre, formed by linking two or three boats together, & laying boards from one to the other for a floor, & spreading an awning overhead & at the sides. A group of natives was assembled here, & gazing no doubt with delight at the fantastic appearance, & uncouth gestures of the performers; and listening to the discordant jargon of gongs, fifes, etc.

We found the Consul at home, & passed an hour with him very agreeably. He occupied quite a pleasant situation, & appeared to be as comfortable & contented as a foreigner could be in a country which affords him so few of the sources of comfort & contentment which are open to him in his own country. The name of Mr. Abeel having been mentioned, I asked the Consul where he resided while he staid at Bankok, & was shown a small bamboo house on the river's bank, supported by piles, which was occupied not only by Mr. Abeel but also by Mr. Gutzlass [Karl Friedrich August Gutzlaff], a German Missionary & his family.[19] Mr. Silveira was a bachelor, & had no one living with him except his Secretary, a young Frenchman.

I made inquiries of the Consul respecting the medical profession, & was told that although there were many of the natives who were called physicians, yet there was no medical science among them. There were some works by natives on the subject of medicine, but foreign medical books were entirely unknown there; and their own were made up of instructions for employing charms & the various arts of incantation. There were no hospitals in the country, & when the poor who were unable to provide for themselves were sick, they were laid at the gates of the pagodas, & suffered to remain there without any other assistance than what an occasional act of charity might bestow, until they recovered by the efforts of nature, or death relieved them from their sufferings. The principal diseases that prevailed at Bankok were bilious fevers, but I did not learn that the yellow-fever had ever prevailed there.

No apothecary establishment was to be found in a city containing 450,000 inhabitants; and when I wanted a piece of camphor for the Prah Klang, I had to send to him, & request him to procure it.

In the evening I received a message from the Prince Chroma Kuhn, step-brother to the King, requesting me to visit him & see one of his men who had been badly hurt. I went, accompanied by Mr. Wells, our junior Midshipman, to whom the prince had taken a great liking, & shown all the attention in his power. The Prince was about 23 or 24 years of age, & appeared to be altogether an untutored child of nature. In all his actions & conversation he appeared like a child, though he manifested a kind & amiable disposition. His residence was of a very ordinary character for a Prince, consisting of several separate buildings of small dimensions, constructed in a very clumsy manner of brick, & plastered on the outside. The principal building, or palace, appeared to consist of only one large room which, however, was closed so that I did not see the interior. On two sides of this building was a corridor, verandah, & in this the Prince held his levees, & there he had a rostrum similar to that of the Prah Klang. Surrounding the corridor was a low brick wall, on which a mat was spread for us to set upon. Chairs were scarcely known in Siam, & never will be among the natives, so long as kneeling shall continue so much in fashion. We had to wait sometime for the Prince to make his appearance, & when he did appear, he showed not the least degree of acquaintance with what we term politeness, & good-manners. His behaviour was precisely that of an awkward, uncultivated boy, who had never been in a situation to learn the customs & manners of civilized society. He had learned a little English, so that we could understand each other sufficiently for me to do what was necessary for the person whom I had been called to see. The patient was at some distance from the Prince's residence, & it being dark, it was necessary to carry a light, & for this purpose the Prince himself brought a candle & put it into my hands, intending, as it appeared, that I should carry the light myself, instead of ordering one of his servants to carry it, of whom there was a swarm creeping & crouching around him ready to lick the dust from the ground, if it had been his will that they should do so. I mention this small transaction merely to show how ignorant even a Prince of Siam may be of what belongs to good manners. The servants, however, carried the light, & the Prince followed me to the house of the patient, which was a miserable bamboo shed, consisting of only one small room, where men, women & children were huddle[d] together like cattle. I found the patient, a young man, with a bad injury of the knee & ankle, & the whole limb was a good deal inflamed. I had occasion to direct a poultice to be made, but neither the Prince himself, nor any of his servants could be made to understand the process of making or the manner of applying it; so that I had to stay & direct the making of it, & apply it myself. This being done, I took leave & returned home.

March 7th. This morning the presents for the King & the Prah Klang, were examined preparatory to the expected audience with his Majesty; it being customary for the presents to be delivered to the King at the audience, & they are always examined before hand, that it may be ascertained whether they are such as the King will accept. The son of the Prah Klang was the principal person sent to examine them, & from what I could learn, for I was not present, he seemed to regard them with a good deal of indifference. Some of them were costly articles of Chinese manufacture, as silks, crapes, & silver baskets of fillagree work; but these seemed to be little esteemed, the preference being greatly in favour of European & American manufactures. So much, indeed, were European & American articles preferred to Chinese, that even the most ordinary of the former were much more highly valued than the most costly of the latter.[20]

In the afternoon the Prah Klang sent his boat for Mr. Roberts, & desired that the presents intended for him might be delivered at the same time. His request was complied with, & notwithstanding the presents were not such as he would have selected, yet he seemed very willing to receive them. Mr. R. made but a short stay, & when he returned, he informed us that we were all invited by the Prah Klang to the house of his brother, to attend a ball given on the occasion of shaving his son's head; a ceremony of a similar nature to that of putting on the toga among the Romans, by which the individual was transferred from the rank of youths to that of men. The ceremony of shaving the head is considered a very important one among the Siamese, & when circumstances admit of it, is always attended with feasting & merriment.

The Prah Klang was to send his boat for us, & accordingly about 7 o'clock in the evening [March 6][21] the boat arrived, in which we all embarked, though it could conveniently accommodate only four or five. We soon reached the place of entertainment, where we found a large number of people assembled, & the music playing, but the dancing had not yet commenced. The ball room was a spacious hall, a hundred & thirty or forty feet long, about thirty feet wide, & open in front. About one half of the room was occupied by a stage for the performers, which was covered with mats. The room was very well lighted by a large number of lamps suspended from the ceiling overhead, & by torches arranged along its sides. No seats having been provided for us before we arrived, we had to wait in the crowd till they could be prepared. We were then conducted to the place assigned for us, which was at the lower end of the stage, where we had a very good opportunity to witness the exhibition. Here we remained some time listening to the music before the performances commenced. The musical instruments consisted of about 50 pairs of flat pieces of ivory about a foot long & an inch wide; a kind of harp; a haut boy [an oboe]; and several others which I could not see, but which sounded like brass basins. The music made by these instruments, together with that of a few female voices, coarse & unrefined as it certainly was, did not strike my ear more unpleasantly than that of an Italian opera.

At length the performers made their appearance & the exhibition commenced. It would be a useless waste of time to give a detailed description of the performances on this occasion, if I could do it; I shall therefore mention only a few particulars.

We had been told that it was to be a ball, & of course expected there would be dancing; but while we staid, for we did not remain through the whole performance, there was no dancing. The performance consisted, so far as I could judge, in a tragi-comic representation. The principal characters were a King & Queen with their trains, & a band of soldiers. The Queen appeared to have fallen under the displeasure of her husband, & was arraigned before him to receive her sentence. The dresses of the principal performers were quite rich, & for aught I know perfectly appropriate. The King, Queen, & female attendants had their faces whitened with some thing, probably chalk, & they were all barefooted.

All the females had artificial metalic nails on their fingers, about three inches long & curved, to show, probably, that they belonged to that station which is exempt from labour. An essential part of the performance appeared to consist in a kind of chorus, sung alternately by the band of musicians, who at the same time struck their pieces of ivory together with great force, & by the female singers stationed near the upper end of the stage. As soon as the women had finished their part of their chorus, the hautboy, harp & bass-drum struck up & played an air which to my ear was far from being disagreeable. There was no scenery whatever.

Soon after the performance commenced we were presented with coffee, tea & segars. It was observed by the interpreter early in the evening, that the nobility occupied an elevated seat at the upper end of the hall while the American Envoy & his suite had been assigned a place among the rabble, which some of our party were disposed to take in high dudgeon, & were unwilling to stay any longer. For my own part, however, I did not think that any insult had been designed, & therefore considered it best not to manifest any resentment.

After we had spent about two hours in viewing the performance, we were sent for by the host into an upper apartment, where we were invited to partake of refreshments which had been provided for us. These consisted of a variety of sweetmeats, oranges, water-melons, & coconuts, placed on large silver dishes, resting on wodden supports about a foot high.

The host was seated on his stage, raised about a foot from the floor, & received Mr. Roberts & his party with only a slight inclination of the head. Mr. Piedada & Gen. Benidito accompanied us & fell on their knees before the "great man." The room was large, airy, well carpeted & furnished. The host asked Mr. Roberts how he liked the performance, & being told that he was much pleased with it, he seemed highly gratified. We now took leave, embarked again the Prah Klang's boat, & reached home about 11 o'clock.

March 8th. [March 7] This evening we were again invited to the same place where we had witnessed the exhibition the night before, to see another kind of performance which was represented as being much more amusing than that which we had seen. It was determined at first not to go, in consequence of the supposed disrespect with which we had been treated the night before; but the message being very importunate, & supposing it might have an unfavourable effect on the mission, if we refused to go, we finally consented, & were again accommodated with the Prah Klang's boat.[22] The theatre was the same on this occasion, & was fitted up in the same manner as the night before. A complaint having been made to the interpreter, & through him probably to the Prah Klang, of our having been seated on the stage, where we were a good deal annoyed by the crowd; we were now provided with seats on a kind of stage at the back part of the hall, where, although we were elevated above the crowd, we were nevertheless not in so comfortable a situation as that which had been first assigned us.

The performance had commenced before we arrived, & seemed to be only a repetition of that of the preceding evening. This continued but a short time, however, when it was succeeded by a battle fought with swords & spears, which continued a few minutes, & gave place to a feat of tumbling & vaulting, in which the principal performers were boys. Next came a play in which the principal characters were the King & Queen of the night before; and an elephant & a horse, represented by men with the heads of these animals surmounted on their own. Whatever the play itself may have been, the performance was exceedingly tiresome & disgusting, as it consisted in great part of unmeaning & unnatural gestures, which appeared so perfectly childish & ridiculous, that I could not view the performance with any degree of patience. After it had continued about an hour it ended, & another battle was fought which was succeeded by another scene of tumbling & vaulting, which closed the performances of the evening. All I shall say of these performances is, that the battle appeared to be fought with great spirit & dexterity, & the weapons were handled with such quickness that it was surprizing how the combatants should escape injury; and the tumbling & vaulting exhibited as great a degree of perfection, & as extraordinary acts of agility as have probably been seen in any country. I have such an extreme dislike to all such performances, however, that I never looked at them without pain, & will not attempt to describe any of the individual exploits that I witnessed.

With the exception that we were accommodated with a more elevated seat this evening than we had been the night before, we were treated by the host with less attention, in consequence, no doubt, of his having been informed of the complaint that had been made to the interpreter. No tea, or refreshments were offered us, & after we rose to depart, he sent to Mr. Roberts, to say that he was so much engaged as to be unable to see him; intimating that the remark which had been made respecting his not showing himself to Mr. R. at his first visit, had been communicated to him, & showing at the same time, that he disregarded what the American Envoy & his suite might say of his conduct.

March 9th. This morning Mr. R. & Capt. G. paid their first visit to Mr. Silveira, & as I had undertaken to render him some professional service, I accompanied them. As Mr. Roberts had some business with the Consul, the Capt. & myself, with the Consul's secretary, took a walk to see a pagoda, which he said was only about three hundred feet distant. The short walk of three hundred feet, however, proved to be one of three hundred rods, & having taken the middle of the day for it, when the thermometer was nearly 100 in the shade, it was by no means a very pleasant one. Our walk lay along the east bank of the river, & in the course of it we passed through two or three villages, & by several dock-yards, where they were building junks, some of which were of a large size. We passed a Catholic church, situated on a level grass-plot of small extent, & surrounded with coconut trees & bamboo. It was a very neat little edifice, & plastered & white-washed within & without. The interior exhibited fewer images & ornaments than almost any Catholic house of worship that I had seen. This was the cathedral church [Cathedral of Santa Assomption], & the Bishop, with a few of his priests had their residence near by. The Bishop was very old & infirm,[23] & we did not see him; but made a short stay with the priests. One of them was a young Frenchman, who had been only three months in the country. A letter had been received that morning by one of them, as we understood, from Cochin China; in which it was stated that all the christian-priests had fled from the country, in consequence of the persecuting measures of the Government.

At length after winding our way through groves of coconut trees & bamboo, in which were a few scattering habitations, besides the villages that have been mentioned, we reached the pagoda, the object of our pursuit. We now found, however, that we had in a great measure lost our labour, for the pagoda was closed, & we could only see the out side of it. There was nothing about it to deserve particular notice, especially as the city contains so many much superior to it.

The Boat was directed to meet us near the pagoda, & after waiting some time it arrived, & we embarked, & reached the Consul's about 12 o'clock.

March 10th. For four days, Mr. Roberts had been promised an interview with the Prah Klang, for the purpose of coming to some definite under-standing respecting the terms of the treaty. After so long a delay a meeting took place this evening, & a copy of the treaty which the Prah Klang had caused to be made, was brought forward, & a few articles of it were read; but it was so different from the original, of which it professed to be a correct copy that Mr. Roberts would not pay any attention to it, & returned home a good deal exasperated at what appeared to be the duplicity of the Prah Klang.[24]

March 11th. This morning, however, after an interview with the interpreter, it was arranged that another interview should take place with the Prah Klang at 6 o'clock in the evening; and accordingly at that hour a boat was sent,

& Mr. Roberts went, accompanied by Mr. Morrison, who acted as Portuguese as well as Chinese interpreter at all the conferences. Soon after they went, I was sent for to see the Prah Klang, who was suffering a good deal from the rheumatic affection, for which I had visited him before. After examining the patient, who was not so bad as to be disabled from discharging the duties of his office, I took a seat with Mr. Roberts & Mr. Morrison, & remained there till the conference closed, which was not till one o'clock in the morning.

I had therefore a good opportunity to witness the progress of the discussion, & of satisfying myself whether the Siamese Government was really desirous of entering into a commercial treaty with the U. States or not. From what had already taken place, I was prepared to expect great opposition from the Prah Klang to several articles of the treaty; but was happily disappointed at the readiness with which he assented to the terms proposed to him. As the article respecting Consuls had been omitted, in consequence of the determination of the Prah Klang, repeatedly expressed, not to allow any, the only strenuous opposition that he made, was to a clause in one of the articles respecting duties; which proposed that a vessel arriving in a port of Siam with only a part of a cargo, should pay the measurement duty only in the same proportion. This was objected to, & certainly with some appearance of justice, on the ground that it would be impossible to determine what proportion of a cargo such a vessel might have on board, & to adjust the duties properly; and thus troublesome disputes would arise, which it was desirable by all means to avoid. This point was debated for a considerable time, Mr. Roberts insisting on the propriety & justice of pro-portioning the duty to the amount of cargo, though without proposing any method by which it could be done in a manner that would be satisfactory to both parties; and the Prah Klang insisting on the other hand, on the great difficulty of ascertaining whether a vessel with a part of a cargo, ought to pay three fourths, or only one fourth of the full amount of the measure-ment duty. And he urged, besides, that it had always been their custom to exact the full amount of the measurement duty, whether the vessel had a full cargo or not. In order, however, to comply as far as he could with the wishes of the American Envoy, he would consent that a vessel with a part of a cargo, should pay only 1300 ticals; but this was so small a reduction, that Mr. R. said it would not answer the desired purpose, & proposed 800 ticals instead of the 1300, which was the highest that a vessel with a part of a cargo could afford to pay. The Prah Klang said this was too great a reduction, & therefore he could not agree to it. The conclusion finally was, that the clause in question should be struck out, which would leave all vessels, whether full freighted or not, subject to the full amount of measurement duty.

The manner of measuring a vessel for the purpose of levying the duty gave rise to some discussion; but it was agreed, that a vessel with only one deck, should be measured on the upper side of this deck at its middle, & from one bulwark to the other; and that a vessel with two decks should be measured across the lower one in the same manner. The measurement was to be according to the Siamese fathom of 96 inches their measure, but equal only to 79½ English inches [78 English inches, according to the treaty]; and for each fathom, measured as just described, a duty of 1700 ticals was to be paid, with the exception of a vessel carrying specie, on which the duty was to be 1500 tical. The tical is equal to 61½ cents.

All the discussions that arose in the course of this conference were carried on with more patience & coolness on the part of the Prah Klang, & with a more manifest desire to enter into a commercial treaty with the U. States than had been expected. He appeared, however, to make no effort to fix his attention upon the business before him, or to impose the least restraint upon his actions, which were frequently very ludicrous for one in his situation. It was indeed amusing, to see a minister of his high rank, while negotiating an important treaty with a foreign Envoy, lying sometimes on his back with his hand hold of his feet, & sometimes on his face extended at full length; then perhaps, kneeling & leaning forward on his cushions, & thus by turns assuming almost every variety of uncouth posture. In the course of the evening he drank a good deal of tea, & smoked, first a cigar & then a long pipe, & chewed the arica-nut masticatory with but little intermission. We were also presented with tea, cigars, sweetmeats, & fruits.

There was less parade on this occasion than at our first interview, though at this time, every person present except ourselves, & the assistant Prah Klang, was either on his knees, or lying prostrate on the floor; and not one of them spoke to the Prah Klang, without making the salam.

The articles of the treaty being thus separately considered & agreed to, & the preamble as dictated by the Prah Klang, being also read & assented to, we took leave & reached our quarters about half past one A.M.

March 12. In compliance with the request of Mr. Silveira, I made him a visit this morning, & after performing the professional service that was required, I remained an hour or two with him, for the purpose of obtaining information respecting the country, the Government, & the people. The result of these inquiries, together with all my other inquiries on these subjects, will be found on a subsequent page.

I reached home a little before 12 o'clock, & found that there had been a fire at a little distance from our residence up the river; but it appeared to be extinguished, & nothing more was apprehended from it. In a short time, however, it broke out again, & very soon raged with such fury, that it became evident nothing could stop it till it reached the open space in front of our residence, where it would find no more materials to feed upon. The buildings being all constructed of bamboo & palm-leaves, & the weather having been long dry & excessively hot, the progress of the fire was extremely rapid. In the course of an hour from the time it commenced, its work of destruction was completed. Next to our residence the buildings were most compact, & here the fire raged with the greatest fury. Fortunately our house was fire-proof, or it would had shared the fate of the rest. The wind was in a direction to drive the flames from us, but the heat was so great, notwithstanding, as to raise the thermometer in our dining-room to 111°.

We had now an opportunity of observing one important advantage which the floating houses possessed over the others; for as soon as it became evident that the fire would spread, the floating houses nearest to it were cast loose from their moorings, & floated down the river, where they were entirely out of danger. Others immediately followed, & in a little time the river was covered for some distance with floating habitations, making their escape with the favouring tide from the devouring element. The same good fortune, however, did not attend all those who sought the safety of their habitations, by allowing them to float down the river; for either not taking the alarm soon enough, or being too long in loosing them from their moorings, the fire caught them, & several of them as they floated down, were wrapped in flames & soon consumed. In one of them were three Chinamen, confined to their beds by sickness; and being unable to help themselves, & receiving no help from others, they were burnt to death.

Our residence was a secure place of refuge for many of the poor sufferers, to which they fled, men, women & children, with the few articles which they had been able to save from their burning houses. Among the sufferers were our interpreter, Mr. Piedada, & a man by the name of Domingo, who could speak a little English, & who had been attending upon us from the time of our arrival at Bankok in the character of deputy-superintendant. The former occupied a very comfortable house, which was furnished in much better style than most of the Siamese dwellings; but with the exception of a few articles, every thing was swept away. His condition, however, was not near so bad as that of poor Domingo; for as he held an office under the King, his loss would in a great measure be made up to him, & besides, he had no children to cause him additional distress; but Domingo was not only stripped of every thing he possessed in the world, & left completely destitute, but he had a family of children, two of whom were very bad with the small pox, & he was utterly unable to provide anything for their comfort.

It is the duty of the Prah Klang, according to the custom of Siam, whenever a fire breaks out in the city, to be present at it, & direct the measures proper for stopping it; and on this occasion, as soon as the fire had begun to rage with considerable violence, he made his appearance riding on a sort of hand barrow, attended with his cup-bearer, or a man carrying a gold cup, probably containing his tea, & surrounded by an armed guard. He passed through our front yard, where he was set down, after proceeding a little distance on foot, & viewing the ravages of the flames, & giving directions for some buildings to be torn down, he came back into the yard, where [he] stood some time viewing the progress of the flames. While standing here, Mr. Roberts went to him, & invited him to walk up into the dining-room & set down. He excused himself by saying that he was obliged to attend to the fire. Shortly afterwards, however, he passed through the dining-room to the verandah on the other side, where he remained a few minutes watching the fire. Several of the officers were there, but he seemed not to take the least notice of them. He then passed through the room where I happened to be standing. I saluted him in the manner of our country, & he returned it with due civility, & then sat down, surrounded by his guard, servants etc., all on their knees, earnestly watching all his motions. When he went away, his attendants all followed him, bending & crouching as much as possible; as if they were afraid of committing a capital crime by approaching towards an erect posture in the presence of their master. He had on no other clothing than the serong, & on his feet he wore Chinese slippers with wooden soles. No Roman Emperor ever assumed a more haughty carriage or looked down with greater contempt upon those around him than did this semi-barbarian; who is himself subject to the will of a master whose one word could any moment deprive him of his life. I have thus entered into unimportant minutiae, because they serve to elucidate the Siamese Character, & customs.

The principal sufferers by the fire were the christians, who were descendants of the Portuguese, & lived together in a society by themselves.[25] The number of houses destroyed, was from 150 to 200. About sunset I took a walk with Mr. Roberts among the burning ruins, & saw with painful feelings, families scattered about on the ground among the coco-nut trees, without food or shelter; while here & there an anxious father & mother were searching among the smoking ruins of their late dwelling for a little rice to keep their children & themselves from starving. The family of Domingo, consisting of a wife & three or four children, were found in this destitute condition, without any other shelter than a mat stretched on poles, & with only a mat spread on the ground for a bed. Two of the children, as I have already mentioned, were ill of small-pox. Poor Domingo was standing by his wife & children, & on viewing their forlorn condition, the poor fellow's sympathies were excited to such a degree, that he beat his breast for agony.[26]

March 13th. Early this morning, the houses which had escaped the fire by floating down the river, were floated back, & placed in the situations which they had previously occupied, which was done with surprizing expedition, & without their having sustained any injury. Some of the piles, however, to which they had been moored were burnt, & it became necessary to replace them by others. The mode of fixing them was this; a heavy piece of timber was suspended from the top of the pile, or as near the top as could conveniently be done, & then as many men as there was room for stood on this piece of timber, & jumped upon it altogether, until it was sunk to the requisite depth.

A party consisting of Mr. Roberts, Lieutenants Purviance & Brent, the Marine officer & myself, made an excursion up the river today, to see the extent of the city in that direction, & to examine such objects as we might meet with deserving of notice. The first object that we saw which induced us to land, was a pagoda about a mile from our residence on the east bank of the river. The extent of this pagoda, together with its environs, which were planted with shade-trees & very pleasant, indicated that it was one of rather a superior order. These pagodas are very different structures from those of China, & in my opinion designed for different purposes; for while the latter are of an octagonal form & generally nine stories high, the former resemble christian houses of worship in their form, & are never more than two stories high. These are designed exclusively for religious worship, but the Chinese pagodas appear to me to be designed for other purposes, as I have already remarked in speaking of Canton.

The pagoda which we stopped to examine so nearly resembled a christian house of worship in its exterior, with the exception of the roof, & the gilding about the windows & doors, that we might readily have taken it for one had we not known the contrary. To describe the roof so as to convey an adequate idea of it, is not easily done. It consisted of three stages or grades, rising one above the other to the height of about a foot, & each upper grade commencing five or six feet from the edge of the next lower one. From each angle of the roof formed by these several breaks, a sort of spire projected out obliquely, four or five feet in length, & being bent upwards, they gave the building the ludicrous appearance of being provided with horns. The gable-ends, the cornices of the roof, the doors & window-shutters, displayed an abundance of gilding, laid on in a fantastic manner, so as to represent, besides Budda, several other grotesque figures.

At a small distance from the principal building, were several other structures called pachadas [prachadas or chedi], which appeared to be designed solely for ornament. They were of a pyramidal form, but of different magnitudes, & all terminated in a long slender spire. Some of them were plain, but others were decorated with gilding & a variety of figures of man & beasts, some of which appeared to be made of plaster, but others were the work of the sculptor. The height of these pachadas varied from ten to a hundred feet or more. They were all made of brick & plastered & white-washed. We could not gain admission into the pagoda, and therefore I can say nothing of its interior.

Having gratified our curiosity here, we crossed over to the other side of the river, for the purpose of viewing the arrangements that were making for burning the body of the late second King, who died a short time before our arrival. We landed near the stable of the white elephant, & stopped to see him. He was about the midling size, weighing probably five thousand pounds, & judging from the length of the tusks, I supposed he had not attained his full size. His colour, instead of white, was a dirty brown, which was probably owing to the neglect of his keeper in washing him & keeping him clean. The eyes were unnaturally small, of a pink colour & kept constantly in motion like those of an albino; and hence I am led to conclude, that the peculiarities of the animal were wholly of the albino character.

In our way to the place where the body of the Second King was to be burned, we passed another elephant stable, where there were six of those [huge] animals confined, some of which were larger than the white one which we had just seen. They were all so secured by means of stout ropes to a frame-work firmly fixed in the ground that they could not change their position in the least. Their tusks were each encircled with several silver rings, intended no doubt for ornament.

We next proceeded to view the funeral preparations, which we found to be magnificent & expensive beyond what we had formed any idea of, & certainly far beyond what reason could approve. The principal structure was a kind of tower, one hundred & fifty feet high as I judged, having a broad base, & tapering gradually to a point at the top. It was constructed of large pieces of timber of immense length, raised on end & covered with mats instead of boards. Over the mat covering was laid a covering of copper-gilded paper, in imitation of gold leaf, especially on the roof & about the base of the structure; which at a distance exhibited a rich & dazling appearance. It was only at a distance, however, that it presented such an appearance, for on a near inspection the imitation of gold leaf was found to be so coarse, & the workmanship so clumsy, that we saw no reason to admire any thing about it except the magnitude of the work.

In the centre of the tower, was a mass of brick work about eight feet high on which the body was to be burnt; and high above this was a canopy in the form of the crown worn by the Kings of Siam; that is, broad at the base, & tapering gradually to a slender spire, which ran up to a height that was altogether disproportioned to the base.

This tower was surrounded by eight others, at the distance of four or five rods from it, & constructed in the same manner, but much smaller. A kind of shed extended from one of these towers to another, which formed an enclosure to the central one, & which was designed, besides, for the immense crowd of people, who were expected to be present at the obsequies of the King. Outside of these towers again, & at the distance of eight or ten rods from them, was another row of smaller ones, & of a structure somewhat different from that of the others. The number of these was not completed, so that I could not tell how many there were to be. These, as I afterwards learned, were designed merely for ornament.

In order to complete the description of these preparations so far as may be desirable, I ought to take notice of the flooring of the area included within the eight towers above mentioned. It was made of broad bamboo splints, which were wove together like a mat, & being raised a few inches from the ground, it formed a neat & comfortable carpet, on which a variety of theatrical performances were to be exhibited.

The scite of these costly & entensive preparations, had been a paddee, or rice field from which a large number of poor people probably derived their subsistence; and which was certainly appropriated to a much better purpose, while yielding support to hundreds than while serving only for the funeral rites of one. We were informed, however, that all these works, & every thing used for the King's funeral, were to be removed, so that the ground which they occupied might be again put to the same use as before.

Having gratified our curiosity there, we returned to our boat, the heat having become too intense to admit of our extending our rambles farther. We left the city by the same gate through which we had entered it, & which was guarded by a number of posts fixed in the ground so near together that, a man could scarcely squeeze himself through between them, & also by a huge pile of rubbish & offal. The principal streets through which we had passed, were of sufficient width & paved with brick; but the buildings were generally miserable hovels, constructed of bamboo & palm leaf, each consisting of two apartments like the floating house already described.

Letter from Batavia

[The portion of Dr. Benajah Ticknor's journal that would have been chapter X is missing. We can follow the remainder of his stay in Bangkok only through an occasional mention of his name in Edmund Roberts's *Embassy to the Eastern Courts.*

On March 18, Dr. Ticknor was on hand for the presentation of Edmund Roberts to the king of Siam in a very colorful ceremony; afterwards, he watched while Roberts fed bananas to the sacred white elephant. The American mission also toured the celebrated Wat Phra Keo within the palace grounds.

On March 29, Ticknor accompanied Edmund Roberts and the Reverend John Taylor Jones, a recently arrived American missionary, to "the temple of the golden sandal tree" [Wat-Rat-cha-O-Rot], about six miles up the Khlong Bangkok Yai. Here Ticknor saw an extensive complex of temples, viewed a sixty-three-foot reclining Buddha, and observed the daily life of the more than 150 monks who lived in the wat. On their return home along the river, they stopped and witnessed monks carrying out the ceremonial burning of the dead.

The visit of the American mission to Bangkok closed on April 2 with attendance at the royal funeral procession of the second king. This procession, which included fabled animals made of bamboo and papier-mâché, in addition to flag bearers, musicians, princes on horseback, and seven hundred men representing angels surrounding the upright body of the deceased, would have no doubt elicited an interesting comment from our staunch New England Protestant.

On April 4, 1833, the *Peacock* left Siam and sailed to Singapore, arriving May 1. Young John Robert Morrison, the interpreter, was discharged and paid $600 for his services; he returned immediately to Macao.

After a ten-day stay, the *Peacock* sailed to Batavia (Djakarta) in Java. It was here that Benajah Ticknor had the leisure to write his old friend Congressman Elisha Whittlesey of Canfield, Ohio. His letter, included in the Elisha Whittlesey Papers at the Western Reserve Historical Society in Cleveland, Ohio, partially fills the gap in his journal.]

U.S. Ship *Peacock*
Batavia, July 3, 1833.

My Dear Sir,

We arrived here on the 5th. of June after a tedious passage of 26 days from Sincapore. The Schooner *Boxer* was here waiting for us, and had been here about 4 months. From her I received the package of Documents which you had the goodness to send me, and for which I return you many thanks. No letter accompanied them, at which I was much disappointed; and I was even more disappointed at receiving no letters from my wife. Not a letter has reached me since we left home, and now I do not expect any before we return to Brazil. It is really distressing to be so long, probably but little short of 2 years, without receiving intelligence from one's family & friends.

During our stay here, which is but 2 days short of a month, our officers & men have been quite healthy, though this, you know, has been considered one of the most unhealthy ports in the East, and indeed in the whole world. The *Boxer,* however, has not been so fortunate for she has lost her Surgeon [Dr. A. E. Kennedy] & 3 men here, all of dysentery. My Assistant [Dr. Edward Gilchrist] has gone to the *Boxer,* so that I am left alone; but so long as my own health continues good, as it is at present, I shall be able to get along without difficulty. It is said that Batavia is much more healthy than it formerly was, and there undoubtedly is less sickness and mortality; but this is owing, in the first place, to the removal & death of a large proportion of those who were liable to the diseases of the climate, and in the second place, to a change in the habits & mode of living of those who remain. The city of Batavia consists of 2 parts, one of which is called "the Town", & the other "the Country." The former is situated immediately on the bay & in the neighbour-hood of extensive marshes; but the latter is situated from 2 to 5 miles back from the bay, and in a great measure beyond the reach of the marsh effluvia. The town is the place of business, but nobody resides there except the Chinese & Malays, who are proof against the pestilential influence of the climate. All the Europeans & Americans reside in the country, and only come into town to transact their business. Formerly they resided in the town, and were perhaps 5 times as numerous as they are now; and consequently the sickness & mortality were far greater then, than they have been, since the town has been abandoned as a place of residence, and since the number of foreigners has been so much reduced. The town, however, is still enveloped by an atmosphere as pestilential as it ever was, and it is now considered about as fatal to pass a night there as it was during the period of the greatest mortality. No foreigner ever spends a night in the town, without being soon afterwards attacked with fever. But the country is really delightful, and comparatively healthy. The residences of the foreigners are like palaces, large, airy, & extremely neat & commodious; and surrounded by extensive yards containing a great variety of shade & fruit trees and flowering shrubs, among which the most conspicuous are the cinnamon, nutmeg & palm. The ground is level as far as the eye can reach, and the roads are equal to any in the world. There is no place, probably in the world, where luxury & the worst kinds of dissipation are carried to greater excess than they formerly were here; and it is to these causes that Batavia is more indebted for its bad reputation, than to the influence of its pestilential climate.

It is expected that we shall sail from here in a week for Qualah Battoo, from whence we shall probably proceed to the Persian Gulf. We still flatter ourselves with the hope of being at home within 8 or 9 months, and most happy will be the day, when I shall again tread the soil of my native country, provided I should find my friends alive and in health. To that event I am constantly looking forward with an anxiety that cannot be expressed. A naval life is becoming more & more irksome to me every day, and until there is a radical change in the Navy, no man of regular habits can find any satisfaction in it. My best respects to Mrs. Whittlesey & the family. Most truly yours, B. Ticknor.

CHAPTER XI

Off the Arabian Coast

[In this incomplete part of the Journal, Benajah Ticknor continues the story of the homeward voyage of the U.S.S. *Peacock* after she left Anjer in the East Indies on July 28, 1833.]

[August 18-19.] . . . of being caught by the N.E. monsoon before we could reach Muscat.[1] But notwithstanding the time was so short that with the most rapid progress that could possibly be calculated upon, we could barely make the visit to Mocha & reach Muscat before the period when the monsoons usually change; yet as we had found the wind more favourable than we had reason to expect, and as the Capt. considered it his duty to visit the R.S. [the Royal Sultanate of Mocha] or at least to make an effort to do so, before he returned home, it was finally, at the last moment, determined to make the attempt. The course from the Straits of Sunda for Muscat & Mocha, is the same during the prevalence of the S.W. monsoon, until arriving near the longitude of the former place; so that, if it was found on reaching that point, that we should probably be too late for the R.S. we could keep away for Muscat, thus no time would be lost. The course that is recomend[ed] for either of these places while the S.W. monsoon is blowing, that is, from April to the latter part of September, is about west between the parellels of 9 & 11 degrees of south latitude, where there is a steady & fresh S.E. trade-wind.

    This course we pursued, and our progress was so rapid, being at the rate of 160 or 170 miles a day, that when we arrived at the longitude of Muscat, which is about 58°, on the 15th. day after leaving Anjer [August 12]; it was determined to push on as fast as possible for the R.S. Our course now inclined more to the north, so as to intersect the equator in longitude about 50°, about 3 degrees to the westward of Cape Guardafui, the southwestern boundary of the entrance of the Arabian Gulf. We continued to be favoured with a fresh S.E. trade, & on the 17th. of August we crossed the equator in longitude 49°-55' & then shaped our course to the northward for the Cape which I have just mentioned.

Immediately after leaving the Straits of Sunda we experienced a considerable change of temperature, as we had anticipated, which was exceedingly agreeable to our feelings, and renovating to our health & spirits. I speak now of the influence of this change on the officers, for on the men it produced quite different effects, & occasioned a large increase of the sick-list. These effects appeared in the form of dysentery, and the cases of this disease increased so that before the date under which I am now writing, the number of sick amounted to 32. During [this] period, one death occurred from the [disease]; but that was of a man from the *Boxer,* who had been labouring under the disease for 2 months before he came under my care, about the time of Dr. Kennedy's death.[2]

The range of temperature, during the period of which I have been speaking was from 78 to 83, & the weather was uniformly pleasant. The barometer rose to 30, immediately on our leaving the Straits of Sunda, and taking the S.E. trade wind; and it continued at that height most of the time till we were within 7, or 8 degrees of the equator, when it began to fall, & continued gradually falling, as we advanced to the north.

Before leaving Batavia, there had been a good deal of debate between the officers of the *Peacock* & *Boxer,* as there always is when the officers of two vessels meet, on the subject of the sailing of their respective vessels. It was found, however, by experiment, that the schooner was a much better sailer than the ship, especially in light winds & in a smooth sea.

Aug. 20. About 6 o'clock in the afternoon of this day which was the 23rd from Anjer, we made land, a little to the southward of Cape Guardafui. After crossing the equator the wind freshened & continued to do so as we [advanced] to the north, & approached the [coast] of Africa. For two or three days before we crossed the line, the wind began to veer gradually to the southward, & as we advanced its direction continued to change till it reached the S.W. point, & became the regular S.W. monsoon.

From the time we crossed the equator till we made the land, our progress was at the rate of about 200 miles a day; and it was more rapid on that day, than at any time before during the passage. The monsoon had now become so fresh as almost to amount to a gale of wind; & as we were running before it, the ship rolled very much, & was extremely wet &

uncomfortable, as indeed she had been during the whole passage. While pursuing our course in this manner, & with quite a rough sea, an accident happened, which was very near being followed by troublesome, if not disastrous consequences. This was the parting of the wheel ropes, while the ship was under a full press of sail, & going at a very rapid rate. The officer of the deck immediately ordered the relieving [t—] in the ward-room to be manned, by which the ship could be steered without difficulty or danger, until new wheel-ropes could be provided. But owing to the hurry & confusion of the moment, it was so long before they could get command of the helm in the ward-room, that the ship began to broach to, that is, to assume such a position as would have brought her head directly [towards] the wind, when all the sails would have been taken aback, and the masts would probably have been carried away, & the ship & all on board [might] have been lost. But happily just at [the] moment when the sails began to sh[red] in the wind, command was obtai[ned] of the helm, and we escaped from a very critical situation.

The view which we had of the land was quite indistinct on account of the haze which enveloped it. The land was high, & presented quite an even, level surface at its summit; at least the [line] which seemed to mark its summit in the horizon, deviated but very little from a horizontal direction. A few hours before making the land, the wind died away, & we remained becalmed till about 8 o'clock in the evening, when a favourable breeze sprung up, & we pursued our course towards Cape Guardafui, which was about 50 miles distant.

Aug. 21. At 9 o'clock this morning we passed Cape Guardafui, and entered the Gulf of Arabia, after a passage of 23 days from Anjer; in which time we ran the distance of 3993 miles. We found ourselves within 6 or 8 miles of the land this morning at day light, & the atmosphere being clear, we had a very distinct view of it for a considerable distance. A chain of high mountains presented themselves to the sight [at] the distance of 20 or 30 miles from [the] coast; and appeared to consist of [rocks] & a brown earth, on which there was [not] a vestige of verdure to be seen. The coast along which we were running consisted of a perpendicular wall of the same materials, rising to the height of more than a thousand feet. The Cape, Guardafui, which bounds the Arabian Gulf on the S.W. is a perpendicular bluff of this description, which rises to the hight, as I judged, of 500 feet. Not a green thing was to be seen on it, or any where along the coast. We passed the Cape & began to shape our course to the westward.

From what Horsburg & other writers say respecting the navigation of the Arabian Gulf we were prepared to expect now constant & strong westerly winds, and consequently to make our way by beating from the Cape to Mocha, a distance of 600 miles; a prospect which was very far from being agreeable.

Aug. 25. At sunrise this morning we found ourselves near "Burnt Island", on the African shore, from which we were directed to take our departure, and shape our course across the Gulf to the coast of Arabia. Burnt Island is situated near the coast, and constitutes the westernmost limit of accurate surveys of that part of the Gulf. Our longitude by chronometer at 12 o'clock this day, was 46°-41´, & latitude 11°-46´ north. The bearing of the island at 6 o'clock in the morning was S.E. by E. distant 7 or 8 miles. From this time till noon we ran about 20 miles on a course nearly N.W.

There is another land-mark on the African side, which is deserving of notice & which we passed on the second day after we entered the Gulf. This is Cape Felix, which projects out to the northward, a perpendicular bluff 3 or 4 hundred feet high, & very similar in appearance to Guardafui. The two capes are about 25 miles apart and both, as they were laid down on the charts, agreed very well with our chronometers. From Cape Guardafui to Burnt Island, we ran along within a few miles of the coast, so that we had a very distinct view of it; and a more dreary comfortless prospect I have never beheld. A chain of mountains runs along at a little distance from the coast, which varies in height from 500 to 4 or 5000 feet, and present to the eye a brown surface of naked rock & barren earth. In the whole distance of more than 300 miles, from Guardafui to Burnt Island, not a single green thing is to be seen on these desolate & sunburnt mountains. And with one exception, the prospect between the waters of the Gulf & the mountainous [terrain] was equally cheerless.

On the third day after we entered the Gulf, we passed a level piece of ground of small extent immediately bordering the gulf, where there was a small village, & grove, probably of the date & other species of the palm tree. With this exception the coast appeared to be quite as barren as the mountains. We found the heat while running along this coast almost in-supportable, especially at night, when the light breeze came from the land. As soon as we arrived within the influence of this burning African coast, we immediately experienced a great change in the temperature, the thermom-eter rising to 90° & remaining nearly or quite at that height through the night as well as the day. This is higher than I ever knew the thermometer before on ship-board, except once, and that was in the bay of Panama in December 1819.

From what is contained in books respecting the navigation of the Arabian Gulf, we expected that as soon as we passed Guardafui, to meet with strong westerly winds, which would render it necessary for us to make our way to the Straits of Babelmandel by beating; but to our surprize, we experienced light favourable breezes, until we reached Burnt Island, & stood over to the other side. There appeared to be a regular succession of sea & land breezes along the African shore, the former blowing from N. to N.N.W. & the latter from S.W. The sea-breeze usually set in about 7 or 8 o'clock in the morning & continued till about 4 in the afternoon, when it died away & was succeeded by a calm, which continued till 9 or 10 o'clock in the evening. The land breeze then set in & continued till near sunrise. While the sea-breeze prevailed, the heat was quite tolerable, notwithstanding the thermometer stood at 90; but when the land wind came off from the burning surface of rock & sand, the heat was almost suffocating, and during the night there was not one moment's comfort, whether sleeping or waking. And our situation was rendered the more uncomfortable by being on an allowance of water, which afforded us only one quart for drinking during the 24 hours. This would be considered by many at home as quite an ample allowance; but to us who were breathing the suffocating air from the African deserts, and perspiring almost in streams from every pore, it was scarcely sufficient to allay the thirst for one hour. I have been on a shorter allowance of water than that, and in a hot climate too; but I do not think that I ever suffered so much from thirst before.

Our course from Guardafui to Burnt Island, was a little to the southward of west, in order to take advantage of the current, which was said to set to the westward at the rate of 2½ miles an hour. We were disappointed, however, with regard to the current as well as with regard to the winds; for it was evident that we had not the assistance of any current, until the day before we reached Burnt Island, & even then, the current must have been very weak, if there was any at all.

Aug. 26. At 12 o'clock today, we made Cape Aden on the Arabian coast, at the distance of 8 or 10 leagues. The distance across the Gulf from Burnt Island to Cape Aden is about 140 miles; and we ran the greater part of it with a fresh southwesterly breeze. Cape Aden is high, uneven & barren, and appears at a distance like an island. On the western side of it is a deep bay, and back from the Cape, at the bottom of the bay is said to be a small

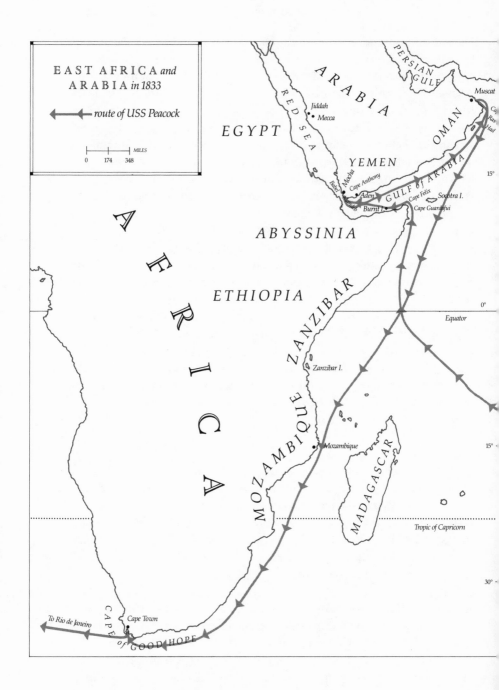

EAST AFRICA and
ARABIA in 1833

⬅️ route of USS Peacock

MILES
0   174   348

ARABIA

PERSIAN
GULF

Muscat

RED SEA

Jiddah
• Mecca

EGYPT

OMAN

Cape Ras al
Had

YEMEN

15°

Mocha
Bab Cape Anthony
el
Mandeb Aden GULF OF ARABIA Cape Felix Socotra I.
Burnt I. Cape Guardafui

ABYSSINIA

AFRICA

ETHIOPIA

ZANZIBAR

0°

Equator

Zanzibar I.

MOZAMBIQUE

• Mozambique

15°

MADAGASCAR

Tropic of Capricorn

30°

CAPE
To Rio de Janeiro Cape Town

of GOOD HOPE

town of the same name with the Cape. We now shaped our course for the Straits as near as the wind would permit, and by sunset we had a view of Cape St. Anthony, at the distance of 18 or 20 leagues from C. Aden. According to the charts, the line of coast between these two points, is nearly straight; but according to our observation, it forms quite a deep curve, the waters of the Gulf extending back several miles, and forming a capacious bay. Between the two capes that have just been mentioned, but nearer to the former, is another cape which also deserves to be mentioned. It consists of several prominences of different elevation, and which, when first seen, appear like rocks rising out of the water. The longest & highest of these points is probably from 800 to 1000 feet, & they all together appear to form an island. This Cape, the name of which is ——— [probably Cape Ra's Imran] divides the large bay that I have mentioned into 2 unequal parts.

In the course of this afternoon we passed 2 native vessels from Mocha, probably, which were of a different construction from any vessels that we had yet seen.[3] They had but one mast & one large sail, which was managed in the manner of the Chinese; that is, by hoisting & lowering the yard to which the sail is attached. They were considerably higher as well as broader at the stern than at the bow, which gave them a most awkward appearance, and must have rendered them very dull sailers. The deck appeared to be an inclined plane from the stern to the bow, which, with its disadvantages possesses the convenience of allowing the water to run off readily, and may thus in some degree contribute to the cleanliness & healthfulness of the vessel. It ought to have been observed when speaking of Cape Aden, that our situation at the time of making it, which was 12 o'clock, was north lat. 12°-24′ - long. 45°-11′ & the bearing of the Cape was about N.W.

Aug. 28. Yesterday morning we found ourselves within 8 or 10 miles of the cape that I have described between Aden & St. Antony, having made no progress during the night. The latter cape was in view, 20 or 25 miles to the westward of us. In the course of the forenoon a breeze sprung up from the S.W. & continued nearly 24 hours. Although we had to make our way by beating, yet we advanced considerably in the course of the day, and before night were some distance to the westward of Cape St. Anthony.

About 4 o'clock yesterday, three or four sails were seen advancing towards us in the direction of the straits; and as soon as they discovered us, one of them fired three guns, which caused us to put ourselves in a fighting attitude. The schooner being a faster sailer than the ship, was ordered to make sail towards these vessels, and speak them if possible. In the meantime we went to quarters, and remained so, until the schooner had spoken one or two of the vessels, when it became evident that no hostilities were designed against us, and we were released from a situation, which in such extreme heat of the weather, was exceedingly uncomfortable. Between 8 & 9 in the evening the schooner sent a boat to us with a Lieut. who reported that the vessel which fired the 3 guns was the English Brig *Nautilus* in the service of the E.I. Company, & that the other vessels were merchant men under her convoy. The reason of her firing was, that she took us for the Company's cruisers, & the 3 guns were intended as a signal. She was from Mocha the day before, where she had remained 3 months. Mocha was represented as being in a wretched state; the Turks having recently taken possession of it, and as usual on such occasions among Turks & Arabs, murder & robery were perpetuated without restraint. Provisions of all kinds were said to be extremely scarce, and no fruit was to be had there except a few dates. There had been four American vessels there in the course of the season, but they had all left some time before. One of them, it was stated, had been trading on the coast of Africa, where she left one of her boats & several of her crew. The boat was sent ashore for some purpose, and before it could return to the ship, so fresh a breeze sprung up that the ship was unable to reach the place where the boat landed; and the poor men were consequently left to their fate. We did not learn where they were left, nor the time, when otherwise perhaps, measures would have been taken to afford them assistance. The English Captain stated that foreigners were treated at Mocha in a very insulting & abusive manner by the Arabs; but that the Turks were disposed to treat them with civility.

We made considerable progress during the night, and when the breeze died away this morning, we were not more than 30 miles from the entrance of the Straits. About noon a breeze sprung up from the S.W. which continued through the afternoon, and enabled us to make such progress, that at sunset we had a distinct view of the Straits, & their boundaries on both sides. A little to the eastward of the Straits, is Cape Babelmandel on the Arabian side, the extremity of which is quite low, & extends out some distance into the Gulf. The appearance of Cape St. Anthony is very similar to this. All the capes that I have mentioned on the Arabian side, as well as the coast between them where we had a view of it, presented the same aspect of perfect barrenness & aridity as the African Coast. On the highlands not a single green thing was to be seen, and on the low ground only here & there a few scattered date trees. At the distance, probably of 30 or 40 miles back from the coast we could discern, though very faintly, a chain of mountains extending east & west as far as we could see. A dense mist or smoke enveloped these mountains most of the time, but when it broke away so as to allow a tolerably clear view, they also presented a brown, sunburnt, barren surface, with broken rugged tops, some of which rose to a very considerable height.

Aug. 31. During the night of the 28th the wind continued light, and we found, at day light that for 12 hours we had made no progress; owing to the current setting from the R. Sea [Red Sea] through the straits. It had been the intention to pass through the narrow strait, but the wind being unfavourable for that, we shaped our course for the large strait, where there is room to beat; so that vessels can pass through this strait with a head wind which they cannot do through the narrow one. These two straits are formed by the island Babelmandel, which is situated a little to the northward of the cape of that name. This island is of small extent, and presents quite a smooth even surface & some appearance of vegetation, though it seemed dry & parched from the extreme heat of a vertical & unclouded sun. This island is quite low, the highest part of it, which is near the centre, not being more than 200 feet high. From this there is a gradual descent to the two extremities, which rise very little above the level of the water. The geographical position of this island, is north latitude 12°-28′ E. Long. 43°-29′. It divides the Strait of Babel mandel, or Babelmandel (Gates of death) into two straits, the narrow & the broad, as I have already mentioned. The first is on the Arabian side, & is about a mile in width. With a fair wind this is the best rout to Mocha, the distance being less than through the other. The broad strait is 10 or 12 miles in width, & is bounded on the west by the African shore; which presents there the same gloomy aspect of a naked, rocky sunburnt surface that I have already described. Near this shore are several small islands called the Brothers, which are also perfectly barren like the adjacent coast.

During the forenoon of the 29th. the wind was quite light, and there being a strong current against us, we made no progress at all; but in the afternoon the breeze became quite fresh and though directly ahead, with the current still against us, yet in the course of the night we gained about 20 miles towards Mocha. Yesterday morning the breeze, which had continued quite fresh through the night, became so moderate, that for several hours, we were unable to stem the current; but in the afternoon we were favoured with a land-breeze from the N.E. which enabled us to shape our course directly for Mocha, and it continued till about 7 o'clock in the evening, at which time we were near enough to see the lights in the city. A short time before this breeze sprung up a signal was made to the schooner to make all sail for the port; and by sunset she was several miles ahead of us. Our course, while the wind favoured us, was nearly north, and within 3 or 4 miles of the Arabian coast. About half way from the Straits to Mocha is a hill on the Arabian side, of considerable height, called Zee-Hill, which is put down on the chart as a land-mark. A few miles to the northward of this hill commences a grove of date-trees, which extends to the city, & is the only verdure that is to be seen along the coast, between the Straits & the city.

About 8 o'clock in the evening the wind died away, and after two or three hours calm, it came out from the N.W. and continued in that direction through the night. There is a bank or shoal extending out some distance to the S.W. from the town, which is considered rather dangerous, & vessels are directed not to approach nearer to it than the depth of 14 fathoms water. We had about 16 fathoms on the S. western edge of this bank, when the wind shifted, & we were obliged to stand off to the westward. During the night we continued to advance to the northward, and at day-light this morning the town presented itself to our view at the distance of a few miles, and the wind being fair, we came to anchor at the distance of 2½ miles from it, at 6 o'clock, A.M.

I shall close this chapter with a statement of the latitude & longitude of the capes & islands from the entrance of the Arabian Gulf to Mocha, which are [of] most import to the navigator, and the position of which has been satisfactorily ascertained.

	Lat.	Long.
Cape Guardafui	11.50 N.	51.32 E.
Cape Felix	12.50	50.00 42 miles from Guardafui
Burnt Island	11.14	47.28
Cape Aden	12.43	45.14 on the Arabian side
Cape St. Anthony	12.39	44.16
Cape Babelmandel	12.40	43.31
Island of Babelmandel	13.38	43.29
Mocha	13.20	43.20 40 miles from the Sts.

CHAPTER XII

Mocha and Muscat

As the schooner had so much the advantage of the ship in sailing, and was so much in advance of us when we lost sight of her in the evening, we expected to have found her at anchor when we reached the harbour; but to our surprize, she was still almost out of sight to the leeward of the port, and with but a slender prospect of getting in before the next day.

Very soon after we anchored, we were visited by an old Arab who called himself Admiral Blanket, after an English Admiral of that name who was at Mocha in 1799.[1] He could speak English tolerably well, and manifested a good deal of shrewdness. When questioned about America, he said that America was the only nation that could fight the English, & was the first to build a steam-boat; thus showing that he was not entirely ignorant of the events that have transpired in the other hemisphere.

About 8 o'clock the junior Lieut. & Purser [Francis B. Stockton] were sent ashore to the Governor's with a complimentary message from the Capt. & to see about procuring supplies, & also to make an arrangement respecting a salute. They returned about 12 o'clock, having seen the Pacha and transacted the business on which they were sent. The Pacha returned a very polite answer to the Capt.'s message & offered to furnish him with such things as he might require, & would exchange salutes at any time the Capt. might choose. They met with an English agent who went with them to the Pacha's & treated them with much politeness. He invited the Capt. & officers to dine with him at three o'clock that afternoon; and seemed disposed to show us every possible attention.

Accordingly at a little past two, a party consisting of the Capt. Mr. Roberts, Lieutenants Purviance, & Brent, the Purser, Marine officer, three Midshipmen & myself, left the ship for the purpose of dining with the Agent. On our way from the ship to the shore, we had a full view of the exterior of the town, which gives one a more favourable opinion of it than he finds verified on a nearer inspection. The buildings appear at a distance to be made of a brown sand-stone, as they all exhibited a dusky brown colour; which is owing, however to the plaster with which the walls are covered. The most conspicuous object in the town, is the Great Mosque, which stands near the centre of the town, and is surmounted by a tower of very considerable height, which is the first object in the town that is visible on approaching it by sea, and serves as an important land-mark in entering the harbour. We landed on a wooden pier which extended out about 20 rods, and after walking nearly half a mile through narrow crooked lanes & under a burning sun, we arrived at the residence of the Agent where we met with a very kind & polite reception. He was a native of Surat, and of course an English subject, but he could not speak English, or any language except Arabic. He was a Mussulman & manifested a strict adherence to the precepts of the Prophet; but showed none of that prejudice towards christians, which is a very general & a very conspicuous trait in the character of rigid Mahometans. His name was Scheich Thie [Sheikh Tayeb Ibramjee]. He appeared to be about 30 years of age & had a countenance which indicated intelligence & good nature. Being a mahometan, his beard was suffered to grow unmolested, and it formed a thick, black bushy appendage to the face, which was an object of pride, and had consequently received much care & attention.

The room into which we were conducted, after passing through a kind of stable in the lower story & up a dark, crooked flight of stone steps, was in the second story & in the west side of the building against which the sun was darting his most powerful rays. This room was small, badly ventilated, and the heat was almost insupportable. The thermometer, in the coolest situation in the room, stood at 94. The walls of the house were of brick, from three to four feet thick, & plastered & whitewashed both within & on the outside. The windows were small, & few in number for a climate so intensely hot as that is, and they were rendered still less useful by being provided with a heavy lattice work, instead of glass.

Two objects appeared to have been in view in the construction of these thick walls; one was, to afford greater security against the attack of an enemy; and the other was to afford the greater protection against the heat of the sun, which is nowhere more intense, I believe, than it is there.

The Scheich was affable, and ready to communicate all the information that was asked for. Conversation was carried on through a native interpreter who spoke English very well, and appeared to possess considerable intelligence. The inquiries that we made of the Agent related principally to the Government & commerce of Mocha. The change that had recently taken place there in the government, appeared to be regarded by the Arabs as a great calamity, as the Turks proved to be hard & oppressive masters. The Turkish force which took possession of the town was small, and their object was accomplished with but little bloodshed.

The commerce of Mocha was represented as being in a declining state, the causes of which were not satisfactorily pointed out. Coffee is the most important article of export from Mocha; and the whole amount exported in the year that we were there (1833) did not exceed, according to the Agent's account 8000 bags of 305 pounds each, that is, 2,440,000 pounds. The price of coffee at the time of our visit was about 12 cents a pound.

With respect to the duties on foreign commerce there, we learned from the English Agent, that Americans are not permitted to trade there on the same terms that the English do. The latter are entirely exempt from what are called port charges, while Americans are compelled to pay three hundred dollars on every ship of large size, and at the same rate on smaller vessels; and they pay moreover a duty on their cargoes of a half per cent more than the English. This is the consequence of the English having a treaty there, while we have none, and our countrymen are obliged to trade on such terms as the existing government may choose to adopt. Mr. Roberts told the Agent that this discrimination between the English & Americans was unjust & ought to be done away at once. The Agent assented to the truth of this remark, & said, that as soon as affairs were put into a regular train there, such regulations would be established with regard to American vessels as would be satisfactory. The population of Mocha, including people of all descriptions was said to amount to twelve or fifteen thousand. The town was quite healthy at the time of our visit, and had been so for about 2 years. It had suffered severely from the cholera about three years before, and a large proportion of the population was carried off by it.

At a little past 4 o'clock we sat down to dinner, which consisted of a few plain dressed dishes of mutton, fowl, & rice. The Scheich favoured us with his company at the table; but he ate very little, & drank nothing. As Mahometans are not permitted to use wine, nor indeed any kind of intoxicating liquor, we carried our wine, beer, & brandy with us; which were repeatedly offered to the Scheich, but he could not be induced to taste of them. This prohibition of the Prophet is certainly a most salutary one in a climate like that of Mocha, where the effects of stimulating drinks must be particularly destructive.

The fruit season being past, we were almost entirely deprived of what would have been a very great luxury to us in a climate so intensely hot, and where the water is so brackish that no one except the natives can drink it, unless he is suffering extremely from thirst. The Scheich was able however, to place before us two kinds of fresh fruit, namely, the pomegranate, and a kind of grape called the sultana. The former is a most ordinary kind of fruit, such as no one would eat, if he could get any other; but the latter is exceedingly delicious, and if they had been in sufficient abundance, I should have desired no other fruit. They were scarce, however, being produced only in the interior at a considerable distance from Mocha. Those which we ate were sent to the Scheich from Sennah [Sana], a distance of 12 days journey from Mocha. We ate some cheese made in the country, which was of a much better quality than a good deal of cheese that I have eaten in America.

Immediately after dinner the Scheich sent to inquire whether the Pacha was at home, and on learning that he was, several of us improved the opportunity to call upon him. The Scheich & the Interpreter accompanied us, & after a walk of 10 minutes, through narrow, dirty lanes, we arrived at his residence, which was a large four story building, situated near the water. The Pacha occupied the upper story, and to get there, we had to grope our way up a long, crooked flight of stone steps, from which every ray of light was excluded, in order to render the occupant within the less easily accessible, & consequently the more secure. In ascending & descending this dark crooked passage, it very readily occurred to me that murders might be committed there with great facility & without danger of detection, & considering the character of the people, it was not difficult to imagine that the walls against which I put my hands to feel my way, had been often stained with human blood.[2] After winding along this dark passage till we were nearly out of breath, we reached the upper story, and passing through a small open court where the Pacha's guard were stationed we entered his appartment, & were received with due politeness. The room was small, with a divan running along three sides of it & covered with a carpet, on which we were requested to be seated. We had no sooner seated ourselves than coffee was brought in & served around to us in small china cups containing about half a gill, placed in larger cups of silver.

The Pacha was a large, stout made man, with large mustachios, and a long Mahometan beard. Being a Turk, his complexion was much lighter than that of the Arabs, and though he exhibited rather a sterne severe countenance, yet it was by no means destitute of the lineaments of kindness & good nature. His name was Ben-al-mas, & it was said that he was a rebel from the government of the Pacha of Egypt.[3] He had collected a force of about 3000 men with which he had taken & plundered Guddah [Jiddah], on the R. Sea above Mocha, and had taken possession of the latter place about 7 months before our arrival there. In order to render himself the more secure in his newly acquired possessions, he pretended that he had made his conquests in the name of the Sultan of Constantinople. His situation, however, was extremely insecure, notwithstanding his pretence of acting under the authority of the Grand Seignior, of which he was so well aware, that it was said he had proposed to take passage in the English Brig *Nautilus,* which we spoke outside of the Straits.

He professed much pleasure at our visit, & manifested a friendly disposition towards our countrymen. He inquired respecting the health of the officers & crew, and how long we had been from home. The subject of the discriminating duties between English & American vessels was brought forward in the course of conversation by Mr. Roberts; who told the Pacha, as he had done the English Agent, that it was not only unjust, but also impolitic; inasmuch as it would have the effect to lessen the amount of American commerce. The Pacha seemed fully sensible of this, and said in reply, that this measure was not his, that he found it in operation when he came there; but that as soon as affairs were settled, he would make such regulations respecting American vessels as would be satisfactory.

We had expected, on visiting a Turkish Pacha, to meet with a good deal of pomp & dignity, as well as with a considerable display of costly decoration, both in his dress & in his appartment; but we were quite disappointed, for every thing we saw was perfectly plain, & exhibited nothing of that splendor in which Turkish Governors are said so much to delight. The outside garment of the Pacha was a robe of coarse cotton stuff, fastened at the middle with a broad belt. He wore on his head a high cloth cap, of a red colour, instead of a turban. His feet were naked. The carpet which covered the floor of the room as well as the low wall or divan on which we sat, was of an ordinary kind, and the velvet cushions appeared to be old, worn, & dirty.

In the small open court adjoining the appartment of the Pacha, was stationed his guard, consisting of about 20 men, both Turks & Arabs. They were all stout, fierce looking fellows, who apparently would think no more of striking off a man's head, than they would of clipping their beards. Each one of them wore a heavy girdle or belt about the waist, in which were fixed one or two pair of heavy pistols, & a dagger; and by his side was suspended an enormous scimetar, with which he could sever a man's head from his body at one stroke. Most of these men wore the same kind of cap as the Pacha himself, & they were all provided with sandals or slippers for the feet, but these they were obliged to leave at the door of the Pacha's appartment, whenever they had occasion to enter it, none of his servants being allowed to approach him except barefooted.

As we were about to take leave, the Pacha proposed to furnish horses for us to ride about the town, if we desired it; but most of us preferred walking notwithstanding the extreme heat, and only two or three of the Midshipmen accepted the Pacha's offer.

Having finished our visit to the Pacha, who at our parting, called on Allah to protect us & return us in safety to our country & friends; we spent an hour in rambling about the town. We found one hour quite sufficient to gratify our curiosity with a survey of every thing in the town that was worth seeing; at least every thing that we were permitted to see, for the object which we were most desirous to see, namely the Great Mosque, was closed against all but the faithful. We had a view of the exterior of it, but there was nothing in that particularly deserving of notice. It occupied quite a large space on the ground, but it was low, with a roof consisting of a large number of low domes, and the high tower in the centre, of which I have already spoken. Most of the buildings are from 3 to 5 stories high, & are made of brick, & plastered & white-washed on both sides. The lower or ground story is generally occupied as a stable; and every thing about the houses exhibits an appearance of great negligence & inattention to cleanliness. The houses are badly lighted & ventilated, the windows being few & small; and these are in a kind of balcony which projects out two or three feet from the walls and are closed by a coarse, heavy lattice work, which in a great measure excludes both air & light. All the dwelling houses have flat roofs, on which the inhabitants sleep in the open air, with no other bedding than a few mats. If it rains during the night, which it very seldom does, they seek no shelter from it; but remain with their naked bodies exposed to it, & receive from it a high degree of refreshment.

The streets of Mocha are all extremely narrow, dirty, crooked, and without pavements or side-walks. We passed through the bazar, or market-place, where we found a great crowd of the wretched inhabitants, some disposing of the trifling products of their industry, & others procuring such of the necessaries of life as their scanty means enabled them to pay for. The bazar is not more than 8 feet in width, & has a roof of palm leaves to exclude the burning rays of the sun; but the heat, notwithstanding, and the vitiated air from such a throng of people crowded together in this narrow space, we found to be almost unsupportable. Each side of the passage was lined with stalls, where a variety of small articles, chiefly articles of food, were exposed for sale. Among the crowd of people assembled here, were to be seen Turks, Arabs, Georgians, Abbasynians etc. etc. The complexion of the first, was that of the north of Europe; the Arabian complexion was considerably darker nearly of the Chinese hue; the Georgian complexion seemed to be a model of every thing that is excellent in the human complexion; but the face of the Abbasynian equalled in blackness the most perfect jet.

From the bazar, our guide took us a little distance out side of the town, to give us a view of the subburb, called Semele, which we found to consist of only a few miserable dwellings, built of palm leaves, in the form of a small haystack. Having now seen all that was worth seeing, and it being after sunset, we returned to the residence of the Scheich, greatly fatigued with our walk, short as it had been.

In the course of our rambles through the town, we passed several females in the streets, all of whom had their faces thickly veiled; though from their general appearance, I do not think there would have been the least danger of their fascinating any of the strangers with their beauty, if it had not been veiled. These, however, were probably women of the lower order, and therefore much less genteel in their appearance than those who belonged to the higher ranks, and who were entirely concealed from the view of strangers.

I had here an opportunity of seeing an animal which I had never seen before, namely, the camel; and a more uncouth, ill-looking animal I never did see. They appeared to be emaciated to the last degree; so that their skin, which was without hair, & of a dirty ash colour, scarcely covered their bones. Then crouching down with their legs doubled under their bodies, either to receive their loads or to take their food, they seemed almost as unlike living animals as can be imagined; and a stranger to the sight would have been but little more surprised, to see a heap of dry bones rise up & walk, than to see these poor starved creatures rise up with the heavy burdens which they were made to carry. The principal food with which they are supplied, is a kind of large bean like our horse-bean; and these were given in the smallest possible quantity that would serve to keep the animal alive. They place themselves in the same position to eat, that they do to receive their loads; at least all that I saw eating were in that position. The foot of the camel is very broad, flat and appears to consist of a soft, yielding substance, and is thus peculiarly fitted to traverse the sandy plains & rocky mountains of Arabia.

As we returned from our walk & the evening shades began to envelope the town, & the heat became less intense; we found the streets thronged with people, lounging on their settees & regaling themselves with coffee & tobacco. These are among the chief luxuries of Mahometans, and in these they seem to indulge without the least restriction.

The country about Mocha, as far as we had an opportunity of seeing it, is perfectly barren, except a narrow strip adjoining the coast to the southward of the town, where there were a few stunted date trees; but they were destitute of fruit, the fruit season being past, as I have already observed. In the town itself there was not a single shade-tree, or other green thing to be seen.

While some of our party were thus gratifying our curiosity in walking about the town, the rest were gratifying theirs in making an excursion on horse back outside of the town, and did not return to the place of rendezvous till it began to grow dark. This proved to be rather an expensive ride, notwithstanding the horses were voluntarily furnished by the Pacha; for when the Purser settled the accounts of the ship with the Agent he found a charge of two dollars for each of the horses that had been used. We found, however, that this was the custom of the place, for it was expected that, when any thing was received as a present, the full value of it would be returned by the person who delivered it. The pacha made several presents to the ship, but he expected & received presents in return, which made the articles at least quite as dear as if they had been obtained at the market, by purchase. Our party being at last all assembled at the house of the Scheich, we took leave of him, and with a guide set out for the landing place, where our boats were waiting for us. The gate by which we entered the town, was now closed; so that we were obliged to take a circuitous route by another gate, and were half an hour in reaching the boats. I ought to have mentioned that a high, thick brick wall surrounds the town, and that ingress & egress are very difficult after sunset, at which time the gates are closed.

In going aboard we had a fresh breeze blowing in our faces; but as it came from the heated surface of Abbasynia, which was not far distant, it was hot & suffocating, and of course contributed very little to our comfort. My seat in the boat was such that one side of my face was exposed to the spray which frequently broke over us, and when I got on board the ship I found that side of my face encrusted with salt. From this circumstance I conclude that the water of the Red Sea must contain a larger proportion of salt than common sea water; for I have often before been more thorughly drenched with sea water than I was then, but never found my self enveloped in a [———] of salt before. We reached the ship about 8 o'clock, completely satisfied with Mocha, and not a little exhausted with heat & fatigue.

Sept. 1. Notwithstanding this was Sunday it was nevertheless a day of great bustle & commotion. It had been determined to sail in the evening, if the wind showed favour, and a good deal was to be done in order to be ready. In addition to this, the Pacha had engaged to pay us a visit at 8 o'clock in the morning; and to put the ship in proper order for his reception & inspection, required the labour of all hands with holy-stones & scrubing-brushes for several hours. The Pacha with the English Agent, & Capt. G. Mr. R. & Capt. Shields [Lt. Commander William R. Shields], were to breakfast in the Ward-Room; and consequently there was not only a good deal of preparation to be made, but our breakfast must be an hour or two later than usual, a circumstance of no little importance to those of us who rose early & made breakfast their principal meal. After every thing was ready, however, for the Pacha, & we were impatiently waiting for him, a message was received from him, stating that on account of indisposition, he should not visit the ship. The Scheik, however, favoured us with a visit about 9 o'clock, and was accompanied by the junior Lieut. & Purser who remained on shore during the night. These gentlemen slept on the roof of the house, in the open air, and passed the night, very comfortably. The Scheik appeared to be well pleased with the ship, and after a stay of about an hour he took leave of us and returned to town.

At about 11 o'clock the night before, the *Boxer* succeeded in reaching the anchorage; and we had the company of Capt. Shields & several of his officers to breakfast in the W. Room, as well as Capt. G. & Mr. R. Our Capt. manifested on all occasions a great willingness for the W. Room to entertain all the company that came on board, although the company might be properly his, and it therefore belonged to him to entertain them. Until the period of which I am now speaking, he had not in a single instance entertained his visitors in the Cabin; but always found means to transfer the trouble & expense of entertaining to the W. Room. It is always expected that the Commander of a ship of war, will at least bear his proportion of the trouble & expense of entertaining company, and in most instances he is forward enough to do it; but our Commander was so bent upon saving money, that he was very willing the reputation of the ship, so far as it depended upon entertaining visitors in a proper manner, should be maintained at the expense of others. This may seem too trifling a matter to deserve any notice; but it serves to show certain traits of character, & therefore I mention it.

Being able to obtain very few supplies at Mocha, we had but little to do to get ready for sea. The purser returned to town with the Scheik, for the purpose of settling the accounts, and was to be ready to return on board at 3 o'clock in the afternoon, at which time a boat was to be sent for him. In the course of the day all the officers who had not been ashore the day before, had an opportunity of gratifying their curiosity with a visit to the town; and by sunset, all had returned on board, and we only waited for a breeze to take our departure.

About 7 o'clock in the evening, a light breeze came off the land from the eastward, and we weighed anchor & stood out of the harbour; rejoicing most heartily to take leave of a place, which, notwithstanding we had been desirous to see it, afforded so little, nevertheless, to repay us for what we suffered from the extreme heat, & want of supplies.

Sept. 3. Contrary to our expectation, we had a head-wind in leaving the Red-Sea as well as in entering it; so that, instead of passing through the Straits in a few hours after leaving Mocha, as we had expected, it was not till this morning about day light, that we left the Straits behind us, and found our selves again in the Arabian Gulf. We made our exit from the R. Sea through the narrow Strait, which has already been described; this being a shorter route, and the wind being more favourable for this than for the other.

I shall here insert the few additional remarks that I have to make respecting Mocha. The importance of Mocha as a place of trade for our countrymen, must be very small; the whole American commerce there not being more than sufficient, as I believe, to employ three or four ships, of three or four hundred tons burden. The principal articles of export from Mocha, besides coffee, are Gum Arabic, Myrrh, & Galbanum, or Frankincense.

As a place for supplies, Mocha is of no importance, at least during a considerable part of the year. The only article of live-stock that we were able to procure there of any value, was sheep; and these were indeed of a superior quality. The lovers of mutton pronounced this to be equal to any they had ever eaten in America. These were a different kind of sheep from any I had ever seen before; the head & neck being perfectly black, while the body was white, & covered with short hair instead of wool. The principal peculiarity, however, consisted in the structure of the tail; which was a broad flat, circular expansion, consisting of fat, & weighing sometimes 8 or 10 pounds. The price which we paid for these sheep was about $2.00 a piece. Some bullocks were sent on board by the Pacha, but they were so lean as scarcely to be fit to eat. Poultry & eggs were not to be had, except in very small quantity. The fowls, of which we procured a few, were small, & cost at the rate of a dollar for 15. Neither vegetables, or fruit were to be had, except dried dates of a very ordinary quality.

English enterprize, always alert, and ready to embrace every opportunity for promoting the interests of commerce, has seen the advantages that would result from navigating the Red Sea with a steam-boat; and accordingly they had one plying at regular periods between Mocha & Suez, and touching at the most important intermediate ports. The boat performs two trips in the year leaving Mocha in the months of October & February; and was usually about 8 days in running from Mocha to Suez. By this route news could be received from Europe in a much shorter time than by the Cape of Good Hope. By the former news could be received at Mocha from England or France in 30 days, while by the latter, it would require at least 100. From Mocha to Bombay, the passage during the S.W. monsoon, that is, from April to September, is not more than 20 days; so that news from England would reach Bombay by the way of the Red Sea in one half the time that would be required to go by the Cape.

The climate of Mocha, as I have already observed, is extremely hot, but probably not unhealthy. From the time of our entering the Arabian Gulf, until after we left the Red Sea, the thermometer was 90 + upwards; and on the day that we spent at Mocha, it stood at 93. This extreme heat was accompanied with a dryness of the atmosphere, which seemed to absorb the moisture of the body with great rapidity, and cause a most distressing thirst. I do not recollect that I ever suffered so much from thirst before, although I have been on a shorter allowance of water, & in a hot climate too; but in that climate there was some moisture in the atmosphere, which in some degree lessened the demand for drink.

Sept. 13. From the time of our leaving the Red Sea, until this date, nothing occurred deserving of notice. The wind was fair & the weather pleasant, and though our progress was not quite so rapid as was expected; yet it was sufficiently so for our comfort, being at the rate of 5 or 6 miles an hour. A principal object of our anxiety had been, after it was determined to go first to the Red Sea, to reach Cape Ras-el-Had, which bounds the entrance of the Gulf of Persia on the S.W. before the monsoons should change; and we had the satisfaction at daylight this morning of seeing the land in the vicinity of the Cape, & before noon we had a view of the Cape itself.

The coast as far as we had a view of it, presented quite a rough, & sterile aspect, being broken into low, pointed hills, most of which appeared to be rocky & barren; but here & there was to be seen a hillock crowned with a patch of verdure. A considerable distance back from the coast, a chain of rugged broken mountains was to be seen, which rose to the height, in some places, of 4 or 5 thousand feet.

We saw here a considerable number of boats employed in fishing for sharks, probably on account of their fins which are considered by the Chinese a great delicacy, & for which they pay a high price. The mode of taking this ferocious inhabitant of the sea, was entirely new to us, and seemed to be attended with no little danger. The harpoon was the instrument used, but instead of being thrown by a man standing in the bow of the boat as it is in taking whale, the man who used it jumped into the water when near enough to the shark, with the harpoon in his hand, and then commenced the attack. This was done several times within a little distance of the ship, and several of the officers saw it; though I had not an opportunity of seeing it myself.

At the same time that we were engaged in looking at these shark-fishing boats, we saw between us & the Cape, much the largest shoal of porpoises that I ever beheld. Indeed, I much doubt, whether all the porpoises that I ever saw before, would equal the number that were present here at one view. For a considerable distance around us the water appeared to be alive with them; and by their antic movements, they occasioned an agitation in the water which would probably have been taken for breakers, if we had not known the cause of it.

Soon after we made the land the wind died away, and during the day we made but little progress. Our position at noon was, lat. 22°-03′—long. by chron. 59.52. The chronometer was found to be correct by the position of Cape Ras-el-Had, which at this time bore N. by E. from us, & was judged to be about 20 miles distant. In the course of the afternoon we advanced near enough to the Cape to have quite a satisfactory view of it; and we found it to consist of low table land, which appeared entirely destitute of every thing like vegetation. A little distance back from the Cape are hills of considerable height, which nowhere present any appearance of verdure, but bore marks of being composed wholly of rocks & sand.

Sept. 18. After passing Cape Ras-el-Had on the 13th. our progress became very slow, in consequence of light winds, calms, & a strong adverse current. Indeed, it was only during the night that we could make any progress, for then, we were favoured with a land-breeze from the S.W. which took us along at the rate of 4 or 5 miles an hour, but through the day there was scarcely sufficient breeze to enable us to stem the current. Our course was generally within 5 or 6 leagues of the Arabian coast, so as to take advantage of the land-breeze, and also to ascertain our progress by the bearings of the several land-marks.

The coast continued quite low, until we had advanced about half way to Muscat, that is, about 60 miles, from the Cape when a mountainous ridge commenced which rose by a very gradual ascent; till it reached the height of 3 or 4 thousand feet. The base of this mountainous ridge was washed by the waters of the Gulf, and it presented every where a most barren & cheerless aspect.

On the 16th at sunset, we found ourselves within 25 miles of Muscat, and felt quite confident of reaching the port the next day; but the wind being of shorter duration than usual, & the current stronger, our expectations were disappointed. Before the land breeze died away, however, we had advanced so near to the harbour of Muscat, that we could see the vessels lying at anchor, and were seen ourselves from the shore. A boat was now sent off to us, with an officer, to ascertain who & what we were, & what was the object of our visit. He was told that our ship was an American Sloop-of-war, & that we had a Minister on board, who had business to transact with the Iman. Having obtained this information, he returned to communicate it to those who had sent him.

Soon afterwards the wind entirely died away, and the ship was so rapidly drifted towards the shore by the current, that we were obliged to anchor. It was about 9 o'clock in the morning when we anchored, and about 10 o'clock, a boat was despatched to the town with the junior Lieut. & Purser, for the purpose of paying the Captain's respects to the Imaum, and making arrangements for a salute, and for obtaining supplies. During their absence, an Arab came on board, who spoke English very well, and who bore the rank of Capt. [Said bin Khalfan][4] & appeared to be in the confidence of the Imaum. Among the subjects of conversation between him & Mr. Roberts, (for the visit was intended principally for him) that of a letter which the President of the U. States received a short time before we sailed, from this same Imaum, was one; and great surprise was manifested at what Mr. R. declared to be the tenor of it. This was, that Americans were permitted to trade freely at all the ports with the Imaum's dominions, as the English & French were, with the exception of Zanzibar on the coast of Africa, from which they were entirely excluded. It was certainly not the intention, the Capt. said, to exclude the Americans from Zanzibar, but on the contrary, the Imaum was desirous that they should be encouraged to trade there; as he intended to make that his principal place of residence, and therefore wished to encourage the trade of all foreign nations. This letter was written by an Englishman in the employ of the Imaum, and it appeared very evident that, in order to favour his own countrymen, he had inserted the clause in question without the knowledge of the Imaum, & even in direct opposition to his intentions.[5]

Early in the afternoon a light breeze sprung up, and we got under way with the prospect of reaching the harbour in a short time; but the breeze soon died away, and we were carried from the port by the current to the rate of 2 miles an hour. Fortunately for the gentlemen who went in the boat the schooner was several miles nearer to the town than we were; and when the boat was seen coming out of the harbour, the schooner was ordered to take her in tow, & bring her to the ship; which she did, & reached the ship about 4 in the afternoon.

They had been favoured by the Imaum with an interview, and were much pleased with the hospitable & friendly manner in which they were treated. He expressed great satisfaction at our visit, and offered to afford us every facility for procuring a supply of water & fresh provisions. One of the Imaum's Generals accompanied the officers as a pilot for the ship, who seemed to be [a] very amiable & intelligent man. He had travelled considerably, & could speak English, but not so well as the Capt. of whom I have mentioned. One trait of his character was very fully displayed, which was a strict regard to the duties of his religion. A little before sunset, he went to the first Lieut. & told him that he wished for a bason of water, that he might wash his face & hands & pray to his God. A bason of water was furnished him, which he took on the quarter deck, and after washing his face, hands, & arms, & feet, he took off the sash which he wore round his body, spread it on the deck, and then standing on it with his face towards the setting sun, he began his devotions; which he continued a short time in a standing posture, & then kneeled down, & bowed his face to the deck twice, remaining in that position at each time, about half a minute. He then rose on his feet, and after another short prayer, kneeled down again as before, bowing his face twice to the deck; and this was repeated four times before he had finished his devotions. About an hour afterwards, the same ceremonies were again performed with the exception of the ablution. What a reproof was the conduct of this Mahometan to us Christians! He was not ashamed to perform his devotions to his God, even in the midst of strangers; and those to whom he knew to be enemies to his religion, but we, who profess our belief in the true Religion, never condescend to perform any acts of devotion, nor do we ever call on the name of our God, except to profane it.* If the Mahometan is so punctual in the performance of the duties of his false religion, what ought to be the conduct of Christians? If the former prays, four times a day, and performs the ceremonies prescribed by his religion ought not the Christian to pray at least once a day, and perform some of the most essential duties prescribed by his religion?

Early in the evening a breeze sprung up from the S.E. which gave reason to expect that we could reach the harbour before it died away; but it continued only a short time, and left us when within about 4 miles of the harbour. We were consequently obliged to anchor, and remained at anchor till this evening, when we were again favoured with a breeze which enabled us to make some head way. About this time just before the breeze sprung up, however, a pilot, sent by the Imaum, came on board, to take the ship into the harbour, although the navigation was so plain, that there was not the least necessity for a pilot. Between 7 & 8 o'clock in the evening we got under way, and at 10, came to anchor in the harbour of Muscat.

Sept. 19. The prospect which presented itself to our view this morning, was quite as dreary & forbidding as any that I ever beheld. Before us, and at the distance of half a mile was Muscat, apparently a small village, consisting mostly of miserable dwellings, & situated in a small recess among the rocks; about 2 miles to the westward stood Mutrah, similarly situated to Muscat, but still more wretched in its appearance. A solid mass of rugged, brown rocks, from two to three hundred feet high, rose abruptly from the water, and extended as far as we could see, leaving here & there a small recess, which was occupied by a few miserable dwellings.

Finding that we were not at the proper anchorage, the ship was warped in this morning, and moored within a quarter of a mile of the town. We found in the harbour, 6 or 7 corvettes, forming a part of the Sultan's navy, and one merchant-vessel, a French ship from the island of Bourbon. The Frenchmen had spent 17 days there very unpleasantly, both on account of the climate, and of not meeting with any body on shore with whom they

---

*I speak here of those belonging to the ship.

could hold any satisfactory intercourse; and they were therefore greatly delighted at our arrival.

A salute having been agreed upon, it was fired at 1 o'clock, consisting of 17 guns. The same number was immediately returned by the fort near the town. The reverberation from the rocks was like the loudest thunder, and it was repeated several times at each report, as the sound struck against different parts of the immense mountain of rock.

At 4 o'clock in the afternoon, Mr. Roberts, accompanied by the Capt. paid a visit to the Imaum,* whom he found to be so strongly prepossessed in favour of America, that the principal articles of the treaty were agreed upon at that interview; and there was a prospect, that in the course of a few days the whole would be concluded. This was cheering news to us all, as we had expected to be detained there some time, which we had dreaded very much from what we had been told of the extreme heat of the place; and from what we experienced on arriving in the port, we had reason to believe that all our anticipations would be reallized.

Sept. 22. This day had been fixed upon for the officers both of the ship & schooner to call on the Sultan; and accordingly at 4 o'clock in the afternoon we went ashore, and were met at the landing-place by the interpreter, Capt. Calaphon, who was to introduce us. We were conducted some distance through very narrow, & most dirty & filthy streets, some of which were covered to exclude the sun; till at last we came to the residence of the Sultan, which was a large comfortable building, at least, comparatively comfortable, for there is no such thing in Muscat as real comfort to those who have lived in a temperate climate. The Sultan was seated in his audience hall when we arrived, and chairs were arranged on each side of his for the guests. On our entering the hall he rose from his seat, and advanced several steps to receive us by the hand, and when the ceremony of introduction was over, & we were all seated, his Highness entered immediately into conversation. He made inquiries respecting our visit to Mocha having learned that we had been there. But the principal topic of conversation was a report which he had received that day by vessel from Zanzibar, that several French ships of war had just arrived at Madagascar, and that a force consisting of 60 sail was said to be fitting out in France, and destined for the East.

In a few minutes coffee was served around, in small glass cups holding less than half a gill, which were placed in larger ones of china ware. After

---

*Whose name is Seid Seyed Ben-Sultan.

the coffee sherbert in tumblers was passed around, which was the first that I had ever tasted. It seemed to me to be nothing else than sweetened water with a small proportion of rose water. But whatever its composition was, it was cool & refreshing. Immediately after partaking of these refreshments, we took leave of the Sultan, being highly gratified with our visit, and of course, favourably impressed towards his Highness. He appeared to be about 50 years of age; but more active & vigorous than a man of his age could be supposed to be in a climate so intensely hot & debilitating as that of Muscat. He was rather above the middling height and well proportioned. His countenance was expressive of intelligence as well as of a mild, amiable disposition. His manners were very easy and agreeable. In his dress & in every thing else that we saw, there was an appearance of great plainness. His outer garment consisted of a dark-coloured robe, which was fastened around the body by a broad cotton girdle or sash, in which he carried a small dagger. His turban was of coloured cotton stuff and very large, & must have been uncomfortable. The feet & legs were naked, except a smaller part of the feet that was covered by a pair of slippers or sandals.[6]

The audience-hall was perfectly plain, being furnished only with a coarse carpet. It was about 20 feet long & 12 wide, and fronted the water. A guard of 15 or 20 men was in attendance on his Highness, who were armed in the usual manner, with daggers in their girdles, & sabres hanging by their sides.

As we left the Sultan's it was proposed to go to his stables to view of his horses, and we accordingly went. In going to the stables we passed through a considerable portion of the town, quite enough, at least, to satisfy our curiosity; for the more we saw of it the more were we disgusted with it. The streets rarely exceeded four feet in width, & were unpaved, & extremely crooked, & filled with a variety of rubbish. In the course of our walk we passed several shops, but they contained only a few coarse articles such as hemp, cordage, & sacks of dates. At last we reached the stables at the other extremity of the town from that where we landed; and very glad was I to reach the end of so uncomfortable a walk, for my health had been quite bad for some days, and I should not have gone ashore at this time, had it not been for the purpose of paying a visit to the sultan, for which there was not likely to be another opportunity.

Some of the horses looked very well, & received very high encomiums from those of the party who professed to understand the excellences of a horse; but for my own part, I could not perceive any peculiar excellence in any of them. Two of them were said to have cost the Sultan $6000. They were bays, stout made, & about the middling height. But the best horse that I saw there, did not appear to me to be superior to those that are valued in America at two or three hundred dollars.

Being a good deal fatigued with our walk, and having no desire to traverse those narrow, dirty streets again, we sent for our boat to meet us at the stables, and when it arrived we embarked and soon reached the ship, heartily glad that we had concluded a visit which required us to submit to the torture of wearing our most uncomfortable cloth uniforms.

Sept. 23. In passing from the boat to the ship last evening one of the officers dropped his sword overboard; and this morning two divers were employed to go down to the bottom & search for it. The depth of the water was 48 feet. They both plunged at nearly the same moment from the bow of their boat, which was not more than 3 feet above the water, and in an instant were out of sight. I observed my watch to see how long they would remain under water, and was surprised to find that one [of] them was under two minutes & three seconds. The other was under only one minute & three seconds. The one who staid under longest was a boy about 16 years old. As the sword was not found the first time, the search was repeated, but they remained a shorter time under water than before. A third attempt was made which was very near proving fatal to the boy; for when he rose to the surface he was helpless and evidently drowning. His companions instantly sprang into the water, and seized him as he was about to sink and got him into the boat; where he was made to disgorge the salt water that he had taken in, by being held with his head downwards, and after a little time he was so far recovered that he was left to himself.

Sept. 24. I witnessed this morning a singular method of taking small fish practised by the natives, but which only those could practice who are expert in diving. The small fish caught in the manner that I shall describe, collected in shoals about the ship, where they were caught to be used as bait for the large fish, which were caught with a hook & line. A sort of cast-net was used for procuring this bait, which, when spread out on the surface of the water covered a space of 10 or 12 feet square. A cord was attached to its centre, by which it was drawn up. Three men were employed in managing the net. All of them standing in the bow of their boat, one of them threw the net in such a manner that it lay spread out on the surface of the water to its full extent for an instant when it began gradually to sink; & when it had descended low enough to enclose the fish, that is about 10 feet, the other two men dove down on opposite sides of the net, for the purpose of closing the mouth of it & thus securing the fish which it might have enclosed. One of the two came up as soon as they had closed the mouth of the net, but the other kept the closed net in his hand and was drawn up with it. The fish thus caught were thrown into a large oblong basket attached to the side of the boat in such a manner, as to be about half full of water. Thus they were kept always alive & fit for use.

We began to have some fears today, that the business of the treaty would not progress so rapidly as we had expected; for the Interpreter reported to Mr. Roberts some alterations & additions proposed by the Sultan; to which he could not assent. Mr. R. stated to the Interpreter his reasons for not agreeing to the propositions of the Sultan; but as these might not be altogether satisfactory to his Highness, there seemed to be a door opened for a discussion which might occupy considerable time.

Sept. 25. Much to our satisfaction the Interpreter came on board this morning, and communicated to Mr. R. the Sultan's assent to all the terms of the treaty except one, which related to vessels wrecked within his dominions, or pulling into one of his ports in distress. It was provided by the article to which the Sultan objected, that if any American vessel should be wrecked within the limits of his dominions, and the crew & cargo were saved, the former should receive such protection & support from the Sultan as their circumstances might require, and the latter should be stored & well taken care of; for all which he should present an account of his expences, which would be paid by the Government of the U.S. but no duties should be charged on the goods, thus accidentally thrown ashore. So, likewise, if a vessel should put into one of his ports in distress, and it should be necessary to land her cargo, it should be well stored & taken care of, all the expense of which would be paid by the Government of the U.S. but they would pay no duties on such goods, unless they should be disposed in the same manner as if they had been landed on purpose for sale.

To all that related to expense in this article, the Sultan absolutely refused his assent. It was not the custom of the Arabs, he said, to receive pay for the assistance which they might have rendered to persons in disstress. When English & French vessels had required his assistance in such circumstances as specified in the article of the treaty, it had always been granted to the fullest extent; but he had received no compensation for it, and he certainly should not treat Americans less kindly than he had done the people of those nations.

Mr. R. found no difficulty, of course, in modifying the article in question, in such a manner, as to suit the Sultan's views, and all the others having been agreed to, nothing now remained but to execute the translating & copying.

October 1, 1833. Day before yesterday the treaty was concluded; so that nothing remained to detain us longer in port, but to prepare the ship for sea & finish taking a supply of wood & water. When Capt. Calaphon came on board with the treaty, which the Sultan had signed & sealed, he brought from his Highness a valuable sword as a present to Capt. Geisinger, or as was pretended, in order to evade the law which forbids any officer to receive a present from any foreign prince or potentate, for the Captain's son; and a cashimere shawl for the wife of Capt. Shields. The shawl was said to be of the nominal value of from 3 to 6 hundred dollars, and for ought I know it may have been really of great value; but it was impossible for me to see that it was superior in any respect to a merino shawl that costs 20 dollars. And as to the figures & colours, they were in such taste, that I think none of our city-ladies would be willing to wear it in the street. But although it might not be exactly to our taste, yet as an expression of the Sultan's generosity, it was duly estimated & thankfully received.

Yesterday in the afternoon, an English ship, a cruiser of the E.I. Company, called the *Amherst,* arrived in the harbour of Muscat from the Persian Gulf. The Capt. came on board the *Peacock* & spent the evening. In the course of conversation he learned that our officers had planned an expedition to the hot springs about 20 miles from Muscat; and he endeavoured to dissuade them from it, by representing the danger with which it would be attended. Parties of English officers, he said, had at different times visited those springs, and notwithstanding they used every precaution against the influence of the climate, yet in every instance the expedition proved fatal to several individuals of each party. He therefore advised them, by all means, to abandon the expedition, and it was concluded accordingly to give it up.

One of the officers of this ship had been at Bassorah [Basra] in Persia a few months before, and he stated that the accounts of the ravages of the Plague at that place last year, were substantially correct. It was supposed that seventy thousand of the inhabitants of the city were carried off by it. Many people died in the streets, where their graves are still seen, for wherever they died, there they were buried. So unsparing were the ravages of the pestilence, that the city was almost entirely dep[op]ulated.

The *Amherst* had despatches from Europe by way of Constantinople as late as July, but the only important information that we received from her was, the restoration of peace in Europe.[7]

For the last few days the Sultan has been collecting troops from the interior, and it is said that he has now about five thousand assembled at Muscat. Their destination is said to be Zanzibar, whither his Highness is preparing to sail in about 2 weeks. It is probable, however, that some fears are entertained of a hostile visit from Ibraham Pacha[8] of Egypt, who was expected at Mocha with a force sufficient to retake the place; and that the Sultan was preparing to receive him, in case he should make an attempt on Muscat.

The ship, for the last few days has been thronged with natives from morning till night; some of whom are persons of rank & consequence, but the greater part belong to the lower classes. The former are in general decently clad, and conduct themselves with propriety & decorum; but the latter are extremely shabby & filthy in their dress, and in their manners they were bold & intrusive. This was particularly the case with those wretched beings, who have undergone a denaturalizing mutilation, for the purpose of being employed in the Sultan's harem. Several of these miserable wretches visited the ship repeatedly, & because they belonged to the Sultan's family, they seemed to consider themselves privileged to go wherever they pleased about the ship without ceremony. Accordingly they directed their course first to the cabin, and if they met with a repulse from the sentry stationed at the cabin-door, they were disposed to resent it, and were not easily prevented from accomplishing their purpose of forcing their way into the cabin. None, however, whatever their appearance might be, were wholly excluded from the cabin, or prohibited from viewing any part of the ship which they wished to see; but after having been once admitted into the cabin, & allowed a sufficient opportunity to gratify their curiosity there, they were not permitted to repeat their visit. I speak of the lower classes, including those members of the Sultan's family of whom I have already spoken; for all others were of course allowed free access to the cabin whenever they came on board. Several of these visitors belonged to the Sultan's navy, and they were very minute in their examination of every thing they saw.

Among those who visited the ship, was a considerable number who came for medical assistance, on account of diseases of the eyes, and effections of the skin, which appear to be the most prevalent complaints there. The first especially were much more general than I ever observed it in any place before; insomuch that it was quite rare to meet with a person who had both eyes sound, & a large proportion of the lower classes of the inhabitants were blind with one eye, and not a few had lost the sight of both. Most of the cases for which my assistance was required, were such as admitted of no effectual treatment, at least, during the short time that we expected to remain there; and of course I prescribed for only a few of them. From what I could learn, I was led to conclude that there were no physicians in the place, though it was said, that there were surgeons belonging to the Sultan's ships then lying in the harbour.

With regard to the great prevalence of diseases of the eyes at Muscat, the causes of it were quite obvious; which were, intense heat & light, and the acrid dust from the rocks & sands, over which the wind usually blows some part of every 24 hours, in the direction of the town, and carries with it a quantity of that hot, acrid dust, from which the lower-clases of the people have no means to protect their eyes.

Oct. 5. Yesterday was the day which had been fixed upon about a week ago, for receiving a visit from the Sultan, and during the interval, nothing has been done but to prepare the ship in the best possible manner for his reception. In order to show off to advantage the ship must be painted both inside and out, and the guns & all the iron work about the ship must receive a black coat of coal-tar, the most horrible offensive material in existence; so that, besides the constant annoyance of paint & tar brushes, which were employed in all directions from morning till night, and required one to be incessantly on the watch to avoid them, we have been enveloped during the whole of this period in an atmosphere but little less offensive than that of a Gas Factory. At last, however, the disagreeable business of preparation was completed; and yesterday, at 4 o'clock in the afternoon, we had the honor of receiving the Sultan on board. He was accompanied by the Interpreter, Capt. Calafaun, 7 or 8 gentlemen whose rank I have not learned, and a guard consisting of 12 or 14 men, some of whom were eunuchs. All these wore small shields on their left arms, and were armed in the Arabian fashion, with short daggars in their belts. Two of the ships boats were employed to bring the Sultan & his suit. All the officers of the ship, & Capt. Shields of the schooner were assembled on the quarterdeck, to receive him. He was met at the gang-way by the Capt. and after he had shaken hands with all the officers, he & his suit were conducted to the chairs which had been placed for them on the after part of the quarter-deck. After remaining there a few minutes, he was conducted below, first to the gun-deck, of which he took a survey, making such remarks on what he saw as evinced considerable knowledge of seamanship, then to the birth-deck & ward-room, and lastly to the cabin. A table was set in the cabin & abundantly supplied with refreshments, consisting of fruits, sweet-meats, sherbert, orgeat etc; of which, however, his Highness partook very sparingly. Coffee, made as near to the Arabian taste as possible, was served around, but neither his Highness or his suite did more than barely taste of it. As soon as his suit had finished the coffee, he signified his wish to leave the ship. The boats were accordingly ordered to be ready, and having taken leave of each officer individually by shaking hands, he went into the boat, followed by his suit and advanced slowly towards the shore. Two other boats were employed to carry the guard, & as soon as they were all at a sufficient distance from the ship, where they were all directed to lie on their oars, a salute of 21 guns was fired, and at the same time the yards were manned by the crew, all dressed in white. As the last gun was fired, the men on the yards gave 3 cheers, which were returned by the men in the Sultan's boat, & this was followed by 1 cheer from the men on the yards, which concluded the ceremonies on our part. As the Sultan passed the schooner, which was lying between the ship and the town, he was again saluted with 21 guns. Both our salutes were promptly returned by the forts.

Thus, in the course of half an hour passed the important event, on account to which the ship had been kept in a state of constant bustle & confusion for a week.

A few particulars, however, remain to be mentioned as connected with the Sultan's visit, since they serve [to] develope in some degree, certain traits in the Arabian character. The first relates to the medical profession, and is an evidence that the character of a physician is now, as it formerly was, highly respected by the Arabs. I happened to be standing between 2 guns on the gun-deck, when the Sultan passed along, & as he came opposite to me, the Interpreter stopped him, and introduced me as "el hakkem," or doctor of the ship, & observed to him that I had been for some time sick; on which his Highness expressed much regret, and said, that if I would go on shore he would be glad to furnish me with a house, where I would be much more comfortable than on board the ship. Would any surgeon of a foreign man-of-war, in one of our ports, receive such particular attention from the President of the U.S. or from any of our Governors or others high in office? I mention this incident, not because I happened to be the object of the Sultan's special notice, but only to show that the medical character is considered by the Arabs as entitled to peculiar attention.

The second particular that I notice, is the custom of the Arabs, &

probably of all Mahometans, of putting of their shoes, or rather sandals, at the door of a room which they are about to enter, & going in bare-footed. Accordingly when the Sultan went into the cabin, he left his slippers at the door, as did all his suit, and went in with naked feet. What the origin or object of this custom was, I did not learn, though I am inclined to believe that it originated with Mahomet, and that its object was cleanliness. The Arabs use no chairs in their apartments, but have their floors covered with mats or carpets, on which they are in the habit of spending much of their time in sitting & lying; and in order to preserve them as clean as possible, the custom of which I am speaking was probably adopted.

I shall mention one other particular, and that for the purpose of showing the Sultan's generosity. It was the duty of our first Lieut. to conduct his Highness about the ship, which duty he performed so much to the Sultan's satisfaction, that he sent him the next day by Capt. Calafaun, a very fine cashmere shawl for his wife. And at the same time, he presented to each of the 2 Lieut^s who attended on him in the boat, a bottle of otto [attar] of roses; to the one, for his wife, & to the other for his sister, having learned some time before, that the officers could not receive any thing for themselves, but that they would receive as much as he chose to give them in the name of their *children, wives,* or *sisters.*

Oct. 7. This day was fixed upon for taking our departure from Muscat, and accordingly there was a good deal to be done, as there always is on the day of sailing, whatever time may have been spent in making preparation. It had been the intention to sail the evening before, but on Mr. Roberts paying a visit to the Sultan for the purpose of taking leave on that day, he learned that the letter which his Highness was to write to the President of the U.S. had been forgotten; but his Highness promised that it should be ready by 7 o'clock the next morning. It was about 12 o'clock however, before Capt. Calafaun came on board with it, and then it was not translated, nor could he translate it, he said, on account of its high figurative style, in less than 3 days. He endeavoured to convey to Mr. Roberts, as correct an idea of its contents as he could, from which Mr. R. made out a translation in his own language, which probably expressed with sufficient accuracy, the meaning of the orginal. It was, indeed, most highly figurative & hyperbolied & therefore in the true Arabian style, as will appear from the following expression. After addressing the President in the usual oriental style, he says "on a fortunate day, & at a happy hour, I had the felicity to receive your letter, every word of which was as clear as the sun, & shone forth like the stars of heaven". He then goes on to compliment Mr. R. with whom he had concluded a treaty of friendship & commerce on such terms as he proposed; which treaty, he will on his part most faithfully observe, and will do all in his power, to preserve it inviolate so long as the world shall last.[9]

All our business at Muscat was now brought to a close, & we only waited for a favourable breeze to take our departure. In the afternoon a light breeze sprung up from the land, & at 5 o'clock we weighed anchor & stood out of the harbour. While getting under way we fired a salute of 17 guns which was immediately returned by the forts. Capt. Calafaun accompanied us out of the harbour, & when about 2 miles from the town he took leave of us & was taken ashore in one of our boats.

I shall now conclude what I have to say respecting Muscat & its inhabitants. But little remains, however, to be said on these subjects, in addition to the remarks which have already been made. The town of Muscat is not so large as Mocha, but the buildings are in the same style, and like those of Mocha, appear to be in a decaying state. The Sultan's palace is of course the best building in the place, but even this is quite ordinary in its external appearance. It stands fronting the harbour, is four stories high, and has two large wings, probably for the use of his guard, eunuchs & servants. The Sultan had about 30 wives, it was said, & consequently there must have been employment for a considerable number of eunuchs & servants.

I could not obtain any satisfactory information respecting the population of Muscat, but I suppose that it did not exceed 7 or 8 thousand. The government is of course a military despotism, the Sultan being the only source of power. But he was said to exercise his power with mildness & moderation, & to enjoy the good will & affection of his subjects. His countenance & manners were certainly those of a mild, amiable man; and the conduct of his officers & servants was such as to show very clearly, that the master was not a tyrant, whose cruelty they had constant reason to dread.[10] Of the extent of the Sultan's dominions, I obtained no information, nor of the country, or its productions. The state of my health was such all the time that we remained at Muscat, that I was unable to go about & make those inquiries, & gain that information which I otherwise should have done. I was but twice in the town, & then only for a few minutes—once to call on the Sultan, & again to procure an article or two of medicine.

The principal articles of export from Muscat, are coffee, dates, wheat, & medicinal gums. The coffee & wheat are not produced in that province, but are brought, the former from Mocha, & the latter from Persia. The price of coffee there was the same as at Mocha, that is, 12 cents a pound, & the price of wheat was at the rate of about 50 cents a bushel.

As to supplies, we fared much better at Muscat than we had reason to expect. The beef was of a better quality than any we had met with during the cruise, & at the rate of —— a pound. The sheep were equal to those of Mocha, though of a different kind, and cost from $1.50 to $2.00 a head. Fowls & eggs were in sufficient abundance the former at the price of $2. a dozzen, & the latter, at the rate of 130 for a dollar. The only fruit that we made much use of was grapes, these were very fine & not dear. Dates, indeed, were in great abundance, but they were far inferior to the grapes. These were of two kinds, white & purple, both of which were large & sweet. Our table was supplied every day with excellent fish, which were caught in great abundance in the harbour. We were also plentifully supplied with milk, and better milk too, than we had tasted before, from the time we left home.

The water that we took in there was very good, & furnished us at the expense of the Sultan. It was taken from an immense cistern at the back part of the town, and carried to the boat in goat skins. We used our own casks but the Sultan employed a boat & boat's crew for the purpose; so that our men were saved a most disagreeable, as well as hazzardous service. The Sultan also furnished us a supply of wood at his own expense. The town & harbour of Muscat appeared to be well protected by fortifications; for wherever a place could be found for a fort, either on the sides or tops of those mountains of rock, there they had been constructed, at an immense expense of labour, & with no small degree of military skill. One of the largest of these forts overlooked the town, & occuppied the summit of a mass of rock, nearly 300 feet high. A great number of watch towers were seen occupying these elevated situations, from which an advancing enemy could be seen at a great distance. Most of these works of defence, however, like the town itself, appeared to be crumbling into ruins; & several of them had become entirely useless.

The climate of Muscat is one of the hottest in the world. Fortunately for us, we did not arrive there, until the season was so far advanced, that the heat began to abate; but even then, we found it intensely hot, the thermometer usually standing, in the coolest situation in the ship, at 90 & upwards, which was nearly equal to 100 on shore. There was sometimes a light breeze, but rarely enough to mitigate the heat. During the 19 days that we remained there, the sun was never obscured by a cloud for a single moment. The change of temperature from day to night was very trifling, so that it was impossible to enjoy any comfortable sleep, except on the upper deck in the open air. I continued, however, to occupy the apartment assigned me below the 2d. deck, where I lay drenched in perspiration during the whole night; until I became so much exhausted, that I was obliged to exchange it for a cot on the gun-deck. To the kindness of one of my mess-mates I was indebted for this exchange, which contributed very materially to the restoration of my health. The apartment from which I was thus enabled to make my escape, was situated in the side of the ship, & so far back, as to admit of no free circulation of air, and was otherwise so entirely destitute of those accommodations which an officer's state-room ought to possess, that it was scarcely fit to be used as a dog kennel.

Here I shall take occasion to observe, that a sloop-of-war is totally unfit to be employed on a long cruise in hot climates, like that for which the *Peacock* was destined; because it is impossible that a ship of that class can possess those accommodations for the officers & men, which are indespensably necessary for their health & comfort, & at the same time, carry a sufficient supply of water & provisions. No vessel of a smaller rate than a frigate, should ever be employed on such a cruise; for none of a smaller size can afford the requisite accommodations. An officer's state-room in a hot climate should by all means be provided with an air-port; for, without this it is impossible that it can be sufficiently ventilated. It is also equally necessary that there should be air ports in the stern, without which there cannot be a sufficient circulation of air through the ward-room. Had our ship been a frigate, possessing the comforts & accommodations that I have mentioned, instead of a small, confined sloop-of-war, we should have suffered much less than we have done, & our situation would consequently have been comparatively a pleasant one.

To return to the climate of Muscat. The year there is divided into two seasons, summer & winter. The former commences in April & continues till November, when the winter commences & comprises the rest of the year. There is a good deal of rain during the winter, & the weather is so cold that woollen clothes become necessary. It is said that snow falls on the mountains in the interior. The general range of the barometer during our stay at Muscat, was about 29.70. There was a diurnal rise & fall, however, of about the tenth of an inch; it being highest early in the morning, & lowest in the afternoon.

During the last week of our stay at Muscat, we were greatly annoyed by visitors, who came off in great numbers to see the ship; and from morning till night she was thronged with them, sometimes to such a degree that it was difficult to get along the decks. Much the greater part of these visitors were people of the lower classes, & were quite destitute of a sense of propriety & decorum. A large number of them were of a class denominated "banyans," who were distinguished from the others by red turbans, & rings in their ears.[11] These banyans were generally shop-keepers on a small scale, and hence their title, which, I am told signifies a trader. They were generally stout, athletic-looking men, but disgustingly dirty in their dress, which consisted of the serong like that of the Siamese & a frock fastened around the waist by a girdle or sash. These garments were generally cotton & originally white; but by long use & neglect of washing, they had assumed quite another complexion.

In the course of my short walks in the town, I passed several females in the streets, all of whom wore a sort of mask, to shield their faces from the gaze of the other sex. But these masks, from the design, no doubt, of their wearers were so made, that they concealed only a small part of the face. They consisted of a piece of cotton or silk, 6 or 7 inches square, with 2 openings for the eyes, so large, as to admit of such a view of the countenance, as easily to determine its pretensions to beauty. I saw none however, which had the least right to set up such a claim, though no doubt there are many in the houses of the Sultan & his officers of a very different description.

Judging from what I saw of Muscat, I should conclude that very little foreign trade was carried on there; but we were told, that at a certain season of the year, the harbour is quite thronged with foreign vessels, and that commerce is then very active. This season comprises the months of February & March.

The harbour of Muscat is secure against all winds except the N.W. which sometimes blows with great violence during the winter, and raises the water in the harbour to such a height, as to fill the lower story of the Sultan's palace. The ordinary rise & fall of the tide is 4 or 5 feet.

CHAPTER XIII

Mozambique to New York

We left Muscat, as I have already said the 7th. of October, at 5 o'clock in the afternoon, with a favourable breeze, which continued till we had gained a sufficient offing, when it died away & we remained becalmed during the greater part of the night. There was a current in our favour however, and the next morning we found ourselves about 30 miles from Muscat. As soon as we were fairly clear of the harbour of Muscat, we began to experience a change of temperature, & I passed that night much more comfortably than I had done any one before for 3 weeks.

Oct. 21. On this day we had to perform the melancholy office of committing to the deep, the remains of one of our officers, Midshipman Roumford [Midshipman Lewis Henry Roumford], who died after an illness of ten or twelve days.[1] This was the first death that had occurred among the officers, and was so sudden & unexpected as to make an unusual impression on the minds both of officers & men. The disease which proved fatal to this young officer, was a fever, of a character nearly resembling that of yellow fever, and which attacked him soon after we left Muscat. For several months preceding his death, Mr. R. had exhibited a bloated, sallow countenance, indicating considerable derangement of his health, & particularly disorder of the biliary organs. This was owing, I have no doubt, in a very considerable degree, to the habit of smoking segars, which he indulged more or less every day, notwithstanding he was repeatedly warned of the serious effects that would be likely to result from it. He frequently observed to Dr. Gilchrist, during this period, as I learned after his death, that he suffered much from a depression of spirits, which he was unable to account for, as he had no reason for melanch[oly] feelings. This mental depression led him to spend much of his time below, in a state of inaction, which he ought, on account of his health, to have spent on deck in the open air taking vigorous exercise. He continued to perform all the duty required of him, however, and seemed not to be aware that he was labouring under any disease, nor did I hear the least complaint from him after leaving Batavia, until the commencement of his last illness. During our stay at Muscat, he was in the habit of bathing almost every day & of remaining a long time in the water, and he also exposed himself unnecessarily to the extreme heat of the sun. These, no doubt, were among the causes of the disease, to which he fell a victim.

Mr. R. was a young man of very amiable manners, & a well cultivated mind, and had the good will of all on board. His parents, I understand, reside in Germantown in Pennsylvania, where his father is teacher of a very respectable seminary.

Oct. 27. This day we entered the southern hemisphere again, after a passage of 20 days from Muscat. Thus far, our progress had been much more rapid than we expected it could be, for it being the period of the change of the monsoons, we had reason to expect a succession of calms & light winds for 15 or 20 days, until the N.E. should be regularly set in. We were most favourably disappointed, however, in meeting with no calms of consequence, and in having our sails almost constantly filled with an easterly or south-easterly breeze. On leaving Muscat, it was the *expressed* intention to stop at Zanzibar, a place belonging to the Imaum of Muscat, near the African coast, in about six degrees of south latitude; but having advanced so much more rapidly than we had anticipated, and the Capt. having orders from the Government to visit Mozambique, a Portuguese town on the African coast, about 600 miles to the southward of Zanzibar, we began, some days before crossing the equator, to shape our course for the latter place.

Until we arrived within a few degrees of the equator, we had very fine weather, by which we were greatly renovated, after the intolerable heat of the Red Sea & Persian Gulf. Scarcely a drop of rain fell till we were within four or five degrees of the equator, and the temperature was such as to be just agreeable to our feelings, though high enough to have been considered very hot, if we had not been exposed for some time to the broiling heat of the Arabian deserts.

Nov. 6. After crossing the equator, we had to contend for some days with adverse winds, which rendered our progress rather slow, and during this time the weather was rendered quite unpleasant by frequent rain-squalls. This scene changed, however, when we had reached the 4th. degree of south latitude, the wind then becoming fair & the weather pleasant. For 4 or 5 days, until we had advanced to about the 12th degree of latitude, the wind was steadily from the S.E. but then it began to change its direction to the northward, and soon became the regular N.E. monsoon; and greatly to our satisfaction, we advanced on our homeward passage at quite a rapid rate.

At day-light this morning, we made the African coast to the northward of Mozambique, and shortly afterwards had a view of land-marks which were supposed to designate the harbour. This proved to be a mistake too, which was very near leading to the destruction of the ship. For being very confident, from the land-marks above mentioned and especially from seeing the Portuguese flag flying on what was taken to be a fort at the distance of 2 or 3 miles from us in the supposed situation of the town, that this was the harbour of Mozambique; we ran in with a fresh breeze, & under full sail, until we were in less than 4 fathoms water & within a half cable length of a rocky shoal, on which the water was but 12 feet deep. It was now evident that this was not the harbour of Mozambique, and as soon as practicable, on discovering the mistake, the ship was rounded too, the topsails were backed, and an anchor was let go, which fortunately stopped our farther progress towards the rocky shoal. By these prompt & judicious movements the loss of the ship was prevented, there is every reason to believe, for in one minute more, if we had stood on, she would have struck upon the rocks in 12 feet water, where it would have been impossible, in all probability, to get her off. After she was brought up by the anchor, however, we felt ourselves quite secure, although the water where we lay was so shoal, that we could even see the anchor lying on the bottom, and at the stern of the ship, the depth of water was only 17 feet. Our situation now was such in relation to a point of land a little distance to the leeward of us, that in order to clear it, the ship must be warped some distance to windward; and the means for accomplishing this were immediately put in operation. A small anchor, with a stream cable attached to it, & a hawser joined to that, was carried out the length of both of these; and very fortunately by means of these we gained a position, from which we could make sail, and go clear of the point of land above-mentioned. To gain this position, required the labour of 3 or 4 hours, on account of having to advance directly against a fresh breeze; and before it was accomplished, it became necessary, on account of the ship going astern, from sufficient force not having been applied to the hawser, to let go another anchor. At last, however, we reached the desired point, at about 3 o'clock in the afternoon, & six hours after the first anchor was let go, and spreading our sails to a fresh breeze, in ten minutes we were entirely out of danger.

This unpleasant occurrence might have been prevented, perhaps, had the schooner, which had been sent in before us to point out the harbour, communicated the information which she had gained; for having run in till he had only about 5 fathoms water, Capt. Shields became satisfied from the shoalness of the water, that we had mistaken the harbour, and tacked & stood out. Supposing that his tacking & standing out would be considered by Capt. Geisinger a sufficient signal to prevent his running in, he omitted to make any other; and besides, he had intended to speak us as he passed us while we were standing in, but he was unable to do this; so that we remained ignorant of the danger into which we were running, until we were in the midst of it, as I have already described. Before he tacked & stood out, Capt. S. sent in a boat with a Lieut. to sound, so that he might report with certainty respecting the harbour. But before the boat had sounded to any distance, we had run in, discovered the danger & escaped it. The boat proceeded on to the place where the flag was flying, and after an absence of about an hour she returned, & the officer reported that he had landed at a small Portuguese settlement, and learned, that the river Quintanigo [Quintangone] emptied itself there, & formed what we had erroneously taken for a harbour, and that Mozambique was 2 or 3 hours sail to the southward.

I am thus particular in mentioning all the circumstances relating to this occurrence, in which the schooner was concerned; because a disposition was manifested to charge all the blame, (if there was any justly chargeable upon any one) of our running into danger, upon Capt. Shields. But I am fully of the opinion, that neither Capt. S. nor any one else could be justly charged with blame. The entrance of this supposed harbour so nearly resembled that of Mozambique, as laid down on the chart, that a stranger might easily mistake the one for the other; so that Capt. Geisinger cannot be justly censured, in my opinion for attempting to run in. And with respect to Capt. Shields, if all the circumstances that have been mentioned, are taken into consideration, together with the reasons on which he acted he appears to me to be equally free from fault.

As I have already observed, we had a view of the African coast to the northward of Quintanigo, and as far as we could see, it was low, nearly level, and clothed with verdure; but whether with forest or jungle, could not be determined. At the distance of 8 or 10 miles from the coast was a ridge of small elevation, running parallel with the coast; in which was one of the land-marks that was represented as an important one in designating the harbour of Mozambique, and which was the principal cause of the occurrences that I have been describing. This was a more elevated portion of the ridge, of a mile or two in extent, level on the top, & therefore called "Table Hill". The bearing of this table-land was about the same from the mouth of the Quintanigo river, that it was supposed to be from the harbour of Mozambique, that is, about west; and the small islands which constituted the other land-marks of the latter, were also found, at least, they were supposed to be found at the former; and hence the confidence with which we attempted to run in.

We made our escape from the unpleasant situation that has been described, about 3 o'clock in the afternoon, and with a still favourable breeze, shaped our course for Mozambique, where we arrived in about an hour from the time we made sail, and at the end of the 30th. day from Muscat.

The principal entrance to the harbour of Mozambique, is formed by Pamony Point on the north, and by a small island called St. George's on the south. On the latter was a small fort, on which the Portuguese flag was flying. Soon after we passed this island, a pilot came on board, and took us up to the anchorage, at the distance of about half a mile from the town. We found there two Portuguese ships which left Rio Janeiro early in August, and had a passage of about 60 days. In one of these ships was a very intelligent gentleman who spoke English well, and who informed us that there had been a disease prevailing at Rio, which had carried off a good many people, and which we were led to suppose was Cholera; but were afterwards told that it was not Cholera, but a kind of typhus fever, which had been confined principally to the outskirts of the city.

As usual, a boat was despatched immediately after we came to anchor, with an officer to the chief authority of the place, with the Captain's respects, and a message stating the object of our visit, and proposing to exchange salutes. The junior Lieutenant, Mr. Brent, was the officer employed on this occasion, and he was accompanied by the Purser, who acted as interpreter, and also made arrangements for the supplies that we stood in need. They returned a little after sunset, and made a very favourable report.

Nov. 8. [Nov. 7] At 10 o'clock this morning, a salute was fired according to agreement, consisting of 15 guns, which was immediately returned by the fort. Water being the article that we most wanted, and with which we could be least expeditiously supplied; measures were taken as soon as practicable this morning, to commence watering immediately and to obtain the necessary supply in the most expeditious manner, that the ship might be ready for sea as soon as possible. For this purpose 2 large boats belonging to the fort were employed, with black crews, by which means the labourious business of watering would be accomplished with the desired expedition, and at the same time our own men would be exempt from a kind of duty, that is always attended, in a tropical climate, with more or less danger. The water with which we were supplied was rain-water, and came from a long cistern or reservoir in the centre of the fort. From the cistern was a subterranean conduit leading down nearly to the landing place, where a gun was placed horizontally in the bank, through which the water was discharged. Here the casks were filled, and rolled down to the boats, which, on account of the shoalness of the water, were obliged to remain at a considerable distance from the shore; so that it was a labourious task to get the large casks, each weighing at least half a ton, on board of them. The water was excellent, and raised from the cistern by means of a large pump worked by negroes.

In the course of the day, the Capt. & Mr. Roberts, together with Capt. Shields, called on the Governor, by whom they were received and treated in a very polite & friendly manner. The government of Mozambique was vested in three persons, viz: 1. Frei Antonio Jose Maia; 2. Joaquin Xavier Dinez Costa, Judge, or Ouvidor; 3. Colonel Francisco Henriquiz Ferrao. The first of these was called Corregidor, and was the person to whom the visit of ceremony above mentioned was made. As these individuals derived their authority from the reigning monarch of Portugal, they of course professed to belong to the party of Miguel, though it was manifest from the manner in which they expressed themselves in relation to the affairs of Portugal, that in reality their wishes were in favour of Don Pedro. The town of Mozambique presented a much more pleasing exterior than I had been led to expect, and the prospect of the bay as well as of the adjoining coast, also far exceeded my expecting. It is very possible, however, that this may be attributed in some degree to the contrast between the scenery here and that at Muscat, where the view was wholly confined, except towards the water, by a mountain of rugged & barren rocks. That part of the town of Mozambique of which we had a view from the ship, consisted of buildings constructed in the Portuguese fashion, of brick or stone, neatly plastered & white-washed on the outside, which gave them a very pleasant appearance. Among these were the public buildings, which were very plain, but sufficiently large and commodious. Some of the buildings, public or private, were more than two stories high, & they all had flat roofs.

On the other side from the town, and across a fine bay from 2 to 3 miles wide, we had a view of the African coast from west to north, which presented a verdant and cheerful appearance, with here & there a snow-white dwelling-house along the border of the bay, which contrasted very agreeably with the surrounding verdure. "Table-Hill," which I have already mentioned, was also a conspicuous object, at the distance of 8 or 10 miles, and the only high-land that was to be seen. Its bearings from the ship as she lay at anchor was about N.W. The hight of this hill, I judged to be about 1000 feet.

Nov. 8. This morning I went on shore in company with Capt. Shields, & Lieut. Poor [Lt. Charles H. Poor] of the schooner, for the purpose of taking a survey of the interior of the town; which was accomplished to our satisfaction in about 2 hours. We landed at a pier, made of stone & earth, and extending out about ten rods, and forming a very convenient landing-place. Capt. Shields being desirous to purchase some gold chains & rings which he had seen the day before, we went to the house of the Banian who dealt in articles of that kind, of whom the Capt. purchased 2 chains & a ring. The 2 chains, or rather cords, (for they were of the form & size of small twine) were double, & each about half a yard in length; and these, together with the ring, weighed nearly an ounce & a quarter. The price of the whole was $24. which was considered very cheap. They were supposed to be cheap, because the material of which they were made, was procured from the Africans who brought it from the interior & disposed of it at much less than its real value, and because the work was done at Mozambique. The work, however, of the chains especially, was very coarse, and if I am not mistaken in my judgment of female taste, they will not be very highly prized as ornaments for a lady's neck.

We procured a guide from the Banian and pursued our rambles about the town; principally, however, in that part of it which could not be seen from the ship. This part of it presented quite a different appearance from that towards the anchorage, the buildings here being constructed principally of poles stuck in the ground, with a roof of palm-leaf thatch, and a floor of the bare ground. These dwellings were inhabited wholly by blacks, who constituted, indeed, almost the whole population of the place.[2] In this part of the town we found the walking very bad, there being no pavement and the sand deep; and we made our exit from it as soon as we could. The town of Mozambique is situated on an island about a mile & a half long from north to south, and not more than a quarter of a mile wide. Almost the whole of the island is occupied by the town. The European population occupied the northern part of it, & the blacks the southern. The former, as I have already observed, lived in houses constructed of brick or stone, and of a very decent external appearance; and several of the streets in that part of the town were well paved so that it was very comfortable walking there.

In the course of our walk, we passed through several small bazars, or markets, which were kept almost exclusively by negro women. These bazars were very scantily supplied, affording nothing scarcely, besides a few dried fish, some dried fruits, a few vegetables, & several kinds of manufactured articles like cakes & sweet meats. The island of Mozambique is entirely barren, & all the supplies for the town, except such as are imported, are brought from the adjoining coast. But the soil there is quite barren & unproductive, being little else than sand; so that, if it were not for the supplies obtained by sea, the town would hardly be able to avoid starvation. Indeed, according to the statement of some of the officers there, they were reduced almost to a state of starvation, when the two Portuguese ships which I have mentioned arrived, and brought them supplies.

Notwithstanding the apparent scarcity of food, however, in the bazars, and notwithstanding the cruel treatment which the blacks are said to receive from their Portuguese masters; all the blacks that we saw, and we saw, I believe, almost every one in the place, appeared nevertheless, to be in a very good condition, and as contented & happy as any people that I have ever seen. I could not discover that they seemed to be in want of any thing, which they considered necessary to their happiness. A supply of their daily wants, and the gratification of their animal appetites, appeared to be all that they required, to constitute as great a measure of enjoyment as they were capable of, without a higher state of moral and intellectual improvement. This, however, is no argument for slavery, but on the contrary is a strong argument against it as I conceive; because, if it is the effect of slavery, so to brutalize the human mind, as to make it satisfied with the gratification of the mere animal appetites, as appears to be the case from the facts which have been stated; then certainly we must conclude, that slavery is an evil of the worst character, and that if the blacks are capable of such a degree of mental improvement as to render freedom a blessing to them, it is criminal in the highest degree, to deprive them of it, notwithstanding they may seem to be contented, like brutes, to wear the chains of servitude.

Having seen as much of the town as we wished, with the exception of the fort, which we designed to visit in the afternoon, we returned on board at about one o'clock in the afternoon. According to agreement, Capt. Shields called for me at 5 in the afternoon, and we paid a visit to the fort; the only object on the island deserving of any particular notice. This fort was said to have been constructed by John de Castra, 250 years ago.* It is situated on the northern extremity of the island; and so constructed, as to protect both the harbour & the town. We landed directly at the fort on the beach, where, however, the water was so shoal, that we were obliged to be transported some distance on men's shoulders. The gate of the fort we found guarded by several soldiers, and we waited there till a message could be carried to the commanding officer & permission obtained for us to enter. In a little time an officer came and conducted us through the gate, & up a long flight of stone-steps to the quarters of the commanding officer. He received us at the door & treated us with due politeness. It was on my introduction to this gentleman, that I was first apprized of my unhealthy countenance; for on my being introduced as the Surgeon of the corvette, he exclaimed with more surprise than good manners, "what, a doctor, and look so bad"! As to indications of bad health, I might have returned the compliment, for his countenance had much more of the sickly cast than mine; and he exhibited, besides, symptoms of great nervous disorder, his features being distorted as if by a paralytic affection, and he was incessantly grating his teeth, as if agonized with pain. I mention these particulars, however, not to pay the gentleman for his compliment to me; but to show the bad influence of the climate, for that was the cause of those indications, of ill-health which I have mentioned. The Major, (for that was his rank) said himself, that the climate of Africa was too much for any European to endure for 4 years, the length of time that he had been there; and that he had applied some time before, for permission to return home. The room in which we found the Major, was sufficiently large, but without furniture, dark & gloomy. After a stay of a few minutes, we took leave of him and under the guidance of a young Lieutenant; proceeded in our survey of the fort.

To give a description of it; would be useless labour, and therefore I shall not attempt it. It is constructed of stone & earth, and is of great extent in proportion to the size of the town. So far as I was capable of judging, it appeared to have been well planned, and the work well executed. It was provided with every thing that properly belongs to a fortification of such

---

*Not being able to refer to any account of John de Castra, I cannot vouch for the correctness of this statement.[3]

extent, as magazines of arms & ammunition, armoury, officers quarters etc. etc. Including a small water battery, guns were mounted on the fort, all of which were brass, except thirty, and most of them very old. They were of various caliber, from 108 to 10 pounds. For the largest, balls of stone were used instead of metal, as being much lighter & more easily handled. The gun-carriages had been in use, as we were told, 20 years, but notwithstanding, they appeared to be still sound and fit for service. In one of the angles of the fort a gun was shown us which had been struck by lightning and its pomillon [pomelion], or the knob at the breech, broken off; and at the same time, the sentinel at his post a little distance from it, was killed.

In the centre of the open space enclosed by the walls of the fort, was the large reservoir from which we obtained our supply of water as already mentioned, and from which the town also obtained its principal supply. Every thing that we saw in the fort, exhibited an appearance of neatness and good order, quite creditable to the officers belonging to it. The number of soldiers belonging to the fort, and those stationed in the town, was about 800, of whom 300 were Europeans, & the rest natives.

Having finished our survey of the fort, we walked to the town, about a quarter of a mile distant, where we remained a short time before returning on board. During this short stay, I had an opportunity of making farther observations on the condition of the blacks; for it being after sunset, and their labours of the day being ended, great numbers of them were collected in the streets, and spending the evening in their accustomed sports & amusements, apparently with as much satisfaction, as if there were nothing wanting, to render their condition the happiest in the world.

Nov. 9. This afternoon, I made another trip on shore, in company with Lieuts Cunningham & Sinclair, & the Marine officer, from our ship, & Lieut. Benham [Lt. Timothy G. Benham] of the schooner. Our principal object was to take a walk through the town, which some of the party had not visited before, though it was also the intention to make some purchases, & collect some shells, if such as were wanted should be met with. For the purpose of accomplishing the latter object, we stopped at the house of a merchant or banian, which was near the principal church of the place, and while some of the party were employed in examining the articles offered for sale, the rest of us, perceiving the doors of the church open, were led by our curiosity to take a view of its interior. On entering the door and looking towards the altar, we observed in a small side-gallery a man arranging some ornaments, who immediately invited us to walk around and go up to his room; but as we did not readily understand him, he sent a boy to serve as our guide, who led us through an open court adjoining the church, and up a long flight of stone steps into an appartment adjoining the gallery above-mentioned. Here we were met by the priest, (for it was the priest himself who had kindly invited us to walk up) who received us with the familiarity and hospitality of an old friend. Not content with the usual mode of salut[at]ion even among friends, he threw his arms around us, and I believe went so far with one or two of the party as to kiss them. Orders were immediately given for refreshment to be prepared for us, and in the mean time he took us into his study, where however, we saw but very little of what properly belongs to a clergyman's study. By this time the rest of our party had joined us, and the spirits and good humor of the priest seemed to be raised almost to the highest pitch. In his study, where we were all now assembled, were some fine specimens of coral, and to testify his good will towards us, he took one of them and dividing it into small pieces & with the playfulness of a child, fixed one in the button hole of each our coats. Coral, shells, and pictures constituted the principal contents of the study, there being very few books, and these mostly formularies of devotion in latin. While in the study he showed us a paper on which was written the name of the Purser of an English sloop of war, which had visited Mozambique the preceding August; and he gave us to understand in a very significant & ludicrous manner, that the said Purser got drunk and was obliged to remain there until he became sober.

On leaving the study we found a table provided with the liquid refreshment that had been ordered, which consisted of a bottle of cordial prepared at the island of Bourbon, and we were not allowed to rise from the table till we had disposed of the whole of it. Not one at the table appeared to relish it so much as our entertainer himself, who smacked his lips at every draught & pronounced it to be very good. Having finished the bottle of cordial, we made an attempt to go, but our reverend host was so urgent for us to stay longer, that we were obliged to gratify him; and taking Lieut. Benham with him into a back-room, he returned in a few minutes with a bottle of muscated wine, which he insisted upon our drinking before he would permit us to go. He was not backward, however, to do his part towards emptying the bottle of its delicious contents, and by the time it was finished, the friendly feeling and good humor of the priest were excited to the highest pitch.

His object in taking Mr. Benham with him into the back-room, was to make inquiries of him respecting the state of affairs in Portugal, in which he was no doubt deeply interested. He was desirous to know what progress Don Pedro was making, and whether there was a prospect of his ultimate success. Although he did not express any wish in favour of Miguel, yet it is probable he would have done so if he had made known his real sentiments on the subject; since Miguel has shown a dispos[it]ion very friendly to the catholic clergy.

Learning that we were desirous to procure shells, our kind-hearted priest had a quantity brought in which he distributed among us, and which, though quite ordinary, we thankfully received. When he found we must go, he accompanied us down into the church, and pointed out to us such objects as he supposed would be most pleasing to us; and among others, the seat which had been prepared for the Governor; for the following day was Sunday, and a festival of the Virgin, on which occasion the Governor was to be present; an occurrence which we had reason to suppose was very unusual. Three armed chairs were placed in a row for his Excellency, and covered with yellow silk; all of which he was to occuppy in succession according to the different stages of the service. Three kneeling stools were also provided for him fronting the altar, which he was likewise to use in succession, as the priest informed us by going through the process himself. The interior of the church presented nothing to the view, however, deserving of particular notice. Its dimensions were small, and there was much less display of ornament & imagery than is usually met with in catholic churches. Our curiosity detained here but a short time, and at last we took leave of the merry priest, better pleased with his hospitality and good humor, than with his temperance and piety.

After leaving the church we pursued our walk toward the lower part of the town, where we expected to meet with the articles which some of the party were desirous to purchase. While stopping at a house where these articles were offered for sale, I observed on the opposite side of the street, and just within a gate which opened into a garden of considerable extent, two women labouring at a hand mill; and found on going to them, that here was practised that mode of grinding to which the declaration of our Savior alluded, when he said that, "two women shall be grinding" etc.;[4] for here were two women grinding their corn in the same manner, no doubt, that was practised in Africa & arabia, in the most primitive times. One of the women turned the crank which gave motion to the mill, and whose task was consequently a laborious one. The other was employed in feeding the mill, and removing the meal. The work which such a mill would perform in a day, must be very small, not exceeding, I should judge, a bushel of grain; but even at this rate it would supply a large number of people with such a quantity of materials for bread, as they would absolutely require. I say materials, because there are several other articles in those countries of which bread might be made besides corn, in case that should fail, as rice, millet, etc.

It being now nearly sunset, and not being in the least desirous to remain on shore in such a place after dark, we directed our course back to the landing place, and reached the ship about 7 o'clock in the evening.

Sunday Nov. 10. This day was spent by most of the officers of the ship, and by the Capt. & one of the Lieutenants of the schooner, in a visit to the African shore two or three miles distant across the bay. The party left the ship between 9 & 10. o'clock and returned about sunset. They all returned in high spirits, and exhibited an abundant flow of good humor, having met with a very hospitable Portuguese, who invited them to his house where he entertained them with an excellent dinner, and a plenty of port wine which they praised very highly. It was very evident that the wine was at least such as they were quite willing to drink; for the effects of it were sufficiently manifest in their conduct & conversation. In the course of the day they had made a considerable collection of shells, which were brought on deck and distributed both among the individuals of the party, & the officers who had remained on board. This proved to be an unlucky transaction, for it led to a violent contest between Capt. G. Capt. S & Mr. R.

The conflict commenced between the two last by Mr. R. casually observing that there were some shells in the boat of which he would like to have a few, and requested Capt. S. as they were in his boat, to do him the favour to have them preserved for him. This was like putting fire to a powder-magazine, for Capt.S. instantly flew into a violent passion, and went on deck & ordered all the shells to be brought out of the boat & placed on deck, and all his boat's crew to be searched, lest they might have concealed in their clothes an article of so much importance. When all this was done, the shells were taken into the cabin, where the other two gentlemen were at tea; at which Mr. R. was both surprized & offended, as the request which he had made had been expressed in a friendly manner, and he had not the least suspicion but that it would be so received.

Thus commenced the conflict between Mr. R. & Capt. S. which, however, was not very violent, and was soon terminated, by Capt. G. entering the lists with Mr. R. on account of some expressions which he thought were intended to reflect upon him. The contest now became very warm, and was continued for a considerable time without the least cessation; in the course of which they fought over again the same ground which had been the scene of contention many times before. This contest was maintained with great warmth until the parties had exhausted all their weapons, when it terminated, as all their previous contests had done, in favour of Mr. R. because he fought only in self-defence, and in maintaining his just rights. But hostilities did not cease, for no sooner was Capt. G. obliged to cease discharging his battery at Mr. R. than he opened a heavy fire upon Capt. S. which was returned with spirit & effect.

The points in dispute between them, were of the least possible importance, and such as none but a most captious & quarrelsome man would ever have noticed. This contest continued until the parties came to close quarters, and Capt. S. declared his intention of requesting a court of inquiry to investigate his conduct, if Capt. G. persisted in charging him with a neglect or violation of duty. This led to a parley, which was soon followed by a treaty of peace, and about 12 o'clock at night the parties separated on the most friendly terms, having regained their senses so far over a bottle of wine, as to discover the fact, that they had quarrelled without any cause, which discovery so delighted them, that they became so excessively kind & loving, as to render their reconciliation almost as sickening as their quarrel had been odious.

I have detailed the particulars of this disgraceful scene, to show from what perfectly insignificant causes violent quarrels arise among those men, whose rank and office are such, as should raise them altogether above the influence of those causes. It may also be seen from what had been said, how easily men are thrown into violent quarrels while excited by wine; for had not those gentlemen been drinking the excellent Port-wine of their hospitable Portuguese entertainer, until they were considerably excited, it is certain, that the disgraceful scene which I have described would not have occurred. At least, if any misunderstanding had taken place on a subject of so little importance as a few shells, it would have been managed with such decorum, that it should not have been heard by all the officers in the ship. But as it was, although the precaution was taken to close the cabin-door, the contention within was so loud, that not only those on the quarter-deck, but those too who slept on the gun-deck, had an opportunity of hearing almost every word that was said. My birth was on the gun-deck next to the cabin, where, for about 3 hours, I was compelled to listen to the angry combattants though I endeavoured all I could to avoid it. Here, I dismiss a very disagreeable subject, which would not have been dwelt upon in such detail, had it not been to show, how like mere children men allow themselves to act, who are vested with a rank & consequence which should require them to exhibit a very different character.

Nov. 12. The ship being in readiness for sea the evening before, we took advantage of a land-breeze from the S.W. & at six o'clock this morning, weighed anchor & stood out of the harbour. The pilot who took us in was also employed to take us out; and a pilot more prompt & apparently better acquainted with his business I had never seen.

A few additional remarks remain to be made respecting Mozambique, to render my account of that place as complete as circumstances would admit of. In the first place, with respect to the government, I have already observed, that the powers of government were vested in three individuals by the King of Portugal; but these powers embrace all the Portuguese settlements on the African coast, of which there are several, though none equal to Mozambique in importance, which is therefore the seat of Government. The tenure of office at Mozambique, both civil & military, from what I could learn, was during the pleasure of the King; which, from a variety of causes, must have been very uncertain, to the great discontent, and frequently great injury of those who held offices there. One of the causes to which I have alluded, is the greatly diminished importance of those possessions, and the little inducement consequently for any one to hold an office there; so that when one is sent there either as a civil or military officer, he is in danger of being compelled to remain until the climate renders him incapable of discharging the duties of his office. Military officers, however, after three years residence there are entitled to promotion; but this would be a small compensation if they were obliged to remain in a situation where they would be certain of losing their health if not their lives in a few years.

The cause which has produced this change in the Portuguese possessions in Africa, and rendered them now of comparatively small importance, is the abolition of the slave trade; for it was by this inhuman trafic principally, that they acquired any importance in the first place, and maintained it till a recent period. This was especially the case with Mozambique the principal seat & centre of this trade. As the Portuguese settlers there derived all their wealth and consequence from their success in the slave-trade, it was therefore for their interest to promote quarrels among the different tribes of natives, that prisoners might be made to supply the market with slaves. Hence the different tribes of natives in the neighbourhood of the Portuguese settlements, were kept in a perpetual state of warfare, to gratify the cupidity of a few savage adventurers. The number of slaves exported annually from Mozambique, until humanity interposed effectually in favour of the wretched Africans, was twenty or thirty thousand. The trade in slaves is now entirely suppressed, so that the few Portuguese who reside there are forced to resort to other means for their support.[5]

The principal & most profitable branch of business that is carried on there at present, is dealing in ivory. This is by far the most important article of export from Mozambique, and in consequence of the cessation of the slave-trade the quantity brought into market has greatly increased; for since the natives have ceased to prey upon one another to gratify the avarice of a handful of unprincipled adventurers, with a lucrative trafic in their fellowmen, they have turned their attention to the peaceful occupations of life, and are beginning to derive an encouraging profit from them. The amount of elephant's teeth exported from Mozambique in 1833, was stated to be ten thousand arrobas, or three hundred & twenty thousand pounds. The price of the largest teeth which are the best, was at the rate of about seventy-eight cents a pound. Besides elephants teeth, a considerable quantity of the teeth of the hippopotamos, or river horse were exported; but this is considered an inferior kind of ivory, and is sold for about twenty-five cents a pound. The only other articles of export deserving of notice, are gum benjamin & colombo root;[6] but the trade in these is of but little importance.

The population of Mozambique at the time of our visit was probably about three thousand, of which about five hundred were whites, and the rest blacks. A large majority of those, however, who were classed, under the term whites, might with equal propriety have been included in the other class; since they exhibited very conclusive marks of their affinity to the sable race.

At the present time Portugal derives no pecuniary advantage whatever from her possessions on the eastern coast of Africa, and there is no probability that they will ever again become a source of profit to her, though to individuals they may afford the means of immense wealth, as they have done heretofore, as well as yielded a profit to the government. But benefit in another way is derived from them, which is probably considered by the monster of cruelty who at present rules Portugal with a rod of iron, of equal importance to the greatest pecuniary profit; and that is from their serving as places of banishment for all those who happen to fall under his suspicion. Mozambique was the principal place of exile for those unfortunate individuals, whose patriotism had led them to express sentiments in favour of their suffering country; and many have arrived there since the savage Miguel commenced his reign. Some of these were seen by our officers, to whom they related their calamities, and the causes which had led to them, in the most pathetic terms.

The climate of Mozambique is unhealthy at all times, but it is particularly so at the change of the monsoons in the spring & fall. What the diseases are which prevail there, I did not learn from any medical authority; but they are probably remittent fever and dysentery. At the time of our visit, which was after the N.E. monsoon had set in, the weather was pleasant, and the place quite healthy. During our stay, there was a regular sea and land breeze in the harbour; the former blowing from the N.E. to S.E. through the day, and the latter from W. & S.W. through the night. The thermometer never rose higher than 84, which to us was a very comfortable temperature, after the intense heat of Mocha & Muscat. I have already observed that the bazars or markets of Mozambique were very scantily supplied with provisions; and

[The remainder of Dr. Benajah Ticknor's journal of the voyage of the USS *Peacock* has not survived. On December 5, 1833, the *Peacock* arrived in Cape Town, South Africa, for a stay of several weeks. Leaving Cape Town on December 21, the ship had an uneventful crossing of the Atlantic and arrived in Rio de Janeiro on January 17, 1834, followed 2 days later by the USS *Boxer*. It was not until April 10 that the *Peacock* was released from the Brazilian Squadron and allowed at last to sail the final leg of the voyage. In New York harbor on the afternoon of May 25, 1834, Dr. Benajah Ticknor reached the end of his journey of 42,150 miles, 412 days at sea, and two years, two months, and 17 days away from home.]

Notes

Introduction

1. Benajah Ticknor to Elisha Whittlesey, December 31, 1831, Elisha Whittlesey Papers, Western Reserve Historical Society, Cleveland, Ohio.
2. Levi Woodbury to E. Whittlesey, January 7, 1832; B. Ticknor to E. Whittlesey, January 14, 1832, and March 2, 1832, Whittlesey Papers.
3. From a letter of Norman Ticknor (Benajah Ticknor's brother), March 18, 1869, quoted in *Old Times in Windham* (Windham, N.Y.: Hope Farm Press, 1970).
4. B. Ticknor to E. Whittlesey, August 29, 1818, Whittlesey Papers.
5. Journal I, 10, Benajah Ticknor Papers, Manuscripts and Archives, Yale University Library, New Haven, Connecticut.
6. B. Ticknor to E. Whittlesey, October 11, 1834, Whittlesey Papers.
7. B. Ticknor to Edmund Roberts, May 31, 1834, Edmund Roberts Papers, New Hampshire Historical Society, Concord, New Hampshire.
8. B. Ticknor to E. Whittlesey, December 24, 1835, Whittlesey Papers.
9. Ibid.
10. J. N. Reynolds to Amasa J. Parker, September 4, 1836, Edmund Roberts Papers, Manuscripts Division, Library of Congress.
11. Included among a group of quotations in Memorandum Book, 1832, Roberts Papers, Library of Congress.

Chapter I

1. The USS *Peacock,* entered on the naval register as a "rebuilt" ship, was actually a new ship laid down in the New York Navy Yard in 1828 to replace the first USS *Peacock,* an aging survivor of the War of 1812. The *Peacock,* a sloop of 559 tons, 118' long with beam 31'6", carried twenty-four guns. After a maiden voyage in the Caribbean, the *Peacock* was now beginning its first major cruise. In 1835, the *Peacock* made its second voyage to the Far East when Edmund Roberts returned the ratified treaties to Muscat and Siam. She was sunk in 1841 while on the Wilkes Expedition (Howard I. Chapelle, *The History of the American Sailing Navy* [New York: W. W. Norton and Co., 1949], 356–58).

2. Commander David Geisinger (1790–1860), born in Maryland, was appointed a midshipman in the U.S. Navy in 1809. He had distinguished service during the War of 1812 and rose to lieutenant by the end of 1814. He was appointed commander on March 11, 1829. After the voyage of the USS *Peacock,* he continued his career in the navy and became captain in 1838. For several years he commanded the Naval Asylum in Philadelphia, the school for midshipmen that preceded the Naval Academy. From 1855 until his death, he was on the reserve list of officers (*Appleton's Cyclopaedia of American Biography* [New York: Appleton and Co., 1887], 2:623).

3. The ward room was the messroom assigned to officers in a warship. It also served as the center of off-duty social life for all officers under the rank of the commanding officer.

4. Francis Baylies, a former congressman from Taunton, Massachusetts, had been appointed by President Andrew Jackson to negotiate a settlement with Argentina over its seizure of three American seal-fishing vessels in the Falkland Islands in 1831.

5. Evidently Ticknor's initial diagnosis was wrong. When he revised his journal, he pointed out that the sea "was sufficiently rough to cause Mr. Baylies a fall that fractured one or two of his ribs, & consequently occasioned him considerable suffering" (Revised Journal II, 5, Ticknor Papers).

6. Francis Baylies, *An Historical Memoir of the Colony of New Plymouth* (Boston: Hillard, Gray, Little and Wilkins, 1830), 2 vols.

7. In a letter from Port Praya, Edmund Roberts assures his daughters that the crew is mindful of religious duty "and every Sabbath all the crew have been mustered on the quarter-deck, dressed neat & clean, and prayers and the Scriptures have been read by our excellent Surgeon, Dr. Ticknor, a very worthy man and a good Christian, and a very strict Episcopalian" (E. Roberts to his children, April 12, 1832, Roberts Papers, Library of Congress).

8. Don Miguel, the younger son of John VI of Portugal, had usurped the throne of Portugal in 1828, while the heir, his older brother, Don Pedro (Pedro I of Brazil), was still in Brazil. A war ensued between Miguel, representing the forces of absolute monarchists, and Pedro, who had favored a more liberal government upon his accession to the throne in 1826. While Ticknor was at Port Praya, Don Pedro was in the Azores organizing a fleet and army to invade Portugal to overthrow Miguel (H. V. Livermore, *A New History of Portugal* [Cambridge: Cambridge University Press, 1967], 258–79).

9. When recopying his journal four years later, Ticknor omitted his rather unsophisticated objection to the waltz.

10. Ticknor is probably describing trachoma, a serious eye disease endemic in Africa and the Middle East in the nineteenth century.

11. Bilious fever was a medical description of a severe fever accompanied by vomiting and diarrhea. It could apply to any number of undifferentiated tropical diseases such as malaria, hepatitis, or amoebic dysentery. Ticknor's reasoning is an example of the miasmatic theory of disease which dominated medical thinking before advances in bacteriology later in the nineteenth century established the germ theory of disease.

12. On April 9, 1832, Commander Geisinger donated from the ship's stores one barrel of beef, two barrels of pork, and one each of bread and rice to the starving inhabitants of Fogo (David Geisinger, Notes of a Cruise on board the United States Ship Peacock, David Geisinger Papers, MS. 1283, Maryland Historical Society, Baltimore, Maryland).

Chapter II

1. During the ceremony, crew members disguised as King Neptune and his court ruled the ship and put all uninitiated personnel, including the officers and important passengers, through merry and often embarrassing rites. Much drinking ensued, and this probably caused Ticknor's distaste for the ceremony.

2. Ticknor probably read a sermon by Joseph Stevens Buckminister, a brilliant young Unitarian clergyman of Boston who died in 1812 at the age of twenty-eight. His writing was available in *Sermons by the late Rev. Joseph S. Buckminister, with a memoir of his life & character* (Boston: Wells, 1821).

3. The dispute between Argentina and the United States resulted from the seizure of three American vessels by Louis Vernet, Argentinian governor of the Falklands, in July, 1831. The original dispute became a serious disturbance in December, 1831, when Commander Silas Duncan of the USS *Lexington*, encouraged by the American consul George W. Slacum, but without U.S. government authority, sailed to the Falklands to investigate. Duncan accused the Argentinians of piracy, sacked their settlement, and brought seven Argentinians back to Montevideo in chains aboard the *Lexington* (Julius Goebel, Jr., *The Struggle for the Falkland Islands* [1917; reprint, Port Washington, N.Y.: Kennikat Press, 1971], 435–55).

4. Commodore George W. Rodgers commanded the Brazilian Squadron, the permanent American naval group stationed off the coast of South America to protect American merchant ships from pirates. Although on a special mission, the USS *Peacock* was still subject to Rodgers's authority in these waters.

5. Wright may have been fired in a dispute over his pay. He had written Edward Livingston, secretary of state, to protest "the mode of settling his account, as adopted by the auditor of the Controller." When his commission was later annulled by the U.S. chargé d'affaires and his nephew Robert Clinton Wright appointed temporary consul, Wright whipped off another letter to Livingston, disputing the fact that he had been judged to have a "troublesome disposition" (William Wright to Edward Livingston, September 12, 1831 and January 18, 1832, Department of State, Despatches from United States Consuls in Rio de Janeiro, Brazil, 1811–1906, RG 59, T 172, roll 5, National Archives [NA], Washington, D.C.).

6. Charles Darwin was living in a cottage here in May and June of 1832, collecting animal specimens on walks similar to those that Ticknor and his friends took. He was equally excited about the beauty of the bay and as a naturalist so overwhelmed by the abundance of new specimens, he was "scarcely able to walk at all" (*Journal of Researches into the Natural History and Geology of the Countries visited During the Voyage of H.M.S. Beagle Round the World* [New York: Harper and Brothers, 1846], 1:33).

7. Ticknor had first visited the Botanic Garden in 1821. In contrast to Edmund

Roberts's enthusiastic remarks about their visit to the garden in *Embassy* (24–25), Ticknor was more circumspect. On his first visit he was disappointed to find not the world's largest collection of "Oriental exotics" (as he had been told), but rather a limited collection of trees and shrubs from China and the East Indies, which caused him to dismiss the Botanic Garden as "only the King's Pleasure-garden, and as such, it was well worth a stranger's attention" (Journal I, 172, Ticknor Papers). Darwin was equally blunt in his diary by saying that the name Botanic Garden "must be given more out of courtesy than anything else; for it really is solely a place of amusement" (Nora Barlow, ed., *Charles Darwin's Diary of the Voyage of H.M.S. "Beagle"* [New York: Macmillan Co., 1932], 64).

8. Ticknor is probably referring to Bishop José Caetano da Silva-Coutinho (Robert Walsh, *Notices of Brazil in 1828 and 1829* [London: Frederick Westley and A. H. Davis, 1830], 1:367).

9. Don Pedro became emperor of Brazil in a bloodless revolution in 1822 and was forced to abdicate by the Brazilians on April 7, 1831. A contemporary account of this period in Brazilian history attributes Don Pedro's abdication to "his never having known how to become the MAN OF HIS PEOPLE,—in his never having constituted himself entirely and truly a Brazilian" (John Armitage, *The History of Brazil, from the Period of the Arrival of the Braganza Family in 1808 to the Abdication of Don Pedro the first in 1831* [London: Smith, Elder and Co., 1836], 104–5).

10. This same Dr. Coates is the principal source of a lengthy description of medical education and types of disease prevalent in Brazil in 1829, in Walsh, *Notices of Brazil* 1:391–417.

11. Another stranger noticed the corpulence of shopkeepers in Rio de Janeiro and attributed it to elephantiasis. Ticknor was familiar enough with this tropical disease to have remarked on it if he had observed it (ibid., 1:411).

12. American merchants in Brazil complained of increased port and custom regulations as well as the collection of duties on vessels that stopped only for protection from bad weather. The U.S. government had recognized Don Miguel's government in Portugal in 1829, which greatly offended Emperor Pedro I and the Brazilians and affected relations between the countries for several years. The abdication of Pedro I in 1831 did not solve the trade problems, and the revolutionary upheaval during the 1830s contributed further to the strained commercial relations between the United States and Brazil (Lawrence F. Hill, *Diplomatic Relations between the United States and Brazil* [Durham: Duke University Press, 1932], 72–85).

13. When Pedro I abdicated in 1831 in favor of his five-year-old son, Pedro II, a regency of three men was established. During the power struggle to control the young emperor in early 1832, José Bonifacio Andrada e Silva, the leader of the 1822 revolution in Brazil and tutor to the royal children, and his brother, Antonio Carlos de Andrada, who presided in the House of Delegates, led the opposition to the permanent three-man regency (Daniel Parish Kidder, *Sketches of Residence and Travels in Brazil, Embracing Historical and Geographical Notices of the Empire and its Several Provinces* [Philadelphia: Sorin and Ball, 1845], 1:60–61).

14. On April 3, 1832, a revolt of troops, first at Forts Santa Cruz, Villegagnon, and later in the city of Rio de Janeiro, was successfully put down (ibid., 61).

15. A semaphore telegraph was a hand-operated system of signaling that used signal arms or flags.

16. This geographic feature was named after Vicount Hood (Samuel Hood, 1724–1816), admiral in the British navy, who had been a renowned naval officer during the American Revolution and the Napoleonic Wars.

17. Copaiba balsam is an aromatic, acrid resin obtained from several species of South American shrubs of the genus *Copaifera*. It was used as a stimulant or diuretic in medicine.

18. On November 16, 1768, during his first voyage of exploration, Captain James Cook anchored the *Endeavour* off the Isle of Cobras. Forbidden by a suspicious Portuguese viceroy to go ashore to carry out repairs, Cook was forced to careen his vessel with all crew and passengers aboard. Evidently ropes attached to iron rings in the rock aided in heeling the ship (J. C. Beaglehole, ed., *The Journals of Captain James Cook on his Voyages of Discovery* [Cambridge: Hakluyt Society, 1955], 1:24).

Chapter III

1. Edmund Roberts remembered a different ship. "As we passed the British line of battle ship Plantagenet, the band of musicians struck up our national air of 'Hail Columbia'" (*Embassy*, 24–25).

2. The HMS *Beagle*, commanded by Captain Robert FitzRoy, was on a surveying expedition along the coasts of South America and in the Pacific from 1831 to 1836. Young Charles Darwin, a civilian, was employed as the expedition's naturalist.

3. Napoleon escaped from Elba on the French brig *Inconstant* on February 26, 1815.

4. Ticknor had lived in Canfield, Ohio, before entering the navy and was related by marriage to the Canfield family. He wrote from Montevideo to his friend Elisha Whittlesey in Canfield about this chance meeting of an old acquaintance (B. Ticknor to E. Whittlesey, June 22, 1832, Whittlesey Papers).

5. Dr. Joshua Bond was the American consul at Montevideo. He was living temporarily in Buenos Aires during the Falkland Islands incident.

6. Roberts took the view that the dispute between the United States and Argentina arose out of the unlawful seizure of American vessels by Vernet and "from the proper and spirited conduct of Captain Duncan, commander of the Lexington, in removing the colony to Montevideo, and thereby, most effectually cutting off all further depredations upon our commerce" (*Embassy*, 25).

7. Ticknor is hinting that Francis Baylies will be overly influenced by the former American consul George W. Slacum. (Slacum had angered the Argentinian government and been dismissed as American consul because of his role in sending the *Lexington* to the Falkland Islands.) He may or may not have been aware that Slacum and Dr. Joshua Bond were engaged in a bitter feud. This feud stemmed from Bond's siding with Rodgers on the decision to release the prisoners. Ten days after Rodgers's death, Slacum and Bond quarreled further over the Falklands dispute. When Slacum found out that Bond had applied for his job, he called Bond "a damned rascal." With this, Bond challenged Slacum to a duel. On the morning of the duel, Bond and his second were arrested. Slacum escaped and hid out with

Francis Baylies until he could leave for the United States (Dr. Joshua Bond to Capt. Edgar S. Hawkins, October 8, 1832, Department of State, Despatches from United States Consuls in Buenos Aires, Argentina, RG 59, M 70, roll 5, NA).

8. Evidently Geisinger did not share this view. In 1836, when petitioning the secretary of the navy for payment of unforeseen expenses incurred on the voyage of the *Peacock*, he complained of the "very great deprivation of the usual personal comforts & conveniences of a naval commander in taking out Mr. Baylies, & his family to Buenos Ayres, by being thrown out of my Cabin for 3 months & having to sleep on the Gun Deck...." (D. Geisinger to M. Dickerson, April 21, 1836, Geisinger Papers, MS. 1283).

9. John C. Zimmermann, a U.S. merchant of German origin, was the leading partner in Zimmermann, Frazier and Co.

10. The USS *Boxer*, commanded by Lt. Commander William R. Shields, was ordered to accompany the *Peacock* to the East Indies. The schooner was to carry the gifts for the monarchs of Cochin China, Siam, and Muscat and to serve as a faster, lighter ship for carrying the American diplomatic mission directly into Hué and Bangkok. Because of delays in assembling the gifts in New York and damage to the hull of the ship in Rio de Janeiro, the *Boxer* was still far behind schedule at this point.

11. War was almost continuous in Argentina after the revolution of May, 1810, which freed the provinces of the Rio del la Plata (essentially Buenos Aires and surrounding territory) from Spain. In the war of Banda Oriental, 1810–14, Argentina drove the Spanish out of Montevideo. From 1814 to 1824, Argentina was involved in war against Spain in Upper Peru; this war achieved the independence of Peru, Chile, and Bolivia. From 1825 to 1828, Argentina fought Brazil over possession of Uruguay and finally had to agree to the independence of Uruguay. Disputes within Argentina during the 1820s resulted in civil war, which ended in 1829 when Juan Manuel Rosas became governor of Buenos Aires and started a dictatorship that continued until 1852 (F. A. Kirkpatrick, *A History of the Argentine Republic* [Cambridge: Cambridge University Press, 1931]).

12. This incident marks the beginning of the estrangement between Ticknor and Geisinger that becomes more noticeable as the voyage continues.

13. Edmund Roberts, who had lived in Buenos Aires years before, remarked on the melancholy changes in life brought about by the loss of friends during the many revolutions.

> The splendid churches were shorn of their ornaments and a few solitary priests, superannuated and on the brink of the grave, were seen tottering through the deserted aisles and cloisters, where hundreds had once been, and where the resounding of my own footsteps now made me start, and look back to see if any of the departed had returned to wander within their former haunts, and deplore, though they were wont to be called holy, their numerouse imperfections. (*Embassy,* 27)

14. A letter from Buenos Aires described a great dust storm of February 10, 1832: "After eleven minutes and a half, the rain began to fall in very large black

drops, which had the effect upon the white walls of making them appear, when the sun again showed itself, as if they had been stained or sprinkled with ink" (quoted in Woodbine Parrish, *Buenos Ayres and the Provinces of Rio de la Plata,* 2d. ed [London: John Murray, 1852], 127–28).

15. Elephantiasis is a tropical disease caused by filariae (parasitic worms). It is characterized by extreme swelling of the legs and rough, thickened, elephantlike skin on the affected limbs. The swelling stems from the parasite's invasion and blockage of the lymphatic glands, but this was not known before 1877. Ticknor's diagnosis of dropsy or edema of the lower limbs caused by too much to drink (acute alcoholism) could have been correct since advanced cirrhosis of the liver causes swelling of the feet and legs.

16. Edmund Roberts likened Montevideo to "a vast cemetery; . . . I therefore left it, better satisfied to wander ten thousand miles over a trackless and stormy ocean, than to remain in a city whose former inhabitants were spread in dust amid its ruins" (*Embassy,* 27).

17. Another traveler was more precise in describing "the most disgusting of all sights." The cattle were let out of a corral two or three at a time, then lassoed, and a man on foot cut the ham strings of the cows. Their throats were then cut, and the animals bled to death. They were skinned and cut up on the spot, with meat heaped up in carts and taken away, "many choice bits falling from the carts unheeded by the way" (Peter Campbell Scarlett, *South America and the Pacific; comprising a Journey across the Pampas and the Andes, from Buenos Ayres to Valparaiso, Lima, and Panama* [London: Henry Colburn, 1838], 1:87–93). Charles Darwin had a similar reaction, describing the scene as "horrible and revolting: the ground is almost made of bones and the horses and riders are drenched with gore" (*Journal of Researches* 1:156).

18. This incident happened when Sir George Macartney, Britain's first ambassador to China, stopped at Tristan da Cunha on December 31, 1792, on his way to China.

Chapter IV

1. During the Napoleonic Wars, the British and Dutch fought over the East Indies. The British, under Sir Thomas Stamford Raffles, controlled Java from 1811 to 1814, when it was returned to Holland during the Congress of Vienna. Raffles moved to the English enclave in Bencoolen in West Sumatra and attempted to extend English rule over the whole island. After Raffles took Singapore in 1819, and its advantages as a center of trade for the Indies became known, British policy changed. In a treaty between the English and Dutch in 1824, the Dutch agreed to an exchange: the Malay peninsula and Singapore became English possessions and all English settlements in West Sumatra became Dutch (Louis Fischer, *The Story of Indonesia* [New York: Harper and Brothers, 1959], 19–36).

2. Ticknor is making a comparison to the American habit of abusing alcohol.

3. Roberts refers to her as the mother of the rajah and is even more shocked than Ticknor. Comparing his horror at seeing her to Macbeth's upon seeing Banquo's ghost, Roberts painted a detailed picture of wretchedness:

...her gray elf-locks scattered by the wind—her eyes running with rheum—her face and hands covered with dirt—her body loathsome with leprous spots; contrasted with her dark Malay skin, gave her a truly hideous appearance; added to this, a solitary long black tooth projected over her under lip, and her trembling and attenuated frame displayed the influence of that baneful narcotic, opium, to which she was addicted. (*Embassy*, 33)

4. The quicklime, known by its Hindustani name, *chunam*, is an aid in the release of the narcotic effect of the areca nut when the combination of leaf, nut, and lime is chewed. The repeated use of quicklime caused the excoriating effect on the mouth that Ticknor described.

5. In his account of the visit to the resident, Roberts makes no mention of any other officers accompanying him and Commander Geisinger (*Embassy*, 32–38).

6. The first Lancastrian school was established at Bencoolen by Sir Thomas Stamford Raffles in 1819. This system of education had been started in 1801 by Joseph Lancaster (1788–1838), an English Quaker, in a London school for poor boys. Being too poor to hire assistants, Lancaster devised a method for older students to teach younger ones. Discipline was maintained by rewarding children with badges of merit rather than using excessive corporal punishment. He improvised school materials and developed a rote system of learning mathematics. He believed in a Christian but nonsectarian education. Lancaster's ideas, spread by his writing, became extremely popular in England and America (Sophia Hull Raffles, *Memoir of the Life and Public Services of Sir Thomas Stamford Raffles* [London: James Duncan, 1835], 2:62); *Dictionary of National Biography* [Oxford: Oxford University Press, 1967], 11:480–81).

7. "The translation was made and published, many years since, at the expense of the pious and well-known philanthropist, Robert Boyle, when the place was under the jurisdiction of the British Government...." (Roberts, *Embassy*, 36).

8. The resident was Thomas Parr, who was assassinated in 1807. His secretary was Charles Murray. Parr, sent from Bengal by the East India Company to govern Bencoolen, had upset the local chiefs by reforming the administration of justice without consulting them and by forcing the natives to cultivate both coffee and pepper exclusively for the Company. Angered by his contemptible manner toward them and his horsewhipping of the son of a local chief, the Sumatrans plotted to kill him. Parr ignored all warnings and continued to live at his estate three miles outside of Bencoolen. In the middle of the night, the assassins entered Parr's bedroom to seize and behead him. Mrs. Parr tried to defend him with her body and caught the blade of the sword, severing most of her fingers. Murray rushed to their aid and was wounded. Afterwards the murderers left, stealing nothing and making no further attempt to kill Parr's wife or Murray. Murray subsequently died of his wound (C. J. Brooks, "English Tombs and Monuments in Bencoolen," *Journal of the Straits Branch of the Royal Asiatic Society*, no. 78 [June, 1918]: 51–53; John Bastin, ed., "Journal of Thomas Otho Travers 1813–1820," *Memoirs of the Raffles Museum*, no. 4 [1957]: 102).

9. When the *Peacock* first arrived in Bencoolen, Lt. Sinclair brought word from the Resident that Downes had been successful at Kuala Batu.

> By this boat we heard of the entire destruction of Qualah Battu, by the Potomac, which happily precluded the necessity of an unpleasant visit, and saved the officers and crew the painful duty which would otherwise have devolved on the Peacock. The demolition of this place struck terror into the inhabitants of all the native ports on the coast, and will doubtless produce a salutary effect. (Roberts, *Embassy,* 32)

10. The *Potomac,* disguised as a Danish merchant ship seeking to trade opium for pepper, had entered the harbor of Kuala Batu on February 5, 1832. Convinced by tales he had heard from the British at the Cape of Good Hope that no reparations would be forthcoming, Downes deviated from his explicit instructions to enter the port, make an inquiry, and then demand reparations. Only if the town refused to produce the murderers of the crew of the *Friendship* or give an indemnity for the stolen property was he free to attack the forts and burn the town. Before dawn the next morning, Downes sent a force of 282 marines and navy men to beseige the forts and demand the surrender of the native chiefs. When the surprised Sumatrans fought back, the marines killed everyone in the forts including women who fought beside their men. The town was then bombarded out of existence. Two Americans were killed and nine wounded (James W. Gould, "Sumatra—America's Pepperpot, 1784–1873," pt. 2, *Essex Institute Historical Collections,* 92, no. 3 [July, 1956]: 229–35; Francis Warriner, *Cruise of the United States Frigate Potomac Round the World during the Years 1831–1834* [New York: Leavitt, Lord and Co., 1835], 65–91).

11. Ticknor was genuinely shocked at the attack on Kuala Batu and the great loss of life. When he revised this journal, he included this paragraph almost word for word. The contrast is most marked when compared with his censorship (by deletion) of his opinion of Commander Silas Duncan's role in the Falkland Islands incident in chapter III. Ticknor, of course, could not know in August, 1832, that much similar criticism of Downes's action would appear in the American press and in Congress (Gould, "Sumatra," 236–37).

12. The training of Eurasians to work as clerks for the East India Company or to hold posts in the government of Bencoolen was well established by the British during the eighteenth century. The Dutch only continued schools which had been started earlier by Sir Thomas Stamford Raffles (John Bastin, *Essays on Indonesian and Malayan History* [Singapore: Donald Moore Books, 1965], 154).

13. When he revised Journal II, Ticknor inserted the following correction:

> Subsequent information, however, which could not be discredited, showed that I had judged too favourably. It happened, as we were informed, that the Resident had occasion, not long after we left, to visit a settlement of the natives at some distance from Bencoolen; & while there he made use of the authority which he was enabled to exercise, to order the men on some duty at a distance from their homes, & in

their absence took improper liberties with their wives & daughters. This led to measures of revenge, the result of which I have never learned. (Revised Journal II, 83, Ticknor Papers)

Roberts, citing the same offense, gave more explicit detail of Knoerle's fate. On a journey to Palembang, Knoerle was murdered for revenge "at the instigation of some of the principal rajahs of Bencoolen. His body was literally cut in pieces, and then burnt with great exultation, by the perpetrators and their friends" (*Embassy*, 37–38).

14. Knoerle may have been inclined to boast unduly about his fearlessness. Another white man, Captain R. Salmond, gave an account of an earlier crossing in 1818: "Thus we reached Palembang in twelve days from leaving Bencoolen, being the first Europeans who had crossed the island in any direction." They found less difficulties than expected and were not menaced by the natives at all ("Diary of a Journey across the Island of Sumatra, from Fort Marlborough to Palembang, in 1818," *Memoirs of the Raffles Museum*, no.4 [1957], app. 1, 166).

15. The price of pepper had reached a high of $10.75 a picul in 1823, but had steadily declined to less than a third of that price by 1829. The result of oversupply and declining prices in both Europe and America proved disastrous for the pepper trade (Gould, "Sumatra," pt. 2, 228–31).

16. Ticknor may have taken the lax morals of a port for the attitude of all Sumatran parents toward the chastity of their daughters. William Marsden, an authority on Sumatra, insisted that the chastity of daughters was more zealously guarded among the Malay people than anywhere else because an unsullied daughter represented the chief means of making a prosperous match. Prostitution of daughters was chiefly seen in seaports where sailors and other less scrupulous Malays came together. "From the scenes which these seaports present, travellers too commonly form their judgment, and imprudently take upon them to draw, for the information of the world, a picture of the manners of a people" (*The History of Sumatra*, 3d. ed. [London: J. McCreery, 1811], 261).

17. The *Boxer*, carrying twenty-four boxes of gifts, did not even leave Rio de Janeiro until late October, 1832. Through delays in forwarding, a shipment of rifles and muskets intended as gifts was sent from Philadelphia to Canton via the merchant ship *Eliza* in November, 1832 (John M. Baker to Edward Livingston, November 1, 1832, Department of State, Despatches from U.S. Consuls in Rio de Janeiro, 1831–35, RG 59, T 172, roll 5, NA; W. C. H. Waddell to E. Livingston, November 27, 1832, Records of the Department of State, Communications From Special Agents, 1794–1906, RG 59, M 37, roll 10, NA).

18. Roberts described their visit to Forsaken Island, evidently the unnamed island northwest of Crockatoa [Krakatau]. Hearing a sound resembling a waterfall, they were sure that they had discovered water only to be disappointed to find that the sound came from the singing of locusts (*Embassy*, 39).

19. Crockatoa is the island which virtually disappeared in a great volcanic explosion in 1883.

20. Roberts explained in detail what was routine to Ticknor.

Immediately all hands were piped to quarters—the battle-lanterns lit, fore and aft—the gun-deck cleared of hammocks—the two-and-thirties loaded with round and grape shot, and runout—the slow matches lighted and placed in their tubs—the marines ranged along the quarter-deck, and the powder boys stationed from the magazine to the gun-deck—the surgeons in the cockpit were displaying a fearful array of bandages; and in five minutes the ship was ready for action. (*Embassy*, 41)

21. Ticknor may be referring to the ballet that was traditionally a part of Italian opera. While in Rio de Janeiro in 1821, he attended the theatre and saw "in imitation of the Italian stage . . . a species of dancing, at which the innate modesty of a wild native of the forest, would have blushed with shame." He was horrified by the sight of young girls, dressed in tutus and tights, leaping and pirouetting across the stage. He never thereafter referred to Italian opera with anything but disgust (Journal I, 265–68, Ticknor Papers).

22. Ticknor is describing the Javanese gamelan.

23. Lt. Colonel Charles Cathcart, quartermaster general of the British army in India, was the first British envoy to be sent to the emperor of China. He died on his way to the East, off the coast of Java, and was buried in Anjer on June 10, 1788.

24. Ticknor's footnote refers to Aeneas Anderson, *A Narrative of the British Embassy to China in the years 1792, 1793, and 1794*, 2d ed. (London: J. Debrett, 1795), v, 71. Evidently Ticknor used this book while writing his journal, and misread Anderson's account of Lord George Macartney's stop at Anjer to view this grave. Ticknor thought Lt. Col. Cathcart was accompanying his brother, Sir William Schaw Cathcart, to China; Anderson, however, had merely inserted "brother to Lord Cathcart" as a means of identifying Lt. Col. Cathcart to his readers.

25. Another visitor to Anjer in 1832 observed: "The Javanese, indeed, are so far from being rigid Mahommedans, . . . there is considerable difficulty in discovering whether they have any religion at all" (George Windsor Earl, *The Eastern Seas or Voyages and Adventures in the Indian Archipelago in 1832-33-34* [London: W. H. Allen and Co., 1837], 69).

26. James Horsburgh was hydrographer of the East India Company and the leading British navigational authority on sailing to the East Indies and China.

Chapter V

1. Roberts evidently had scenes of this nature in mind when, after his return in 1834, he sent suggestions to the secretary of state for a second mission to Cochin China and Asia. He concludes that the last and most important point is the selection of the commander of the Naval ship.

He must be a gentleman in the strictest sense of the word—a sober — discreet & moral man — of a good disposition . . . nor a Drunkard nor a quarrelsome man — he should be a good navigator & a strict disci-

plinarian — The Agent or Envoy should have his rights defined, settled
& acknowledg'd by the Commander before leaving the U. States — He
should be unquestionably entitled to one half the Cabin . . . it is quite
time this point was clearly & distinctly & unequivocally settled — for
the Agent is frequently & in the most insulting manner told he is
admitted there by sufference.

Geisinger voiced his own complaints when he petitioned for additional pay because
of the inconvenience of sharing his cabin with Roberts during the two-year voyage
(Edmund Roberts to secretary of state, July 3, 1834, Records of the Department of
State, Communications from Special Agents, 1794–1906, RG 59, M 37, roll 10, NA;
Geisinger to Dickerson, April 21, 1836, Geisinger Papers, MS. 1283).

2. Henry Parkman Sturgis (1806–69) of Russell, Sturgis and Co., the leading
American mercantile house in Manila, was the nephew of James Perkins Sturgis of
Canton. His assistant, Josiah Moore, was later American consul in Manila.

3. Francis Warriner, an eyewitness to the attack of the *Potomac* at Kuala Batu
and a staunch defender of Commander Downes, pointed out that if American traders
had treated the Sumatrans fairly, the president would never have had to send a frigate
to chastise them. He excused the officers of the *Friendship* from this charge, but
pointed out that the natives had been "robbed and cheated in by-gone days" and
over time "the vials of wrath were poured out upon the heads of the unfortunate
crew of the Friendship" (*Cruise of the Potomac,* 97–98). The Americans cheated the
natives by using false weights and justified doing so by claiming that they were
making up for the Sumatrans' adulteration of the pepper with sand or stones (Gould,
"Sumatra," pt. 2, 230–31).

4. There is no evidence that the American force surrounding the forts at Kuala
Batu made any effort before attacking to find out the murderers of the crew of the
Friendship or to demand reparations. The order was to capture the rajahs first and
talk afterwards about who was guilty of attacking the ship (Gould, "Sumatra," pt.2,
235; Warriner, *Cruise of the Potomac,* 81–92; Jeremiah N. Reynolds, *Voyage of the
United States Frigate Potomac in the years 1831, 1832, 1833, and 1834* [New York:
Harper and Brothers, 1835], 105–20).

5. The effect was only temporary. There was an attack by Sumatrans on an
American brig, *Leander,* in 1833, and another vessel was taken in 1839 (Gould,
"Sumatra," pt. 2, 235–36).

6. The imperial commissioner of Canton ordered the *Potomac* to leave upon
discovery that she was a warship. Jeremiah Reynolds noted: "This order is always
made to every armed vessel, though not the least attention is paid to the mandate
of his celestial majesty's commissioner" (*Voyage of the Potomac,* 344). In 1819, the
Chinese had issued a similar order to the first U.S. naval vessel to visit Canton.
Nervous American traders had urged the captain of the *Congress* to comply. By the
time the USS *Vincennes* paid a visit to Macao in 1830, American merchants were
eager to have periodic visits from U.S. men-of-war to remind Chinese pirates and
petty bureaucrats of the consequences of interfering with American trade (Charles
O. Paullin, *American Voyages to the Orient, 1690-1865* [Annapolis, Md.: United
States Naval Institute, 1971], 32).

7. Ticknor's acceptance of this point of view was surprising in light of his Protestant background. His view, however, was that of other contemporary writers. One exception was Lt. Charles Wilkes, who did not agree that Spain had been able to maintain its ascendency over the other tribes by religion alone. It was "more easily accounted for, from the Spaniards fostering and keeping alive the jealousy and hatred that existed at the time of the discovery between the different tribes" (Charles Wilkes, *Narrative of the United States Exploring Expedition during the years 1838, 1839, 1840, 1841, 1842* [Philadelphia: C. Sherman, 1844], 5:311).

8. Charles S. Stewart, *Journal of a Residence in the Sandwich Islands, during the years 1823, 1824, & 1825*, 2d ed. (New York: John P. Haven, 1828). This is a highly laudatory book about the work of the American Protestant missionaries in the Hawaiian Islands, written by one of the missionaries.

9. Ticknor is referring to the feud between Jones, a wealthy American merchant in Hawaii, who acted as American consul from 1820 to 1838, and the Protestant missionaries of the American Board of Commissioners for Foreign Missions. The missionaries had introduced strict morals as well as education into a society once willing to trade its women and commodities like sandalwood for a few trinkets or alcohol. Through education and influence, the missionaries persuaded the Hawaiian royal family to enact laws that ended the licentious life-style of seamen and native women and caused interference in the heretofore unrestricted trade. Jones and his fellow merchants sided with the traders (such as McDonald) in the belief that the missionaries were telling the Hawaiians that the traders were cheating them. After 1826, because of his feud with the missionaries, Jones became embroiled in political conflict with the rulers of Hawaii. He was so preoccupied with trade that he often ignored his consular duties of protecting the rights of American seamen. When Captain W. C. B. Finch visited Hawaii in 1829 and encountered the quarrels between American merchants and missionaries, he concluded that the American government should send to the islands "salaried consuls, or a chargé des Affaires . . . restricting them from all participation in business," since while the consuls continue to be merchants, "their influence is comparatively small or nothing." This opinion was quoted in Charles S. Stewart's second book, *A Visit to the South Seas, in the U.S. Ship Vincennes, During the Years 1829 and 1830* (New York: John P. Haven, 1831), 2:276. This mild criticism of a merchant-consul caused McDonald to accuse Stewart and Finch of "ill treatment of Mr. Jones." However, neither Stewart nor Finch attack Jones overtly in the book. See also Harold Whitman Bradley, *The American Frontier in Hawaii* (Stanford: Stanford University Press, 1942), 89–93; W. Patrick Strauss, "Pioneer American Diplomats in Polynesia, 1820–1840," *Pacific Historical Review* 31 (February, 1962): 21–22.

10. When Ticknor revised his journal, he inserted a footnote on McDonald's veracity. "Of this man I afterwards heard such unfavourable reports in Siam, that I consider his statements & assertions as not entitled to belief" (Revised Journal II, 116, Ticknor Papers).

11. When the *Potomac* arrived in Hawaii in August, 1832, Francis Warriner found himself a witness as merchants and missionaries paraded their opposing points of view before Commander John Downes. Warriner, sympathetic to the missionaries, summed up the underlying conflict: "The foreign residents oppose the gospel because

it teaches the natives better to understand their rights, and prevents their being so easily imposed upon" (*Cruise of the Potomac*, 242).

12. This letter evidently was not sent to the Navy Department since no copy of it can be found in "Letters Received by the Secretary of the Navy From Commanders, 1804–86" (RG 45, M 147, NA), and other miscellaneous naval records. Ticknor noted in his revised journal that the letter "though ill-received, & the cause of very unjustifiable conduct on the part of the Capt. produced, nevertheless, the desired effect; for the crew did not go ashore on liberty, & the ship was ordered to be got ready to leave the port as soon as possible" (Revised Journal II, 121, Ticknor Papers).

13. Ticknor is describing the conservative treatment for cholera, used by most physicians in 1832. He administered laudanum (opium) to quiet the bowels and stem diarrhea. Cajeput oil was used as an antispasmodic and a copious quantity of brandy was given as a stimulant. Morphine sulphate was the standard painkiller; ammonium carbonate was a stimulant; and camphor combined with tincture of opium (paregoric) was a sedative. As a further aid to stop the spasms, the physician kept the patient warm by rubbing the limbs with volatile liniments such as warm turpentine and by applying sinapisms (mustard plasters) to the body. Ticknor differed in his treatment in that he did not bleed his patients or purge them with calomel. For the history of the medical treatment of cholera, see Charles Rosenberg, *The Cholera Years* (Chicago: University of Chicago Press, 1962), 66–68; Norman Longmate, *King Cholera: The Biography of a Disease* (London: Hamish Hamilton, 1966), 76–79.

14. "The Romulus, Harding, from New York to China, passed Anjier 27th Sept. after encountering a series of Gales, during which she sprung a leak, and threw overboard 27 tons of lead, 53 tons spelter, & 16 tons iron" (*Lloyd's List* no. 6830, London, March 19, 1833).

15. The seaman was Charles Peterson, whose death is recorded by David Geisinger in Notes of a Cruise, October 7, 1832, Geisinger Papers.

16. Edmund Roberts, who was living ashore during the *Peacock's* visit to Manila, did not witness the first deaths from cholera aboard ship. Reluctantly he came on board:

> To be compelled to leave a comparatively healthy and pleasant abode on shore, for a floating hospital, tainted with a highly infectious atmosphere, was painful and dangerous, but such was our lot; for thirty sick-hammocks were slung on the starboard side of the gun-deck, when we weighed anchor, and a panic was visible in the countenances of nearly the whole crew. (*Embassy*, 64)

Roberts's descriptive account of the first case of and death from cholera on the *Peacock* was taken directly from this passage in Ticknor's journal.

17. In his revised journal, Ticknor inserted the remedy that appeared to be "the most efficacious." After a hot bath, he gave the patient a mixture of tincture of guaiacum volatile, tincture of cinchona compound, and tincture of opium (Revised Journal II, 125, Ticknor Papers).

Chapter VI

1. The *Lintin* was one of the best-known opium storeships anchored off the island of Lintin. It was owned by Russell and Company, the dominant American company in the China trade. From 1831 to 1838, the ship was commanded by Captain Frederick W. Macondray, originally from Raynham, Massachusetts. Ships arriving from India and Turkey would deposit their opium aboard the *Lintin* before proceeding up to Canton. Chinese smugglers bought opium chits at a counting house in Canton (such as Russell and Co.) and paid in silver. They presented their chits plus a small bribe to the crew of the *Lintin,* received their chests of opium like any other commodity, and smuggled them ashore. The merchant house got a commission on each chest of opium sold and the storeship a demurrage fee. The Chinese opium dealers took all the risks of smuggling and bribing officials for the prohibited sale of opium in China while the American merchants gained the hard currency needed to fill their ships with tea, silk, and porcelain for the voyage home. Most American merchants considered the trade completely legitimate because it was conducted entirely offshore outside of Chinese jurisdiction (Jacques M. Downs, "American Merchants and the China Opium Trade, 1800–1840," *Business History Review,* 42 [Winter, 1968]: 418–42; Jonathan Goldstein, *Philadelphia and the China Trade, 1682–1846* [University Park: Pennsylvania State University Press, 1978], 49–50).

2. One of those ladies was Miss Harriet Low, the twenty-three-year-old niece of William Henry Low, head of Russell and Company in Canton. She had accompanied her uncle and Aunt Abigail from Salem, Massachusetts, to Macao in 1829, to be her aunt's companion. Harriet was attractive, well-read, independent-minded, and witty. She was visiting her friends Capt. and Mrs. Macondray in the hope of getting over her broken engagement to a Philadelphia artist, William W. Wood. In her diary on November 9, 1832, she noted:

> About 2 o'clock the Sloop of War, Peacock arrived here, anchored pretty near — Capt. M. boarded her and Capt. Guysinger, Mr. Roberts and the first Lieut. Mr. Cunningham came and dined with us, very pleasant & gentlemenly men. Mr. Roberts a fine looking man, looks like a clergyman a statesman or anything great you can name. they all made many pretty speeches at the pleasure of seeing ladies, meeting their country women etc—but oh I am sick of professions and pretty speeches.

After dinner they walked on shore and rowed back to the ship in bright moonlight. When dancing was then proposed, she wanted to retire to her cabin, but since only two women were present she felt that she had to hide her feelings and go on dancing (Journal of Harriet Low, 5:28, Low-Mills Papers, Manuscripts Division, Library of Congress).

3. The *Good Success* was a British ship owned by Jardine, Matheson and Company and principally engaged in carrying opium from Bombay to Canton. It arrived in Canton on May 20, 1832 (*Lloyd's List* no. 6827, London, March 8, 1833).

4. Dr. Robert Morrison (1782–1834), the first Protestant missionary to China, was also interpreter for the East India Company. He was well known in the West as

the first translator of the Bible into Chinese. Rev. Elijah Coleman Bridgman (1801–61) and Rev. David Abeel (1804–46) arrived in Canton in 1829 as the first two American Protestant missionaries. Because of ill health, Abeel left his job in Whampoa in 1831 as chaplain to American seamen under the auspices of the American Seaman's Friend Society and traveled throughout southeast Asia investigating the need for missions for the American Board of Commissioners for Foreign Missions. He was in Siam when Ticknor arrived in Canton.

5. Cholera outbreaks on ship or shore forced physicians to reconsider the almost universal use of venesection for treatment of fevers of any kind. The surgeons of the British navy used a vigorous application of venesection to cure malaria, yellow fever, or any other bilious intermittent fever. Until the symptoms of Asiatic cholera classified it as a separate disease and were widely recognized, the British naval surgeons' remedy of choice was the lancet. During the 1830s as cholera penetrated Europe and America, many doctors began to question the universal application of bleeding, but it remained part of conservative treatment of disease in the United States throughout the 1840s (Christopher Lloyd and Jack L. S. Coulter, *Medicine and the Navy, 1200–1900* [Edinburgh: Livingston, 1963], 4:173–81; Longmate, *King Cholera*, 78–79; Rosenberg, *The Cholera Years*, 66, 151).

6. Bishop Reginald Heber (1783–1826), Anglican bishop of Calcutta and author of the missionary hymn "From Greenland's Icy Mountains," died suddenly on March 4, 1826, while on his way home from Madras. His wife, Amelia Heber, was devoted enough to the memory of her husband to edit and publish in 1829 and 1830 two volumes of his sermons and write his biography, *Life of Reginald Heber, D.D., Lord Bishop of Calcutta* (1830), 2 vols. (*Dictionary of National Biography*, 9:355–57).

7. Capt. Alexander Grant was master of the *Hercules* and "store-keeper of Messrs. Jardine, Matheson & Co.'s opium afloat" (H. B. Morse, *The Chronicles of the East India Company Trading to China, 1635–1834* [Oxford: Claredon Press, 1926], 4:364).

8. Harriet Low and her aunt were the first *American* women to visit the hong (trading house) of Russell and Company in Canton (November 6–30, 1830). Earlier that year, three English women—Mrs. Baynes, wife of William Baynes, the president of the Select Committee of the East India Company, and the wives of merchants Henry Robinson and Christopher Fearon—had attempted to visit their husbands in Canton. They had been driven out of Canton by the threat of the mandarins to stop all trade with the East India Company (Katherine Hillard, ed., *My Mother's Journal* [Boston: George H. Ellis, 1900], 75–82; William C. Hunter, *The 'Fan Kwae' at Canton before Treaty Days, 1825–1844* [reprint, Taipei: Ch'eng-wen Publishing Co., 1970], 119–21).

9. Harriet Low noted in her journal on November 14 that three officers from the *Peacock* joined in a party of twenty on the deck of the *Lintin* for supper and dancing. When the party broke up at 2:00 A.M., she complained of fatigue because there was "no spring to the deck." However, Harriet pointed out that only "the gents waltzed" since she was *"too light* headed for such *evolutions"* (Journal, 5:29a, Low-Mills Papers).

10. The *Panther* and *Lion* were owned by Edward Carrington and Co. of Providence, Rhode Island.

11. Edmund Roberts, accompanied by Harriet Low and Mrs. Macondray and several officers from the *Peacock,* had a similar walk on Lintin Island on November 9. He had an impression of barren hills, desolate landscape, and loathsome people.

When we entered the village, (containing about twenty or thirty huts,) every man, woman, and child, turned out to see the barbarian ladies and gentlemen. A more ragged, filthy assemblage was, perhaps, never before seen. We hurried through, obliging them not to press too closely upon us, fearful some of their old acquaintance, apparently the rightful inheritors of their persons, might contrary to our wishes, transfer themselves to us. (*Embassy,* 67)

12. Whitmore is giving Ticknor a slightly garbled version of the ongoing conflict between a French Catholic mission, which arrived in Hawaii in 1827, and the American Protestant missionaries. After the French mission, which consisted of three priests and several lay brothers, began to make a significant number of converts among the Hawaiians, the Protestant missionaries became alarmed and began to urge the Hawaiian government to deport them. In 1829, Queen Kaahumanu, siding with the Americans in seeing a political as well as a religious threat in the Catholic converts, forbade her people to attend Catholic services. Many Hawaiians continued to defy the law and practice their religion. Two of the French priests were deported to California in late 1831, and the natives who refused to give up Catholicism were sentenced to work on a coral wall outside of Oahu. There is no record that French females were involved. When the USS *Potomac* arrived there in June, 1832, "some forty natives, men, women, and children, were confined at hard labour, on a coral wall. . . . And this punishment was inflicted because they were Catholics, and would not change their religion for that of the missionaries of the island!" Commander Downes, citing the American toleration for all religious faiths, was able to persuade the queen and her chiefs to stop the persecution (Reynolds, *Voyage of the Potomac,* 418; A. Grove Day, *Hawaii and its People* [New York: Meridith Press, 1968], 106–9; Bradley, *The American Frontier in Hawaii,* 185–209).

13. Harriet Low wrote a full account (very similar to Ticknor's) of this excursion. She noted that the party consisted of

Capt. Macondray, Dr. Ticknor of the 'Peacock' Makay, Crockett, Wilson, Daily, [Tish], & myself with about 15 attendants, carrying provisions, a band of music. . . . The sun was rather hot and the roads rough and steep. We however reached the Peak at ½ past 2. they give three cheers, I have the honour of being the first lady that has reached the Summit. (Journal, 5:31, Low-Mills Papers)

14. Harriet's version adds a note of playfulness. "We descended on the opposite side, where the grass was very long. Some of the gents sat down and slid from

the top to the bottom of the first ridge—I slipped down supported by two gentlemen—" (ibid).

15. "Darby and Joan" is a reference to a ballad written by Henry Sampson Woodfall and first published in *Gentleman's Magazine* in March, 1735, in London. Woodfall was a printer apprenticed to John Darby, to whom, along with Darby's wife, the song refers. A verse from the song illustrates Ticknor's allusion: "Old Darby with Joan by his side, / You've often regarded with wonder; / He's dropsical, she is sore-eyed, / Yet they're ever uneasy asunder" (John Bartlett, *Familiar Quotations* [Boston: Little, Brown and Co., 1980], 663; *Dictionary of National Biography*, 21:861). Ticknor replaced "Darby and Joan" with "Chinaman and his wife" when he revised his journal. He may have thought the reference too remote for his audience or too vulgar. Harriet Low did not hesitate to use "Darby and Joan" and she may have been the source for the allusion as well.

16. Harriet Low also recorded what happened when she came to the "little Cottage just big enough to hold the ancient Darby and Joan." Arriving back on the *Lintin* about 6:00 P.M., Harriet concluded her exciting day: "The gentlemen of our party took tea with us. having a band then more from *Bravado* than any thing I stood up in a *quadrille*. but for once, my strength was gone. I sneaked away to the Cabin below and reposed my weary limbs upon a couch—" (Journal, 5:32, Low-Mills Papers).

17. Major William Fairchild Megee, one of the most colorful and successful merchants in Providence, Rhode Island, at the end of the eighteenth century, had made his fortune in the China trade. Suffering financial reverses in the early 1800s, he attempted to recoup by delivering a cargo of slaves from Africa to Buenos Aires. After this voyage failed, Megee arrived home deeply in debt and was forced to declare bankruptcy in 1807. By 1810 he had turned up again in Canton with neither wife nor debts. He spent the remainder of his days as an innkeeper in Canton (Jacques M. Downs, "The Merchant as Gambler: Major William Fairchild Megee [1765–1820]," *Rhode Island History* 28 [Fall, 1969]: 99–110).

18. More knowledgeable observers disputed the idea that these were observatories. Elijah Bridgman found that the Chinese considered these towers of no other use "than to keep off evil spirits from the neighboring country" (*The Chinese Repository* 1, no. 6 [October, 1832]: 221). William C. Hunter, admiring the same pagodas on the river, remarked: "If you ask a Chinaman its object or use, he replies that it is 'Joss pigeon,' and you are as wise as you were before. In reality, the Chinese believe that these buildings bring prosperity on the region and ward off evil influences" (*The 'Fan Kwae,'* 85).

19. William C. Hunter, a young American clerk who was working for Russell and Company at Canton in 1832, records this same story in *Bits of Old China* (London: Kegan Paul, Trench, and Co., 1885), 72. His date for the incident is 1655.

20. John R. Latimer (1793–1865), a Philadelphia merchant, had been living in Canton since 1824, when he joined the longtime American trader Benjamin Wilcocks. By 1827 Latimer had become sole owner of a trading house that was deeply involved in the opium trade. He was an extremely hospitable and generous person who often entertained visiting American naval officers at his luxurious quarters in the American factory on the banks of the Pearl River. Accounts of his hospitality

toward officers of the *Potomac* in May, 1832, may be found in Reynolds, *Voyage of the Potomac*, 347; and Warriner, *Cruise of the Potomac*, 205.

21. Dr. James H. Bradford (1802–59), a physician from Philadelphia, lived in Canton from 1822 to 1835. He conducted a medical practice for independent merchants and shared quarters in the American hong with John R. Latimer.

Chapter VII

1. Dr. Alexander Pearson, surgeon of the East India Company, introduced vaccination for small pox in 1805. He trained a Chinese surgeon to superintend the infirmary and instruct other physicians in the technique of inoculation. By the time he left Canton in 1832, a very large and successful vaccine institution was in operation (William Lockhart, *The Medical Missionary in China* [London: Hurst and Blackett, 1861], 120).

2. An almost exact description of the vaccination infirmary appears in the journal of Dr. Peter Parker, American medical missionary and diplomat. Parker pointed out that the Chinese authorities offered premiums of $.50, $1, $2, or $3 to parents for successful inoculations. "There were about half a dozen men employed in inoculating, taking the virus from the most healthy child that could be selected among those who were returned, for the premium" (Journal of Peter Parker, November 6, 1843, 7, American Board of Commissioners for Foreign Missions Papers, 16.3.8., vol. 1, Houghton Library, Harvard University, Cambridge, Massachusetts).

3. Dr. Robert Morrison, an ordained Presbyterian minister, was sent to China in 1807 by the London Missionary Society. Because of opposition from the Chinese government, he successfully converted only ten Chinese to Christianity, but he opened the way for Western scholarship on China by his writings and by compiling the first English-Chinese dictionary.

4. Elijah Coleman Bridgman, of Belchertown, Massachusetts, and a graduate of Amherst College, arrived in Canton in 1829. His immediate task was to learn to speak Chinese, and his early years there were spent almost entirely in study of the language. In 1832, with the help of Robert Morrison and Morrison's son John, he started a monthly newspaper in English, *The Chinese Repository*, which became the richest single source of information to the West about social, economic, and cultural life in China.

5. Bridgman had a school of five boys who took care of his rooms in return for English lessons, taught by reading from the Bible and Christian books. Bridgman hoped to convert the boys by teaching them English. In between teaching and giving public worship, Bridgman found time each day for two hour-long classes in Chinese with his own teacher. The rest of his day was spent in study, devotion, and prayer (E. Bridgman to his parents, March 28, 1831, and E. Bridgman to his mother, October 27, 1832, Elijah Coleman Bridgman Papers, Belchertown Historical Association, Belchertown, Massachusetts).

6. Stevens had been sent to Canton in 1832 by the American Seaman's Friend Society to replace the ailing Rev. David Abeel.

7. Ticknor had a seal made for his letters. The base is ivory and the actual seal, depicting the head of a peacock entwined with a serpent, is carved in mother-

of-pearl. A Latin motto, *cassis tutissima virtus* [the safest protection is virtue], encircles the head of the peacock. He also bought two small Chinese paintings for his family.

8. Morrison was highly suspicious of Episcopalians because he felt himself a religious and perhaps social outcast among them. In a letter written to the London Missionary Society, he gave vent to his feelings that the bishop of Calcutta and the Episcopal chaplains of Macao conspired "to teach Europeans & Pagans that the ministration of the Gospel & the ordinances of Christ's Church, in the hands of non-episcopalians, are invalid" (Robert Morrison to T. Fisher, April 6, 1834, Council for World Mission Archives, China, box 1, vol. 2, School of Oriental and African Studies Library, University of London, England).

9. When Ticknor rewrote his journal in 1836, Robert Morrison had been dead for two years. He revised this defense of Morrison in a subtle way. The text is essentially the same as originally written, but Ticknor now writes entirely in the third person. He attributes all conclusions about American morality to what Dr. Morrison probably observed, omitting entirely the more personal "I" (Revised Journal II, 154–56, Ticknor Papers).

10. Ticknor is referring to the 1828 petition of the East India Company to the viceroy to limit all trade in Canton to the seven members of the Chinese cohong, who were approved by the government. Americans such as John R. Latimer and Daniel W. C. Olyphant, who traded with competing shopkeepers in silk and tea, were outraged by the attempt of the British to extend their monopoly. After two months of intense pressure by the American merchants on the hong merchants, the Chinese viceroy was forced to allow the Americans the right to trade with shopkeepers for silk and other commodities. Evidently this dispute had not been forgotten by Latimer and the other American traders, and Morrison, being the Chinese interpreter for the company, probably received a share of the obloquy (Morse, *Chronicles* 4:168–73).

11. Latimer also liked to serve more mundane American food to homesick seamen. In a letter to his brother Henry, Latimer mentioned that he got a constant supply of hominy from one of Dr. James Bradford's friends. "I make excellent corned pork in my own house in the winter, and have delighted some of the Officers of the Peacock who are from the South—with hog and hominy" (John Latimer to Henry Latimer, December 27, 1832, John R. Latimer Papers, University of Delaware Library, Newark, Delaware).

12. Ticknor may have been influenced in this expectation by Elijah Bridgman or some of the merchants in Canton. Bridgman discussed the Chinese attitudes toward foreigners in *The Chinese Repository*. He reminded his readers that little had changed in a government policy of harassing foreigners since a Dutch traveler had described being pelted with dirt on a walk in 1771. He pointed out that children are brought up from infancy to

> insult & maltreat foreigners; as soon as they can read, they see the abusive proclamations of the government, pasted up on the very walls of the foreigners' own houses. . . . With such education and such examples placed before them, is it to be wondered at, that instead of

having improved, we find them grown worse. . . . (vol. 1, no. 7 [October, 1832]: 214)

13. Foreign merchants, being an inferior class in the eyes of the Chinese government, were forbidden to ride in sedan chairs and thus suffered a double indignity.

14. Several instances of foreign merchants having to force their way into the city of Canton to deliver a petition are recounted in Reynolds, *Voyage of the Potomac,* 352.

15. Edmund Roberts also visited the Honam temple with Rev. Elijah Bridgman as his guide. From textual differences and the fact that Ticknor did not include Roberts in his account of the excursion, I would judge that they went on separate trips, but their tours were virtually the same. Roberts used the same Morrison pamphlet, without acknowledging it, to identify and name parts of the temple. A close reading of both texts will show that Ticknor was more open than Roberts to new experiences (see *Embassy,* 70–73).

16. In 1816 Robert Morrison served as Chinese interpreter to Lord Amherst, a British ambassador, in an unsuccessful attempt to open diplomatic relations with the Chinese emperor. The mission returned to Canton on January 1, 1817.

17. Every Western traveler was impressed with the swine.

We next visited the *Jos-pigs,* ten or twelve in number, the most gouty *squeaks,* perhaps, the whole empire could produce. These were mostly presents from devotees, and supported by the Church, and fed most enormously. They had become so fat that many of them could not rise, and seemed to breathe with difficulty; some were so old that their faces were covered with immense wrinkles, and blotches of fat. They are never eaten, and of course die a natural death. (Reynolds, *Voyage of the Potomac,* 349)

18. Independent English traders as well as American merchants chafed under the monopoly of the East India Company. The Chinese, a rigid, highly authoritarian culture, preferred to deal with one entity in controlling the foreign barbarians. But the pressure for free trade was too great and Parliament in 1833 revoked the charter of the East India Company trading to China.

19. This figure is evidently not far from the actual amount. The combined value in dollars of opium imported into Canton in 1831, by British, American, and other merchant ships was $13,022,703 (Morse, *Chronicles* 4:271).

20. At a dinner party given by John R. Latimer for the officers of the *Potomac* in May, 1832, Latimer left the table for a few minutes. On his return, he told the officers that he had just made a sale of opium for two thousand dollars, and he praised the business efficiency of the Chinese in this trade (Reynolds, *Voyage of the Potomac,* 353).

21. Two other foreigners in China viewed the Chinese differently. Harriet Low wondered, upon hearing about Chinese being victims of disasters or being killed, why the foreigners in Macao were so indifferent. "It must be that we have no sympathy

with them, they appear to me to be a connecting link between man and beast, but certainly not equal with civilized man" (Journal, 5:69, Low-Mills Papers). Edmund Roberts summed up his impression:

> Of all uncouth figures, that strut their little hour upon the stage of life, a China-man is surely the most grotesque animal. A loose shirt for his outer and principal garment—his bagging breeks, added to his white slouching stockings, made of cotton cloth, filled with wrinkles— his black cloth slippers, with a white sole half an inch thick—his shaved head, with his long plaited cue, streaming out when he runs, like a ship's pennant in a brisk breeze—his elongated and stupid eyes; . . . present him as the most unprepossessing figure ever beheld—the most awkward looking biped in the universe. (*Embassy*, 159)

22. Roberts had spent his time in Canton shopping for presents for the kings of Cochin China and Siam. The American gifts, shipped on the *Boxer*, had failed to catch up with him. He also sought the advice of Dr. Robert Morrison on how to conduct himself before an Oriental monarch. In a simple but firm letter, Morrison listed eight rules to follow in his diplomatic mission. The most important were to tell the truth, never to agree to kowtow (bowing before the monarch by kneeling and touching forehead to the ground), and to demand strict reciprocity in all agreements. Morrison also suggested that Roberts hire his young son, John Robert Morrison, as interpreter. He cautioned that young Morrison should be designated as "private secretary" since the term "interpreter is often treated, by the inconsiderate with contempt." Roberts went to Macao to meet and pick up John R. Morrison (R. Morrison to E. Roberts, November 20, 1832, and November 24, 1832, Roberts Papers, New Hampshire Historical Society).

23. John Robert Morrison, born in Macao on April 14, 1814, was actually eighteen years old. He was fluent in Mandarin Chinese and had already begun to do translation work for independent British traders in Canton as well as to assist his father with his work as interpreter for the East India Company. He was also an accomplished writer for *The Chinese Repository.*

Chapter VIII

1. The *Ann* was a ship owned by Jardin, Matheson and Company, British independent merchants who were the greatest rivals of the East India Company in the China trade.

2. Remittent fever was one of the major classifications of fever used by all physicians in the nineteenth century. It was described as a fever that went up and down (remission), but was never wholly absent, usually over a course of eight days. Often the patient was afflicted with "bilious vomiting," hence the name bilious remittent fever (William Buchan, M.D., *Domestic Medicine; or, A Treatise on the Prevention and Cure of Diseases, by Regimen and Simple Medicines* [Berwick: William Lochhead, 1816], 143–44).

3. This harbor was about 120 miles south of the capital of Hué. By anchoring at Vunglam, Roberts had to violate another of Robert Morrison's eight rules for success of diplomatic missions—"carry up the ships as near the Capital as practicable, and reveal as little to inferior officers as possible" (R. Morrison to E. Roberts, November 20, 1832, Roberts Papers, New Hampshire Historical Society).

4. Roberts's account of the visit to Cochin China is taken almost entirely from the report of his secretary, John R. Morrison, "Journal and Conversations with the Officers of Government During the Stay of the mission at Vunglam in Cochinchina." Morrison wrote in detail about the questions the mandarin posed. His acceptance of the old man is in marked contrast to Ticknor's attitude. "He then took leave after having drunk a little wine. The old man was throughout lively and cheerful. As he wrote Chinese pretty well, it was easy to hold intercourse with him" (Roberts, *Embassy,* 174).

5. Dates in brackets are taken from the official report of the mission as it appears in Roberts's *Embassy,* 175–79.

6. The surprising fact that a Vietnamese Catholic priest could converse in written Latin was a direct result of the influence of French Catholic missionaries who had entered the country during the reign of Emperor Gia Long (1802–20). French advisors had greatly aided Gia Long in consolidating his rule during a civil war, and afterwards the country was more open to Western ideas and education. John White, a Yankee captain who had tried unsuccessfully to open trade with Cochin China in 1819, was amazed to find mandarins who spoke Latin at Turon Bay. He wrote that "the mild and unassuming manners of the Christian missionaries endeared them to the natives, and procured them many proselytes, who were instructed in the principles of Christianity, through the medium of the Latin language; and of this number were two of the chiefs who came on board of us at Turon" (*A Voyage to Cochin China* [1824; reprint, Kuala Lumpur: Oxford University Press, 1972], 80–81).

7. There were two mandarins from Hué, accompanied by a judge (undergovernor) of the province, plus two interpreters (Roberts, *Embassy,* 180–81).

8. The mandarins pointed out that the address on the cover of the letter was incorrect and hence their chief minister (the minister of commerce and navigation) could not give it to the king. "The country, they said, is not now called Annam, as formerly, but Wietman, (in Mandarin dialect, Yuenan) and it is ruled, not by a king, (wang) but by an emperor (hwang-te)." Morrison included the Chinese characters for these titles in the official report from which this passage is a direct quote (Roberts, *Embassy,* 182).

9. The expressions in the letter that probably enraged Edmund Roberts the most were the references to him as (1) a "petty officer" and (2) deputized by the president of the United States to "entreat earnestly for a friendly intercourse." Young Morrison, who was completely familiar with the subtleties of official language, pointed out in a note that "petty officer" was "an expression used by inferior officers, in corresponding with superiors, when referring to themselves" (Roberts, *Embassy,* 183).

10. Ticknor is referring to the well-known failure of the British embassy under Lord Amherst to achieve diplomatic relations with the emperor of China in 1816.

The Chinese considered Lord Amherst simply a tribute bearer, as they had the Macartney mission in 1793. Robert Morrison had been Lord Amherst's Chinese interpreter and probably warned Roberts of this pitfall in Oriental diplomacy.

11. This humorous exchange was not included in the official report that Morrison wrote (*Embassy*, 184–85), but Roberts included this incident in a general discussion of Cochin China later in his book as an example of the ignorance of the mandarins (*Embassy*, 225).

12. Roberts gave a complete description of the dishes and expressed a similar distaste for unsanitary food preparation.

> The feast was brought on the board in handsomely varnished and gilded cases; to all outward appearance, it was very neat and cleanly; but we could not divest ourselves of the idea, that it was cooked in the uncleanly vessels we had seen on shore, and that it had come in contact with the filthy paws, dirty nails, and heads filled with vermin, which we had seen on shore: we therefore, barely tasted of one article, the confectionary. (*Embassy*, 189)

13. The argument between Morrison and the mandarins was over the mandarins' insistence that the minister of commerce and navigation in Hué had to have a translation of the president's letter to the king before he would agree to deliver it. By the end of the day the mandarins attempted to bully Morrison by saying that since he had read Chinese literature, he was familiar with their court etiquette and should explain it to the American envoy. The success or the failure of the mission would rest entirely on Morrison. Morrison's only comment was: "To this absurd language no reply was returned" (Roberts, *Embassy*, 193–96).

14. Morrison was told by the mandarins that since the president was elected by the people and did not have the actual title of king, "it behooved him to write in a manner properly decorous and respectful" and therefore the translation of the letter had to be examined "in order to expunge improper words." Morrison replied that the president was inferior to no one, and stalked out of the meeting (Roberts, *Embassy*, 201).

15. Cochin China was at that time a tributary state to China.

16. Roberts recounted this scene with glee. Obviously fed up with the mandarins' references to his inferiority, he decided to give them as titles every geographical point in New Hampshire. Using Morrison as interpreter, Roberts began with Portsmouth and proceeded through all the towns and counties until the mandarin, weary with writing a whole page of Chinese paper and complaining of headache and seasickness, acknowledged that Roberts was fully the equal in titles to the prime minister, and fled the ship. "The whole scene was certainly most ludicrous. Some of the gentlemen could with much difficulty restrain their risible faculties, while others walked out of the cabin, being utterly unable to refrain from laughter, while I kept a most imperturbable countenance until the whole matter was concluded" (*Embassy*, 218).

17. John White summed up in angry terms all the frustrations of trying to trade with the Vietnamese without a commercial treaty and pointed out that "the

rapacious, faithless, despotic, and anti-commercial character of the government, will, as long as these causes exist, render Cochin China the least desirable country for mercantile adventurers." Roberts owned a copy of this book and Ticknor may well have read it (*Voyage to Cochin China*, 246–47).

18. John Crawfurd (1783–1868), authority on Malay language and culture, British administrator in Java, and noted author, was sent by the governor-general of India on a diplomatic mission to Siam and Cochin China in 1821. His book about the mission was the main reference used by Edmund Roberts in his negotiations with the Vietnamese. Ticknor seems to have misunderstood the trade arrangements accepted by Crawfurd in Cochin China. Crawfurd was more than pleased to accept the same measurement duties agreed to by the Chinese. There is no reference to any clauses giving the emperor and his ministers a monopoly of trade. However, in Siam, British merchants had to compete with royal monopolies. Crawfurd sought to have an onerous eight percent ad valorem import duty lowered so that the British would have a better chance against these monopolies. Ticknor, in his earnest defense of the Roberts mission, may have confused the two trade negotiations (John Crawfurd, *Journal of an Embassy to the Courts of Siam & Cochin China*, 2d ed. [London: Henry Colburn and Richard Bentley, 1830], 1:396–417; 1:221–22).

19. Edmund Roberts made the same conclusion (*Embassy*, 221).

20. Roberts declared that "the inhabitants are without exception the most filthy people in the world" (*Embassy*, 220). Both Ticknor and Roberts echoed the more polished opinion of Crawfurd: "This neglect of personal cleanliness they perhaps carry to a greater length than any of the nations of the further East" (Crawfurd, *Journal* 2:281).

21. Neither Roberts nor Ticknor was aware that Emperor Minh Mang (Gia Long's son), fearing French and British colonial expansion, had decided to avoid any commercial treaty with a Western power and had essentially closed his court to any European or American influence (Alastair Lamb, *The Mandarin Road to Old Hué* [London: Chatto and Windus, 1970], 235).

22. This is a group of islands in the Gulf of Thailand, the largest of which is Kaoh Tang, 10°18′ north latitude, 103°7′ east longitude.

Chapter IX

1. Chang and Eng, born to a Siamese mother and a Chinese father in the province of Samuth Songkram in 1811, were joined facing each other by a flap of skin at the lower end of the rib cage. They were otherwise normal in every way. At age eighteen, they were taken to Europe and America by an American captain and exhibited as a monstrosity. The medical term "Siamese twins" is derived from this case.

2. José Piedade was captain of the port of Bangkok and an aide to the phraklang, the foreign minister of Siam.

3. Piedade probably used this story to strengthen his own position as interpreter in the negotiation between the phraklang and Roberts. John Crawfurd, who spoke Malay, chafed at having to use the assigned Siamese Malay interpreter, named Luang Kochai-asá-hak. This was a minor factor in the failure of Crawfurd's mission

in Siam. His difficulties with the Siamese stemmed from the British attempt to avoid being drawn into a war between Siam and a Siamese tributary, the Malay sultanate of Kedah. The sultan of Kedah had fled to British territory at Penang, and the British angered the Siamese by giving asylum to the sultan. The Crawfurd mission in 1822 could not achieve any trade agreement in the face of the unresolved conflict over Kedah (Crawfurd, *Journal* 1:113; Lamb, *The Mandarin Road,* 237–38).

4. Ticknor neglected to include John R. Morrison, Roberts's interpreter and secretary.

5. When John Crawfurd was received there on March 26, 1822, the governor's house was virtually the same. Evidently no special effort had been made for the American mission (Crawfurd, *Journal* 1:112–13).

6. The factory had been built for the Scottish merchant Robert Hunter on the west bank (left bank when ascending) of the Menan River, directly in front of Wat Prayurawongse, on property owned by the phraklang (R. Adey Moore, "An early British merchant in Bangkok," *Journal of the Siam Society* 11, pt. 2 [1914–15]: 22). Ticknor again refers to the residence being on the right bank of the river. His usual meticulous sense of direction may have been thrown off by the U-shaped curve of the Menam River at this point. The site is occupied today by a modern government building, off-limits to tourists.

7. Chaopraya Phraklang had been foreign minister under Rama II. He had been closely allied with Prince Chesda, the son of a minor wife of Rama II, and retained his post as foreign minister when Prince Chesda became Rama III in 1824. In 1830, the king appointed him the governor of southern Siam, and the phraklang occupied both important offices during the reign of Rama III (Walter F. Vella, *Siam under Rama III, 1824–1851* [Locust Valley, N.Y.: J. J. Augustin, 1957], 6–7).

8. Roberts was referring to the practice common at that time of the king preempting trade for the benefit of the royal monopolies. Crawfurd had complained of this in his unsuccessful commercial treaty negotiations in 1822.

9. Captain Henry Burney (1792–1845), a British army officer, was sent by the governor-general of India to Bangkok in 1825 on a diplomatic mission to negotiate a commercial treaty and to ensure the neutrality of the Thai court in the war between the British East India Company and Burma. Captain (later Major) Burney, who was born in India, had become fluent in the Thai and Malay languages while stationed in Penang. His language skill and knowledge of Asiatic customs contributed to his success in negotiating the first British trade treaty with Siam in 1826 (*The Burney Papers: Bangkok, 1910–1914* [Farnborough: Gregg International Publishers, 1971], vol. 1, pts. 1–4, i–iii).

10. Prior to Roberts's arrival in Bangkok, the phraklang had been given specific orders about bedding: "The Officers of the See Tamruat are to provide three bedsteads for use of Emin Rabad [Edmund Roberts] and the two lesser noblemen. The Office of the P'ra Klang Wiset is required to provide silken mosquito nets, whilst the P'ra Klang Nai Office is entrusted with supplying three mattresses, three sheets, three pillows, and six bolsters for their use." For a translation of Rama III's order, see Chula Chakrabongse, *Lords of Life: A History of the Kings of Thailand* (London: Alvin Redman, 1960), 168.

11. Part of the quarrel was between the phraklang and Silveira, who refused

to give up to the phraklang the valuable land on the Menam River occupied by the Portuguese consulate (J. H. Moor, *Notices of the Indian Archipelago and Adjacent Countries* [1837; reprint, London: Frank Cass and Co., 1968], 204).

12. The residence of Carlos da Silveira was located on the bank of the Menam River at the present site of the Portuguese embassy, 26 Bush Lane.

13. The discussion between Roberts and the phraklang about a vessel paying partial duty for a partial load and the article exempting American debtors from prison or corporal punishment is not recorded in the official record made by John R. Morrison. Roberts, perhaps influenced by the success of naval diplomacy at Kuala Batu, went well beyond his instructions in threatening a declaration of war (Journal, and Conversations with the Officers of the Government etc. during the stay of the Mission in Siam, 64–67, Roberts Papers, Library of Congress).

14. In the official reports of the Crawfurd and Burney missions, there is no mention of wives, but Crawfurd did present his six-year-old son at court. Silveira aided both Crawfurd and Burney and doubtless met the wives.

15. Major Henry Burney gave an account of this incident in his official report of the mission. The two Muslim interpreters were more insistent on his removing his shoes than were the Siamese. He silenced their objections by saying that if "our shoes were removed, I should insist upon their turbans being taken off" (*The Burney Papers*, vol. 1, pts. 1–4, 39).

16. Emperor Minh Mang, jealous of the political influence of Christians during his father's reign, began to move to an anti-Western, anti-Christian position upon ascending the throne. He was thwarted in the complete eradication of Christianity while Le Van Duyet, the governor of the south of Cochin China, protected the French priests and converts. When Le Van Duyet died in 1832, Minh Mang ordered all Christians to abandon Christianity on pain of death. During 1833, Christians were persecuted throughout the country and a French priest (Father Gagelin) and about twenty converts were executed (Lamb, *The Mandarin Road*, 283–84).

17. Burney recorded in his journal that the phraklang paid him 120 ticals from the wang na (second king). When Burney sought to refuse the money, the phraklang explained that it had been observed that the British used animals almost completely for food. Since it was repugnant to the Siamese to take the life of an animal, they wanted the British to accept the money and provide their own food. Burney then acquiesced (*The Burney Papers*, vol. 1, pts. 1–4, 54).

18. Crawfurd stated that when he was in Bangkok (1822), the phraklang had forty wives (*Journal* 2:62).

19. Karl Gutzlaff, a remarkable Prussian, had been sent by the London Missionary Society to Siam in August, 1828. He lived there preaching, teaching, dispensing medical care, and translating the Christian message into Siamese until 1831. David Abeel, the American missionary who arrived in Bangkok a few days after Gutzlaff left, wrote with appreciation about Silveira's aid:

> This gentleman entertained the missionaries during the early part of their first visit—assigned them a house on his own lands—and when they were opposed by the Catholics, and through them, by the native authorities, continued their warm friend, notwithstanding the threat-

ened loss of all his property, and the menace of expulsion from the Siamese dominions. (*Journal of a Residence in China and the Neighboring Countries from 1829-1833* [New York: Leavitt, Lord and Co., 1834], 207–8)

20. The gifts most coveted by the Siamese were guns and items of European or American manufacture. By having to substitute Chinese items readily available in Bangkok for the missing American gifts, Roberts achieved less of an impression in the Siamese court. It was even suggested that the Siamese did not believe Roberts's story about the *Boxer* not arriving in China before he left (Moor, *Notices*, 203).

21. Roberts describes this event as happening on the nights of March 6 and 7.

22. Roberts makes no reference to any slight being shown the American party by the host on either night (*Embassy*, 238–40).

23. This was Bishop Sozopolis, a Frenchman from Avignon, who had been in Siam and Cochin China since 1788. At the time of Crawfurd's visit in 1822, the bishop was sixty, still quite lively, and unfazed by his isolation from Europeans. Roberts also recorded a visit to the bishop, accompanied by Dr. Ticknor and Silveira, but gave no date. Roberts found that the bishop had almost forgotten his own country. "He was very infirm, and in his second childhood; sans teeth, sight dim, sans every thing" (*Embassy*, 278; Crawfurd, *Journal* 1:248).

24. The phraklang defended the changes in the treaty by comparing the process of making a treaty to that of "a person purchasing an article, which he endeavours to obtain as cheap as possible, while the owner wished to sell it at as high a rate as he can obtain for it: & so a medium price is fixed." Roberts took issue with this parallel and pointed out that he

> had considered most of the articles to have been agreed to, in the previous conversation respecting them, on the 5th inst[ant]. The Prahklang answered, that what was to last as long as Heaven & Earth shall endure c'd not be concluded so hastily, and that he could not have agreed to the proposals on the previous occasions, as he had not then had opportunity of consultation with the other Chief Ministers. (Journal during the Stay at Siam, 76–77, Roberts Papers, Library of Congress)

25. The descendants of the Portuguese lived in the area immediately surrounding the Church of Santa Cruz, near the site of the American mission on the western bank of the Menam River.

26. Some fifty to sixty of the victims of the fire took shelter in the grounds of the American mission and were fed by the Americans for a considerable time. Bamboo to rebuild their houses was supplied by the king and phraklang. Their more fortunate neighbors donated rice and other small articles (Roberts, *Embassy*, 241).

Chapter XI

1. Ticknor is writing about the problem of sailing vessels being caught by a change in the monsoon winds, which determined all movement in crossing the Indian Ocean.

2. This is Seaman William Cooper of the crew of the *Boxer,* who died August 11. Dr. A. E. Kennedy, an assistant surgeon in charge of medical duties on the *Boxer,* died in Batavia on June 14 (Notes of a Cruise, June 14, 1833, and August 11, 1833, Geisinger Papers).

3. The vessels were dhows, which plied the waters between Africa and Arabia.

Chapter XII

1. Admiral John Blankett, whose flagship was HMS *Leopard,* commanded British naval forces in the Red Sea from 1798 until his death near Mocha in 1801 (*Dictionary of National Biography* 2:667).

2. Roberts expressed the same thought, perhaps a little more dramatically. "In passing through the entrance, up this narrow stairway, the scene of so much bloodshed at different times, we were strongly impressed with the idea, that the lumps of dirt and the spots on the walls, were the blood and brains of many a victim; and however erroneous the opinion might be, we imagined every thing about the palace smelt of blood, as though it were the shambles of wretched human beings" (*Embassy,* 345).

3. Ben-al-mas, dissatisfied with his post in the army of the Egyptian pasha Mehemet Ali, collected an army of Copts, Turks, Egyptians, Arabs, and Abyssinians, and marched from Cairo eastward. He captured and pillaged cities along the Arabian coast of the Red Sea, including Jiddah, the gateway to Mecca. He conquered Mocha on March 16, 1833, and his Bedouin followers plundered the city for three days (Eric Macro, *Bibliography on Yemen and Notes on Mocha* [Coral Gables, Fla.: University of Miami Press, 1960], 62).

4. Said bin Khalfan, called Capt. Calaphon or Calafaun by Ticknor, was an Arab merchant at Muscat who acted as a translator for Seyyid Said bin Sultan. As a reward for his service to the American mission, he was later appointed the local agent for the United States, but the sultan refused to accept him as a representative of a foreign state (Norman R. Bennett and George E. Brooks, Jr., eds., *New England Merchants in Africa: A History through Documents 1802 to 1865* [Boston: Boston University Press, 1965], 159).

5. Roberts is referring to the letter that the imam of Oman, Seyyid Said bin Sultan, had addressed to the U.S. government and sent via a ship captain from Salem, Massachusetts, whom Said met in Zanzibar on February 9, 1832. This letter, which has disappeared, evidently reiterated the sultan's desire to negotiate a trade treaty with the United States as had been discussed when Edmund Roberts first met Said bin Sultan in Zanzibar in January, 1828 (N. R. Bennett, "Americans in Zanzibar, 1825–1845," *Essex Institute Historical Collections,* 95 [July, 1959]: 243–46).

6. Seyyid Said bin Sultan, this agreeable, unpretentious man whom Ticknor met, was one of the most successful Arab rulers of an empire extending from Muscat in Oman on the eastern tip of the Arabian Peninsula to Mozambique in East Africa. Having murdered his uncle to seize the throne in 1804, Said bin Sultan ruled Oman in an enlightened way until his death in 1856. He described himself as primarily a merchant and developed a modern navy to protect his African slave trade and his

clove plantations in Zanzibar. After 1822, he cooperated with the British in the suppression of the slave trade outside his African and Asian possessions, losing a great deal of profit as well as prestige in the eyes of the other Arabian slave traders. He sought to develop trade links with the Americans to offset a dependence on the British and in the hope of securing weapons for his continual fight with the Portuguese in Mozambique. His suggestion to Edmund Roberts in 1828 of a trade treaty with the United States probably fitted this strategy (Wendell Phillips, *Oman: A History* [London: Longmans, 1967], 84–111).

7. Since the July Revolution (1830) in Paris, Europe had been swept by other revolutionary upheavals in Italy, the Germanic states, and Poland. By 1833, more conservative governments were once again restoring order.

8. Ibrahim Pacha was the eldest son of Mehemet Ali, the ruler of Egypt. He was much feared throughout the area because of his ruthlessness in suppressing anyone who might challenge Mehemet Ali's power in northern Africa and eastern Arabia.

9. Ticknor's example of the colorful language of the letter is essentially correct. For the official translation of the letter from Said bin Sultan to Andrew Jackson, October 7, 1833, see Records of Department of State, Communications from Special Agents, 1794–1906, RG 59, M 37, roll 10, NA.

10. Ticknor's generous praise of Said bin Sultan was echoed by Lt. James Raymond Wellsted, an Englishman who traveled extensively in Arabia in 1831:

> The government of this prince is principally marked by the absence of all oppressive imposts, all arbitrary punishments, by his affording marked attention to the merchants of any nation who come to reside at Muskat, and by the general toleration which is extended to all persuasions: while, on the other hand, his probity, the impartiality and leniency of his punishments, together with the strict regard he pays to the general welfare of his subjects, have rendered him as much respected and admired by the town Arabs, as his liberality and personal courage have endeared him to the Bedowins. (*Travels in Arabia* [London: John Murray, 1838], 1:7–8)

11. The banyans (banians) were natives of India who had fanned across Arabia and East Africa in search of trade. They remained a separate merchant class living along the coasts of the Indian Ocean, never intermarrying with the Africans. In Africa, banyans were given the monopoly of trade between Mozambique and the Portuguese possessions in India (Mabel V. Jackson Haight, *European Powers and South-East Africa* [London: Routledge and Kegan Paul, 1967], 43).

Chapter XIII

1. Edmund Roberts describes the scene: "A short distance to the eastward of the island of Socotra, in the Indian ocean, he was laid in his watery grave. The solemn and sublime service of the Protestant Episcopal church was read by our worthy

surgeon, Dr. Ticknor; the main-topsail being aback, and the colours hoisted half-mast" (*Embassy,* 366–67).

2. Ticknor walked through Black Town; the thatched dwellings that he described were owned by free blacks rather than slaves. A similar description appears in a contemporary book: William F. W. Owen, Capt. R. N., *Narrative of Voyages to explore the Shores of Africa, Arabia and Madagascar* (London: Richard Bentley, 1833), 1:190.

3. The site of Fort S. Sebastiao was chosen in 1558 by Joao De Castro, one of the greatest Portuguese viceroys of India. Actual construction of the fort began ten years later when an engineer became available (James S. Kirkman, *Men and Monuments on the East African Coast* [London: Lutterworth Press, 1964], 210).

4. "Two women shall be grinding together; the one shall be taken, and the other left" (Luke 17:35, King James Version).

5. By 1833 the slave trade was virtually suppressed in Mozambique, a port more vulnerable to the British navy, which enforced the Treaty of 1817 forbidding the slave trade. Under that treaty, Portugal had the right to trade in slaves only with her colony of Brazil. However, when Brazil became independent in 1825, Portugal did not bother to apply the prohibition against the slave trade to her ex-colony, and the trade continued unabated from the less conspicuous ports of Quelimane and Inhambane, south of Mozambique (Haight, *European Powers,* 226–30).

6. Gum benjamin or benzoin is a resin that was used in the nineteenth century as a stimulant and expectorant in medicine and as an ingredient in perfume. Columbo root, a native plant of Mozambique, was used medicinally as a bitter tonic.

Index